ADVANCE PRAISE

"I would pay to read any of Richard Burger's insights and interpretations of modern China. To have him explore China through its sexual history, practices, hang-ups, and business ambitions is a particular treat. His writing has been distinguished by its combination of empathy and edge, two traits that come through very clearly in this book."

James Fallows, national correspondent at the *Atlantic Monthly* and author of *China Airborne*

"In telling a great story of the history of sex in China, Richard Burger peels back the curtain on the private lives of the world's most populous nation."

John Pomfret, author of *Chinese Lessons: Five Classmates* and *The Story of the New China*

"A complex and fascinating story [told] in a surprisingly engrossing way. Detailed descriptions of intimacy are handled in a sensitive yet matter-of-fact manner, never vulgar and always thoughtful. The reader is treated to an engaging, readable progression - providing a window into the history of and attitudes to sex in China from China's earliest written chronicles to the astonishing cultural changes of the past 40 years."

Jan Ziff, CBS news host and former State Department correspondent for the BBC

"A wonderful book. A rich exploration of the intimacies, physical and emotional, that have bound Chinese together over millennia of history."

James Palmer, author of *Heaven Cracks, Earth Shakes* and *The Bloody White Baron*

D0099336

"Highly recommended for those with an interest in Chinese culture or in how human sexuality shapes and is shaped by a society."
Lisa Brackmann, author of *Rock Paper Tiger*

"*Behind the Red Door: Sex in China* offers a wonderfully salacious and thoroughly entertaining guided tour through the five thousand years of Chinese history that you are not going to read about in standard accounts of the subject. The book will be an especially useful supplement to traditional textbooks for students of Chinese history."
Peter Vernezze, author of *Socrates in Sichuan*

"In this humane, lively, and fluent exploration of a vast topic, it is astonishing how much ground Burger covers: the long shadow of Confucius, a taxonomy of mistresses, the zero-sum premise of ancient Daoist sex manuals, the etiquette of 21st-century dating; and the varying effects, sometimes subtle and often conscious, which authoritarian power has exerted on the Chinese pursuit of Eros."
A. E. Clark, translator, *Tibet's True Heart*

"Incisive, funny and courageous, Richard Burger's writing provides a unique look at Chinese society."
Mei Fong, former Pulitzer Prize-winning correspondent at *The Wall Street Journal's Beijing bureau*"

"Combining a wealth of historical research with revealing interviews and forthright observations, *Behind the Red Door: Sex in China* is a nuanced study of China's shifting sexual landscape. Richard Burger's analysis of differences between China and the West in attitudes towards and practices of sex, including homosexuality, is eye-opening."
Xujun Eberlein, author of *Apologies Forthcoming*

This book is dedicated to my parents.

BEHIND THE RED DOOR
By RICHARD BURGER

ISBN-13: 978-988-19983-2-3

Published by Earnshaw Books Ltd. (Hong Kong).

BEHIND THE RED DOOR

SEX IN CHINA

RICHARD BURGER

EARNSHAW
BOOKS

NOTES

Most of the Chinese words in this book appear in Romanized pinyin, today's standard format.

Monetary figures are usually presented as Chinese yuan, followed by a conversion to the United States dollar.

All translations are from sources listed in the Bibliography.

CONTENTS

ACKNOWLEDGMENTS

Sex in China: Behind the Red Door could not have been written without the valuable help of friends, mostly in China, who helped me verify much of the material, assisted with translation and offered editorial advice. I would like to offer special thanks to Jeremiah Jenne, Dean of China Studies at IES Abroad Beijing Center and a Ph.D. candidate in Chinese history, for his help with the material on imperial China. I would also like to acknowledge author Lisa Brackmann for the time she spent reviewing the manuscript and offering important editorial suggestions. Brendan O'Kane generously helped with translations and shared his knowledge on the life of Edmund Backhouse, and Zheng (Silvano) Yuantao provided invaluable assistance for the chapter on same-sex love. Researcher Zhang Na was instrumental in conducting and translating the interviews held in Chinese. Special thanks must also go to ethnographer Tricia Wang for her insights into the world of China's migrant workers and residents of China's countryside, to Dr. Chong Kee Tan, a researcher of Chinese literature, and finally to Niklas Dougherty for his superb graduate thesis on China's sex trade.

I also owe a debt to my friends and relatives who provided suggestions, insights and support including Ben Miao, James Palmer, Nick Wheeler, Marianne Friese, Jeremy Goldkorn, Kaiser Kuo, Derek Sandhaus, Dave Lyons, Bob Page, Rick Cullison and my parents.

I would especially like to acknowledge my editors, Jessica Li and Graham Earnshaw, under whose watchful eyes this book was made possible. Chapter by chapter, page by page they helped to guide the book along and offered unending support and encouragement. Thanks, too, to the researchers and staff at

Earnshaw Books, who also made important contributions. It was Graham Earnshaw, my publisher, who initiated this project and developed the original concept for it. He was the seminal force behind the book, without which *Sex in China: Behind the Red Door* could not have been written.

INTRODUCTION

Every year, thousands of Chinese women pay for an operation to restore their hymens shortly before their wedding so that husbands can see blood on the sheets on their honeymoon night. Brides-to-be who cannot afford the 4,400 yuan operation (about $700) can walk into one of China's 200,000 sex shops or go online to buy a cheap artificial hymen that seeps artificial blood when punctured. Although the percentage of Chinese women who engage in premarital sex has skyrocketed in urban areas from 15 percent in 1990 to more than 50 percent in 2010, conservative attitudes toward sex, even in big cities like Shanghai, remain largely intact. To most Chinese people, virginity matters, and husbands look forward to their wedding night when they can deflower their young virgin brides. For some husbands, the absence of blood on the sheets can be grounds for divorce.

It has become a tired cliché that China is a "land of contradictions," but it is only a cliché because there is so much truth to it. China's ruling Communist Party oversees an economy that is in many ways aggressively capitalist, runs a socialist society filled with Western icons like McDonald's, iPads and

Mickey Mouse, has democracy "with Chinese characteristics" while regularly arresting human rights lawyers and a vigorous and lively Internet community that is just as vigorously censored and manipulated by the party's propaganda arm. Corruption is both rigorously banned and blatantly everywhere. The contradictions related to sex in contemporary China are just as dramatic. Opposing forces always appear to be pulling at each other. Looking at a Chinese newspaper one day you might get the impression China is as sexually liberated as Sweden, and the next you might think China is actively engaged in sexual repression.

In 2009, authorities launched a 15-day crackdown on the huge prostitution business in the southern China manufacturing hub of Dongguan. Hundreds of arrested prostitutes were marched down the street tied to a leash, their photographs broadcasted throughout the country. Others sat on the sidewalk, their heads in their hands, weeping. The raids were major national news. And yet, any man in China seeking sex-for-sale can probably find it within walking distance, be it at a karaoke bar, barber shop or massage parlor. Most of the brothels busted in "strike hard" campaigns as in Dongguan are back in business a few weeks or even days later, though they may have changed their address.

There are now gay bars in most of China's first and second-tier cities, and usually a bathhouse or two as well. In 2009 a gay male couple held a symbolic wedding a few blocks from Tiananmen Square in Beijing, and a photograph of the two men in a passionate embrace was splashed across the front page of China's largest newspapers, all mouthpieces of the ruling Chinese Communist Party (CCP). Other gay and lesbian marriages across the country followed, and were covered positively. But until relatively recently gay bars and establishments were frequently shut down with no notice. In 2009 police raided a popular "gay park" in Beijing and detained eighty men. A similar park in Guangzhou was raided three times the next year and a hundred men were also arrested. Bathhouses are frequently shut down during major national events such as the annual National People's Congress or the Beijing 2008 Olympic Games.

Weddings in China are nearly as sacred and revered an event today as they were in ancient times. While many of the rituals, such as being carried to the wedding ceremony in a sedan chair, have been updated, vestiges of traditions that date back two-thousand years remain intact, including the selection of an auspicious wedding date by a *feng shui* master and the bountiful all-night wedding feast with foods selected for their association with good luck. For most Chinese, even homosexuals, the very idea of not marrying is incomprehensible; a child's primary obligation to their family is the provision of offspring within wedlock. But at the same time, divorce rates have soared in China since the 1990s, with infidelity being the most common reason for separation. Hundreds of thousands of wealthy Chinese men keep "second wives" (*ernais*), a throwback to the practice of concubinage, and millions of married Chinese men of all social strata pay for sex on a regular basis.

For most of the past 100 years, talking about sex in public in China has been taboo. Still, in 2004 a healthcare website distributed postcards that were displayed in bars and restaurants across the country telling men and women there was no problem with masturbation. The Chinese expression for autoeroticism is "shooting planes," and the front of the postcard features a large anti-aircraft gun pointing at a plane in the sky. Directly above, the text reads: "If you shoot planes too often, will your barrel get blocked?" Flip to the other side, and it says, "Of course not; both men and women can masturbate. It is normal and does no harm." Are the Chinese hyper-shy about sex or surprisingly liberal? As the expression goes: It's complicated.

The story of sex in China, from thousands of years ago to today, is an astonishing one. No society has swung more dramatically from extreme sexual openness to prudish orthodoxy and then to the sexually ambiguous atmosphere we see at present. This transformation has gone back and forth many times, and there is no single clear trajectory leading from sexual openness to sexual repression and back to relative openness. Even within the same imperial dynasties, China's attitudes toward sex kept shifting. And during some of the most sexually repressive periods, Chinese artists created some of the most sexually graphic art and literature. These contradictions have been there throughout China's sexual history, and they are alive and well today.

There is no arguing that China is in the midst of a sexual revolution, the beginnings of which can be traced back to the start of Deng Xiaoping's policy of "reform and opening up" in the early 1980s. However, it did not really take off and become a true "revolution" until the 1990s. The initial opening only lifted the dark curtain of repressed sexual expression that fell over China from the Communist victory in 1949 through the late 1970s. It took several more years before sex education was introduced in China's classrooms and many biology teachers today are still so squeamish on the subject that they skip it all together.

But the changes underway are palpable. Today in China's cities you will see public displays of affection that would have been unthinkable as recently as ten years ago, let alone during the time of Mao. Young Chinese couples are holding hands, walking arm in arm, and they may even enjoy a brief kiss. But as is always the case when discussing sex in China, there are qualifiers. Public displays of affection are still rare in China's smaller towns and villages, and even in the big international cities like Beijing and Shanghai many young couples refrain from touching one another. Still, the ice has certainly broken and more Chinese young people are rejecting the long-held tradition of keeping their affections to themselves outside of their homes.

China's sexual revolution is real, but what kind of sexual revolution is it? It is tempting to look at China and conclude it is going through the same type of sexual revolution that swept the United States and much of Europe starting half a century ago. In the West, sexual expression was tightly repressed before and during the Victorian period, followed by a loosening up as people gained new political freedoms and societies liberalized. This process was a slow one, and it wasn't until the 1960s and 1970s that we saw the bubble burst, with young people suddenly "doing their own thing" and shedding many of the sexual inhibitions of their parents. Entertainment became increasingly risqué, and nudity and language that would have been considered obscene just a few years earlier became widely accepted. Co-ed dorms opened at universities, young people started having sex earlier, and erotica was everywhere. The door was opened for people in the West to express their sexuality as they saw fit. Openly gay bars proliferated after decades of operating in secret. Pornography and books that had been banned became available to anyone who wanted them. Sex clubs, mainly underground but well known to the public, became a regular feature of major Western cities, at least until the advent of AIDS in the 1980s. These changes were part of an overall movement of political and cultural liberalism, a willingness to challenge authority and traditional societal norms that suddenly seemed passé. It was a revolution fought on several fronts, and it swept through Europe and the United States at roughly the same time (although Europe tended to be more open-minded about sex earlier than the United States).

According to the popular narrative, China has generally followed this same course, the key difference being that it was a couple of generations late to the party. How tempting it is to chart China's sexual revolution as if it paralleled that of the West. For the past thirty years, so the story goes, after a quarter century of a sexual blackout under Mao, the world was witnessing a long-overdue opening up of Chinese sexual freedom, growing in tandem with the economy and the slow but steady loosening of control over citizens' private lives.

But was it really this simple? Matthew H. Sommer, in his book *Sex, Law and Society in Late Imperial China* cautions us: "This ideal of erotic liberation has influenced some historical studies of sex in China, which seem to assume that the only important story is one of a struggle between individual freedom and narrow-minded repression." But China is not the West, where individual freedom has long been highly prized, and Sommer and other historians argue that such assumptions in regard to China are simplistic. Neither China's creeping sexual repression under the Qing nor the country's gradual unfolding of personal liberties in the late twentieth century follows the more linear model seen in the West.

To understand why China's sexual revolution cannot so easily be explained by Western Enlightenment notions of ever-increasing freedoms and individual rights we need to briefly survey how China got to where it is today.

China was for many centuries a society of extraordinary sexual openness. More than two thousand years ago, Daoists were celebrating the performance of sex with as many young women as possible to extend the lives of male practitioners. Sexual intercourse was seen as fundamental for the sharing of Yin and Yang essence. Ancient sex manuals detailed techniques for bringing women to multiple orgasms in order to siphon off the "female essence" released by their vaginal secretions. Men of means kept concubines, and at times prostitutes were registered by the government. Emperors kept harems that numbered thousands of women, and more than a few kept young male lovers as well. Same-sex love was acceptable, as long as those who practiced it maintained their familial obligations.

While there was a loosening and tightening of these sexual norms at different points in China's history, ancient China was in many ways one of the most sexually open societies the world has ever seen, particularly from the male perspective. The pendulum swung, unevenly, from unprecedented sexual liberalism under the Tang Dynasty (618 - 907) to repressive orthodoxy under the Qing Dynasty (1644 - 1912), with lots of back and forths in between. Puritanism reached its peak in the Mao era, when prostitution was all but eradicated along with almost all public references to sex.

INTRODUCTION

If by the late nineteenth century the sexual landscape had grown dim, after Mao took power in 1949 it soon went absolutely black. For many years, the slightest display of intimacy outside the home was taboo. Marriage was a monogamous relationship between one man and one woman. Premarital sex and homosexuality were strictly forbidden as the CCP wrapped its people in a cocoon of chastity. Men and women wore drab, gender-neutral clothing, and sexual desire was looked on as a selfish and bourgeois indulgence. To discuss anything about one's personal life and romantic longings was unimaginable. Sex education in school was forbidden, as were all forms of erotica and sex-related books.

An interesting exception was the numerous research papers on sex that circulated among the highest party members in the 1950s. These reports indicate that while the government was intent on creating a society that was basically sexless outside of their homes, it was still concerned with keeping its citizenry sexually satisfied. Sexual contentment was seen as an important pacifier to keep the society stable and harmonious. Although the communist government distributed some pamphlets on the importance of a healthy sex life, they still stressed the importance of sex for the purpose of procreation. The pamphlets were only circulated in a few cities, however, and most Chinese never even saw them.

The stifling of sexual expression seemed to reach its apex during the Cultural Revolution, when Mao sent forth his Red Guards to destroy the *"four olds"* – Old Customs, Old Culture, Old Habits, and Old Ideas – and threw the country into a decade of chaos and terror. Sexual asceticism became the law of the land, and those who sought sexual pleasure outside of marriage faced brutal punishment. The editors of an exhaustive book on sex during the Cultural Revolution, *Report on Love and Sex among China's Sent-Down Youth*, lamented, "We were robbed of our youth, ideas, hopes, and love. In terms of love, people were criticized and struggled against, put in jail . . . All books about

7

love were labeled pornographic, all songs about love labeled low-class. Men and women in love were considered hoodlums."

Gender differences were broken down as girls in Mao's Red Guard wore their hair short and donned the same quasi-military uniforms as boys. Androgenized females were encouraged to be as brutal as their male comrades, and often led the charge beating suspected "rightists" with leather belts. Their role was to be devoted only to total and unending revolution and class struggle, undistracted by physical desires. One of their top priorities was to purge the country of pornography, considered the most dangerous import of "spiritual pollution" from the West. Dirty jokes and profanities were forbidden.

And yet there are more than a hundred memoirs from the period telling stories of the sexual urges and romantic yearnings of young male and female Red Guards, set free to roam the country under no parental supervision and frequently experimenting with sex. According to feminist studies professor Emily Honig, many female Red Guards were sexually molested by their male comrades. Many of Mao's foot soldiers, male and female, were exposed for their sexual "immorality" and subjected to cruel interrogation sessions and beatings.

Girls in particular were vulnerable to scorn if caught having sex, and were paraded down the street with a pair of worn-out shoes tied around their neck, a metaphor for their being "damaged goods." Despite the ban on sexual thought, young male Red Guards frequently exchanged handwritten pornographic books, and there are many recorded instances of male Red Guards molesting women as they terrorized the population. So to label the Cultural Revolution as a time of complete sexual austerity, despite its battle against sexual expression, is not entirely accurate. Experimental sex and private displays of affection may have been banned but they certainly did not cease to exist.

After the Cultural Revolution ended in 1976 life slowly returned to normal, and the reforms of Mao's successor, Deng Xiaoping, would soon loosen the Communist Party's chokehold on sex. The 1980s saw the return of prostitution open the door to a new sexual chapter. As foreign businessmen flooded into China to seek their fortunes, a huge prostitution industry developed and thrived, despite occasional government crackdowns known as "*Sweeping the Yellow*" ("yellow" in Chinese stands for vice). The demand for prostitution increased as migrant laborers moved to the big cities to find work. China was slowly loosening the reins, recognizing the need for citizens to find sexual satisfaction. Censorship under Deng never stopped, and there were many violent crackdowns on vice and pornography, but Mao's eradication of prostitution was over.

It was not until the 1990s, as the Communist Party continued to give citizens greater personal freedoms, that a truly visible sexual revolution swept the country. Homosexuality was decriminalized and gay bars began to sprout up in the international cities. Western influence was everywhere and attitudes toward sex began to change. But the tug of war between conservative values and China's new-found sexual freedom was always pulling in opposite directions. "*Sweeping the Yellow*" campaigns continued and the government never ended its efforts to keep its sexual revolution in check. In 2010 there were a series of arrests targeting wife-swappers, and the war against pornography, especially in the age of the Internet, took on a new aggressiveness. The government would not stop interfering with people's sex lives entirely. Any sexual revolution would be on its terms.

It needs to be remembered that for all its progress and modernization, China's government remains an authoritarian one that does not hesitate to meddle in the lives of its citizens. That is not to say the leadership is homogeneous; some members of China's huge Communist Party and government apparatus are pushing for greater social and political reforms, but the conservatives often seem to have a greater say.

Today, movies and books are still heavily censored or banned altogether for "lewd" content. The media report that an army of 30,000 censors watches over China's Internet to protect the people from "unsafe" material, which is defined not only in terms of pornography and gambling but also in terms of comments, articles and websites that reflect negatively on the party and its leaders and question in some way the political status quo. Thousand of sites the censors deem harmful simply will not load in China. This includes many blogs, Youtube, Facebook and Twitter. Social media can rally the masses, and what the Chinese Communist Party fears most is an uncontrolled assemblage of citizens, as it saw in Tiananmen Square in 1989. But at least in terms of sexual material, it appears to be a losing battle. Anyone in China with a Wi-Fi connection can download porn to their heart's content, and anyone using a virtual private network can visit any of the banned sites. Millions do every day.

The decision by the government to allocate a high degree of social and sexual freedom to its citizens is an intentional and self-protective one. The government knows that when the people are prosperous, and when they feel they are free to do in their private lives as they choose, they will be less concerned with political matters and will be more willing to leave the government alone. This concept is not really anything new for China, where for thousands of years the average citizen played no role to speak of in the nation's governance.

China's leaders have decided they can allow people a considerable degree of personal latitude, as long as society accedes to the government's claim to complete power. Democracy advocates in China, like Nobel Peace Prize winner Liu Xiaobo, can still receive lengthy prison terms for urging Western-style political reform. References to democracy on Chinese microblogging and social networking sites are routinely censored (though this can be compared to a game of whack-a-mole). So far the strategy of increased personal freedom in exchange for limited political freedom has worked, despite occasional grumblings from netizens about censorship, corruption and social injustice. If these grumblings grow too loud, censors do all they can to squelch them.

In the book *Sex and Sexuality in China*, China scholar Elaine Jeffreys examines the argument that in China "talking about sexuality may be neither inherently liberating, nor diametrically opposed to the interests of power," and that perhaps "the recent proliferation of sex-related discourses in the PRC constitutes an extension rather than a curtailment of the CCP's disciplinary power." She questions the narrative common in the Western media that China is on a steady path to "Western-style sexual and political liberation."

Greater freedom, ironically, can mean greater control. Mao recognized this in 1950 when his government rewrote the marriage code to give women greater equality and the right to marry whomever they chose. The actual effect was to accelerate women's entry into China's workforce, one of the Party's goals, and to weaken the male-dominated family structure, transferring power from the family to the state. Arranged marriages were banned (on paper) and young people were encouraged to choose their own spouse, though always with the active participation of their family. Divorce, while legal, remained impossible without official approval. Although divorce rates rapidly increased, it was still a difficult process and many thousands of requests were denied. Mao's emancipation of women under the mantra *"Women hold up half the sky"* was an important landmark for women in China but many of the gains were theoretical. Post-Mao revisions of the marriage code, which continued into the twenty-first century, did eventually give the Chinese true freedom to marry and divorce as they wished.

An early sign of growing personal freedom was seen in the early 1990s with the advent of new radio programs featuring advice hotlines, such as the wildly popular call-in show "Midnight Whispers," which started broadcasting in Shanghai in 1996. Citizens called to discuss previously taboo topics like extramarital affairs and unrequited love, and the programs enjoyed a huge listenership throughout much of China. People finally had an outlet to talk about sex without fear of being watched by the government or by their family. Both men and women participated, men usually seeking sexual advice, women more likely to discuss family and marital stability. This program was a major step in giving the Chinese people a sense of sexual freedom, and similar type shows were soon producing self-help books people could buy anywhere. The dissemination of knowledge not only helped spread sex education, but it also created a sense among Chinese citizens of being connected, of realizing they were not alone with their problems.

Kathleen Erwin, author of an analysis from 2000 of what such phone hotlines have meant for China, reminds us, however, that the advice these shows dispense comes from either party cadres or specially selected experts. The shows, she argues, are an example of "the *disinterested interest* that the state maintains in monitoring the populous." The state encouraged the hotlines, and used them to convey information that was within the sphere of mainstream Chinese discourse. As China shifted more toward a market economy, commercial businesses began to sponsor the programs, but only in cooperation with the government. As Erwin noted, "The dual but joined hands of the state and of the market could be found in the operation and structure of hotlines, pointing to the complicity of state and capitalist interests in the promotion of hotline counseling." To see the hotlines purely as proof of sexual liberation is naive.

Prostitution, too, is an area where at first glance it seems the people have considerable freedom of choice with little government interference. There are occasional "strike hard" campaigns directed at brothels and pornography and gambling rings, but usually prostitutes are left alone, and when there are raids the brothels soon re-open. The reason for the relatively cozy relationship between prostitution and law enforcement is that they often work together. The police depend on the bribes they are paid by karaoke bar owners and massage parlors. When they do launch a raid, it is often at the bequest of higher authorities, and the local officers frequently warn the brothels and karaoke bars in advance to keep the money flowing. The government and the prostitution industry are closely intertwined.

In 2003, a female sex blogger known as Muzimei rocked the country with her tell-all blog that gave the names of the men she slept with. Millions of Chinese women felt liberated by her open discussion about her sex life, and the joy of pure sex with no commitments. While her blog was soon shut down, many copy-cat blogs followed in which women discussed their sexual exploits and even posted erotic photographs of themselves. Some were censored; others were left alone. The Chinese government still appears confused about how to handle the groundswell of sexual expression and its proponents like Muzimei. It approved a gay pride event in Shanghai, but not a parade. In 2004 it closed down a performance of *The Vagina Monologues* in Beijing, but the show was allowed to come back in 2009. To this day, Chinese television shows that appear to the government to be too sexually risqué are "modified" to remain within limits set by the state. Just as in the imperial days, the government's attitude toward sex seems to be in a state of permanent flux.

The sexual revolution has left the countryside relatively untouched. Most twenty-somethings have moved from their rural villages to find work in urban areas. Tens of millions of young migrant workers who move to towns and cities often frequent Internet cafes where they use social media to find dates and make friends. They are part of the sexual revolution, even if they do not experience it in their hometowns. The Chinese people are trying to balance their new sexual liberties with old traditions and customs they are reluctant to abandon. The Internet has added a whole new dimension to the lives of these young people, making sex easier to find and allowing them to express themselves in ways that would have been impossible a mere twenty years ago. At the same time, China has to deal with the challenges that come with sexual liberation, such as unwanted pregnancies, sexually transmitted diseases and HIV/

AIDS, which are all a part of this story.

China's transformation from the sexual dark ages of the 1950s to a time when bloggers can detail their sex lives for all to see has been breathtaking. Thirty years ago, gay men and women holding symbolic weddings in public and young couples walking down the streets arm in arm would have been unthinkable. All of these changes make it a confusing time for the Chinese people, but it appears they are going to emerge the better for it, like other societies that made the transition from sexual repression to liberation. Whether China's sexual revolution ever truly mirrors that of the West, with near-equality between men and women, freedom of expression without censorship and the notion that all people have the right to choose their own sexual path, remains an open question.

In his book about a trip up the Yangtze, *The River at the Center of the World*, Simon Winchester writes of "the delicious strangeness of China," and nowhere is this strangeness more manifest than in the country's improbable sexual history. Drawing together China's past and present attitudes toward this most basic human necessity and arriving at a neat conclusion is impossible. Any discussion of sex in China can only be suggestive. There are no universal truths or absolutes. Every point an observer makes can be argued and contradicted. The best we can do is pull together the various conversations on what sex and sexuality in today's China means, and hope to offer as balanced a picture as possible.

SEX IN IMPERIAL CHINA

A complete history of sex in imperial China would require several volumes at the very least. But at the heart of China's attitudes toward sex throughout most of its history is the concept of balance and harmony, Yin and Yang. The concept, which dates back at least three thousand years, was developed and expanded upon during the Zhou Dynasty (1046 – 256 BC), when the foundations of Chinese philosophy were laid out by Confucius (551 – 479 BC), the founder of Confucianism, and Laozi (sixth century BC), the founder of Daoism. Daoism, an umbrella term for a wide-ranging set of beliefs and practices, was influenced as much by the brilliant philosopher Zhuangzi (369 – 286 BC) as by Laozi, and was practiced by China's leaders and educated classes for centuries. It is key to understanding attitudes toward sex in ancient China.

It was in the Han Dynasty (206 BC – 220 AD) that the terms Yin and Yang came to dominate the philosophical lexicon. Yin and Yang are complementary to one another and interdependent despite being polar opposites: male and female, light and darkness, heaven and earth, creation and destruction. The symbol of Yin and Yang, a dark Yin and a white Yang bound together like two tadpoles flowing in a rotating symmetry, suggests a continuous circle, the flow of existence moving in synchronicity. Everything exists in harmony, balanced by Yin and Yang, which is at the core of Laozi's incredibly influential text the *Dao de Jing* (most likely written by a composite of authors over several centuries). The philosophy of the *Dao de Jing* permeates Chinese thinking, from thousands of years ago to today. It is the basis for Chinese medicine, for Chinese martial arts and *tai ji*, and for *feng shui* and geomancy. Yin and Yang is a concept that affects practically every aspect of China and other Asian countries, including the Chinese people's outlook on life itself.

The origin of Yin and Yang, goes back much further than Laozi. The ancient Chinese text the *Yijing* (*I Ching*), one of China's first and most important philosophy texts, is largely based on the concept of Yin and Yang, whose continuous interaction accounts for the origin and the destruction of all phenomena on earth. All human beings are made up of *qi*, or vapor, undifferentiated matter that manifests itself in two opposite but interconnected forms, Yin and Yang. Yang represents male energy, powerful, creative, active and bright, while the dark Yin represents female energy, passive, weak and destructive. Yet, although Daoism does see the male as enjoying higher status than the female, the female Yin is in no way "bad" or inferior to the male Yang. They represent opposite poles of existence, but they flow together in a dynamic, natural cycle, always seeking harmony with one another.

The *Yijing* is resoundingly sex-friendly, viewing sexuality – the ultimate co-joining of Yin and Yang – as something to cherish:

The constant intermingling of Heaven and Earth gives shape to all things. The sexual union of man and woman gives life to all things.

The interaction of one Yin and one Yang is called Dao (the Way, or Supreme Path or Order), the resulting constant generative process is called "change."

The two most influential philosophies in China's long history are Confucianism and Daoism, the latter of which later evolved into China's first indigenous religion, complete with priests, temples and worship rituals. Confucianism remained a secular religion-philosophy, a set of principals to live by. Both were strongly influenced by the notion of balance and harmony, of Yin and Yang. Both advocate distinct gender roles in which women were expected to yield to men, although Daoism treats women with a greater degree of reverence.

Confucius believed that sex, like eating, was a necessary human function, the main purpose of which was to produce children to continue the family lineage. He never wrote of sex as something bad or shameful, but he did believe it was an act performed by a man and a woman in a monogamous relationship. He acknowledged the importance of sex and in the Confucian Analects wrote, "I have not seen one who loves virtue as he loves sex." He did not condemn concubines, however, especially if the actual wife failed to bear a male heir. Confucianism even includes a set of rules dictating how a husband should interact with his concubines. Confucius' teachings include relatively few references to sex, which he seemed to dismiss as a distraction from what really mattered: order, discipline, harmony, ritual, filial piety and obedience, both to the male head of the household and to the state. His most influential follower, Mencius (372 – 289 BC) was an advocate of the people's right to seek sexual pleasure and in the Confucian classic *The Works of Mencius* is quoted as saying, "To enjoy sex is the desire of human beings."

Daoism, on the other hand, is an active, participatory way of life, and offers practical guidelines for followers to attain self-betterment and inner peace. The *Dao de Jing* flows from reflections on the nature of the Dao (the Way). Mystical in nature, Daoism lays out a program of herbal medicine and aphrodisiacs, deep breathing, magic and astrology, and a scientific theory of the origin of the universe and its five elements – wood, fire, metal, water and earth – all based on the concepts of Yin and Yang.

While these are at the heart of Daoism, and of Confucianism as well, the philosophy took many twists and turns over the course of Chinese history and there is no single definition that can encompass all of what Daoism came to stand for. It has many subsets and branches, and it took a new course when it became a true religion under the Han Dynasty. Volumes can be written on its influence on Chinese medicine, design, art, the Chinese character and even Chinese cooking.

Daoism celebrates sex as a vital force for men to improve their health, to find tranquility, and to gain longevity or even immortality. Its sexual techniques, described in sex manuals that go into the finest detail, are meant for the benefit of the individual, in contrast to the Confucian notion of all human endeavors serving to benefit the family and the state. Yin and Yang form the basis of these ancient texts, and are even used to describe human sex organs, *yangju* meaning penis and *yin dao* meaning vagina. According to an early Daoist classic, the *Taiping Jing* (*The Canon of Peace and Tranquility*), "Through the way of copulation between husband and wife, the Yin and Yang all obtain what they need and Heaven and Earth become peace and tranquility. Based on one Yin and one Yang, Heaven allows both man and woman to exist."

Lovemaking was seen as an art, and Daoist texts describe the sex act in highly descriptive language. The penis is sometimes referred to as the Jade Stem, Coral Stem, Male Stalk, and Heavenly Dragon Pillar. The vagina is called the Coral Gate, Jade Gate, Jade Pavilion, Golden Lotus, and Receptive Vase. The clitoris is described as the Pearl on the Jade Stem or the Jewel Terrace.

All-important for a fulfilling life is *qi*, the vital energy of existence, which Daoists sought to manipulate through specific sexual practices to gain eternal life and happiness. The intermingling of Yin and Yang during sexual intercourse increases *qi* and thus longevity and health. Since sex is a fundamental human necessity, Daoism teaches sexual intercourse maintains the order of nature and brings continuous benefits.

For Daoists, sex was essential for enhancing a man's *qi* and for gaining a woman's Yin essence, which would bring him a longer life. This is achieved by bringing the female partner to orgasm multiple times to share her Yin and nourish the man's vital powers. In order for this process to work, it was essential for the man to conserve his *qing* – the concentrated form of *qi* that in a man is semen and in a woman vaginal juices. All human beings, Daoism teaches, require a balance of Yin *qi* and Yang *qi*, and the best way to attain it is by absorbing the *qing* of a member of the opposite sex through sexual intercourse. The goal is for a man to take in his female partner's precious Yin *qing* while conserving his own *qing* through techniques that control ejaculation. Premature ejaculation would deprive the woman of the multiple orgasms that allow her to share her Yin essence. Frequent ejaculation would bring on a loss of *qi*, so Daoists believe ejaculation must be controlled. Each time the man performs intercourse without ejaculation, his senses grow sharper, sickness vanishes and he gets closer to attaining immortality.

Male masturbation, or at least ejaculation, was discouraged, as it lessens the male's supply of Yang essence. Daoism viewed male homosexuality as pointless, as it was seen to rob men of their Yang essence without bringing them any precious Yin. Sex between women was fine, as they were seen as having an infinite supply of Yin essence. (Male homosexuality nevertheless thrived in the Zhou Dynasty and was practiced openly for many centuries by the nobility and the upper classes and even the middle and working classes.)

Daoist sex manuals go to great lengths to instruct men how to desensitize the penis so intercourse can be enjoyed longer. They also teach men how to control ejaculation by "injaculating," diverting the flow of semen inward instead of out of the body. The man achieves this by pushing down on the pressure point between the scrotum and anus right at the moment orgasm begins. When pressed firmly enough, this blocks the flow of semen through the urethra and diverts it into the bladder and recycles it into the blood. Once in the bladder, Daoism teaches that the semen moves into the bloodstream to strengthen the mind. (Scientifically this is not the case and this practice is not recommended.)

This self-control is believed to retain the man's vital energy and allow him to maintain his erection longer. The man can still enjoy his orgasm and experience the pleasure of pressing on his prostate. But saving his Yang *qi* was not enough. The male also needed to be sure his female partner reached orgasm to emit her Yin *qi*, so Daoist sex manuals go to great lengths instructing men how to please their sexual partner and hopefully bring her to orgasm multiple times. Gaining precious *qi* and *qing* were the keys to a man's health and long life. Without it, he might become sick or even die. And the woman had to make herself available for intercourse voluntarily, with a great sense of pleasure and arousal. If she were forced into sex or not enjoying it, there would be no sharing of the Yin essence, or of her *qing*.

One Daoist text offers explicit instruction for avoiding ejaculation while arousing the female partner:

In the Daoist master's sexual "battle" [to give the woman an orgasm while avoiding ejaculation] his enemy is the woman. He should begin by touching her vulva, kissing her lips and tongue, and touching her breasts, making her highly aroused. But he should keep himself under control, his mind as detached as if it were floating in the azure sky, his body sunk into nothingness. Closing his eyes, he should not look at the woman but maintain an utter nonchalance so that his own passion is not stirred.

When she makes sexual movement, the man must remain still rather than take any action. When her hand actively touches the penis, the man avoids her caress. The man can employ stillness and relaxation to overcome the woman's excitement and movement.

But while stimulating the woman sexually is essential and beneficial to her, most of the benefit in Daoist sex techniques –

health and longevity – was for the male. The Daoist sex manuals were written by men for men, and the woman was essentially an object used by the man for the sake of his own well being. Despite the emphasis on pleasing the woman and bringing her to orgasm, the woman remained subservient, submitting to the power of her male partner's Yang.

Deep-breathing, taking an array of medicinal herbs and performing a regimen of stretching exercises based on the movements of cranes and tortoises were also used by Daoists to help delay male ejaculation, preserve *qi* and enhance energy recirculation. These techniques were designed to tranquilize the mind so the man could totally control his body as he engaged in intercourse and foreplay. To put off climax he was instructed to copulate with leisurely, shallow thrusts, being sure to delight his partner. An excerpt from the Daoist sex manual *True Manual of the "Perfected Equalization,"* explains how to achieve satisfaction in coitus without ejaculating, changing positions to keep the female aroused.

When she gets very aroused and excited and her desire for the penis is strong, he changes his posture, lies on his back and lets her take the woman-superior position and move actively. He keeps still, closing his eyes and mouth, withdrawing (his) hands and feet, compressing the seminal duct between his fingers while concentrating the mind – this is the way a turtle withdraws into itself. As to the serpent swallowing its prey, he is like a turtle withdrawing into himself, it will first suck and nibble at its victim till it is completely powerless, then swallow it never to let it go again . . .When she is almost ready to climax, he returns to the man-superior position. Then, when she has had her orgasm, without ejaculation he repeats the battle again and again until she is exhausted.

By having sex with as many women as possible without ejaculating, a man could build up a copious supply of *qi*, bringing him an array of health benefits. If he kept having sex with the same woman, her Yin would diminish and the sex act would not bring him the benefit of shared Yin *qi*. Ideally, he would have multiple partners who were virgins, preferably adolescents between 14 and 18, as Daoists believed they were rich in Yin essence. The Daoist sex handbook *The Secrets of the Jade Chamber* instructs men that those who sleep with young virgins can live to be 3,000 years old.

In modern times, sex counselors around the world use Daoist sex techniques to treat sexual dysfunction and improve patients' libido (though the "injaculation" technique is no longer considered beneficial). Daoist-inspired techniques of foreplay and stimulation are staples of modern sex therapy. The art of controlling a man's orgasms to prolong and enhance sexual pleasure was being taught by Daoists two thousand years ago, and is used today to treat premature ejaculation. While Daoist sexual techniques may not bring immortality or freedom from all disease, there definitely are benefits to approaching sex from a Daoist mindset, in which blissful sex with lots of mutual stimulation results in the harmonious joining of each partner's "vital energy." Daoism teaches that sex is natural and in no way sinful, and that engaging in it correctly leads to emotional and physical nourishment for both partners, leading to greater energy and awareness, and a more fulfilling life.

Several Zhou Dynasty rulers had embraced Daoism as a guiding philosophy. The Qin (221 – 207 BC), China's first imperial dynasty, ruled with an iron fist and initiated a shift to a Confucian culture. Sex outside of marriage was no longer celebrated. Unmarried girls were kept secluded from men, while married women enjoyed relative freedom. Many married women, however, carried on illicit affairs, and they were even permitted to engage in conversation with their husband's male guests – provided she stand behind a silk curtain.

As is so often the case in ancient China, there were different forces at work, namely the conservatism of Confucianism and the tradition of sexual openness described in the country's earliest historical records. Confucianism and Daoism influenced one another and borrowed from one another in regard to Yin and Yang and the role of the woman, and they existed together in what was at times an uneasy alliance. Many educated Chinese applied the conservative Confucian doctrine to their family life, and practiced Daoism in their private life. The wealthy and those born to royalty continued to keep harems and carry on affairs, and there was still a good deal of sexual license. Ancient texts indicate that adventurous princes kept boys for homosexual pleasure, though the practice was hardly widespread during the Qin Dynasty. Concubinage was accepted, and Confucianists even wrote a set of guidelines for concubines, instructing them how to dress and behave. They saw the chief role of concubines as bearers of sons.

Under the Han Dynasty, Daoism flourished once again and began to be practiced as a true religion, though Confucianism also came into its own. The royal family believed the mystic rituals of Daoism would endow them with magical powers and longevity and they surrounded themselves with Daoist alchemists and magicians. Many of the great Daoist sex handbooks were written during this period. The Han, despite their belief in Daoism, modeled their empire on Confucianism to ensure political stability due to the philosophy's emphasis on order and obedience. Confucian texts from the time laid down stricter gender guidelines. Men were supposed to be segregated from women, and there was a general rule that a husband and wife should only have physical contact when they were on their marriage couch, though women did have a vested right to demand sexual pleasure. Despite the stricter rules, the Han period was one of sexual laxity. There are many tales of debauchery and sexual sadism practiced by the princes of the royal family, and several of the Han emperors were bisexual and had countless harem ladies along with their boy lovers. It was a time of change for China as a new middle class emerged, buoyed by burgeoning foreign trade. High-end brothels opened to accommodate merchants and the educated with their new wealth. The prostitutes would sing and dance for their customers, who came not just for sex but also for dining and drinking. Following the entertainment, the customer would often spend the night and enjoy intercourse with a prostitute.

China's culture, along with its sexual openness, reached its peak during the Tang Dynasty, a wonderful period of artistic achievement and liberalism. Erotic art and literature flourished under the Tang. Prostitution was institutionalized and its practitioners registered with the state. Men of letters and the upper classes nearly all had courtesans to sing and dance for them and accompany them outside of their home. Often these relationships were platonic, the courtesan providing entertainment and prestige, and a welcome break from family life. Chinese literature from the time is rich with stories of wealthy men and their relationships with courtesans. It was during this period that several of the Daoists sex manuals teaching men how to avoid premature ejaculation and bring their female partner to orgasm multiple times were written. Many Tang texts celebrated the sex act in near-pornographic detail. At the same time, many Buddhist monasteries were looked on by Confucians as havens of vice, which many were. Fang Fu Ruan, in his book *Sex in China*, notes a study that indicates "many [Buddhist] nuns really resembled prostitutes and their temples brothels."

This celebration of sex continued under the first emperors of the Song Dynasty (960 – 1279), but change was in the wind toward the end of the Song, when China's view of sex and erotica began to take a turn from openness to prudishness. The teachings of Zhu Xi (1130 – 1200), a Neo-Confucianist of enormous influence, became the imperial ideology of the late Song Dynasty and the Yuan Dynasty (1279 – 1367), and its ramifications have never entirely worn off. Zhu was instrumental in popularizing Neo-Confucianism and successfully advocated the adoption of an orthodox version of the philosophy as the nation's secular religion.

No previous interpretation of Confucianism was as strict

or rigorous as Zhu Xi's, which stressed social harmony, sexual monogamy within wedlock only, and the strict separation of men and women. R. H. Van Gulik, author of the groundbreaking *Sexual Life in Ancient China*, describes how worldly desires were to be suppressed: Neo-Confucianism would be the law of the land, and it was the duty of the authoritarian state to exercise strict censorship and to inculcate all citizens with its values. Ch'eng I (1033 – 1107), another influential Neo-Confucianist, summarized the movement's philosophy: "Discard human desires to retain the heavenly principles." The puritanical Neo-Confucianists did not appear overnight; they had been making the case for greater adherence to Confucianist doctrine during the Tang Dynasty, but now they were finally winning endorsement from the state.

It was during this period that foot binding, the origin of which can probably be traced to the fifty-year period between the Tang and Song dynasties, became widespread, limiting women's mobility and freedom. It began with courtesans in the late Tang Dynasty, moved on to elite women in the Song Dynasty, and then to the masses by the Ming (1368 – 1644) and Qing Dynasties as parents believed that binding their daughters' feet would increase their chances of finding a good husband. Most women who underwent the procedure did so willingly, despite the constant pain that resulted, as it was the fashion of the time, and the practice would continue until the twentieth century.

Neo-Confucianism called for a strong central government based on strict moralistic principles. It was during the Yuan Dynasty, founded by Mongol invaders, that Neo-Confucian doctrine became truly prevalent among the Chinese as they sought to protect their women from sexual coercion by the invaders. Women were segregated and kept out of sight. Remarriage of widows was frowned upon. Men began to keep their sexual lives a secret, as boasting of relations with a prostitute became grounds for punishment. All performances that included erotic entertainment were banned, and those who disobeyed the order were punished severely.

The war on sex continued into the early Ming Dynasty. This can be partly explained as a result of hyper-nationalism that followed China's liberation from the invading Mongols. The new freedom generated a major revival in Chinese art, which was produced in great quantity and with the highest artistic standards, but this was accompanied by the stifling of independent and critical thought. A period of unparalleled censorship ensued. All erotic fiction, such as the famously pornographic book *The Golden Lotus*, was forbidden, and copies of such works were burned, including their original woodblocks. Some of the ancient classics were only preserved in copies that had been sold in Japan, depriving the Chinese people of a great part of their culture. Penalties for printing banned materials were harsh, including beatings and exile.

The principles of the Daoist sex manuals were still practiced in the privacy of one's home, but the texts, while not banned entirely, increasingly fell into oblivion. Female segregation was enforced with a new strictness, and visitors to Chinese cities were struck by the near total absence of middle and upper class women on the streets. Concubinage continued, but the chastity of women became an obsession.

As always in the history of sex in China, there were contrary forces at work. In the second half of the Ming Dynasty, there was a reaction against Neo-Confucianism and the late Ming was a time of considerable openness, especially when compared to what came before and after. Part of this change was due to a philosophical turn away from Zhu Xi's Neo-Confucian philosophy and toward that of the idealist philosopher Wang Yangming (1472 – 1529). Though a Neo-Confucianist himself, Wang believed that rather than searching for the principle of all things through an investigation of external entities (especially books), one had the capacity to understand this principle by examining one's own heart. Later followers of Wang Yangming took this as an endorsement of an "anything goes" philosophy whereby if one's heart dictates it, it must be right.

The late Ming saw the increased use of woodblock printing, which made commercial publishing viable and led to a flourishing print culture and a general rise in reading. Naturally, sex was a popular subject matter so there was a corresponding increase in the number of erotic texts. Erotic and pornographic novels saw a renaissance and some of the most famous scrolls and drawings depicting every sexual position imaginable, a few even including same-sex acts between men, were created under the late Ming.

A colony of artisans, novelists and artists, along with retired merchants and government officials, found a welcome home in Nanjing around 1550, where courtesanship and prostitution flourished. Many of the late Ming's greatest writings and art originated in Nanjing, which became a hub of artistic achievement. Unfortunately, it soon also became a breeding ground for syphilis, a scourge that was only brought under control during the Communist regime in the mid-twentieth century.

After the collapse of the Ming, repression, censorship and the vilification of extramarital sex came roaring back under the Qing Dynasty. When the Manchus took over, they, along with many Chinese, felt that the philosophical, political, and moral laxity of the late Ming contributed mightily to the dynasty's downfall, and during the Qing there was a new conservatism toward sex. The new dynasty's restrictions imposed on sex went back and forth, enforced more aggressively under some emperors than others, but the trend was very clear: The Qing wanted to make chastity the highest virtue and make the illicit penetration of women, either through rape or adultery, the most heinous crime.

Chastity and the suppression of extramarital sex were seen as protecting the family structure and thus providing greater social stability while increasing the state's control over its citizens' lives. The Qing were determined to whip the country into moral shape, and their campaigns to repress and criminalize "illicit sex" and to engineer an entirely new Chinese attitude toward sex were relentless and largely successful.

Under the most repressive of the Qing emperors, Yongzheng, who ruled from 1723 to 1735, women who fought against rape were rewarded with silver. Men who committed "illicit intercourse" with either a woman or man could be subject to brutal punishment, including beatings, exile and long prison sentences. Informers spied on people to report illicit intercourse. Punishment was partially based on the woman's reaction to the man seeking to penetrate her. If she simply rejected his advances and reported him, the penalty for the perpetrator was less severe than forced rape. If she reacted to attempted rape by committing suicide, she qualified as a "chastity martyr", and the perpetrator could be sentenced to death by strangulation. Extramarital sex with all women was now a serious crime, though concubines and brothels remained in reality largely unaffected. Under Yongzheng, a nationwide propaganda campaign preached chastity as a woman's highest virtue, and countless edicts and announcements were issued glorifying chastity martyrs and urging women to resist forced intercourse.

Prostitution was prohibited, though it was never eradicated, and the practice thrived, especially in treaty port cities like Shanghai and Guangzhou, which were partly controlled by foreign powers following the first Opium War. Wealthy men continued to have their concubines, and brothels continued their operations. Yongzheng also "liberated" the entire class of China's sex slaves – those at the very lowest rung of the social ladder who worked in effect as serfs or entertainers for the wealthy and the nobility – and put them on the same social level as commoners. Known as *"yue,"* this subservient class often consisted of family members of criminals or of prisoners of war or of those seen as enemies of the state, who were punished by penal servitude. Many actors, musicians and prostitutes, long looked upon as the dregs of society, were also counted among the *yue*. This debasement was hereditary, and children born into a family of *yue* inherited their parents' status.

While at first glance it may appear that the sex slaves and servile workers were emancipated by Yongzheng, the motive behind their new status was not one of compassion. Matthew Sommer, in his book *Sex, Law and Society in Late Imperial China*, notes that as commoners, the *yue* were now subject to the stringent new chastity laws; prior to their liberation, the criminalization of extramarital sex did not apply to them. Now, their sex lives were restricted. The government had significantly increased control over the lives of its citizens.

The Qing were obsessed with the act of sexual penetration. Homosexual men who engaged in anal intercourse could, at least in theory, be punished with 100 lashes with heavy bamboo. This was a far lighter sentence than was meted out to men who committed illicit heterosexual intercourse, the main focus of the chastity laws. These laws were completely silent about female same-sex love, which did not include penetration with a penis and was therefore not regarded as criminal. Most of the sex crimes under the Qing, whether heterosexual or homosexual, had to do with male penetration. It was no crime for a man to have sexual desires for another man, only to engage in penetration. Any instance of sexual intercourse outside the monogamous relationship between husband and wife was criminalized. There were exceptions. The relationship between the literati with young male actors ("song boys") which, while illegal on paper, tended to be ignored by the Qing authorities since they saw sex between the wealthy and young actors at the bottom of the social scale as an acceptable form of status domination.

Starting in the early years of the Qing, as the government reinstated Zhu Xi's interpretation of Neo-Confucianism, erotic literature was banned. Once again, original woodblocks were burned so no record of these remained. Citizens caught publishing such materials were beaten and exiled. Hundreds of China's greatest erotic works of fiction were destroyed, some of them forever. The censorship policy was, however, inconsistent, and was relaxed and tightened at various times throughout the

Qing reign. During some periods, reprinted copies of Ming and Qing erotic literature continued to be published and circulated along with new erotic fiction. But the censorship was largely successful, and by the time of the late Qing many citizens had no idea about China's open sexual past. Toward the end of the nineteenth century, lawmakers were increasingly influenced by Western morality, which seeped into China after the second Opium War and taught that extramarital sex of any kind was a sin. Public reference to sex in the late Qing was now taboo and the Chinese became increasingly closed minded on the subject.

After the Qing collapsed in 1911, there were moments such as the May Fourth student movement in 1919 when it appeared China might have been ready to relax its puritanical policies, but liberalizing the sex laws was a low priority for China's new Nationalist rulers and the notion of sexual openness faded away. The age of China's imperial dynasties ended in 1912, but sexual thought control and repression would flourish for many decades to come, and its lingering effects are still seen and felt in the country today.

In 1912, new social and intellectual movements at once championed a liberated approach to love, sex, and marriage while at the same time internalizing foreign "scientific" attitudes toward sexual behavior. For the young reformers and revolutionaries of the May Fourth era, modernity meant relaxing strict controls regulating women's behavior, the ability of young people to choose their own spouse, and the expression of sexuality in literature and drama. One of the first essays published by an idealistic young Mao Zedong was a lamentable tale of a young woman in the countryside who committed suicide rather than marry her arranged suitor, only to have the bride and groom's families argue over who should pay to bury her body.

Mao was not alone. Many of the leaders, both in the Nationalist government and the People's Republic of China (PRC), were members of the May Fourth generation and were strong believers, in theory if not only in practice, of advocating against traditions such as arranged marriage, footbinding, concubinage and prostitution. The 1951 marriage law banned arranged marriage and gave women unprecedented rights to seek divorce. Young female cadres participated in rural reform movements by instructing women in the villages about birth control and family planning.

At the same time, both the Nationalist and Communist governments also inherited the May Fourth generation's conflation of modernity with science, in particular the regulation of the human body. This meant that the new society, while encouraging the liberation of women and a new freedom for young people to avoid arranged marriages, would also be one where the "new citizen" acted in a wholesome, hygienic manner. A stigma emerged against "unwholesome" behavior – such as homosexual sex, patronage of brothels, or excessive sexual activity – as being backwards and feudal and not appropriate in the new social order envisioned by Nationalist and Communist modernizers alike.

DATING AND MARRIAGE

Dating and marriage based on romance and love were practically unheard of in China from ancient times until the 1980s. Casual dating did not exist and took many years to become accepted. Dating as a means of seeking fun or entertainment would have been considered immoral in earlier times. Premarital sex would have been absolutely unimaginable. Even now, most Chinese believe that marrying the wrong person will bring disgrace to the entire family, and the family should play an active role in the process of finding the right mate.

In the 1950s, China passed a sweeping marriage law declaring that marriage must be based on "the complete willingness of both man and woman." But it took some decades before this concept was embraced by the population at large, and in some rural parts of China today the notion of marriage by free choice is still unknown.

Throughout China's history, marriage was an institution designed to continue the family's lineage and fulfill the Confucian ideal of filial piety. In earlier times it was out of the question that young people could make such a vital decision as choosing a life partner. Often marriages were arranged upon the child's birth. Dating etiquette was rigidly structured, starting with a matchmaker presenting the man's proposal to the woman's family. Her family, and especially her father, would make the final decision as to the man's suitability. The couple's stars would be charted based on their birthdates. If they got to the next level, the prospective groom would offer gifts to the woman's family, and finally the matchmaker would determine the best date, based on *feng shui* and astrology, for the wedding itself.

Any discussion about the evolution of dating in China must take into account that there is more than one China. Attitudes toward dating and casual sex in large international cities like Shanghai and Beijing remain markedly different from those in lower-tier cities, let alone villages in the countryside. Dating and one-night stands have only become commonplace in larger cities because of relatively recent Western influences and dramatic modernization. Even so, dating in China remains considerably different than in the West. What we see in China today is a rapidly evolving hybrid of modern Western dating practices and traditional Chinese courtship conventions. And while casual sex is now routine in the big cities, especially now that the Internet makes hook-ups easy, in the countryside and many smaller towns and cities the dating process is still bound by convention.

Professor Li Yinhe, an expert on family and marriage at the Chinese Academy of Social Science, in an interview in 2010, said that in 1989 only 15 percent of people in China had pre-marital sex. Today, she said, more than 60 percent of urban Chinese have sex before they are married.

In China today the family still plays a considerable role in the dating process, providing perspective on whether the potential spouse lives up to their expectations in terms of personality, temperament, wealth, title and education. It doesn't compare to the arranged marriages of times past, but it is a far different cry from how marriages come about in the West. In less developed parts of China, parents may still analyze the couple's compatibility using ancient astrological charting.

But throughout China one thing remains the same: Parents are consulted and usually become actively involved before a couple agrees on marriage. If it actually gets to the point where the woman invites her boyfriend to meet her family it means she expects to marry him, and Chinese men understand this arrangement. If he doesn't intend to marry her, the man will decline the invitation. As soon as the girl hints that she has spoken to her mother about the man, he knows she means business.

"Wuhan is a second-tier city but just like in Shanghai, our parents remain deeply involved in the dating process," said Ada, who was born in Wuhan and now lives in Shanghai. "Your parents won't force you to stop seeing someone, but they might suggest he's not the right man. They want us to marry, to settle down and be happy. In my hometown, many parents will try to introduce a good match for you, and some families will try to force you to accept their choice, others will just suggest it. My mom just called me and tried to set me up with a man she was told about. She won't force me, but she will keep an eye open for me."

Stella grew up in Shanghai and agrees that while the parents might leave to her the final decision of who to marry or not, their opinion still matters:

Parents want to get as involved in your relationship as much as they can. When you date they want to know, where did you go and what did you do? They want details about how the relationship is going and they try to offer you advice. Girls especially value what their parents think of their boyfriends, and if they do not approve the girl may not be happy. I don't have a boyfriend now and my parents are going crazy, so they're telling me everyday, 'You're almost 24, you should be going out to find a boyfriend. Your career is secondary to your marriage.' They think I should prioritize my goals in life and make finding a boyfriend my first priority. It's annoying for me to hear them talk like that because I want to get a degree. Their intentions are good, but they're based on their own judgment and experience and they are trying to force their ideas on me and prove my own ideas are wrong. I try not to discuss this issue with them. Still, it's much different than in the countryside, where the marriage is usually arranged and the girl only meets the boy once or twice before they get married.

Everywhere in China, courtship is typically taken very seriously. Even in the big cities, serial dating is frowned upon, even as it becomes increasingly common. In the eyes of most Chinese, frequent dating with different suitors is a good measurement of the person's character and reputation, signaling they might be immoral or promiscuous. The Chinese still see dating as a means of finding a spouse, and as the first step in a process leading to marriage. Young Chinese rarely date until they have finished high school, and more often they wait until their early twenties. As of 2010, the average age for men to marry was 24 years old, and for women it was 22 years old. Both men and women who are still single in their thirties are looked at with suspicion.

While young singles in many parts of China now date, they are not likely to bounce from partner to partner to size up who makes the best match. Dating is an opportunity to show honor and respect. Often it starts with friends setting up a dinner for a couple interested in one another, with the friends acting as matchmakers, steering the conversation toward topics that reveal the characteristics of the couple so they can weigh whether or not they are a good match. Afterwards, if the girl agrees to go out on a date with the man, she sends the signal that she considers him a viable candidate for marriage.

More casual, serial dating occurs in the big cities, but is still marked by "Chinese characteristics." For example, the woman on the first date may ask her suitor how much money he makes, almost as casually as she would ask him about his day. She will ask about his education and his health (most Chinese women today prefer to marry non-smokers). Stability, loyalty and dependability are important, and the woman wants to make sure her potential spouse will be committed to her, physically and financially, throughout their lifetimes. China's current gender imbalance gives girls the upper hand in the dating process, since she has more potential husbands to choose from. Dating and marrying can be compared to an auction in which the bride will go to the highest bidder, i.e., the man who can offer her the most financial longevity.

Unlike in the West, much of the courtship process may take place outside on the sidewalk if the couple cannot afford to go to a restaurant or Starbucks. If they are in a university together, they may well whisper romantically to each other in a corner of the classroom. Privacy is often hard to come by in China.

The Internet is another factor changing the face of dating in China. Although meeting for the first date is still frequently arranged by family or friends, China now has thousands of dating sites that have become home to millions of young people. Online dating sites and social media are especially useful if the parties live far apart but find they have mutual interests. They get to know each other online first, and then arrange at some point to finally meet, and maybe even marry. (Of course, such sites also lead to lots of hook-ups and one-night stands.) Some of China's leading online dating sites boast millions of registered users, and some charge a small fee to register, making Internet dating a huge business. One of the largest sites, Jiayuan, has more than 50 million paid users, and went public in 2011.

Prior to the start of China's sexual revolution in the 1980s, Chinese couples usually did not kiss or touch one another until the day of marriage. Nowadays, many young, urbane Chinese who have been exposed to Western influences have rejected these traditional virtues. Public displays of affection have become common in big cities, though they are nonexistent in less developed areas. Even in Beijing and Shanghai, many couples feel more comfortable holding hands in a secluded park than on the street, though that is changing. Most single adults in China still live with their parents and if they are going to have sex, chances are they will do it in rented apartments or when their parents are at work. For one-night stands and affairs, couples with enough money often check into cheap "love hotels " run specifically for customers who want to have a quick sexual encounter.

Most Chinese women still believe it is best to date only one man and to marry him. Once the man invites her on a second or third date, he is indicating that he's serious, that he is hoping for an exclusive relationship, and that marriage may be in the cards. If the girl tells him at some point that she likes or misses him, or if she casually touches him, the man knows that she, too, is getting serious.

Despite the liberalization of the cosmopolitan cities, traditional Confucian values still influence young people. Stella, a white-collar worker, notes the ongoing conflict between the sexual revolution and classical values. "In Shanghai, it's hard to generalize because people are more open-minded than in the smaller cities. But even so, there are lots of girls in Shanghai who have no sexual activities with their boyfriends until they get married. Due to pressure to keep their virginity, girls are in a dilemma if their boyfriend wants intimacy, they have to struggle about whether to conform to him or wait until they get married."

In a class by itself is the dating process for young migrant workers who have flooded China's big cities from rural villages. Tricia Wang, a sociologist and ethnographer who has spent years in China studying social trends said in an interview:

The migrant workers have brought the countryside to the city. These young people bring with them strong ties to their families and friends, and often they migrate to a location based on their family knowing someone there. They are still closely tied to their village through these networks. When they are in their early twenties the family puts pressure on them to marry, getting involved, often through their networks, and encouraging friends and relatives to make introductions. If the son or daughter returns to their village with a boyfriend or girlfriend, it usually means they plan to marry.

In the towns and cities, young migrants are free from the watchful eye of their parents and are more likely to engage in premarital sex. If they do, however, it will usually be with the partner they intend to marry. Sex with multiple partners is not common. This is very different from the urbanites, who are more inclined toward casual dating and premarital relations without the expectation of marriage.

Many of these young migrant workers also find partners to "date" in virtual Internet communities. Some of these are similar to the popular Second Life community, self-contained worlds in which virtual partners can live and sleep together, wash dishes together and enjoy a feeling of being connected and being cared for, if only online. Message boards, chat services like MSN and its Chinese equivalent QQ, and a Twitter-like microblogging platform called Weibo offer migrant workers a variety of Internet communities to stay connected and find friends.

These sites are critical to millions of migrants longing for a sense of connectedness and bonding. Young workers from all around China who cannot afford their own PCs flock to Internet cafes where they use these tools to connect with friends, find dates, stay in touch with their families, play games, watch porn and even sleep. For about two dollars they can stay for eight hours in what is a welcome escape from the city outside, which often treats migrant workers with dismissal, if not outright contempt. These digital tools help to urbanize young migrant workers and allow them to have hopes and dreams. Their adoption of technology and greater exposure to the outside world can help move them toward eventual assimilation into China's middle class.

Premarital sex generally does not occur in rural areas for two main reasons: most young people of dating age have moved to urban areas to work, and the lack of privacy in the small villages makes it nearly impossible to carry on an affair.

Yellow Fever

In 2006 an English teacher in Shanghai, later revealed to be one David Marriott from the UK, started a blog that meticulously detailed his sexual exploits, including the seduction of former students. He wrote under the name China Bounder, and his blog was appropriately titled "Sex in Shanghai." The blog left nothing to the imagination. In one typical post Marriott describes his excitement as he prepares to make love to one of his many one-night stands:

And so while she freshened up I lay on the bed, reaching down to pick a pair of panties from the floor, feeling their slick silk texture under my fingers, pressing them to my nose to inhale her scent, and once again running through in my mind what was about to happen.

And he tells what happened in shocking detail, in story after story. Descriptions of intercourse and oral sex and panty-sniffing with a seemingly endless stream of young Chinese girls, all told with a wry wit and a good deal of writing talent, ensured that he would get noticed, both by fellow expatriates and the Chinese. He makes it abundantly clear that he cares nothing for the girls, who are there only to give him pleasure. In one of many humorous if somewhat depraved posts he describes his hunt for a condom that would fit him:

The [drug store] rep told me this was a frequent problem with Western guys, and that as far as she knew nowhere in the city sold a bigger size. But, she said, foreign guys said such and such a line of Durex was the least bad fit; and so we bought a few packets of those.

Anyhow, back to Sweetie and her mouth. The condom being too small, it first of all threatened to come off, sitting as it was on my helmet like – well – a helmet – so I had to pull it further down me, making it yet more tight, and thus constricting me, reducing feeling and making it rather tougher to come, meaning I had to pump her pretty hard and fast, which began to exacerbate her discomfort. But come I did, covered in sweat and roaring.

Yeah, it was a pretty good fuck, and she's a good lover – though her oral technique could do with some improvement.

Such candor and graphic detail, especially from a teacher seducing his own students, was sure to get attention. At first it was the expatriates who took notice. More established English-language blogs began reporting on this newcomer who was pushing the envelope. Some argued he should be congratulated for having the nerve to tell the truth. Others said he was a psychopath. Sex aside, Marriott was a merciless critic of the Chinese Communist Party and Chinese society. His writing style was compelling and often hilarious, and if he had left the sex out, odds are he would have become a popular political blogger.

The reaction of Chinese readers to the blog, not surprisingly, was far different than that of the foreigners. The image of this "Ugly European" spitting in the face of his host nation and repaying it by fornicating with every girl in sight including his students was an assault on the Chinese psyche on multiple levels. The Chinese look down on serial seducers, especially foreigners who are going after Chinese girls. One way a foreigner can guarantee being unpopular with his neighbors is to bring a different girl up to his apartment every night. Also, the Chinese have long seen themselves, with a lot of justification, as victims of Western and Japanese imperialism. This image of the callous Westerner deflowering young Chinese girls aroused more than a hundred years of resentment against exploitative foreigners. When word of the sex blog burst onto the Chinese Internet, the reaction was predictably explosive. On August 25, 2006, Zhang Jiehai, a professor of psychology at the Department of Sociology in the Shanghai Academy of Social Sciences, wrote a blog post bristling with outrage, condemning the sex blogger and raising a rallying cry for his expulsion from China. From the translation by Roland Soong of the "East South West North" blog:

Today, with tremendous anger, I will tell you the story of an immoral foreigner and I call upon all Chinese compatriots to get together and kick this immoral foreigner out of China. This is how it is: Several days ago, a friend told me about a blog run by an English man in Shanghai. I read it and I was shocked, angered and disgusted . . . after I read his blog, I had only one idea: This is intolerable and this piece of garbage must be found and kicked out of China!!!

In his blog, he used extremely obscene and filthy language to record how he – a foreign language teacher in Shanghai – used his status as a teacher to dally with Chinese women, most of whom were his students. At the same time, he did everything that he could to insult, debase and distort the Chinese government and the Chinese men.

. . . This piece of garbage openly declared in this blog that he was only dallying with these female Chinese students. He said, "We don't talk about love, we don't talk about marriage, we don't even talk about being together." Once, he was even shameless enough to say, "I'm tired of her already. A cunt is a cunt. I keep her just so that I can play with her again."

Zhang managed to touch on just about everything that resonates with the Chinese people and makes their blood boil, especially exploitation by greedy, careless foreigners and the blasphemy of a foreigner mocking and ridiculing China. Furious Chinese Internet users leapt to Zhang's call, creating a "human flesh search engine" to track down every detail of the Shanghai sex blogger's real identity and force him out of China. Marriott immediately responded with a long, mocking attack on the professor:

Here's a mouth-frother, here's a bigot, here's a stiff-necked buffoon who, in one ranting article, shows all that is wrong, footling and absurd about modern China. This man is a professor at the Shanghai Academy of Social Sciences. A professor! In this is shown so much that is wrong about today's China. A country's educational system should be home [to] the best and brightest, to those who can think, weigh, balance, judge. And instead what does poor China get? Knee-jerk nationalists like this, myopic, thoughtless, a crass dolt who thinks like a sheep, rages like a hyena, and is impotent like a mule.

Although he was threatened with castration and murder, the human flesh search engine was not successful; Marriott's identity was not uncovered. He did, however, decide it would be best to leave Shanghai and head back to England. He never said specifically why he chose to leave, indicating only that there were "differences between the Shanghai police and me." Marriott later said, "Although it seemed cowardly at the time, not revealing who I was, those Chinese men who wished to protect women did not realize that the women I wrote about would have been torn to pieces by those very same Chinese men if their names had been revealed at that time along with mine." He announced his identity in 2008 as he started to promote his new book, *Fault Lines on the Face of China: 50 Reasons Why China May Never Be Great*, which dismissed China's aspirations to become a global superpower. The book, with its highly critical tone, was a flop and Marriott faded away, his blog eventually closing down in October 2008.

"Would I do it again?" Marriott reflected in a recent interview. "I am not sure that I could. Part of what I was exploring in the blog was the ease with which any Caucasian male who is not wholly grotesque can have a lifestyle in China that would be impossible in the West. I felt that Shanghai people too often looked up to Western people without good reason, just as they looked down to the *nongmin* [countryside dwellers]. In any case I am not sure I would want to do it again. I miss the friendships I had in China far more than the sex."

Most foreign men do not come to China to exploit and deflower young Chinese girls, of course. Thousands of foreigners enjoy happy marriages with a Chinese spouse. These relationships are often based on true love, mutual respect and caring for one another, with no ulterior motives on either side. Often the foreign partner is totally accepted by their Chinese in-laws and becomes a close part of their family.

The issue of what attracts foreigners to Chinese partners and vice-versa is a landmine of a question because nearly all attempts to answer it involve racial stereotypes and generalizations. Nothing lights up the English-language message boards and blogs like the topic of why Chinese women are so interested in white men, and why there appears to be far less interest by Chinese men in white women. There is no scientific data to support any of the multiple arguments, so the best we can do is look at the various theories and trends.

In 2006, of the 9.45 million couples registered for marriage in China, 68,000 were between a foreigner and a native Chinese. In 2005, 8,267 mixed couples filed for divorce, up 42 percent from 2004, according to *China Daily*. A civil court judge in Shanghai told the paper that most divorce proceedings involving foreigners were initiated by the Chinese wives, aged between forty and fifty. Most had been married more than once and were unemployed. A number of these women, the judge said, marry foreign men hoping to immigrate to another country or to enjoy a higher standard of living. Later, when these hopes fail to materialize, they divorce their foreign husbands.

All expatriate men, like China Bounder, know that it is relatively easy to find a Chinese girl for a relationship or a one-night stand, even if the man would be considered strictly average or below average by Western standards. Many Chinese women who date foreigners are seeking security and stability. For a girl from the countryside or small town whose prospects of finding a wealthy Chinese husband are low, even a foreigner on the low end of the pay scale would offer more financial security than a Chinese man in her own income bracket. Thus in the big Chinese cities it is not at all uncommon to see a foreign man who in the West would seem to be no great prize with a much younger Chinese girlfriend. If she is from a poor family, in her eyes the man might be a ticket to a better life, perhaps a visa to another country, and a chance to practice her English.

At the same time, many Chinese women are attracted to foreigners, who tend to be more open and direct than Chinese men and more willing to express their feelings. Chinese men are relatively shyer and more reserved. A Western man is far more likely to say, "I love you" to his Chinese girlfriend than his Chinese counterpart. Chinese men can appear less sure of themselves and more tentative. The outspoken sexologist Li Yinhe, when asked why certain Chinese women are drawn to foreign men, replied, "I've asked that question many times myself. One possibility is [Chinese] men just don't have the confidence."

And then there are the physical considerations. Many Chinese women irrespective of their social status are attracted to Westerners' exotically round eyes and the definition of the bridge of their nose. If online message boards on the topic are any indication, Chinese women are especially drawn to Westerners with blond hair and long eyelashes. Western men tend to have bigger frames and greater height than Chinese men (though certainly not always), which can also make them appear more attractive to certain Chinese women. They are less drawn, however, to foreigners who look overly muscular or dark skinned, as these characteristics imply the men are manual laborers and poorly educated. Some Chinese girls say Chinese men's penises are smaller than most foreigners' and they find sex with the foreigner more satisfying. Regardless of whether this claim is true or not, it is a topic frequently discussed on the Internet.

There is also a category of independent, young, highly educated Chinese women who live almost exclusively in China's cosmopolitan cities and are looking for fun and excitement as opposed to marriage (at least for the moment). These upwardly mobile women frequently go out on casual dates that end up in the bedroom, and many are happy to date Western men. Their standards, however, are the same as those of independent young Western women, meaning they are attracted to handsome, successful, highly desirable men who are usually not too much older than they are. Older, more average-looking expatriates in China will have little success going after these Chinese yuppies.

Chinese women who want a foreign boyfriend or husband make up only a small subset of the population. In 2009, Gregory Mavrides, an American psychotherapist with a Ph.D. in clinical social work who spent eight years in China, conducted a survey of 302 Chinese men and women from 14 different provinces and eight percent from Hong Kong ranging in age from 16 to 30 years old. The study indicated that only 4.2 percent of the 144 female respondents showed any preference at all for dating and marrying a Westerner, while more than 15 percent said they would never even consider it. None had a strong or exclusive preference for foreign men, while more than 30 percent said race didn't matter to them and they could go either way. Nearly 50 percent said they would prefer a relationship with a Chinese man but would consider a foreigner if they believed he was Mr. Right. The most common reasons respondents gave for their unwillingness to date foreigners were that their parents wouldn't approve of the relationship, that the cultural differences would prove problematic in the future, and that communication would be too difficult.

Another reason Chinese girls might hesitate to date a foreigner is that she risks being considered "damaged goods" by potential Chinese suitors down the road. "Once a Chinese guy learns a woman has dated a foreigner, he will be less likely to date her," said Shanghai resident Stella. "In China, we traditionally consider Western people to be more capable and more wealthy than the Chinese. That means Chinese men will have a hard time – at least in their own minds – proving they are as good as or better than the Western guy. This is a serious ego problem for them, and the ones who do date Chinese girls who have gone out with foreigners are those Chinese men who like challenges."

There are many variables at play when it comes to mixed dating that complicate any definitive conclusions about Chinese women's attraction to foreigners. There seems little doubt, however, that security and dependability are major factors, especially for less financially secure women and those who feel they cannot compete for the most desirable Chinese men. In September of 2008, right when the global financial crisis was beginning, the popular Chinese matchmaking site *Hongniang.com* announced the results of an interesting survey of 6,600 women married to foreign men. When asked to score their happiness at a range from one to 100, the average score was 72. When the survey was done again toward the spring of 2009, when the effects of the financial crisis were deeper and more widespread, the 4,400 women who participated in the new survey were far less delighted with their marriage to a foreigner: the average score dropped to 54, with scores of 63 for the group aged 25-30 and 45 for the group aged 31-40. The Chinese and foreign media were fascinated with this story, and a marriage counselor employed by Hongniang said the reason for the drop was that Chinese women were looking for stability and an opportunity to save their money. The latest survey results indicated many were no longer convinced foreigners were a safe bet. (These numbers, as with any online survey, should be taken with a grain of salt. Plenty of Chinese women remain devoted to landing a foreign husband.)

While foreign men in China can usually find a date with a Chinese girl if they try hard enough, foreign women living in Asia have a harder time getting a date with a Chinese man. There are many foreign women happily married to Chinese men, but it is not so easy for them to find a man willing to go out on a date. China remains a male-dominant culture. Chinese men are reluctant to date Chinese women who possess a higher level of education or a higher salary. This reluctance increases exponentially if the woman is a foreigner. A Western businesswoman educated at a Western university will be seen as a threat to the man's ability to be in control.

In 2010 the *Global Times* wrote about this phenomenon, citing an interview with a Chinese man in Beijing, Jack Yan, who dates white women:

A Chinese man with an apparent taste for Western girlfriends, Yan is an anomaly. Take a walk in Sanlitun, Wudaokou, or any of the city's expat-heavy neighborhoods, and you'll see a dozen Chinese women holding hands with Western men. Yan said that none of his girlfriends had ever dated a Chinese man before him.

Raise the question in an expat bar, and you'll hear a lot about what foreigners think of China. Western women, people will say, simply aren't as attracted to Chinese men as Western men are to Chinese women. But many expat women say that they have never been asked out on dates by Chinese men - so the real question may be why Chinese men don't want to date Western women . . .

Yan agrees that Chinese men have trouble approaching foreign women. "I know some Russian girls, and some of my [Chinese] guy friends say, oh, let's have a party full of blonde girls. So maybe four or five girls and four or five guys go out. And then, the girls are there, and the guys are all together across the room," Yan said. "They are afraid to be very aggressive, because, traditionally, those kind of men are bad men, playboys."

Another topic that lights up the expatriate blogs and message boards is whether Chinese men are effeminate, and whether this is a turn-off for Western women. But effeminacy is only in the eye of the beholder. As a commenter on this author's blog remarked:

If a Westerner sees a Chinese man with long fingernails, wearing lacey, floral-patterned socks, a woman's clutch-purse under his arm, riding a pink woman's bicycle or "running like a girl," the Westerner may feel that the Chinese guy is effeminate. However all of these criteria are from Western culture. In China, lacey, floral socks are not the least unmanly.

While most Western men wouldn't be caught dead wearing such socks, if we look at what the alpha male of 17th century Europe was wearing, we find high heels with big fancy bows and lacey stockings.

The same misplaced perceptions can be seen at work even within China itself. Here in Shanghai many men help their wives with the housework, and some guys are quite proud of their cooking skills. However, in other parts of China these traits would be considered evidence supporting the stereotype of overly effeminate Shanghainese men.

Asians also tend to be slimmer than Western men, with smooth arms and legs and less facial hair, factors that contribute to the Western stereotype that Chinese men are less manly. Seen through Chinese eyes, your average Chinese man is not at all effeminate. Most foreign women who participate in the online chats and blogs say this isn't an issue for them, and is mainly a perception of biased Western men. Their main frustration is that Chinese men are too reserved to walk over to them and ask them out. Some of the women feel that Chinese men see them as being too "masculine," too strong, and that Chinese men are only comfortable with a woman who fits the age-old Chinese stereotype of what a wife should be – demure, subservient and less powerful than her husband. Wives of Chinese husbands are also expected to fit into the culture of their families, and Chinese men often feel that bringing a Western wife into their home would be asking too much of their parents. Chinese men also have more hang-ups than Westerners about chastity and female sexuality, and might worry that Western women have had too much sexual experience.

Western women do find Chinese men to date and marry and live a happy life with. But there is little doubt that they will have to try harder than their male counterparts and deal with hurdles built into the Chinese culture.

Tying the Knot

Marriage is a very big deal in China, where the family and its lineage comes first and foremost. Traditional Chinese marriage was not the free union of two young adults, but rather the union of two families of different surnames for the purpose of continuing the groom's lineage. Marriage also offered security for the bride, who ideally became a productive member of her new family and the mother of her husband's children.

In ancient times, marriage rituals were complex and highly formalized. The parents and a matchmaker or other go-between were the key players who negotiated the proposal and betrothal, not the bride and groom. An auspicious date and time for the ceremony had to be selected by a *feng shui* expert to fight off bad luck. Prior to the ceremony the bride would go through an elaborate hairdressing and bathing ritual that symbolized her entrance into the world of adulthood and protected her from evil influences. A special nuptial chamber and bridal bed were prepared the day of the wedding, and visitors would gather there with the bride and groom after the ceremony and tease them with sexy jokes. After the bed was in place, a young male relative or a group of children were invited to play on the bed, a ritual believed to increase the likelihood of fertility. The children would scramble for fresh fruits and nuts scattered across the bed, which was also supposed to bring on fertility.

Everything was dictated by ritual, including the color of the clothes worn by the bride and groom, how they were transported to the wedding ceremony and back home, the use of firecrackers and drums to mark the day, the wedding feast, and the prayers at ancestral altars before the ceremony. Prior to heading off to the wedding ceremony, the groom, clad in a long red gown and red shoes, would kneel at the family altar while his father placed a red cap on his head. The son then paid homage to his ancestors, and then to his parents.

In China today, weddings remain ceremonious but are far less formal and ritualized, and often combine elements of Western and Eastern cultures. There is still a formal meeting of the parents, who negotiate aspects of the marriage, such as the dowry for the groom, which usually consists of daily necessities for the new home, such as furniture. The auspicious date for the wedding may still be determined by *feng shui* or astrology. Before the wedding celebration, a Chinese bride traditionally goes into seclusion with her closest friends, a ritual that gives the bride-to-be some time to symbolically mourn the leaving of her friends and family. Immediately before departing for the wedding ceremony, the groom and his best man come to pick up the bride, while the bridesmaids try, playfully, to keep them out.

On the wedding day the bride might wear a Western-style white wedding gown or a traditional Chinese wedding dress of bright red, or both at different times during the evening. In any case, she will be adorned with beautiful jewelry. The color red, which chases away evil spirits and is associated with good luck, will permeate the event. The invitations will be red, as will the cash-filled envelopes guests give to the wedding couple as a gift, and all gifts will be recorded in a red-covered book. Wedding photos are an essential element of a Chinese wedding, and a photographer will document the entire day, creating an elaborate wedding album that features dozens of pictures of the bride and groom at various locations and wearing several different costumes.

Brides in ancient China were sent to the groom's house on the wedding day by sedan chair or carriage, but this has been superseded by a luxury car decorated with fresh flowers. The ceremony itself is relatively simple, and often couples are married in group ceremonies, especially on auspicious dates. As eight is seen as the luckiest number, mass weddings were held across China on the opening day of the Beijing Olympic Games on August 8, 2008 – 8-8-08.

Following the ceremony, an elaborate wedding banquet is held where friends and family bestow gifts and best wishes on the bride and groom, who in turn provide cartons of cigarettes and bottles of wine for their guests. Wedding banquets are marathon events lasting many hours, and have been known to continue for as long as three days and nights. A huge variety of dishes are served and the type of food is carefully selected. There will always be some fish, as the pronunciation of the Chinese word for fish (*yu*) also means abundance. There will often be chicken and lobster, which, based on ancient symbolism, signifies a good balance of Yin and Yang. During the course of the banquet, the bride will change her outfit several times, a sign of her wealth and status.

The banquet is the highlight of the wedding day, and is almost as important today as it was in ancient times. For an entire month following the wedding the bride and groom celebrate a honeymoon that signals the beginning of their sexual relationship (a custom imported from the West), and the month is often spent traveling so the couple can love each other undisturbed. After the wedding the couple will, depending on their financial status, move in with the bride or groom's family, or into a place of their own. Traditionally, a married woman is expected to live with her husband's family.

In imperial China, women usually did not remarry after a husband's death but took on the honorable role of a "chaste widow" who remained attached to the husband's household and continued to serve his family. The family was also obliged to continue supporting her. On some occasions, the bride would be ejected from the family, who would then try to sell her off as a wife or a prostitute or a servant. If it was the wife who passed away, the husband was expected to remarry soon after the mourning period, especially if his wife had failed to bear him a son. If he already had a son, the decision to remarry was left to his discretion. In today's China, many, if not most, younger widows and widowers eventually remarry, and it is becoming increasingly common for senior citizens to find a new spouse.

The Virginity Obsession

Singer-songwriter Cui Jian, often referred to as China's "Pop King" and "Godfather of Rock," made a short film in 2006 titled

Repairing the Hymen, an attempt by Cui to shake the Chinese people into realizing their notions of female virginity were anachronistic, sexist and unfair. In researching the film, Cui's team investigated three hospitals in Beijing and discovered that every day they performed from three to ten hymen restorations, known as hymenoplasties, for a little less than $300. (Prices have since increased to an average of 5,000 yuan, about $730.)

Virginity still matters in China. Many young Chinese men believe the high point of their wedding night should be the deflowering of their young virgin bride, and since many if not most of them are still virgins when they marry, especially outside of the big cities, they expect the same of their wives. If not, it could mean she was having one-night stands and might be an unfaithful wife, or perhaps she had been a prostitute. The notion that another man has had sex with their bride before they did is unacceptable. And this attitude can be found in the largest cities as well, not just rural areas.

According to a 2010 survey by the National Working Committee on Children and Women under the State Council, more than 22 percent of Chinese people had engaged in premarital sex (sex scholar Li Yinhe says the number is three times higher), and 60 percent were 'relatively tolerant' towards sex before marriage. But the notion of virginity before sex remains ingrained in the Chinese psyche, especially in rural areas. In 2005, unmarried women in a Chongqing village applying for compensation for farmland seized by the government were forced by local officials to take a chastity test because, they argued, only virgins deserved to be compensated.

Virginity and youth have been extolled in China for thousands of years. The ancient Daoist text, *Secret Instructions of the Jade Chamber*, explains the importance of sleeping with a virgin to improve one's health:

Now men who wish to obtain great benefits do well in obtaining women who don't know the Way. They also should initiate virgins into sex and their facial color will get to be like the facial color of virgins. However, man is only distressed by a woman who is not young. If he gets one above fourteen or fifteen but below eighteen or nineteen, it is even more beneficial and fine. However, the highest number of years must not exceed thirty. Those who, though not yet thirty, have already given birth cannot be beneficial to the man. The masters preceding me who transmitted the Way to each other got to be three thousand years old. Those who combine this with medicines can get to be immortals. [Fang Fu Ruan translation]

While contemporary Chinese men may not believe sleeping with a young virgin will extend their lives to 3,000 years, many still believe a woman who has been "defiled" is unworthy of them. Knowing that their husband expects to see blood on their wedding night, many thousands of Chinese women who have lost their virginity, or who have even ruptured their hymen accidentally, are taking drastic steps to ensure their husbands will not be disappointed.

In 2010, the *Global Times*, one of China's most popular national newspapers, ran an exhaustive article on desperate women who are doing whatever they can to convince their husbands of their virginity, buying cheap artificial hymens or turning to relatively expensive surgical hymen restoration. The article reported:

Medical studies have shown that bleeding is not the only signal of a broken virginity. Some women are born without hymens; while others might accidentally rupture theirs long before any sexual activities, either by accident or through sporting activities. Still this common sense fails to reach some Chinese men or their future mother-in-laws.

Many women in China are dumped or divorced after men deflowered them and found no bleeding, which causes many desperate women . . . to fake their virginities.

Three months later, in an opinion piece that followed, a contributing writer wrote:

Extramarital affairs, one-night stands and prostitution complicate sexual relations in China. In an age when virgins disappear in batches everyday, many Chinese men still dream of marrying a girl with an untapped hymen.

Chinese men do not have a preference for a specific shape of hymen, as long as it's intact. It is a security seal and a boundary between ethics and desire. I'm not saying men prioritize virginity above everything else. The mentality of preferring a virgin is understandable.

Take an improper but plain comparison. It's like going to enjoy a feast with a brand new pair of chopsticks. Some may argue, "You are with the girl, not her hymen." Then how do you feel eating a delicious meal with a second-hand pair of chopsticks?

In order to help women make their "chopsticks" first-hand again, offers for hymen restoration kits of every kind are easy to find. Nearly every sex shop offers a variety of artificial hymens of all prices. Signs on sex shop windows throughout China cry out, "Your virginity back in five minutes!" "Your unspeakable secret will be erased!" "No surgery, no shots, no medicine, no side-effects. Only 500 RMB!"

Most hospitals and clinics offer "hymen repair surgery," a simple, 40-minute medical procedure that stitches the hymen back. Minutes after it is done, the woman can stand up and walk out. Hospitals love this operation, as its cost is low and the margins are tremendous. Customers are happy, too; this method guarantees there will be real blood on the sheets. It costs about ten times more than an artificial hymen.

Dr. Zhou Hong, a physician and director of gynecology at a Beijing hospital, told the Washington Post in 2010 that most of her patients for the operation are sexually active young brides-to-be who told their future husbands they were virgins. Some said they wanted to start over; some were victims of rape. Zhou says she is not concerned that women are starting their marriage with a lie: "It's just a white lie," Zhou said, which she blames on men who have unreasonable expectations. "It's unfair to the women. The men are not virgins. But we can't change this male-privileged society."

For Chinese women on a tighter budget, artificial hymens sold in sex shops or online are the preferred method of guaranteeing blood on the sheets. The cheapest version sells for about $15 and consists of a small red plastic insert. The *Global Times* told the story of a young bride who bought the "Virtuous Girl Red" artificial hymen kit and inserted the device a few minutes before consummating her marriage. At first all went as planned. She pretended to be in a bit of pain, and her husband was thrilled to see the blood on the sheets. But after a moment they both noticed a strange, strong odor. The Virtuous Red Girl instructions failed to mention that the "blood" it exuded gave off a nasty smell. The couple soon broke up. To make matters worse, the insert gave the girl a severe case of vaginitis and ended up costing her well over $100 in medical bills. Japanese artificial hymen kits, on the other hand, offer a far more reliable outcome for about $75. A salesman from an online store said artificial hymens were one of his best sellers, and that orders flow in not just from women in China but also from the Middle East, the US and South Korea.

As China continues to liberalize and modernize, perhaps the notion among Chinese men that their wife must prove her virginity will fade away. Cui Jian's film claims that making the bride feel guilty on her wedding night is unfair and a throwback to an earlier, more closed-minded age. But in spite of all the changes China's sexual revolution has wrought, this tradition appears to be stubbornly change-resistant, especially outside the cosmopolitan cities. Chinese men still want to be in charge, and an unbroken hymen helps convince them they are the dominant force in the relationship.

The New Normal: Divorce and Adultery

Polygamy in China goes back to ancient times and flourished throughout the nineteenth century. In the old days, wealthier

Chinese men were frequently married to three or four women at the same time, each with her own role in the household. Usually they shared responsibilities raising the different children. The first wife, however, oversaw the other wives and could tell them what to do. Her children were always given precedence over those of secondary wives.

Today, while there remain a few pockets of polygamy among some of China's minorities, only monogamous marriages between a man and a woman are permissible. China's marriage laws, written in the 1950s and revised several times since, begin:

A marriage system based on the free choice of partners, on monogamy and on equality between man and woman shall be applied. The lawful rights and interests of women, children and old people shall be protected.

Family planning shall be practiced.

Marriage upon arbitrary decision by any third party, mercenary marriage and any other acts of interference in the freedom of marriage shall be prohibited. The exaction of money or gifts in connection with marriage shall be prohibited.

Bigamy shall be prohibited. Cohabitation of a married person with any third party shall be prohibited. Domestic violence shall be prohibited. Within the family maltreatment and desertion of one family member by another shall be prohibited.

It sounds good on paper. But domestic violence remains a common affair, as do arranged marriages (both are now more prevalent in the countryside than in major cities). Adultery runs rampant and many wealthier men practice a more modern form of polygamy by keeping "second wives." Arranged marriages are still common in rural China and its smaller towns and cities. Traditional Confucian values have not been stamped out.

At first glance, the reforms built into the new marriage laws seem to signal a new age of women's liberation and freedom of choice, similar to the end of the Victorian era in the West that eventually led to a sexual revolution. It is important to draw a distinction, however: China's marriage laws were not changed to liberate its people and give them a sense of "inalienable rights" that Westerners cherish. Mao was an idealist, and while he did want to elevate the status of women, the laws were also a tool for shifting power away from the family and strengthening the power of the state. Divorces had to be approved by the state, usually with mandatory counseling and approval from the applicants' *danwei* (work unit), and many of the applications for divorce were rejected by the government. True reform of the divorce process came only in 2003 when the marriage laws were again revised. Getting a divorce became relatively simple, and the divorce rate subsequently soared.

While China has certainly experienced a sexual revolution that began at the end of the Cultural Revolution, the high value placed on virginity continues to limit women's engagement in sex. The wife is still expected to meet her husband's sexual demands, though that is changing. The marriage laws of the 1950s emancipated women and ultimately paved the way for China's sexual revolution, but it has been a long, hard journey. Unlike the sexual revolution in the West that exploded in the 1960s and 70s, China's version was more gradual, and the government always sought to control it, with varying degrees of success, slowly giving its people more sexual freedom to keep them satisfied and ensure greater stability and harmony.

An online survey in 2010, jointly conducted by the Shanghai Academy of Social Sciences and the China Population Communication Center, showed that more than 25 percent of husbands and more than 50 percent of wives considered their sex lives "unsatisfactory"; about a third of middle-aged couples described their marriages as "facing crisis." It is not surprising then that so many Chinese marriages end in divorce.

The divorce rate in China is not high by Western standards but is growing fast. It was in the 1990s that the number of divorces began to accelerate as China continued to liberalize and social tolerance of divorce grew. Although divorce was institutionalized under the Tang Dynasty, it had been traditionally frowned upon. An ancient Chinese proverb warns newlyweds: "You are married until your hair turns white." During the Mao era divorce was relatively rare, and divorced people were seen as eccentric or selfish, as the black sheep of their family.

In contemporary China, with the marriage laws encouraging individuals to choose their own spouse, and with the increasing influence of Western culture and its emphasis on independence and romantic love, many Chinese, especially those in the large cities, now see love as an essential element of a happy, fulfilling marriage. Many of the first to divorce as Deng's reforms took hold were couples who were married during or before the Cultural Revolution, when marriages were still arranged and romantic love was not seen as an important ingredient of marriage. Marriage during this time of revolutionary fever often brought together couples from dramatically different backgrounds, such as intellectuals married to peasants. When the Cultural Revolution came to a close in 1976 they were often eager to seek divorce.

The number of divorces has risen steadily in the new millennium, with one in five marriages now ending in separation. In 2006 the divorce rate was about 1.4 for every thousand people – twice what it was in 1990 and more than three times what it was in 1982. In 2010, the Ministry of Civil Affairs reported that a total of 2.68 million couples applied for divorce, an 8.5 percent increase over the year before. The number of divorces in the first three months of 2011 increased 17.1 percent year-on-year, meaning there were more than 465,000 cases of divorce in that brief period, an average of more than 5,000 per day. Beijing leads the country with nearly 40 percent of marriages ending in divorce, followed closely by Shanghai.

Divorce is no longer the big deal it was forty years ago. Today people feel comfortable talking about their ex-husband or wife, and divorced people are often seen on television matchmaking shows. According to a popular joke in Beijing, people who see a friend on the street no longer use the traditional Chinese greeting, "Ni chi le ma?" – "Have you eaten?" – but instead ask, "Li le ma?" – "Have you divorced?" Divorce in China is now seen as an acceptable alternative to an unhappy marriage and has become a relatively simple process that can usually be finalized within three days. Earlier it might have taken years.

New social and economic freedoms, the rising expectations that women bring to marriage, and extramarital affairs are cited as the main drivers behind the rising divorce rate. About 70 percent of divorces are initiated by women, the *Beijing Evening News* reported in 2011, with the most common reason being an extramarital affair on the part of the husband. Many divorces also occur for financial reasons; in modern China an increasing number of women hold full-time jobs and have become far less financially dependent on their husbands. If the husband's earnings are low and the wife believes he is not shouldering enough of the domestic responsibilities, or if the wife is earning more than her husband and feels disappointed by his inability to make enough money, she may feel more inclined to seek a divorce.

Another reason for divorce is migration and mobility. Migrant workers, after living for years in the larger cities away from their spouses, develop a different attitude toward sex and marriage, and contribute to the growing divorce rate, although a statistical breakdown is not available. Many Chinese people also get divorced due to an unsatisfactory sex life, but traditional Chinese values and the importance of family continue to make the pursuit and enjoyment of sex a secondary concern, especially outside the international cities. Due to these cultural differences, China's divorce rate will probably never be as high as in the West.

Divorced couples often seek a new spouse, and the rate of remarriage among Chinese people who marry each year is quite high, about 10.6 percent in 2009, according to a 2010 white paper, *China's divorce and remarriage rates: Trends and regional disparities.* More than seven percent of divorced couples later have their marriage restored. While the high divorce rate is somewhat counterbalanced by the number of remarriages and restored marriages, the Chinese government has expressed alarm at the soaring number of divorces and its threat to the traditional Chinese family. In 2011, China took controversial steps to discourage divorce, reinterpreting the marriage law so that residential property is no longer regarded as jointly owned and divided equally after a divorce. Instead it will belong exclusively to the spouse who bought it or whose name is on the deed, which is usually the husband, even if the wife helped pay for the property. This means that upon divorce many women might find themselves homeless.

At a time of soaring property prices, real estate is often a couple's most valuable possession, and the revised law has caused many women to consider more carefully whether they really want to get married. Chinese media reported that marriage registrants plummeted as much as 30 percent in some cities weeks after the revised law was announced in 2011. Women rushed to add their names to the deeds, but Chinese newspapers reported that some husbands refused, resulting in the breakdown of the marriage. On China's Internet the measure was dubbed, "The law that makes men laugh and women cry." Many experts denounce the law as a return to feudalism. No matter what the government does to discourage divorce, there is no sign that the divorce rate in China is going to decrease. Too many people now view marriage and divorce as a personal choice and not a family obligation.

In 2007 China Central Television's sports channel ran a lavish promotional event to rebrand itself as China's official channel for the Beijing 2008 Olympic Games. What no one counted on was that in the middle of the live broadcast a famous Chinese TV personality would burst in front of the camera and, in calm, measured tones, accuse her husband, the anchor of the event, of sleeping with another woman. The clip became a huge hit on Chinese video-hosting sites, and on YouTube as well.

Adultery is everywhere in China, where prostitution was legal for thousands of years and where tales of unfaithfulness were a staple feature of literature and art. Many women take it for granted, albeit reluctantly, that this is what men do, as they have done in China since ancient times. And it is men who have the power. In light of China's male-centric culture, it should come as no surprise that adultery is far more tolerated when it is committed by men than by women. Extramarital affairs by husbands with mistresses and prostitutes are seen as uncontroversial, while a woman sleeping with another man might be seen as a scandal. In ancient times adultery for men was institutionalized. It was also the norm for a wealthy Chinese man to have multiple wives or concubines living under his roof, though this was not considered adultery per se. Concubinage continued into the twentieth century. Wives, on the other hand, were expected to be faithful then as now.

Under Mao, concubinage and prostitution were eradicated, and infidelity was considered a crime to be punished harshly (concubinage had been banned earlier in the century but Mao finished stamping it out). Likewise, extramarital affairs all but disappeared under the new communist regime. Until 1980, adultery was a crime punishable by jail under a law against "harming the family." Neighborhood watch committees as well as members of every worker's *danwei* kept their eye on everyone, looking for signs of improper behavior. It was difficult to have an affair but very easy to get caught, and punishment was painful. Offenders were frequently beaten and subject to grueling struggle sessions to help them come to terms with their crime. Mao and his upper echelon, of course, continued their discreet affairs with multiple partners.

As Professor Li Yinhe told the *Guardian* newspaper in 1997, society in the 1990s was becoming more tolerant:

People nowadays can be adulterous without any serious problem. Adultery is even on television soap operas nowadays. Some couples have an agreement to each have lovers . . . Before the nineties, the pressure from people's work unit was very strict. I had one case more than ten years ago of a married woman and a married man who had an adulterous affair. As a result the man was thrown out of the Communist Party, and all the details were entered in his personal file. The woman was dismissed from the Youth League. Nowadays people don't get this kind of punishment any more. And if people are kicked out of the party they won't think it's a big thing.

The phenomenon of rich Chinese men keeping a mistress has soared in tandem with China's explosive growth. Ever since China opened up and became wealthier, and as the marriage laws were relaxed, infidelity has been on an up-tick with no sign of abating. Money has a lot to do with it, especially for men. As more and more Chinese men enjoy a higher disposable income, and as they travel on business trips and spend late nights out socializing at karaoke bars and saunas with their colleagues, the more opportunities they have to turn to prostitutes, one-night stands and, for the wealthiest, a second wife. China's traditional culture of male entitlement coupled with new-found wealth and changes in attitudes toward sex all paved the way for a new golden age of infidelity.

The relatively new phenomenon of the absent husband is in turn leading greater numbers of women to assuage their loneliness and lack of sexual satisfaction by seeking their own extramarital affairs. A survey taken in the early 2000s indicated many Chinese women feel love-starved, and enter into affairs more for romance and attention than sexual craving. Many married women, especially wealthy ones who live in big cities like Shanghai, do seek sex for the sake of sex, visiting bars and nightclubs looking for a one-night stand. Others have full-time secret lovers. The effects of adultery, mainly in urban areas, have eroded the traditional Confucian ideal of a close, disciplined family, and what this might mean for the future of social stability remains to be seen.

A survey conducted in 2004 by the Chinese Sexology Society and the Chinese Medical Association revealed just how dramatically urban Chinese women's attitudes toward sex have liberalized. Most of the women who participated were college educated and lived in large international cities like Beijing and Shanghai. Of the women surveyed, 55 percent were married and 45 percent were single. More than 75 percent of the single participants had sexual partners. More than eight percent of the married women said they had frequent affairs while 32 percent said they had at least one affair. About 59 percent said they never had sex outside their marriage.

Migrant workers in the large cities, far from their homes in the countryside, are also contributing to the wave of extramarital affairs, although no statistics are available. With options for sex highly limited due to their poverty they seek out low-cost prostitutes and carry on affairs with factory colleagues.

When it comes to marital infidelity, nothing has so outraged and energized the public as the highly paid mistresses usually kept by corrupt party officials or the wealthiest businessmen, often from Taiwan and Hong Kong. Known as *ernai* or *xiao san* (little three), these women are often university students or young white-collar workers and usually range in age from 17 to 40 years old. They are paid lavish allowances by their sugar daddy, expect to receive the finest jewelry and fashion accessories on a regular basis, and are usually put up in high-end apartments. For the *ernai*, this is a fulltime job.

The role of the *xiao san* is practically the same, with one key difference: The *xiao san*, who starts out as an *ernai*, is (or claims to be) in love with her client, and usually wants to win him over for herself. They are called "little three" because they come between the "big two" – the husband and his wife. Often the *xiao san* wreaks havoc on the marriage, fighting for the man to divorce his wife and threatening to disrupt his family and his life if he refuses.

"There is a fundamental difference between the *ernai* and the *xiao san,*" explains 22-year-old San Jie, the founder of a website dedicated to gathering *xiao sans* together so they can share stories and seek advice. "*Ernai* never talk about love or marriage. They only go after the money because they want the man's financial support. Most *xiao san* have a steady job and a higher educational background than an *ernai*. *Xiao san* expect to marry the man because they've invested so much, their youth and their love, to the relationship."

San Jie started her website in 2007 because, she said, so many of her friends were *xiao san* living in pain and frustration. It costs 100 yuan to join her online group, the China Association for the Care of Xiao San, which boasts 500 members. The most popular topic in the forum, unsurprisingly, is love. According to San Jie, the most-asked questions include, "Does this man really love me, and if he does, why doesn't he get a divorce and marry me? Why does he still chase me? If he won't divorce his wife why doesn't he let me go?" They also talk about the gifts they receive, how much they are paid a month (usually between 20,000 to 30,000 yuan), and how they can convince their lover to give them more money.

The association has even launched campaigns against husbands who deceive their *xiao san*, spreading their names and photos over the Internet and exposing them as abusers. One *xiao san* interviewed by Hong Kong's Apple Daily in 2011 argued that the ones at fault are not the *xiao san* but the wives, for failing to recognize their shortcomings that lead their husbands to cheat. "Many people hate *xiao san*," she said, and pleaded for the public to better understand the plight of *xiao san* and recognize that the husband is as much to blame as the *xiao san* herself.

*Ernai*s have an easier time of it, living off of their lover and making no pretenses of love. The booming industrial city of Shenzhen is home to so many *ernai* that it and its neighboring industrial city Dongguan have been dubbed "concubine villages." Thousands of foreign businessmen, especially from Hong Kong and Taiwan, as well as wealthy mainland Chinese are constantly there on business, and it has become common for them to keep an *ernai* for companionship and pleasure when they are in town. Drama students are especially sought after as *ernai*s, as they tend to be beautiful. It is common for a mistress in the "concubine village" to live in a comfortable apartment where her lover visits a few times a week (and sometimes only once a month), paying her a regular monthly salary. This is her fulltime occupation, and she spends most of her time watching television, playing cards or mah jong with friends, or commiserating with other mistresses.

Chinese men who can afford an *ernai* are often government officials, and the *ernai* has become a symbol of corruption in China. Many believe the *ernai*s further corrupt officials by demanding they be given a steady stream of gifts and luxuries. As a popular Chinese saying notes, "Where there is corruption, there's sex. And where there's sex, there's corruption."

So many university students have sought jobs as an *ernai* that Chongqing Normal University implemented a regulation that would expel students working as *ernai*s; the rule also applies to *xiao san* and female and male escorts. Most of the students resented the regulation, which they said would be next to impossible to enforce. South China Normal University in Guangzhou instituted similar rules, making illegal cohabitation and damaging married families grounds for expulsion.

Not all Chinese wives are taking this situation sitting down. A number of women hurt by their husband's or father's infidelity have created Internet forums and websites to create their own community. For example, an anti-mistress association started by a few women in Fujian, now has 3,000 members and eight online chat rooms. Members tell their stories and seek advice. Volunteers, including psychologists and lawyers, offer free counsel and help them to either save or walk away from their marriage.

In 2011, Zhang Yu Fen, a woman in Xi'an who was dumped by her husband, started her own website to wage "guerrilla warfare" against unfaithful husbands. Zhang's mantra is, "We, the socially vulnerable, have to get together to eradicate the existence of mistresses . . . Our organization's aim is to punish these husbands and claim the assets we are entitled to." Zhang's call to action led the way to lawsuits against at least 11 adulterous men. Thanks to the video recordings and photographs she collected, the men were punished for violating the marriage laws. Most of them, some leaders in their field, decided to remain with their wives and let their mistresses go. The local media have dubbed Zhang as a "mistress killer."

The government, too, appears increasingly fed up with the nationwide adultery epidemic. China's Supreme People's Court recently approved legislation that would prohibit mistresses from suing their married lovers for reneging on promises of money, property or goods. On the flip side, husbands would not be permitted to seek the courts' help to recoup money and gifts they had given to their *ernai* or *xiao san*. Wives, however, could take the mistress to court to recover apartments, autos, cash and other goodies bestowed on the mistress by the husband. Although the law allows the same rights to husbands whose wives are unfaithful, the legislation is clearly designed to protect women, and the courts tend to rule in favor of the wives.

In a widely publicized case in Henan province in 2009, the judge ordered a mistress to return 330,000 yuan ($51,600) her lover had paid to her during their three-year affair after the wife discovered the payments. She and her husband reconciled and sued the mistress in court, where the judge ruled the husband's payments were illegal because, under the marriage laws, couples must jointly decide how to spend their common property. Some courts, however, have ruled that property must be split between the wife and the mistress.

In its war against adultery, the government also exposes corrupt officials who keep mistresses. In 2009 China's chief prosecutorial body said that 90 percent of all provincial or ministry-level officials found guilty of corruption in the past seven years had engaged in extramarital affairs, some with as many as 100 or even 200 partners. Some Chinese cities have issued edicts warning officials to remain faithful to their spouses. Worried by declining morality, Guangdong province recently made long-term cohabitation by unmarried couples a crime. Adultery per se is not illegal, but anyone found cohabitating with a woman other than his wife could go to a labor camp for two years. (Many are skeptical the law can be enforced.) Bigamy remains illegal in China, and corruption inspectors have targeted several officials for keeping second wives, including the former head of the National Bureau of Statistics, Qiu Xiaohua. He was tossed from the party and publicly denounced as a "vile social and political influence."

Other local governments have launched campaigns to teach girls that they can take care of themselves, without selling their services as *ernai*s. In 2010, the government of Guangzhou announced that all girls in elementary and middle school would take a mandatory class on self-improvement, self-esteem and self-confidence. But with the temptation of a high allowance, a steady flow of gifts and a paid apartment, and with so many wealthy men willing to shell out big bucks for companionship, the *ernai* market looks as healthy as ever.

The government is now trying a new tactic to discourage extramarital affairs: creating a national online database listing all married couples. This will allow mistresses to check out whether their lover is cheating on his wife. The database will first go online in Shanghai and Beijing and is expected to be nationally available in 2015.

For those seeking divorce in China it can be difficult to prove that one's partner actually committed adultery. That is why in recent years detective services have sprung up throughout the country dedicated solely to helping a husband or wife catch their partner "in the act" so they can use the evidence as grounds for divorce. Ding Hanshen, an online detective in Shanghai, explains the process:

We talk to you about when the spouse is most likely to be cheating. Sometimes it is on the way home from work, other times it is on the way to work or on weekends. Together, we will put together a strategy to minimize the amount of surveillance required, while maximizing the chances of catching the spouse cheating. We prepare an agreement, outlining what we will do and how much it will cost. It also states that the matter will be handled with complete confidentiality, before, during and after the investigation is complete. We both sign the agreement and you pay a 50 percent deposit. We will not exceed the budget you authorize without your approval.

Ding Hanshen is a fulltime adultery detective in Shanghai, and it is a job that pays. He compares his work to that of a policeman. First he picks a location where he believes he can catch the spouse and their lover together, and he keeps it under surveillance for as long as it takes, often several days. It has to be a place where he can take a good picture to incriminate the couple. It isn't good enough to photograph them on the street or in a restaurant. They need to be going into a hotel or an apartment. Getting the perfect incriminating shot takes a lot of time and patience. Most cases take him about 15 days to complete.

Clients are willing to pay a hefty sum for this service because under the marriage laws, a wife is entitled to a certain share of her husband's home and belongings if he's caught having a mistress. "Shanghai people love money, and houses in Shanghai are very expensive," Ding Hanshen explains. "It's worth them spending 30,000 yuan ($4,700) on investigating fees to get the evidence to win in court so that they can get more square meters. About 60 percent of my customers come to me because they want to divorce their spouse."

Ding Hanshen charges between 2,000 and 200,000 yuan per case, and says his client base is growing fast. He estimates that 70 percent of those he investigates are proven unfaithful. But married couples aren't his sole source of income; parents, too want to check on their child's fidelity, and especially their in-laws. "One customer wanted us to find out if her daughter-in-law is unfaithful to her husband. They were married for two years and had a child, but now she doesn't come home very often. After a 10-day investigation we found she had a very close relationship with another man. One night after dinner they went to a 'love hotel'. We got pictures of them as they came out at two in the morning."

Ding Hanshen says his oddest experience was when a wealthy man asked him to investigate his wife, but the man insisted he himself had to find her in bed with her lover. When Ding Hanshen followed the pair and saw them enter the man's apartment, he called the client, who came running over and burst into the room, and catching the couple *in flagrante* suffered what seemed to be a heart attack. He recovered a few minutes later and promptly summoned his and his wife's relatives to the hotel room so they could see the proof of adultery for themselves. He forced both the man and his wife to drop to their knees and apologize.

When he was getting started, Ding Hanshen would advertise his services by writing on building walls. Now he gets most of his clients from search engines like Baidu and Google. He says he can earn as much as five million yuan ($790,000) in a year, and that his highest-paying customers are celebrities.

THE SEX TRADE

On September 17, 2003 a group of 268 Japanese businessmen celebrated their fifteenth year of doing business in China by holding a two-day sexcapade with about 500 prostitutes at a hotel in Zhuhai, Guangdong province. What they did not know was that September 18 marked the beginning of Japan's occupation of Manchuria in 1931, a solemn date for many Chinese. The story got leaked, creating an explosion in the Chinese media and lighting up the online message boards. Outrage was widespread, with many condemning the Japanese and the orgy's Chinese organizers for desecrating a sacred day, although it is highly doubtful those involved had any idea of the date's significance. The nationalistic government puffed up the story and kept it alive for days, as it often does with perceived offenses by the Japanese. The men were sent packing and the event's organizers were sent to prison, two of them for life.

This indignation might seem curious considering that on the same day, as it is every day in China, millions of Chinese men were paying money for sex, and no issue was made of it. Even if the "perpetrators" were Japanese, it seemed strange that China, where prostitution pervades so much of contemporary life and where government officials are among the most voracious clients, would make such a fuss over a relatively minor and not very uncommon incident. The main reason, of course, is China's hypersensitivity over anything to do with Japan. To condemn the Japanese men for paying for sex, however, is to hypocritically ignore the fact that despite periodic "cleanup" campaigns, prostitution plays a large role in today's China, socially and economically, as it has for thousands of years.

Women in China, today as in ancient times, turn to prostitution for the same reasons they do everywhere else: to improve their financial situation and to help provide for their families. For many, it is the only way they know to survive. For others, particularly the young and the educated, it is the fastest and easiest way to feather their nest. And while the Chinese outlook on sex has changed dramatically over the past 3,000 years, from extreme open-mindedness under the Tang and Han dynasties to outright prudishness under the Qing, the Chinese people's attitude toward prostitution has remained remarkably unchanged; ever practical, the Chinese people tend to tolerate prostitution even if they disapprove, as they understand it is not going to go away.

Public opinion in China is never monolithic. Some feminist groups today advocate the stamping out of all forms of prostitution, while other groups are demanding its complete legalization. But with sex for sale so ingrained into modern Chinese life and with demand so high from the wealthiest party leaders in Zhongnanhai to the poorest migrant laborers in construction-site shacks, the Chinese people accept prostitution as a fact of life, as it has been throughout China's recorded history (except under the rule of Mao Zedong). Today many Chinese view prostitution as a legitimate aspiration. Sexologist Pan Suiming, one of China's leading experts on prostitution, has said most Chinese see prostitution as "normal" and don't understand why it is not legalized; they see no reason why it should not be available to those willing to pay for it.

Aside from a brief period under Mao Zedong when prostitution was all but eradicated, the world's oldest profession has thrived in China for well over 3,000 years. The earliest reference to prostitutes can be traced to the Shang Dynasty (1766 – 1122 BC), and historians cite China as the first country to license and regulate the industry. Prostitution flourished in the Tang Dynasty, when Chinese culture was at its peak, and became institutionalized throughout the country. Rich men had their concubines, poor men had their brothels, and there were no restrictions. Prostitution was legal, and high-end pimps and prostitutes enjoyed a degree of social status.

Women in imperial China were always considered less worthy than men, and were usually relegated to the position of wife, concubine, servant or harlot. Women were seen as an ornament that adorned the household, an attitude personified by the practice of foot binding. For men of means in pre-modern China, prostitution was a sign of their privileged status and a social necessity. It was not unusual for these men to have multiple concubines. The role of a wealthy man's wife was to bear and foster children, and serve the needs of her husband without complaint. For beauty and sexual skills, he turned to his concubines, usually sold by low-income families to be used at their master's pleasure.

Cohabitating with the husband and often bearing his children, a concubine's status was nearly always inferior to that of the actual wife, though she was still seen as more a family member than a prostitute. Ideally, the concubine would play the role of a spoiled, flirtatious girl and amuse her master. On occasion, if the wife passed away a concubine might take her place, thereby elevating her social status. Chinese emperors often had hundreds and even thousands of concubines, and stories of concubines and their role in the royal court and in wealthy families permeate Chinese literature from ancient times to the twentieth century. The most famous and successful of all concubines was the Empress Dowager Cixi, who, in the latter half of the nineteenth century, clawed her way to the very top through ruthless manipulation to become the most powerful figure in all China.

Still, there were rules when it came to those husbands wealthy enough to afford concubines. It was fine to have sex with concubines, who were part of the household, but carrying on an affair outside the family boundaries was frowned upon, as it could damage the family's reputation and bring disgrace on its daughters, making it difficult for them later to find husbands.

For wealthy men in pre-modern China, prostitution was not only about gratification and social status, but also entertainment. High-class courtesans, the history of whom can be traced back as far as the Han Dynasty, were more entertainers than prostitutes, and were often trained at an early age as musicians, artists, storytellers and performers. Often from wealthy families that had fallen upon hard times, many courtesans, also known as "blue mansion girls," "flower girls" and "sing-song girls," enjoyed considerable status. Their purpose was to entertain their wealthy masters by singing, dancing and reciting poetry. The relationship frequently evolved into a sexual one, and sometimes led to marriage, provided the man of the house lavished her with jewelry, expensive meals and other gifts. Courtesans were often dependent on more than one sponsor to maintain their relatively high style of living and to pay off family debts. They earned substantially more than women in other types of labor.

Men in the middle and upper-middle classes turned to "harlots" (*changji*) for paid sexual gratification. While these women occupied the lowest rung of the social ladder, even they operated within a tiered system, those at the highest level catering to the needs of respected artisans and intellectuals. Often trained in art and music since childhood, *changji* in the higher tiers were usually owned by upper-middle-class families, who selected them for their beauty and artistic skills, and were treated similar to courtesans. Middle-class men had their needs met at respectable brothels, which offered a relatively cozy environment with girls who tended to be clean and attractive, supervised by accommodating madams. Prostitutes from the lowest tiers serviced low-income males and laborers in what were called "whore huts" — rundown, dirty brothels that populated red-light districts.

Starting in ancient times and continuing to the present, sex workers made considerable contributions to China's economy. The wealthy spent lavishly to maintain relationships with their concubines and courtesans. For the middle class, sex was commoditized, and provided income for hundreds of thousands of girls. At the lowest levels, impoverished girls were able to support themselves by meeting the needs of other indigents. The sex trade in China has always been a powerful economic engine, except for the 25 years under Mao, and continues to be one today.

Opening the Floodgates

In 1842 China reluctantly signed the Nanking Treaty, which marked a turning point in the nation's long history of prostitution. The treaty, a product of the first Opium War, made way for the opening of "treaty port" cities, including Guangzhou, Shanghai, Tianjin and Xiamen, to foreigners and foreign business. The economic growth this generated quickly produced a huge new demand for sexual entertainment. Chinese women from surrounding provinces made their way to these cities, whose streets they imagined to be paved with gold, seeking employment as sex workers.

Appropriately dubbed the "whore of the Orient," Shanghai saw high-end nightclubs and brothels spring up to service the hordes of both Chinese and foreign merchants, gold-diggers and seekers of excitement. Vice flourished in the port cities, despite the growing spirit of puritanism that was sweeping much of the country under the Qing. By 1869 there were nearly 500 brothels in Shanghai, the city that lured the most foreigners with waves of Chinese following them to set up shop in the protected foreign settlements. By 1935, the estimated number of prostitutes in Shanghai soared to nearly 100,000 – more than two percent of the city's population. Prostitution was a major industry, especially in the two sections of Shanghai under foreign rule, the French Concession and the Independent Settlement. Most prostitutes were licensed, which brought revenues to the government and helped control venereal disease. In the late nineteenth century, brothels for the wealthy and educated had evolved into social gathering places, not unlike opium dens, where clients shared stories and political viewpoints, enjoyed poetry recitations, flirted with the hostesses and, of course, had their sexual needs fulfilled. Opium was often a regular feature at brothels, which men used to avoid premature ejaculation. Detailed training manuals on the art of sex were used by the best brothels to instruct prostitutes how to walk, when to smile, how to flirt, and how to get the most money from customers. One nineteenth-century text, *Memoirs of the Plum Blossom Cottage*, offered a vivid description of how a prostitute can best delight her customer:

As most males want to deem themselves potent and virile, your primary concern is not to hurt their ego. Since they are your customers, your job is to satisfy their desires, not yours. Let them imagine they have the initiative, though in fact it is in your hands. With someone who does not have the stamina, you must feign satisfaction even though he may discharge the moment he enters you. You can still let his shrunken organ remain inside, embracing and caressing him as if he were the most wonderful man you had ever had. With a customer who has a tiny organ, you have to hold your legs tightly together once he puts it inside you. This will give him the feeling that his every thrust really hurts and yet thrills you. An older customer may find it difficult to keep an erection; in this case you will have to fondle his organ tenderly and gently. Meanwhile tell some sexy stories to give him time to warm up. If this fails to arouse him, you will have to use your mouth to suck it.

Such textbooks were as detailed and thorough as a plumber's manual. Nothing was left to chance, and all possible sexual scenarios were taken into account.

There were various tiers of prostitutes in Shanghai during this period, though at different times and in different sections of the city these tiers blurred and merged. In the 1860s and 1870s, the highest rung were the "flower girls" and "sing-song" courtesans, who were trained in the performance arts and who enjoyed celebrity status for their musical, dramatic and recitation skills. They usually did not provide sexual favors for money and were often successful developing relationships with more respectable clients, who they frequently ended up marrying. Prostitutes in other tiers had their own specialties, some trained specifically to work in high-end brothels, and others at the very bottom who serviced customers in shacks and cheap brothels for pennies.

In 1911 the imperial dynasty crumbled, wracked for years by revolution, and the revolution's leader, Sun Yat-Sen was elected provisional president in December. The Republic of China was established a month later and soon afterwards Qing Emperor Xuantong Puyi and the royal family accepted Sun's terms for abdication. Concubinage was outlawed and the traditional tiers of prostitution began to merge, with the "sing-song girls" gradually fading away, and the high-end prostitutes in brothels taking their place as the first tier. This tiered structure would remain roughly in place until Mao seized power in 1949. Although groups of feminists and intellectuals tried to have prostitution banned in the new Republic of China, the government took little action; the revenues from licensed prostitution were too lucrative to give up.

Mao Drops the Curtain on Prostitution

The Sodom and Gomorrah-like atmosphere of Shanghai and other coastal cities was brought to an abrupt halt after Mao Zedong defeated the Nationalists and became China's supreme ruler in 1949. In the eyes of the communists, nothing could be more capitalistic than prostitution, and it had to be quickly and totally stamped out. One of Mao's first acts was to order the closing of all brothels in China. This policy was carried out aggressively in Beijing in November 1949, resulting in the closure of well over 200 brothels and the arrests of thousands of pimps and prostitutes. Many of the women were sent to rehabilitation centers to be taught working skills, and those who resisted were often sent to jail.

Shanghai, like most other large cities, phased out prostitution more gradually, first controlling and then banning the brothels. The government's budgets and human resources were simply inadequate to deal with the swelling unemployment of complete closure. The government took over the administration of brothels and discouraged male clientele with new legislation restricting prostitution. Gradually the number of brothels in each city decreased to the point where the government felt it could stamp them out altogether and reeducate the prostitutes to integrate them back into the general population. In 1951, a Beijing-style crackdown in Shanghai led to the closure of more than 300 brothels and the arrest of 7,000 prostitutes and pimps.

Over the next few years Shanghai's elaborate sex industry was methodically dismantled and by 1958 had been all but erased. Two years later the authorities ordered the shutdown of every brothel in China. Those who refused to cooperate were arrested. The nation's largest re-education program was implemented in Shanghai, where the number of sex workers stood at 100,000 following World War II. Reeducation usually consisted of one to three years of rehabilitation and job training, after which the girls were given menial jobs. During the Cultural Revolution, there was a furious backlash against these former prostitutes, who were subject to violence and public shaming.

Mao's iron-fist approach to the sex trade was one of his most conspicuous successes. By 1958, the Chinese government could truthfully state that all signs of public prostitution in China had been eradicated. Only an invisible, illegal underground prostitution scene remained. The Party, not surprisingly, had prostitutes available for visiting foreign statesmen and envoys, and also for internal Party use, but this was well out of sight of the general public. In 1964, the government claimed that venereal diseases, too, had essentially been wiped out in China, a claim later verified by a group of visiting Western physicians, including some who had practiced medicine in China for many years. To celebrate this milestone, all of the nation's twenty-nine research centers for sexually transmitted diseases were closed the same year.

Prostitution Bounces Back

The sex trade that had disappeared under Mao came roaring back when Deng Xiaoping initiated China's "reform and opening up" in the late 1970s. The largest mass migration the world has ever seen took place in the 1980s and 1990s as tens of millions of migrant workers from the countryside flooded the cities of China's east coast to work in factories or low-paying construction jobs, and the demand for paid sex soared. At the same time, millions of Chinese people began their ascent from poverty to relative wealth, further fueling the demand for paid sex services. China's bustling economy also began to attract ever-growing swarms of wealthy foreigners, creating a boon for the higher-end sex trade.

China's transformation from a controlled economy to a market economy ensured a resurgence of prostitution. Suddenly everything was for sale, commoditized, and women, like everyone else, followed the money. Once again, prostitution in China became a tiered, hierarchical industry, with women playing the role of hired wives, escorts, streetwalkers and brothel workers, each serving clients of different social rank. Traditionally women became sex workers because they were jobless and uneducated, but in post-Mao China many turned to prostitution because they simply had no alternative and needed livelihood. Debt and a sense of hopelessness drove many thousands of women who would not normally be associated with the sex trade, such as university students, intellectuals and government cadres, to prostitution. This pressure was (and is) exacerbated by the tradition in China of sending money back to one's hometown to help care for their families.

China has always been quick to blame "Western spiritual pollution" for the sex industry's renaissance, and there is a small element of truth to this accusation. Just as with opium in the days of the Nanking Treaty, China's policy of reform and opening up had all sorts of side effects in what had become overnight the world's largest market. At the same time, China became increasingly influenced by Western culture with the renewed influx of foreigners into the country following Deng's reform policies, and the attitude of the Chinese people, especially those in the large coastal cities, toward sex was slowly liberalizing. Sex was becoming less of a taboo, and as the sex business took off, most Chinese simply accepted it as a part of modernization.

But it is wrong to attribute China's blossoming sex trade industry solely to Western influences. A great many sex workers had had no exposure to Western culture before they decided to enter the trade. And prostitution had thrived in China long before any influence from the West. The policy of reform and opening up in and of itself opened the floodgates for the rebirth of prostitution. The market economy suddenly offered new opportunities for sex workers as more Chinese acquired disposable income.

Millions of male migrant workers found themselves thousands of miles from home, with no sexual outlet other than prostitutes. At the same time, urbanization soared. Today well over 400 million Chinese live in cities compared to about 170 million only 30 years earlier. More than 150 million transient workers, mainly young people, are employed in China's cities, and most earn enough money to allow them to seek entertainment and sexual companionship. Where there is a need there is a market, and the sex industry, like so many other industries in China, inevitably opened up and took off.

Despite the resurgence of prostitution under Deng, the central government still declared it to be a serious crime that went against its ideology of moral purity. Thousands of prostitutes and their customers were arrested in various sweeps under Deng, especially in the late 1980s. Punishments were made harsher, and some pimps received the death penalty. That did not prevent more and more poor women from becoming sex workers, enticed by the possibility of earning thousands of yuan a month compared to the average Chinese worker's pittance of a monthly income at the time.

The Sex Trade Hierarchy

As in ancient times, prostitution in China today is made up of a number of distinct tiers based on the role the sex worker plays, the type of customers they service and the environment in which they operate. Although there are many gray areas and tiers within tiers, there are certain basic categories that encompass most sex workers in China. In the mid-1990s the Chinese police broke down the descending hierarchy into seven tiers that still apply today. They reflect the social strata of contemporary China, from impoverished migrant workers to wealthy officials.

Tier 1: *Ernai*

An *ernai*, or "second wife," is a salaried mistress, a sort of modern-day concubine. Wealthy married men, often government officials and businessmen, pay their second wife a steady income in exchange for sex, with no romance or children involved. The man provides her with accommodations and an allowance, buys her gifts and uses her for company and sex. In most instances the details are actually laid out in a contract the two parties agree on before they consummate the relationship. Second wives tend to be young, attractive and well educated, and usually their sole motivation is building a golden nest. Many of today's second wives are university students hoping the man they service will help them find jobs after they graduate. Some second wives, however, depend solely on their "husband's" generosity, and are often let go as they reach their mid-30s. At that point many find themselves out of work and with limited skills, making their life a struggle. It can be argued that an *ernai* is not technically a prostitute, as she is totally exclusive, whereas prostitutes have sex with multiple clients. One witty Chinese netizen remarked on an online forum:

Prostitutes are a bit like a paid public toilet, they're there to fulfill a basic need and anyone who has the money can use them. An *ernai* is like a private toilet – you need to be fairly well off to have one, no one else can use it, and you take much better care of it than a public toilet. And a wife? Well, you wouldn't want to compare her to any kind of toilet at all, because she is your equal.

Tier 2, *Baopo*

Baopo can be roughly translated as "indentured wife" and is similar to the *ernai*. Both groups solicit men of wealth or rank, but rather than living in apartments provided by their client, *baopo*s accompany him for set periods of time, such as on business trips, and are paid an agreed-upon rate for each period. Besides sexual pleasure and company, the *baopo* provides "face" – it looks good for a rich Chinese man to be seen with a beautiful young woman.

Chinese men usually keep the existence of their *ernai* and *baopo* a secret. Since the majority of the clients are government officials, both tiers are closely associated with corruption. This practice has led to an outcry from Chinese feminist groups denouncing second wives as a form of concubinage practiced only by the rich. While the lower tiers of sex workers are in constant danger of harassment or arrest, *ernai* and *baopo* are above the law, protected by the officials or rich clients they service. This rather blatant discrimination against the poor remains highly controversial.

Tier 3: *Santing* escort girls and hostesses

Santing means "three halls," and refers to girls who work as hostesses in karaoke bars, dance halls, teahouses or regular bars. Like a value-added tax, *santing* hostesses charge set fees for each level of service they provide, such as sitting down to talk, having a drink, and leaving the venue together with the client. They also receive a cut on what the client spends at their venue, such as drinks and food. While the police do not see hostessing as prostitution per se, they consider it an activity that promotes prostitution. The hostesses' "accompany first, have sex later" technique makes it difficult for police to catch them in the act of soliciting for sex. *Santing* bar girls tend to be sophisticated and bright and they charge high fees for their services. In the big coastal cities they are extremely popular with foreign businessmen who pay them hefty tips just to have a chat.

Tier 4: *Dingdong* girls

Every man who has stayed in a Chinese hotel, especially those with only two or three stars, is most likely familiar with the *dingdong* girls who slip business cards with sexy pictures under the bedroom doors and who call the rooms at night, usually offering massages. *Dingdong* girls rent rooms at hotels, and if the potential client responds to their calls they'll knock on their door or ring the bell (hence the name *dingdong* girls) and negotiate the price. Call girls also belong to this tier, including college students and others who advertise their services on the Internet.

Tier 5: *Falangmei*

Falangmei refers to sex workers employed in bath houses, saunas, foot massage parlors and other establishments that are, in reality, a cover for whorehouses. Usually the *falangmei* work as masseuses who, once their client is aroused, negotiate a fee for sex services, including intercourse, for a flat market price, usually around 200 yuan ($32). These are the most visible and easy-to-find prostitutes in China. Often they sit in the front windows of their pink-lighted massage parlors in the city's red light district. Much of what they earn goes to the proprietress or pimp running the operation, and the workers depend heavily on tips. They are usually uneducated migrants from the countryside with no other source of income.

Tier 6: *Jienu*

Sex workers in the bottom two tiers differ from the upper tiers in that they are straightforward about exchanging sex for money. They have no ties to any recreational establishment like massage parlors and have no relation to government corruption. *Jienu*, or "street women," solicit clients in public spaces, often outside of hotels and entertainment centers or in parks, railway stations and pedestrian malls. They either work on their own or with a pimp, and their services usually include petting and intercourse. Of the seven tiers, *jienu* run the greatest risk of being arrested by the police.

Tier 7: *Xiagongpeng*

At the very lowest rung of the hierarchy, *xiagongpeng* – literally "down the work shack" – refers to sex workers who service migrant laborers from the countryside working in China's urban areas. Millions of these very low-paid workers have left their wives to work at construction sites. Their loneliness has created a huge demand for cheap sexual services. The *xiagongpeng* who solicit them at their "work shacks" are desperately poor themselves and are willing to perform sexual services for very small amounts of money, or even for food.

The Sin Police: *Sweeping the Yellow*

Prostitution remains illegal in China, as it has since the Qing dynasty, but it is regarded as a misdemeanor unless those participating know that they have a venereal disease, or in the case of physical violence or involvement of a minor under the age of 14. It can be punishable with a warning, a fine up to 5,000 yuan ($785), a signed statement of "repentance," attendance in a reeducation program, or a few weeks in prison. Prison sentences are longer for repeat offenders.

The police created the seven tiers to monitor prostitution at various levels of society and to help them organize periodic sweeps known as "*Sweeping the Yellow*," "yellow" standing for vice such as prostitution, pornography and gambling. *Sweeping the Yellow* consists of cracking down on porn, closing brothels and massage parlors and arresting the pimps, prostitutes and clients. These efforts, however, are often half-hearted, and used mainly to curry favor with senior officials in the hope of getting a promotion. After a few weeks most of the sex establishments are up and running again. Some crackdowns are very aggressive and shops close for months, but the businesses soon reemerge, even if they change their address. As one official once remarked about the "strike-hard" campaigns, "They make thunderous noises, but bring little rain."

The sweeps also take place around major events like the annual National People's Congress and the October First National Day holiday, and when China is on display to the outside world, such as the 2008 Olympic Games in Beijing and the 2010 World Expo in Shanghai. A common belief is that the central government sweeps houses of prostitution and vice before the annual sessions of the National People's Congress in Beijing to keep the behavior of the thousands of visiting cadres in check.

Brothel and karaoke bar owners will often be tipped off in advance before a sweep thanks to their close ties to government officials and the local police eager to collect their protection fees. They tend to turn a blind eye unless the brothels become a base for more serious offenses, such as violence and drug dealing, and when there is a serious crackdown it is frequently carried out under intense pressure from higher-level officials. The authorities depend on income from prostitution, which obviously compromises their ability to police it. This doesn't mean, however, that there are no serious, aggressive sweeps.

One of the more visible crackdowns on vice was the closing down of the entire Chongqing Hilton Hotel in the summer of 2010 because a brothel was doing business in the same building complex. The brothel was raided and altogether 102 persons, including a hotel shareholder and even some public security officials, were arrested and charged with various accounts of prostitution, drug dealing, bribery and organized crime. Though the hotel reopened shortly afterward, it was stripped of its five-star rating. Many attributed the crackdown to an attempt by Chongqing's then populist Communist Party chief Bo Xilai to win political points. Shutting down a Western-branded five-star hotel on vice charges was unprecedented.

Crackdowns on prostitution and pornography also serve a political purpose. Following the Tiananmen Square "incident" on June 4, 1989, for example, the government waged one of its most aggressive crackdowns on vice as part of an overall strategy to repress and control its citizens' lives. By intervening directly into the people's private lives the state was leaving no doubt who was in charge. A year later, *People's Daily* reported the government had cracked down on nearly 80,000 prostitutes and customers. Penalties were harsh, and some received the death penalty.

As with the Chongqing Hilton, not every sweep is half-hearted. In 2009 the prosperous town of Dongguan, Guangdong province, was targeted by the local government for one of the most ambitious sweeps in the country's history. Dongguan is home to thousands of factories, a hub for the manufacture of electronics, textiles, furniture, and nearly every other product one can imagine. It attracts millions of migrant workers seeking low-paying factory jobs, and thousands of foreigner factory owners, managers and gold diggers. Dongguan is almost as famous for its sex industry as it is for manufacturing. With so many day laborers and foreigners, nearly all of whose wives were back home, Dongguan became flypaper for prostitutes.

According to a popular contemporary saying, "Ten thousand girls go to Lingnan [the area covering Guangzhou and Guangxi provinces], millions of whoremasters go down to Dongguan." The city was dubbed "paradise for men." Taxi drivers earned lucrative tips referring and ferrying businessmen to sex parlors. Sexual services were available at every level, from assembly workers to corporate executives. An estimated 100,000 prostitutes work in the city, contributing billions of yuan in revenues to beauty salons and jewelry shops, not to mention hotels and massage parlors.

Many of the women who came to Dongguan to work in factories discovered they could earn more as call girls and hostesses. Prostitution was everywhere and there was little attempt to conceal it. Many Dongguan sex workers actually attend intensive training classes more complex and rigorous than the technical training most factory workers go through. One sex worker told the Guangdong newspaper *The Southern Metropolis Weekly*, "A dozen days of training is enough to take the skin off your knees."

A common joke was to refer to the high standards of Dongguan's sex trade as being measured against the ISO standards organizations use to assess their management systems. Indeed, most hotels and saunas asked customers to rate their experience in an assessment survey to determine which girls might not be performing up to speed. Because of these high standards, saunas felt they had to compete by providing the most plush, opulent surroundings. Many of the saunas had no pools or steam baths, but offered lavish rooms on multiple stories furnished with waterbeds and dance floors.

In the eyes of the government the sex trade in Dongguan had gotten out of control, and a national campaign against vice began in November 2009. The initiative targeted more than 20 provinces and cities, mainly in Guangdong and Fujian provinces, shutting down sex parlors and leaving thousands of sex workers unemployed. As part of the campaign, Dongguan Party Secretary

Liu Zhigeng enlisted public security organizations to use "the hardest measures" to smash kidnapping and gambling rings as well as porn and prostitution operations. On November 9, police raided bathhouses, hotels, massage parlors, karaoke bars and made more than 400 drug and prostitution arrests in all 32 of Dongguan's districts. Two hotels were shut down and dozens of girls were arrested for soliciting on the street.

The sweep lasted 15 days and became a national story when the media released dozens of photographs taken during the raids, including girls trying to cover themselves while their johns sat naked on the bed. Photos of well-dressed women paraded barefoot in handcuffs and tied together like dogs on a leash, and of others kneeling terrified on the street trying to hide their faces, ricocheted across the Internet. One popular online forum started a thread titled, "Shocking photos of police sweeping the yellow – is public humiliation too excessive?" Soon more than 300,000 Chinese had read it and arrived at the consensus that the public shaming of prostitutes was excessive. The crackdown soon won criticism from the Ministry of Public Security for damaging the suspects' personal dignity. Local public security officers were ordered not to march prostitution suspects through the streets. One Dongguan police officer accused of treating suspects with needless humiliation was suspended, and the local police said they had learned from the experience and would reform.

Most prostitutes "went on vacation" for several weeks after the crackdown, but by the end of November, many sex parlors quietly turned their pink lights back on, and sex was available at most high-end hotels, although it was less visible than before the raids. A few weeks later, a journalist covering the aftermath of Dongguan's *Sweeping the Yellow* reported receiving a text message from a brothel, "Winter is over, fresh produce is available, we welcome new and old customers to come and have a taste."

China seems slow to learn from its mistakes. Only three years earlier, in a similar crackdown in the nearby manufacturing hub of Shenzhen, 100 prostitutes and their clients who were caught *in flagrante* were paraded down a main street as police read their names through a bullhorn. This, too, created a nationwide backlash. One outraged lawyer, Yao Jianguo of Shanghai, wrote an open letter to the National Congress: "Twenty years ago, this kind of parade would have been greeted with unanimous applause," he said. "But now it gets more criticism than support because more people realize their rights should be protected. And of course, they have more channels to voice their criticism, like the Internet." The days of the Cultural Revolution are long gone, and with them the interest in public shamings.

A Sex Worker's Story

Lu Jie is an attractive 43-year old divorcee from Jiangsu province with two sons developing their skills at a training college. At first glance, based on her attire and demeanor, you might take her for a housewife. Her career as a sex worker offers a revealing case study of the life of a modern-day prostitute whose career spanned the various tiers, from dance hall hostess to street walker to call girl.

A farmer in the Jiangsu countryside before she moved to Shanghai in 1998, Lu has been a sex worker for 13 years. She fled her life in the field because her husband, to whom she remains legally married, treated her cruelly and refused to give her or their children money to live on. When she first arrived in Shanghai she washed dishes in a restaurant for 1,500 yuan (US $235) a month plus meals and accommodation. When her boss told her she would only get paid if she slept with him she refused and quit the job. Although she had worked there for two months she was never paid a cent.

Acquaintances told Lu that she could earn lucrative tips if she became a sort of escort, accompanying men to watch movies. All she had to do was sit next to them and talk occasionally for 20 yuan ($3.20) per movie. The fee went up if the man wanted to touch her, and the price for a hand job was 50 yuan ($8). She would usually get two men per movie, and they mainly wanted to touch her hands, kiss her face or hug her against them.

As a single mother with two children to raise, the movie theater income allowed Lu to survive, and she continued it for two years. The job was not free of risk. Plainclothes police would occasionally scan the theaters looking for "*xiaojie,*" women who moved from guy to guy, and one day she was arrested after being seen with two different customers. She spent 15 humiliating days in a detention facility in Pudong.

As Shanghai movie theaters were torn down to make way for more profitable enterprises, Lu was introduced to a Shanghai dance hall where she could earn 50 yuan for two hours of dancing in front of a male audience. When the lights were turned out during some of the songs, customers would kiss or touch her for an extra 20 yuan, or receive a hand job for 50 yuan. She worked in the dance hall from 2000 to 2003, when the dance hall industry all but died out, another victim of Shanghai's soaring real estate prices.

When she turned 35, Lu felt she was too old to work in a karaoke (KTV) bar and found work in a barbershop where she offered men massage and hand jobs. Customers, she found, actually preferred having their needs met by an older woman, who they saw as more honest and experienced than younger girls. The job came with serious risks, however, as the police frequently raided barbershops before events like the National Party Congress and major holidays. While her boss had connections with the local police, sometimes police from other districts would carry out sweeps.

In 2004 she was entrapped by a plainclothes officer on the street near the barbershop and was charged with "fishing" for paid sex. She was sent to detention for 70 days that she says she will never forget: She had to endure freezing temperatures and she was forced to work, making shoes and clothing. Lu Jie could not hide the news from her family since upon arrest the police typically send a letter to the address on the arrestee's ID card, though it did not spell out the specific charges. To cover up the truth, she wrote to her sister and lied, telling her she was arrested for mah jong gambling, and asked her to send her 3,000 yuan ($475) to pay off her jailers; otherwise she would have had to stay longer, perhaps up to six months.

"It's not that we want to become 'bad women,' it's this society that forces us to," Lu Jie says. "I have no degree, I'm not pretty enough to be an *ernai*. Can the government offer me four or five thousand yuan a month so my children and I can live and pay for their higher education and provide proper medical care so I don't need to care about money if I get sick? No, it cannot. Under these severe circumstances, I trade myself to survive, even if it's illegal. What do you want me to live on?"

She reserved special anger toward the police. "They have the power. They can sleep with girls without paying. They say to the girls, 'if you have sex for free it's not prostitution, it's only illegal when you take money from the guy you sleep with.'"

After her last arrest Lu decided it was time to get out of the business, and tried to open a small grocery shop. At her request, Lu's husband joined her to help run the store, but soon he stole her money and looted the shop to pay for his affairs with other women. Lu divorced him in 2006 and he remarried 30 days later. Lu said she never wanted a boyfriend or a husband again.

On the advice of friends Lu, now 38, decided to seek out foreign customers, and learned a few key English phrases like "hand job" and "massage". In Chinese eyes, she said, she was old and worn out, but to foreigners she was young and beautiful. She would meet prospective clients at a Hong Kong-style café in Shanghai and recommend her massage services. She would first tell them it would cost 800 yuan, after which it was bargained down to 500 yuan and she would follow the foreigner to his hotel or rental house. If he became aroused during the massage and asked for "special services" she would demand an extra 300-500 yuan, usually for a hand job or blow job.

Lu says she would only engage in copulation if the client's

penis was not too large. If his penis was large and her hand got tired masturbating him she would give the customer lubricant and have him bring himself to climax while whispering sexual words to him. "Foreigners just want to have fun," she says, "which doesn't necessarily mean they have to have intercourse." For those customers who demand sexual intercourse, she frequently refers them to her girlfriends or to barber shops, where the fees are much lower. After she began engaging with foreign customers, she earned about 10,000 yuan a month ($1,500), a considerable sum for an uneducated Chinese worker.

Lu Jie's clients range in age from 18 to 70, the majority being foreign students in Shanghai. She prefers married, middle-age customers as they are more likely to be wealthy and to take her out to dinner. Most are American, European, Canadian or Australian. She refuses to do business with blacks, Arabs and Indians, claiming they are rude and treat her "like an animal."

Lu's life became harder after the 2008 Olympic Games, when China was hit by the global financial crisis. Her monthly earnings fell to 5,000 – 6,000 yuan a month. She now lives with her mother in a seven-square-meter apartment in Shanghai. Her plan is to work as a call girl for a few more years to pay for her two sons to finish their education, and then to move back to her hometown in Jiangsu and open a small shop. "It doesn't matter how much money I can make," she says. "The most important thing is to enjoy life with my family and friends in my hometown."

Lu Jie earns just enough to survive and support her family, but higher-end prostitutes and pimps in China can rake in large sums of money. Their business is nearly always tied to the government, which makes a handsome profit from the payoffs.

The Madams

Thirty-year-old Toni Chen earns his money as a Shanghai "babasan" – a male madam whose job is to bring well-heeled businessmen from around the world to karaoke bars and clubs all over China and set them up with *santing* hostesses. This is a job usually performed in China by women ("mamasans"), but Toni is clearly good at what he does. He says he has thousands of client cell phone numbers and frequently sends them photos of available girls he thinks would be a good match. They also call him directly to make reservations at bars, as he gets them good discounts and knows their taste in women. He is frequently asked to book large groups. Along with customers from his personal Rolodex, Toni makes use of Internet advertising (he claims to be the only babasan in Shanghai using the Internet to attract clientele). Along with being a professional pimp, he sells his customers drugs that prolong their potency like Viagra and other "sex medicines."

Toni usually gets a commission of 30 percent of what the customers spend. The owners also take a generous cut, about half of which they use to pay off officials. "The KTV [karaoke] owners are rich," Toni says. "It costs about 5,500,000 yuan ($870,000) to build up a KTV bar in Shanghai, and the owners are often Taiwanese. They do the best service – they know how to please customers."

When Chinese businessmen want to indulge their business partners, karaoke is the entertainment of choice. High-end KTV clubs are lavish, with large private rooms and excellent sound systems. Going to karaoke with their Chinese colleagues and partners is a must for foreigners seeking to build good *guanxi* – a uniquely Chinese form of bonding and building trust. "Usually Chinese businessmen go to KTV after a banquet," Toni explains. "Sometimes the Chinese won't sign a contract unless they go to KTV together. Sex in KTV is a big business because men like three things: cigarettes, alcohol and women. There are different kinds of KTV. Some are just about singing and talking. At the 'bad' ones you can see girls naked."

Toni's customers pay 600 yuan ($95) just to have a conversation with a hostess, and as much as 1,000 yuan if she's especially beautiful. The minimum for sex is 3,000 yuan. Toni brings the girls in groups and the customer takes his pick. The average customer spends about 1,500 yuan a night, including a hostess' company and alcohol. The most he's ever known a girl to make is 20,000 yuan in a single night for providing entertainment followed by sexual services. Finding girls is easy, Toni says, since KTV can pay quite nicely. "Every day more and more girls call me wanting to be an escort. They see KTV as an ATM, and I hear from a lot of university students and wanna-be stars who need the money. About 90 percent of the ones who call are too young and I tell them no." He says the girls need to be beautiful, well mannered and cultured; taller and slimmer girls are preferred.

Two mamasans work for Toni overseeing his online business. "About 30 percent of my customers come from the Internet," Toni says. "We're very careful about Internet customers because they are strangers. They know the girls we provide are rich, and they've been known to rob or kidnap the escort. For strangers, we only make reservations at KTV. We only do pimping for customers we're familiar with." Toni says he earns about 1.5 million yuan ($237,000) a year as a babasan, which is actually less than what many high-end mamasans make. Usually mamasans earn 300,000 yuan ($47,000) a month, he says, because most men prefer to deal with women. This means babasans have to work harder, and Toni only sleeps from 6am to noon. He says he loves his work: "I get to travel throughout China and meet all kinds of interesting people."

Chen Jian is a partner of a Japanese-style karaoke business with two bars in Shanghai. The bars draw their exclusively Japanese clientele by advertising in Japanese magazines and on Japanese websites. Chinese men, who don't pay as much, are not allowed entrance. Chen boasts that what sets his bars apart from others is the ultra-high-class service offered to customers and their benevolent attitude toward their hostesses.

"For most KTVs, they look at the girls as tools for making money," he says. "The manager won't say good night to the girls and the girls don't respect the managers. In this bar the managers give the girls training every day for half an hour to three hours. Every Tuesday and Friday we teach the girls Japanese for three hours at a time."

Chen never looks for hostesses; they all come to him. The average age of 75 girls he employs is 24, and most of them are from the countryside and send money to their husbands or parents back home. Most do not tell their parents how they earn the money. The girls, Chen says, see the job as a godsend: "How can these girls, coming from rural places with no skills, survive in this city? When they are miserable and I can offer them the possibility of happiness why shouldn't I? Their sense of survival is so strong, it's hard for people to imagine how hard those girls work in this place."

Girls who speak Japanese wear bikinis while others wear school-girl uniforms. They line up and the customer selects the one he wants to entertain him. They pay 1,500 yuan ($235) if they want to take the girl home for sex. The girls wearing bikinis get a 400-yuan tip for working a table, those in uniforms make 300 yuan, of which Chen gets about 10 percent. If within thirty minutes the customer decides to reject the girl, she makes nothing. The girls' income ranges from 10,000 to 70,000 yuan a month. The one thing the girls don't want, Chen says, is to be given time off for holidays. "That would kill them," he says. "All they want to do is make money."

Chen says that beauty isn't always the driving factor behind the customers' choices. "Beautiful girls are too arrogant to provide perfect service. Some customers think it's tiring to be with beautiful girls. Less pretty girls with perfect makeup and a sincere smile might appear more attractive. These girls always feel flattered when they're selected." Chen pays off local officials with free hostess services about twice a month, and pays them cash bribes before major holidays, when the police regularly "sweep the yellow." He says the KTV industry in Shanghai is booming, and that there are too few hostesses that speak Japanese to meet the burgeoning demand from Japanese businessmen.

China's Male Sex Workers

With China opening up to the world and wealthy tourists flocking to destinations like Shanghai and Beijing, the male sex trade industry is booming. Male prostitutes in China are called "ducks" (*yazi*) and they also refer to themselves, in English, as "money boys." While there are no official statistics on the number of money boys in China, their customers know they can always find one easily enough. There are even money boys who are sought by women as well as men. Those looking for female clientele roam the floors of straight bars that are popular with the wealthy, especially tourists, who can afford to pay generously. Money boys whose clients are male homosexuals can be found on the Internet, at the "gay quarter" of public parks, and at gay bars, saunas and massage parlors. Most male prostitutes operate in first- and second-tier cities, where customers can afford to pay anywhere from 300 ($47) to 1,000 yuan ($158) for an hour or two of pleasure.

Of the approximately six million prostitutes in China, money boys make up only a small fraction, and the overwhelming majority service male customers. Those who cater to women usually meet them in high-end clubs and karaoke bars. Female tourists, especially those visiting from Hong Kong and Taiwan, are sought out because they tend to pay the best. The money boy catches their eye and approaches them for a chat. Often the new customer is happy to pay just to have a drink and talk with them, just as many men do with hostesses at karaoke bars. If it goes a step further and they decide to go to a hotel together, the price rises, usually ranging from 600 to 1,000 yuan. Young, white-collar women also seek money boys out at karaoke bars for flirting and sex, as do lonely housewives whose husbands are away.

Most of the money boys who pursue female clients are well educated and often college students who have the clothing and the manners to fit in at high-class venues. Many speak excellent English. They can earn far more as male prostitutes than at an average Chinese desk job, and many see it as an ideal career that gives them lots of freedom. There are, according to the NGO Shanghai Leyi, an estimated 2,000 gay-servicing money boys working in Shanghai, and many thousands more in other Chinese cities. Most are heterosexual young men from poor families in the countryside who cannot find work. As a money boy they can earn anywhere from 2,000 to 20,000 yuan a month, depending on where they work, their physical attributes and their ability to market their wares. Most of them work under the guise of being a "masseur." Some work for prostitution rings and pay a portion of their earnings to a pimp. Others work freelance at parks or gay bars. Others are masseurs at saunas. Their *modus operandi* is similar across the board: They begin by giving the client a massage and slowly stimulate him; then they tell him if he wants more he has to pay an additional tip, usually between 100 and 200 yuan.

The Internet has made it extremely easy for money boys to hook up with male clientele. They also communicate with potential clients using Chinese social media like QQ, and those who can speak some English hang out at gay online chat sites where foreigners go to meet local Chinese guys. Many advertise on English-language websites for gay tourists. Massage services exclusively for men advertise openly on the streets of Beijing and Shanghai, and most of them offer "special services" for an additional charge. Masseurs in gay saunas will also meet their customer's needs, hoping for a generous tip.

Most male prostitutes range from 18 to 30 years of age, and after that they are considered too old to be marketable. While they can earn more than average workers at fulltime jobs, their lifecycle is relatively short, and once they have to give up selling their bodies they have a very hard time finding new work, never having developed any useful job skills. If they work for a prostitution ring, they are always at risk of arrest, as most of the establishments are raided once or twice a year during "*Sweeping the Yellow*" campaigns.

For a number of reasons it is unlikely prostitution will be legalized or decriminalized in China anytime soon, if ever. First and foremost, it greases the palms of local cadres and the police, all of whom garner lucrative bribes from karaoke bars, saunas, massage parlors and prostitution rings. Second, the government has been carrying out an anti-vice crackdown for years now and has made it clear it sees prostitution as an unhealthy influence on Chinese family life. There is no hint that they are about to change their minds. Stories about the closure of prostitution rings and the arrest of customers and sex workers appear regularly in the state-controlled media, which clearly wants to portray the industry as one that tears at the moral fiber of the nation. This strategy reeks of hypocrisy, of course, since it is the well connected and the government officials who most enjoy the services of the high-end prostitutes and *ernai*. And the local authorities depend heavily on the bribes and fines they earn from the sex trade industry.

At a conference in 2005, Chinese sex scholar Li Yinhe made a strong argument for decriminalization of China's sex trade industry, reported by China's news agency Xinhua:

It would be more reasonable to issue licenses to Chinese prostitutes and administer regular physical examinations to them. This will safeguard women's rights and be conducive to the social problems related to prostitution. I believe that day will come. I don't mean to legalize this special trade, but I opt not to view it as a crime. We need to deal with it as a moral issue, or a business based on free will, whether there is money paid or not. We should reserve the right to reprimand it from the prospective of morality.

It's impossible to eliminate the problem by criminalizing it, for that will drive it underground and create a chain of social problems such as gang involvement and police corruption. We should find a solution to it, instead of punishing prostitutes.

Li has pointed out that in the modern world there is no example of a prohibitionist policy that actually works, and that such policies inevitably encourage corruption and more crime, not less. In 2007, the United Nations Committee on the Elimination of Discrimination Against Women also called for the decriminalization of prostitution in China, saying it would end a rampant sex trade that leads to human rights violations against women. Decriminalization would be a huge step forward in the treatment and prevention of sexually transmitted diseases, and would help end the violence and abuse of female sex workers. It would end the shaming of thousands of prostitutes arrested in crackdowns, and improve human rights throughout China. Unfortunately, China does not appear to be listening, and the crackdowns and rising rates of STDs among sex workers show no sign of abating.

China's Sex Trade in the 21ˢᵗ Century

In every major city in China today sex for sale is everywhere. As the Chinese became increasingly wealthy following Deng's reforms, the demand for sex workers of all varieties has gone up and up. While no reliable statistics exist, sex experts estimate the number of active prostitutes in contemporary China at any given time at around six million. Most agree that prostitution contributes between six to eight percent of China's annual GDP, as at least half of the earned income is immediately pumped back into the economy through consumption. Today's prostitutes need to pay for cell phones, apartments, taxis, expensive clothes and cosmetics. Prostitution in China is a cornerstone of the economy, and if it were ended there would simply not be enough jobs to absorb the millions of unemployed sex workers.

According to sexologist Pan Suiming, China's huge prostitution industry and the cottage industries it has generated form a complex economic web:

Although the sex industry is still illegal, it already has a formed system and operative mechanism. Production and distribution of pornography is its advertisement department. The escort services are its exhibition and sales department. The medical treatment of sexually transmitted diseases is its after-sale department. Clients who directly buy sex with money are its core production department. There are many affiliated industries, such as the accommodation, food and entertainment industry. If the added output value of those affiliated industries that derive income from prostitution and escort services is included, the economic scale of the Chinese sex industry expands many times.

It is not only the poor and the desperate who seek out work in China's sex trade. Many professional white-collar workers, university students and aspiring actresses serve as karaoke or nightclub hostesses at night, where they earn lucrative tips from relatively wealthy foreigners and businessmen. Some pimps even boast that they have a waiting list of girls looking for hostess jobs. And China's Internet has made it easy for educated call girls to advertise their services.

Another major contribution to China's sex trade industry is the fact that there are more men in China than women, meaning millions of Chinese men cannot find wives. These men are aptly nicknamed "bare branches" – unmarried men who have nothing attached to them, no family and no children. This is due to China's One-Child Policy, which has led to a huge surplus of men, millions of whom will never marry. The greater the number of unmarried men the greater the demand for sexual services. This phenomenon guarantees that prostitution will continue to thrive. These unfortunate men have little choice but to turn to sex workers to fulfill their needs.

Sex Trafficking and Kidnapping

There is always a dark side to prostitution. Sex workers can be forced to perform humiliating acts, they can be beaten, and johns can simply refuse to pay. While massage parlors and KTV may provide a safe haven, offering security to poor girls who see few alternatives, there is always an element of degradation to prostitution. Workers are also subject to venereal diseases; rates of syphilis in China have soared, growing by about 30 percent per year, largely due to prostitutes servicing migrant workers.

But the darkest side of China's sex trade is the kidnapping and human trafficking of women who are forced into prostitution. (The trafficking of children, especially boys, in China is a related crisis, as is the kidnapping of women for domestic marriage; both are by-products of the One-Child Policy.) Impoverished Chinese women are kidnapped outright or tricked into moving abroad with false promises of legitimate employment only to be forced into prostitution. Southeast Asia, Europe and North America are the primary destinations for the victims.

Many of these women have already been exploited by the sex industry in China. Helpless and frightened, after being pressed into prostitution abroad they are told by their pimps that they'll be treated brutally by the local police if they try to seek help. A report on human trafficking between China and the UK showed that Chinese sex workers found in raids refuse to offer evidence against their exploiters and even return voluntarily to the brothel. The women are familiar with the sex trade in China, where the government frequently sides with the pimps for payoffs, and believe the same situation exists in their destination country and refuse to report their situation to authorities.

The greatest number of kidnappings for shipment abroad occurs in Yunnan province along the Burma border. Some parents, desperate to pay off debts, sell their daughters to sex traffickers, usually for about 13,000 yuan ($2,050). China also has a significant amount of internal trafficking of women and children for sexual and labor exploitation, with estimates running from 10,000 to 20,000 a year. The victims are trafficked primarily from poorer provinces and taken to the large coastal cities, where they are in effect sex slaves. China's One-Child Policy and the resulting surplus of men, set to reach about 24 million in just a few years, has been a driving force behind domestic trafficking.

Men who cannot find brides due to the short supply of women turn to traffickers to provide a woman for marriage. To meet their sexual needs, China has also become a major destination for the import of kidnapped women.

According to a 2010 report from the U.S. State Department, "Women and children from neighboring countries including Burma, Vietnam, Laos, Mongolia, Russia and North Korea, and from locations as far as Romania and Zimbabwe are trafficked to China for commercial sexual exploitation and forced labor. Well-organized international criminal syndicates and local gangs play key roles in both internal and cross-border trafficking."

The Chinese government's response to what the U.S. State Department calls "China's No. 1 problem" has been unsuccessful. Its failure to adequately punish traffickers or to protect the victims of trafficking has only facilitated the crisis. Despite announcing an action plan in 2007 to fight trafficking and kidnapping, the effort is woefully under-funded and has accomplished little. Until China implements harsher sentences against traffickers and does more to protect the victims, the trafficking epidemic will only continue to grow. Human trafficking is big business in China, and is more lucrative than even the trafficking of drugs or weapons. With its relatively light sentencing and lack of enforcement, sex trafficking appeals to organized crime, making it even more difficult to stamp out.

THE FAMILY

Twenty-five centuries ago a philosopher, bureaucrat and educator named Confucius began spreading his beliefs on filial piety and the importance of family, and in so doing managed to shake China into cultural alignments that are still evidenced today. Although highly structured, close-knit families are not unique to China, no society past or present has placed greater value on the family. The Chinese belief that the hierarchical family must be the center of one's life stems from the teachings of Confucius, his followers such as Mencius, and the interpretation of his writing by the Neo-Confucianists that followed him.

Confucius always said he was a disseminator, not an originator, meaning he drew his philosophy from existing Chinese principles, which he pulled together to form a cohesive set of moral values. His philosophy won the endorsement of the Western Han Dynasty (140 – 87 BC) and he came to be known as the "Great Sage." While Confucius wrote little about sex, he always considered it a natural and necessary act to be performed by husband and wife in a monogamous relationship. Like prayer and ancestor worship, sex was to be practiced only in private.

Unlike in many Western religions, sex in China was in no way considered a sin. In *Sexual Life in Ancient China*, R.H. Van Gulik remarks, "It was probably this mental attitude that together with the nearly total lack of repression, that caused ancient Chinese sexual life to be on the whole a healthy one, remarkably free from the pathological abnormalities and aberrations found in so many other great cultures."

Confucius taught that the family, headed by the male responsible for its members' livelihood, was the core unit of society. In his institutionalized role as head of the family, the father exercised supreme authority over all family matters and his decisions in the family's affairs were final. Often the oldest member of the family, such as the husband's father, would also share control over the wife and children. Stability and harmony were the guiding principles of the ideal family. Mothers were highly respected, but were not the decision makers. The family hierarchy was based on age and gender. The most senior male would have the most power while the youngest woman would have the least.

The mother and children were subservient to the father, and upon his death the oldest son assumed his role. This succession led to a method of child rearing in which each new generation was brought up with the same strict values, making it nearly impossible for children to feel or think differently. Filial piety, social order, submission to authority, family loyalty and adherence to ritual formed the bedrock of Confucian values, and they ultimately reached beyond the family to affect the structure of government and most other aspects of Chinese life. After Confucius' ideas took hold, children who were subordinate to their parents could face severe punishment, while those who heroically supported them were idealized in Chinese literature.

In middle and upper class families, each woman had an assigned role within the family hierarchy. Maids and concubines answered to the female head of the household. She in turn was responsible for keeping the household in order, managing its servants and seeing to her young children's education. Nothing was more important for a married Chinese couple than to give birth to at least one son, as he would be the one to carry on the family's lineage. Confucianism teaches that women have a "natural place" to bear children, to yield to others and never place themselves first.

A poem from a Confucian classic, the *Book of Songs* (*Shi Jing*), translated by Gulik, describes how parents received the birth of a son as opposed to a daughter:

When a son is born
He is cradled on the bed,
He is clothed in robes,
Given a scepter as toy,
His lusty cries portend his vigor,
He shall wear bright red knee-caps
Shall be the lord of a hereditary house.

When a daughter is born
She is cradled on the floor,
She is clothed in swaddling bands,
Given a loom-whorf as a toy,
She shall wear no banners of honor,
Shall only take care of food and drink,
And not cause trouble for her parents.

Women were considered to be inferior to men in every way, and a man was supposed to show no interest in his wife once she had left the bedchamber. Confucianism carried this so far that women weren't even supposed to hang their clothing on the same rack as their husband. It would be unthinkable for women to participate in matters outside her household, such as public affairs. A spirit of outright misogyny, however, did not emerge in China until the rise of the Neo-Confucianists starting around the time of the Song Dynasty. This was when the onerous practice of foot binding became widespread. Men would show off their wives' tiny shoes as a sign of their own status, the smaller the better. Under Neo-Confucian doctrine, women were expected to commit suicide when in danger of being raped.

The notion of male superiority and the importance of a female "knowing her place" dominated the Chinese mindset from ancient times through the mid-twentieth century. It continues to influence Chinese people's approach to marriage, dating and sex, even in the big cities heavily influenced by the West, though that idea is slowly changing. Today forced marriages are mostly a thing of the past but children still seek their parents' approval before marrying.

Under the tenets of Confucianism boys traditionally kept on living with their families even after adulthood, carrying on their lives in the same house, though this practice scarcely exists anymore. When girls grew up, however, they were expected to marry and leave home to live with their husband's family. The mother-in-law was the female head of that household and the girls were subservient to her. Chinese families routinely practiced ritual based on Confucian teachings. Veneration was shown to older family members, and even after they died the family believed their spirit continued to exist as they carried on watching over the family. Altars used to make sacrifices to dead ancestors could be found in every home. To not make these sacrifices would lead to bad luck for the entire family. Ancestor veneration, like other aspects of Chinese family life, was patrilinear: A man would revere his male ancestors and their wives. His wife would revere her male ancestors and their wives, but also all of her husband's male ancestors and their wives.

Over the past one hundred years, and especially in contemporary China, there has been a considerable loosening of the Confucian yoke. For example, most young people today are free to choose their own professions, though they may be expected to seek the advice of their elders. Yet, family still matters above nearly all else and most remain paternalistic and extremely tight-knit. Most societies, including those in the West, have a history of paternalism, but few have a family order as hierarchical and as rigid as China's. Chinese people still see their family as their primary responsibility, and believe that everything the family has is to be shared by its members.

While Chinese family values have undergone many changes, certain principles remain the same. The father, for instance, remains the maintainer and protector of the family. He may still have a final say in important matters concerning his children even if he no longer enjoys total control. Surveys of women in contemporary China, especially in large cities like Shanghai, indicate they increasingly see themselves as nearly on an equal footing with their husbands when it comes to family-related decision making. Veneration of older family members and ancestors remains a core value, and children are still expected to support their elders as they age. Many, if not most, working Chinese continue the tradition of sending a portion of their salary back to their parents. It is actually written into modern marriage laws that if parents are unable to work they have the right to demand support payments from their children.

The belief that the family must produce a son to eventually take on the role as head of the family and preserve the family name remains firmly in place. There is strong pressure on the son to marry and continue the family lineage. The Chinese family remains patrilinear, meaning the ancestors that matter are the father, the father's father, etc. Without a son, the lineage ends.

Confucius' beliefs in regard to sex are still a topic of debate. Some have found his philosophy to be "sex-neutral," with little discussion of sex per se. He does, however, acknowledge man's desires and the importance of the husband and wife to have sex, but within the limits of self-control. In the Confucian classic *The Book of Rites*, Confucius is quoted as saying, "Food and drink and the sexual relation between men and women compose the major human desires."

Sex, according to the Confucian mindset, is for the purpose

of producing heirs, and should include a balance of desire and ritual. Confucius never disparaged sex and recognized it as integral to human nature. It can be inferred from his relative silence on sex that while he saw it as necessary for continuing the family lineage he also saw it as distracting people from their moral obligation to focus on social duties. While he was strictly against adultery, he believed it was all right for a man to keep concubines, especially if he had no male heir from his actual wife.

Under the influence of Confucianism, China adopted strict gender roles that started in early childhood. Boys and girls up to ten years of age were allowed to play with one another, but then they went separate ways. Boys went to school and girls were restricted to women's quarters where they learned "womanly" skills such as sewing. Girls were not permitted to participate in family rituals when they were menstruating.

China's family, unlike that in the West, is one of collectivism, of putting family ahead of one's self, and of always striving to find the "middle way." Peace and harmony are what matter most. Western families tend to emphasize individualism. Being adventurous and inventive and exploring new avenues are seen as enviable traits. The passage to adulthood means stepping out into the world, leaving one's family to begin their own household. In China, even today, the family is the anchor of one's existence, and children are expected to help support the family as soon as they start earning an income. Individualism and breaking with traditions are seen as disrespectful.

Many Chinese families still adhere to ritual ancestor worship, an unknown practice in the West. Westerners often pray to whatever god they believe in to seek answers and spiritual comfort. Although Christianity in China is now slowly spreading, the vast majority of Chinese do not believe in god or religion, aside from the secular religion of Confucianism.

There are also striking differences in how the two cultures mourn the death of a family member. In the West it tends to be straightforward, with family gatherings, a religious service and burial or cremation, after which few if any formal rituals are carried out aside from placing flowers on the grave on the anniversary of death. For the Chinese, the mourning process includes elaborate, sequential rituals: crying and wailing announce the death, the corpse is bathed, symbolic goods like paper money are offered, music is often played to put the spirit at rest, and the coffin is formally sealed. Friends and relatives joining the funeral often bring food, as eating brings good luck. How long and how intensely one mourns depends on the deceased's rank in the family. The oldest son, for example, is supposed to mourn a parent's death for months, during which time he wears drab-colored clothes and cannot get married.

In a Chinese family, even today, kinship is of central importance. Children and elders are still addressed according to rank. While in the West we refer to siblings by their name, in China the oldest brother will be called "*da ge*" (big or oldest brother). Each family member is similarly ranked according to seniority, and relatives of the mother hold different titles than those of the father. An uncle on the mother's side, for example, is referred to as *jiujiu*, while on the father's side it is *bobo*. This rigid hierarchical structure is foreign to the West and difficult to comprehend without knowledge of Confucian family values. In the West it can be considered unseemly for children to refer to their parents by their first name. In China, this taboo is extended to all adult relatives. Confucius' moral principles on the role of the family held sway for more than 2,000 years until the Chinese Communist Party took over the country in 1949. While these principles continue to be the cornerstone of Chinese culture, they underwent considerable transformation under the rule of Mao Zedong.

In the early 1900s China was already liberalizing the Confucian ideal of the woman as a subservient second-class citizen. Foot binding and concubinage were banned (though not completely eliminated) and there was a call to recognize women's rights. The reforms under Mao were even more dramatic: Husbands were forbidden to abuse their wives and it became easier to obtain a divorce, at least on paper. Foot binding was now totally eliminated. Forced marriages were banned as was prostitution, and women were encouraged to enter the work force, to join the Communist Party and to pursue educational opportunities. Mao sought to break down the family structure, which, he believed, kept the people oppressed. But the citizens never abandoned the core Confucian principles of a strong paternalistic family based on loyalty and obedience.

Upon assuming power in 1949 the Communist Party was torn by Confucianism. On the one hand, Confucianism's call for submission to authority helped legitimize the party's hold on power, while its rejection of revolution and the overthrow of old ideas was anathema to socialist philosophy. The party took the road of "critical inheritance," recognizing what it saw as the positive and negative aspects of Confucianism. It called for citizens to revere Confucius and his call to uphold traditional authority, while rejecting many of his political teachings. Ambivalently, Mao at first called for the people to continue Confucian principles of moderation and obedience while rejecting its celebration of feudalism and "old" thoughts and rituals that conflicted with socialist ideals.

When communism was radicalized during the Cultural Revolution Mao essentially repudiated Confucianism as he sought to eradicate the "*Four Olds*": Old Customs, Old Culture, Old Habits, and Old Ideas. Every reminder of Confucianism, such as temples, shrines and sacred texts, was to be destroyed, and the state-run newspapers railed against Confucius. Those who were associated with Confucianism were labeled counter-revolutionaries. (It was ironic that Confucian values – strong central authority, harmony between the rulers and their subjects, a rigid cultural climate – were the hallmarks of Chinese communism.) The traditional notion of the highly structured family also fell under attack. Family histories were wiped out when ancestral records were burned, a desecration of the traditional Chinese value of ancestor worship.

As the Cultural Revolution died away, Confucius was quickly rehabilitated and his greatness was once again declared, his shrines restored, his birthday celebrated. Mao's successor Deng Xiaoping saw Confucian values as tools for stabilizing and unifying the country as he pushed China to "reform and open up." Persecution of the traditional family structure was abandoned, although it would never be the same as before communist rule. With the liberation of women, and with many women entering the work force, the family structure was permanently altered, and often grandparents would move in to take care of the children as the mother worked.

The One-Child Policy

The most dramatic change to the traditional Chinese family was the One-Child Policy introduced in 1979 to control China's burgeoning population and ease the strain on China's resources. Ironically, it was the Communist Party that encouraged population growth after coming to power in 1949. Mao, who said nothing was more essential for China's growth than people, decried birth control and in 1958 stressed the need for a larger population in order to fulfill his utopian program, the Great Leap Forward, a policy disaster that was supposed to make China a manufacturing giant but instead led to the starvation and death of tens of millions. In the late 1960s birth control was promoted once again, but the population, after a drop between 1970 and 1976, continued to grow and by 1979 the government felt it had to take more aggressive action.

The draconian One-Child Policy forbids families from having more than one child, although there are many exceptions, often determined by local officials, especially for families outside the big cities. Parents who lost their only child in the 2008 Sichuan earthquake, for example, were permitted to have a second. China's minorities are also exempt, and many wealthy Chinese and government officials have found ways to evade the policy. Contraception and sterilization were dictated by local family planning authorities, which also carried out forced abortions. The measure, innocuously referred to in Chinese as the "family planning policy," shattered the traditional Chinese ideal of a "big family" and created a raft of problems that promise to challenge China for many years to come.

Because of the long-held belief that having a son is necessary to continue the family lineage and support the parents as they age, many Chinese families did everything they could to ensure that their one child would be a boy. Failure to continue the family name was considered a sign of disrespect to one's ancestors. Inexpensive pre-natal sex determination technology lowered the cost of sex selection, and the policy soon led to selective abortion of females and even to the killing of young female children after birth in the hope that the next child would be a male.

Pre-natal sex screening was banned in 1994 but sex experts in China estimate it is still used for about twenty percent of all pregnancies, with the fetus being aborted if it is a girl. Chemical-induced abortion is by far the most common method. If a child is born a girl, she may be abandoned or killed. This selection process in turn has led to huge gender imbalances, with a surplus of men and a shortage of women. A 2010 study conducted by the Chinese Academy of Social Sciences warns that China will have a bride shortage of 24 million by the year 2020.

While there was resistance to the One-Child Policy from the very start, many Chinese still believe it was a painful but necessary measure. With a population above 1.3 billion and limited resources and jobs, the government convinced the majority of the population that there was little choice. The One-Child Policy remains in place today, despite reports that the government is considering relaxing some of its restrictions. Two only children who marry, for instance, are theoretically now allowed to themselves give birth to two children, but many people including government workers are ruled out.

The One-Child Policy has brought other changes to traditional Chinese family life. Individual savings rates have increased, mainly because with only one child to raise the family spends less money, so there is more to invest. Also, with only one child to support them in old age, young Chinese feel impelled to save more for their retirement.

With so many millions of men unable to find wives thanks to the One-Child Policy and the gender imbalance it spawned, many Chinese men are secretly marrying relatives as a last resort. Incest remains a taboo in China, and marriage between men and women with a close blood relationship is forbidden. But in 2002, *Time* magazine reported that in some poorer areas of the Chinese countryside intra-family marriage was becoming so common that these areas were dubbed "incest villages." Men in these villages, which are usually remote and inhospitable, cannot find women willing to move there, and in desperation they turn to close family relatives.

Marriages to first cousins and even siblings due to the lack of females are not unheard of in the countryside. Such marriages have been prohibited for genetic reasons since the 1980s but are still practiced in some villages. Marriages between a man and a woman born to his mother's sister are usually looked on as acceptable since the woman is not a blood-related kin of the father and is seen as an outsider of the family. Marriages between blood-related kin of the father are frowned upon as a form of incest. Such patrilinear marriages, like marriage between siblings, are a cause of shame for the families, which do all they can to keep them secret.

The gender imbalance also seems to have caused an increase in the rate of crime and violence in China. While other factors such as lack of steady employment might influence the rising numbers, there appears to be a direct statistical correlation between crime and the lopsided sex ratio. According to a detailed 2006 study carried out by researchers at the Chinese University of Hong Kong, with help from other schools in Asia, Europe and

North America, violent crimes and property crimes like burglary and theft in Mainland China rose nearly 14 percent between 1988 and 2004 while arrest rates soared by 82.4 percent. More than 70 percent of the perpetrators were between 16 and 25 years old and 90 percent were males. The report concludes:

The rise in the sex ratio has coincided with a dramatic increase in crime ... We find that the sex ratio among those 16 to 25 years old has had a significant, economically and statistically, impact on crime. We estimate that male-biased sex ratios may account for up to one-sixth of the overall rise in violent and property crime during the period 1988-2004, a finding of particular salience given China's demographics. The 2005 by-census indicates that sex ratios at birth have kept climbing, implying that the next decade may see another 10 percentage-point increase in the 16-25 sex ratio.

Although there is no statistical data to lean on, there is no doubt that the One-Child Policy has also resulted in the kidnapping of women, from China and abroad, who are sold as wives to Chinese men unable to find brides of their own. The policy has also led to many families offering up their unwanted daughters for adoption. Usually they are placed in state-sponsored orphanages, from which thousands are adopted internationally and by Chinese parents each year. Many families do not report the birth of these daughters, hoping their next child will be a boy.

Chinese people, especially those in the larger cities where the One-Child Policy is more strictly enforced, seem to exist to pamper their only child. In the city, both of the parents usually work, allowing more money to be showered on their child in the form of toys and gifts and clothes. The child is their treasure and life revolves around them. Single children of wealthier parents often receive expensive gifts such as automobiles. While the Chinese have always looked on their children, boys especially, as their prize possession, the One-Child Policy has carried this caring to a new extreme that many worry can, ironically, have detrimental effects on the child, making it harder for them to adapt to the outside world and prepare for adulthood.

This phenomenon has been dubbed "Little Emperors Syndrome," which might also be called "spoiled brat syndrome." The parents as well as grandparents give the child everything, often spending half the family income on them. They give the child the one last seat on the bus or subway while they stand. They constantly hold the young child and keep them in a cocoon of protection lest they hurt themselves. They cater to their whims.

At the 2007 Chinese People's Political Consultative Conference, a professor with the Chinese Academy of Social Science, Ye Tingfang, warned, "It is not healthy for children to play only with their parents and be spoiled by them . . . the one-child limit is too extreme. It violates nature's law and, in the long run, will lead to Mother Nature's revenge." The attendees concluded the government should abolish the One-Child Policy and compromise by allowing up to two children per married couple. In 2011, Chinese media reported the government was considering moving to a two-child policy, mainly because the population was becoming unbalanced, with too few working-age adults to care for the elderly.

Abortion was officially termed a remedial measure for meeting China's goals of population control in the 1970s, and it remains very easy for a woman to undergo the procedure. In the 1980s and 1990s mandatory abortions were frequently performed in many regions to control population growth, though the practice is far less common today. An abortion in China costs only about 600 yuan ($88). If a woman already has a child, she will be asked by local family planning officials to terminate her unplanned pregnancy by abortion in the first trimester and even as late as the second trimester. If she refuses, she can incur severe fines. More than 30 percent of pregnant women in China undergo an abortion.

Statistics on abortion are hard to come by, but experts estimate

13 million were performed in China in 2008 and approximately 10 million abortion pills, used in hospitals for early-stage abortions, were sold. (The average annual birth rate in China is about 20 million.) Sex-selective abortion is the exception to China's general acceptance of abortion and the practice was made illegal in 1994. According to a 2009 report in the *China Daily* newspaper, government statistics show that about 62 percent of the women who have abortions in China are between 20 and 29 years old, and most are single. The actual numbers are undoubtedly far higher, as these figures are only collected from registered medical institutions.

Yu Dongyan, a gynecologist, told the paper, "Sex is no longer considered taboo among young people today, and they believe they can learn everything they need from the Internet. But it doesn't mean they've developed a proper understanding or attitude toward it." Many, he said, still have an inadequate knowledge of contraception to avoid unwanted pregnancies.

Sex selection accounts for only about 10 percent of the abortions performed. Many Chinese, particularly in rural areas, are unaware of contraception, which can be at least partially attributed to the lack of sex education in schools. Although surveys show that about 80 percent of married couples use some form of contraception, accidental pregnancies occur frequently, and abortion provides the simplest solution, especially when an "abortion pill" such as Mifepristone can be administered during the early stages of pregnancy.

Male Dominance and Rape in China

As a patriarchal society, male rule and privilege were institution-alized in China long ago. Women were subservient to their male masters. Foot binding, concubinage and spousal abuse are all products of a patriarchal belief system. This is not to say that all women in China lived miserable lives in the shadow of their husband or master; many were acclaimed for their musical and performance skills and lived quite luxuriously. In the Han and Tang Dynasties, several women rose to attain tremendous political influence, as did the Empress Dowager Cixi at the end of the nineteenth century. But always central to China's social organization was the belief in the male as the decision maker, with absolute control over the family's women, children and property. Men were entitled to their concubines, courtesans and prostitutes.

Women, on the other hand, were expected to remain chaste until marriage. When asked whether it was acceptable for a widow faced with hunger and poverty to remarry, eleventh century Neo-Confucianist Cheng I famously responded, "It is a very small thing to die as a result of starvation, but a very serious evil to lose chastity toward one's dead husband by remarrying."

Not surprisingly, this type of father-centric belief system has led to violence against women in China as it has in other patrilinear societies. If women grow up believing their role is to support male entitlement, while boys are raised to conceal their feelings and to measure their power by their sexual potency, spousal abuse is practically inevitable.

"Women hold up half the sky," said Mao Zedong, the man who did much to liberate women from their status as second-class citizens. And yet China still displays a double standard for women in cases of rape. Traditional Chinese culture holds that the woman bears responsibility for an act of rape, and even today many Chinese tend to believe if a woman is raped she must have brought it on herself, either by walking alone late at night, visiting a man's home, drinking alcohol, sexually teasing the man or dressing in an enticing manner. A woman who is raped is considered "damaged goods" and is stigmatized even within her own family.

Incidents of spousal rape soared in the years following the Cultural Revolution, when Confucian values were rejected and China waged war against "old thoughts." The Confucian principles of harmony, balance and self-control had been largely stamped out, and when the Cultural Revolution ended this breakdown in values made women more prone to violence from their husbands than ever before. According to one academic research paper in 1987, the incidence of rape in China soared nearly 350 percent between 1979 and 1983.

Official figures for rape in most developing countries are famously hard to come by, and that is especially true for China. Practically nothing is more taboo in Chinese culture, where virginity is highly prized, than rape, and it is not a subject Chinese people are comfortable discussing. In 2007, the U.S. State Department estimated there were nearly 32,000 rapes in China in 2007, though no numbers from the Chinese government are available for that year. The government last released statistics on rape in 2005 and the official number was only 15,000, obviously a gross underestimation.

It is also estimated that only one out of ten Chinese women will report a rape to the authorities. Most of these rapes are carried out by people the woman knows, according to a recent report prepared for the Chinese Academy of Social Sciences. In many instances, the family or the local police will pressure the woman to rescind the charges.

In 1949 the new communist government created the All-China Women's Federation to protect the rights of women and promote equality, though originally it was mainly a tool for disseminating propaganda. Now an NGO, it drafted a proposal in 2009 defining the boundaries of domestic violence:

"Generally speaking, domestic violence means the physical, mental and sexual harm inflicted by family members, which includes physically violating the rights of a person or forcing a person to do things against his or her will, mentally humiliating or coercing a person, sexually forcing or abusing a person, damaging or depriving a person of his or her right of property and other conduct that inflicts physical or mental damage on a person." Along with marital rape, the definition also included violence in the pre-marriage cohabitation period.

A survey conducted in 2011 by the Federation indicated

that the occurrence rate of spousal abuse in China is nearly 25 percent. Although measures to stem the problem have been proposed, there are no specific, systematic laws mandating the legal obligations and punishment for domestic violence and no mention of rape within marriage. Chinese legislators are aware of this problem and 2012 saw the first conviction of a husband for committing marital rape.

While data is scarce, reports indicate that surprisingly large numbers of women in China are victims of domestic rape and violence but never report it. Chinese women continue to remain in abusive relationships, largely due to the paternalistic culture that raises women to be dependent on their husband and to tolerate nearly everything he does. Tolerance, to the wife, is a virtue, and so domestic violence continues in a vicious circle. This mindset is slowly evolving, but the patriarchal system continues to determine the family structure and the role of family members. The problem is far less evident in the larger cities, where there is a greater awareness of the rule of law and human rights.

Linda Wong, Executive Director of the Association Concerning Sexual Violence Against Women in Hong Kong, believes that these attitudes point to a larger inequality in Chinese culture. "Violence against women is rooted in patriarchal gender relations where women are assigned roles based not on their capacity but norms and values that perpetuate male dominance and superiority," she said in 2008. "The gender inequality is embedded in all levels of the society such as employment, education and social status."

The problem is exacerbated by China's lack of meaningful sex education in schools. Classes focus on biology, with little to no discussion on the social aspects of sex or sexual morality. According to the aforementioned 2009 *China Daily* report, more than 70 percent of callers to a pregnancy phone line at a Shanghai hospital knew next to nothing about contraception. Only 17 percent were aware of venereal diseases, and less than 30 percent knew that HIV/AIDS could be transmitted sexually.

More and more support services are becoming available for

abused women, but they generally fail to address the mentality that is at the heart of the problem, namely women's' lack of self-esteem. Linda Wong remarked, "The support services such as psychological counseling, medical, health and legal services are indeed necessary, but these address practical rather than strategic gender needs. They will not put women in greater control of themselves in their own context. They will not change attitudes, behaviors and power structures."

Awareness of rape as a serious social problem in China has grown in recent years, largely thanks to the Internet. A rape story that galvanized the country occurred in 2009, when two police assistants raped an intoxicated young woman who was out celebrating her completion of the college entrance exams. After wining and dining her they took her home, and then took turns raping her as she lay unconscious. The men were given shockingly light sentences of three years in prison, sparking a national outrage that set the Internet ablaze. Sentencing for rape in today's China ranges from three years in prison to the death penalty. Inexplicably, the judge ruled that the men had committed a "temporary crime with no prior planning . . . and had been forgiven by the victim" and sentenced them to three years in prison, the minimum sentence.

This immediately raised eyebrows across the country. A "temporary" crime because it was unplanned? Would an unplanned murder qualify as a "temporary crime," Chinese netizens asked. A large number of online commenters went in the other direction, blaming the girl for getting drunk and allowing herself to be raped, an echo of China's traditional misogyny. Others asked what the victim's "forgiveness" consisted of and how it was obtained. Many speculated that she had been paid off. One commenter wrote, "I for one believe 'money sealed lips.' If this sentence becomes a new example then the next time when a 'temporary crime' happens again, should we give lenient punishment again? If so, we can extend this to the entire country so that the vast [number of] criminals all can say they 'temporarily committed this crime.'" Another asked, "So is there a difference between formal and informal, long-term and short-term when it comes to the crime of rape? . . . What does it mean to describe a crime as temporary, fixed or permanent?"

Many on the Internet complained that the government was more concerned with the appearance of harmony than with the rights of women. The Internet has proven an invaluable tool for reporting violence against women. In 2009, Deng Yujiao, a 21-year-old karaoke waitress in Badong, Hubei province, became a national folk hero when she stabbed a government official to death with a fruit knife and also wounded a second official because they tried to sexually molest her. At first she was charged with murder and held without bail. As the story caught fire on the Internet the government tried censoring references to the case, but it was too late. Deng had become a celebrity, and poems and songs were written about her and her defiance of male domination. The story also resonated with the masses because of the national disgust with government corruption and the men's notion that they could get away with assault because of their positions. The outcry over the Internet was so intense she was finally released on bail and soon the case was dropped altogether.

In 2008, a 50-year-old Beijing official at a Shenzhen restaurant walked into a restroom and molested an 11-year-old girl. He was confronted by the girl's parents outside the restroom and the scene was captured on the restaurant's security video. The man lashed out at them, "Do you know who I am? I was sent here by the Beijing Ministry of Transportation, my level is the same as your mayor. So what if I pinched a little child's neck? Who the fuck are you people to me? You dare fuck with me? Just watch how I am going to deal with you."

The video flashed across the Chinese Internet like lightning, and netizens launched a "human search engine," digging up dirt on the official and spreading his details and photos everywhere. A man who in the pre-Internet age would have simply walked away was publicly humiliated and dismissed from office, although the authorities said there was not enough evidence to charge him with a crime. Cases like these provide a beacon of hope in regard to violence against women, and the government's bending to the outrage of the people could be seen as a new phase in China's reactions to sex crimes. These stories raised the public's awareness and created a demand for justice, while in the past no one would have heard a word about them. Nothing has made the public more aware of government abuse and corruption than the Internet. But for every story of rape and molestation that is exposed on the Internet, there are doubtless thousands of others we will never hear about.

HOMOSEXUALITY

No country has as rich and unusual a history of homosexuality as China. For centuries, China was more tolerant of same-sex love than nearly any other society, rivaled perhaps only by Ancient Greece and Rome. References to same-sex love have permeated Chinese literature since the Tang Dynasty more than 1,000 years ago. Throughout most of its 5,000-year history until the end of the nineteenth century, China has not only tolerated male same-sex love but also celebrated it. As far back as the Warring States (841 BC - 221 BC), when China's history first began to be recorded by trustworthy scribes, stories tell of giving the gift of a young man to ruling lords. Nearly all of ancient China can be called a "golden age" of same-sex love although some eras were more tolerant than others.

It is important to draw a distinction between homosexuality in ancient China and homosexuality as perceived in the West. Throughout China's imperial dynasties, men who practiced same-sex love were not considered deviants, even if their partner was a boy in his early teens. Homosexuality was not a lifestyle choice or an identity or something that could be explained psychologically as it is in the West; it was a behavior that was, at most times in imperial China, considered natural. There was not even a word for "homosexuality," as it was not seen as a person's identity, but simply as an accepted behavior. Those who practiced it were usually married with families and, it is probably safe to say, heterosexual, or at the most bisexual. The nobility, the literati and wealthier merchants were at certain times in China's history expected to have young male lovers, though the relationship was quite different than the one they shared with their wife.

A relationship with a younger man was not so much a matter of love but of status and power. For men of privilege, same-sex love was something to be practiced with boys from lower rungs of society, and the boy would invariably play the passive role. It was the wealthier man or aristocrat who held the power. This is not to say that these relationships did not blossom into long-term love affairs. Often they did. But usually, as the boy grew older, the patron would discard him and seek a younger man. The term "homosexuality" in regard to most Chinese practitioners of male same-sex love is really something of a misnomer, as their sexual life was by no means limited to boys. They had their heterosexual family complete with all the Confucian rituals, and they sought young men for entertainment outside their house.

The phenomenon of same-sex love in China can seem surprising in a nation whose secular religion is Confucianism, which is based on morality, restraint and the belief that procreation is the primary reason for sex. Yet Confucianism never teaches that homosexuality is a sin. In general, as long as a man lived up to his social obligation of getting married and having children, sexual contact outside the marriage, at least for men, was not considered relevant. The Chinese from ancient times through the nineteenth century did not see same-sex love as going against traditional family values and the practice was rarely criticized. It was simply another form of pleasure seeking. Most of China's emperors applied the philosophy of Confucius to their management of the state, with its emphasis on order, obedience and authority, while in their private lives they sought immortality by practicing Daoism, with its celebration of sensual pleasure. Many of these emperors kept male lovers even well into the conservative Qing Dynasty.

Most of the references to homosexuality in imperial Chinese fiction, painting and poetry are of men having sex with other men. Far less common are depictions of female same-sex love, although throughout most of its history the Chinese were broad-minded and accepting of it, though some periods were more tolerant than others. The relatively scant portrayals of lesbianism can be partly explained by the tradition of segregation between men and women in China, and the greater freedom and mobility men enjoyed. Men were expected to go to brothels, to keep concubines and to seek pleasure, while the role of women was to stay at home and submit to the head of the household.

Many descriptions of female same-sex love in Chinese fiction are about women living together as concubines or servants who fall in love. Under Daoism, same-sex love between women was perfectly fine and even to be expected because they lived together in close quarters. Just like men who had sex with other men, those who practiced female same-sex love were not given a gender identity such as "lesbian." They were simply women enjoying the act of physical love. Romantic feelings between women were classified as "sisterhood," not lesbianism. One of the many erotic works from prominent late-Ming fiction writer Li Yu (1611 – 1680) is a short story that includes a relatively rare reference to sex between women, though it is brief and not nearly as graphic as his descriptions of male same-sex love:

So they undressed together and proceeded to compare their treasures. Peeking at one another, they dissolved into giggles. By the time they got into the water, lotus-picking was the furthest thing from their minds. Instead they began lurking about . . . some stood close together and fondled each other's charms, while others hugged and had their way with each other. [Adapted from the graduate thesis of Kimberly Shane.]

Li Yu also wrote a stage play about female lovers, *Loving a Fragrant Companion*, which tells the story of two young women who fall in love. One of the women marries the other's husband as a concubine so the two could live together forever. Another depiction of female-female love can be found in *Dreams of Red Mansions* (*Honglou Meng*) written by Cao Xueqin in the mid-eighteenth century, and perhaps the most celebrated Chinese novel of all time. It includes a story of two actresses who fall deeply in love, and how it is fully accepted by the book's hero Baoyu, illustrating just how tolerant the Chinese once were of lesbianism.

A late-Ming author, Tzu Yang Tao Jen, wrote an incredibly graphic novel of female same sex love, *The Flower's Shadow Behind the Curtain*, which leaves little to the imagination:

First, Dangui, the elder girl, took the part of the "man". She told Xiangyu, "We may not have a penis as a man does, but we can use our fingers just like a penis. Dangui raised Xiangyu's legs, kissed and sucked her nipples, and touched her vulva. She tried to insert her finger into Xiangyu's vagina, but not even her little finger could get in. She wet her finger with her saliva, and finally succeeded in inserting it into Xiangyu's vagina.

At first, the thrusting of Dangui's finger was painful to Xiangyu, but after many thrusts, Xiangyu felt excitement and pleasure. She applauded Dangui, calling her, "my darling brother." At the same time, Xiangyu began caressing Dangui's vulva, and was surprised to find it very wet. She asked Dangui, "Why did you urinate?"

Dangui replied, "This is women's sexual secretion, and tomorrow when I play with you, you will get as wet as I am.

But again, such graphic descriptions of lesbian love in Chinese literature are considerably less common than those of male same-sex love. Female same-sex love was rarely celebrated publicly as was love between men.

About half of the twenty-five emperors of the Han Dynasty (206

BC - 220 AD) were openly bisexual, their relationships with male lovers recorded by historians in rich detail. One such scribe kept a volume titled, "Biographies of the Emperor's Male Favorites," and some of its stories remain alive to this day. For example, the phrase "the cut sleeve," which stems from an episode with the Han Emperor Ai and his favorite male lover, remains code in Chinese for homosexual love even today. The story behind it is well known to many homosexuals in contemporary China, as described by Bret Hinsch in his book *Passions of the Cut Sleeve: the Male Homosexual Tradition in China*:

Emperor Ai was sleeping in the daytime with Dong Xian stretched out across his sleeve. When the emperor wanted to get up, Dong Xian was still asleep. Because he did not want to disturb him, the emperor cut off his own sleeve and got up. His love and thoughtfulness went this far.

Another metaphor for male same-sex love also originated in the Han Dynasty, when one of its rulers, Duke Ling, fell in love with a court official, Mizi Xia, who offered him a half-eaten peach as a gift, causing the emperor to exclaim, "How sincere is your love for me!" The phrase "sharing the peach" has connoted male homosexuality ever since. None of this was controversial at the time. It was fine for the emperor to show deep love for his young male lover. Men having sex with men was a fact of life and most Chinese simply accepted it as such. During the Tang Dynasty, when erotic painting and fiction came into vogue and books became available for popular consumption, stories expressing love between men became common. An early Tang short story, translated by Bret Hinsch, is one of the first in popular fiction to reference anal sex between men:

When Wu Sansi saw his beloved's pure whiteness he was immediately aroused. That night Wu summoned him so they could sleep together. Wu played in the "rear courtyard" until his desire was satisfied.

"Rear courtyard" is an obvious reference to the anus, and it is a metaphor that writers employed from the Tang through the Qing Dynasty a thousand years later. It also comes up in a later Tang Dynasty story about an orphaned boy:

Because of his exceptional good looks, he was repeatedly sodomized. He grew accustomed to this "coupling of skins" and at last found his place as a street boy. He indiscriminately associated with Buddhist and Daoist monks, robbers and thieves, and was a beloved to all of them. Day and night men excitedly played in his rear courtyard. One could hang a bushel of grain from his erect penis and it would still not go down! It looked like the shaft of a miller's wheel, and could be used to beat a drum loudly enough to alarm people. Because of him two of the rogues fought one another over him.

The nobility and the literati – well-educated men who had passed the civil service examination and often worked in coveted roles as officials – frequently kept male lovers from local acting troupes. All of the actors were young men and boys who played both the male and female roles on stage, and the most sought after were those who were smooth and feminine. Often they wore female clothing and always played the female role with their male patrons. While most literary references to male-male love involved relations of an aristocrat or wealthy man with a younger man of lower social status, it was hardly limited to the upper classes, and many stories from the Tang and later dynasties depict homosexual love between ordinary people. One late Ming scholar described in detail how men in the southern province of Fujian lived with one another in a type of same-sex marriage that was blessed by their parents and family, though eventually it was necessary for them to marry women. There are records of male love in nearly all parts of the country, especially during the late Ming and Qing Dynasties.

A change in China's outlook on sex was in the wind in the late Song Dynasty (960-1279 AD) as Neo-Confucianists gained influence and preached a new moral orthodoxy. Soon court historians stopped recording the emperor's exploits with young men, though no doubt such relations continued. While Neo-Confucianism led to drastic new restrictions on women, homosexuality was relatively unaffected. Male prostitution among the common people had thrived in the first half of the Song and would continue to enjoy popularity until the end of the Qing Dynasty in 1911, despite unsuccessful efforts starting in the second half of the Song to suppress it. Male and female prostitution was banned and edicts were sent out restricting officials' behavior with boys. Most of these were ignored and rarely enforced.

In 1610, in the late Ming Dynasty, Jesuit missionary Gaspar da Cruz visited Guangzhou and was shocked at the openness of male prostitution in public:

That which shows the misery of these people is that no less than the natural lusts they practice unnatural ones that reverse the order of things: and this is neither forbidden by law or thought to be illicit, or even a cause of shame. It is spoken of in public and practiced everywhere, without there being anyone to prevent it. And in some towns where this abomination is most common . . . there are public streets full of boys got up as prostitutes. And there are people who buy these prostitutes and teach them to play music and sing and dance. And then, gallantly dressed and made up with rouge like women these miserable men are initiated into this terrible vice.

This raises another important difference between Chinese and Western perspectives on same-sex love. Unlike the West, the Chinese had no religion that taught them homosexuality was a mortal sin. The two cultures saw homosexuality through different prisms. Chinese passing by on the street would most likely have viewed the male prostitutes as providing entertainment that harmed no one, while Western missionaries would see them as sinners committing perverted acts that went against all of

God's teachings. The sin of homosexuality from the perspective of traditional China was that the men would likely not provide their parents with grandchildren.

Perhaps the most intriguing period in the history of same-sex love in China was the second half of the Ming Dynasty followed by the Qing. The first half of the Ming saw an increasingly repressive and reactionary government that can only be described as anti-sex. Neo-Confucian Cheng I (1033 – 1107) led the charge for the suppression of free thought and personal gratification under the mantra "Discard human desire to retain the heavenly principles." Books and erotica were banned and prostitution was forbidden. There are few records of homosexual affairs during the first half of the Ming, or of homosexuality being practiced among the general population.

The second half of the Ming Dynasty, however, witnessed a resurgence of sexual openness and tolerance as the rulers rejected Neo-Confucianism and adopted a philosophy of free sexual expression. Erotic painting, poetry and literature flourished, and the educated and upper classes in the large international cities like Beijing enjoyed a golden age of libertinism. Male same-sex love thrived as never before under the late Ming as China's growing foreign trade and general prosperity boosted citizens' income.

Wealthy men enjoyed a choice between love with a female or male courtesan, and as usual, those who had sex with younger men did so as proof of their status and power. Privileged men carried on affairs with their servant boys, who had no choice but to submit to the head of the household, which remained patriarchal. The attraction to young, feminine boys from acting troupes, known as "song boys," became an obsession for the literati, who were by far the most open in their homoerotic practices, though men in every social stratum, from royalty to manual laborers, sought pleasures with other men. Under the late Ming, male prostitutes, usually working in brothels, sometimes saw more business than their female competitors, who looked with jealousy at the popularity of the catamites.

For the rich and the educated, male same-sex love offered a novel and exciting opportunity to indulge their senses. Prostitution was still illegal in the late Ming (at least on paper) and there are stories of men being punished for having sex with male entertainers during this time, but boys continued to provide an appealing alternative and in general authorities turned a blind eye. Female same-sex love was also widely accepted during the late imperial period; as long as the woman met her family obligations and bore children, the Chinese saw no need to impose restrictions on her private life.

As described in Wu Cuncun's remarkably detailed book, *Homoerotic Sensibilities in Late Imperial China*, young men of beauty and feminine appearance appealed most to the literati. The boys, almost always from acting troupes, took great trouble to make themselves beautiful, oiling their skin at night to ensure a healthy glow, growing their fingernails long, wearing rouge and donning bright flowing gowns to appear more ladylike. The most prized were those between 12 and 14 years of age, before they grew facial hair and their voices changed.

These relationships were decidedly unfair. For the young actors life was terribly difficult. Being at the bottom of the social ladder, the years they spent in the service of male patrons left them without skills and with few prospects for a successful life once they were rejected for being too old. Unlike concubines, who were often treated as family members, especially if they bore the master's children, catamites were discarded like an old shoe, and many became beggars or took on the most menial jobs and died in poverty.

The Qing Dynasty marked the start of yet another reactionary wave of orthodox Neo-Confucianism, which the Manchu conquerors hoped would help restore order and foster morality. Once again erotic art and literature were banned, and the government imposed harsh penalties on those who continued selling or possessing it. Such prohibitions during the 250 years of Qing rule were not consistent; sometimes restrictions on vice were relaxed or ignored, and some of China's most graphic art and literature depicting male-male love was created under the Qing. In *Dreams of Red Mansions*, written in the mid-eighteenth century, the sex-obsessed bully Xue Pan is beaten by his father for having a brief affair with a young actor – not for performing a homosexual act but for disturbing the social order by seeking affection from someone of a lower class.

The most notorious book on homosexuality under the Qing was titled *Pleasant Spring and Fragrant Character*, written in the first half of the nineteenth century, and it goes into astonishingly graphic detail. This excerpt from the banned book, translated by Fang Fu Ruan, describes an encounter between 18-year-old Li Zun-xian and 13-year-old schoolboy Sun Yi-zhi:

Li's penis had reached Sun's anus and was fully erect but could not enter. Despite several attempts in different ways, Li still could not succeed in entering Sun. Meanwhile Sun was screaming with pain and begged Li to stop. Li replied to Sun that he did not want to hurt him, but the real great feeling would come later. Li further told Sun that it would help if Sun moved his buttocks. Sun replied that it hurt everywhere so Li might as well come into him. Li then instructed Sun to hold his own buttocks and press as if to excrete. He would enter Sun at that time. Meanwhile, Li lubricated his penis with his saliva, and with a strong push succeeded in entering Sun. Sun's inside was still quite tight and dry. Li used another strong push and reached to the end. Li then pushed up and down, and in and out with force. Gradually, Sun's inside began to feel smooth and slippery. Li was then able to enter and withdraw at ease. Sun at this point began to feel fluid flooding his inside and had a strong sensual feeling. He then began to move his buttocks up and down until he could hardly breathe and indulged himself in this sensuality. Li knew then that Sun was enjoying himself, and pushed his penis with great force while Sun was resting, catching his breath. It was at this point that Sun reached his sexual climax. Sun uttered 'dear brother' and turned around and kissed Li on the mouth.

But despite the flow of quasi-pornographic stories and novels of the time, the Qing Dynasty was also a time of unprecedented censorship as the state adopted the most conservative Confucian values. Most erotic works were banned as the state sought to restore order and conformity. The powerful second Qing emperor Kangxi banned fornication, which had been illegal on paper for centuries, and also banned sexual relations with boys under twelve. In 1740 the government passed its first edict banning consensual homosexual sex, though it appears not to have been enforced. Despite such repression, intolerance of homosexuality went back and forth under the Qing, and four of Kangxi's successors carried out affairs with men.

So it may seem a paradox that under the conservative Qing rule male same-sex love enjoyed a golden age, and several Qing emperors continued to carry on with male lovers. The advent of Beijing Opera from the late eighteenth century to the middle of the nineteenth century brought more talented young men onto the stage playing female roles (women were not permitted to perform) and the partner of choice for the literati were now "song boys" as opposed to houseboys and prostitutes. Pleasure-seeking officials during this period enjoyed their leisure hours in the company of young male opera performers, usually female impersonators, who began to displace women in entertainment quarters.

Some of these performers had income and were quite particular about their male suitor. The wealthier the patron, the more gifts he would bestow on the young actor. It was in Beijing under the Qing that male same-sex love reached its zenith as many of the literati visibly carried on with young performers. Male prostitutes were still in fashion in other cities, but it was the nation's capital that saw a boom in male homosexuality as never before. Scholars and literati were known to carry out their liaisons with song boys in public, at the same time sodomy was being persecuted in Europe as a mortal sin. In some circles song boys had become more popular than female prostitutes. Same-sex love also underwent an evolution in the nineteenth century, often becoming more about romantic love than domination. Poetry from the time increasingly celebrates affairs of the heart. Still, there was never any question of the yawning gap between the lovers' social status, and it was always understood that the patron's devotion was finite.

The Qing rulers became increasingly fixated on idealized gender roles and the belief that sexual intercourse was to be performed only by married men and women. This led to new laws banning homosexual acts, including serious penalties for homosexual rape, though far more attention was paid to illicit heterosexual intercourse. (Such laws were extremely difficult to enforce in a country as geographically vast as China.) Other forces were also at work in the nineteenth century that buoyed China's growing sexual conservatism. In 1860, the British and French defeated the Qing Emperor in the Second Opium War and Western nations colonized parts of the country, subjecting it to harsh and humiliating treaties. Dr. Chong Kee Tan, a researcher of Chinese literature, explains in a recent article how this defeat changed China's perceptions of sexuality:

[It] was such a devastating blow to Chinese confidence that it unleashed numerous waves of social movements aimed at regaining Chinese national prowess and pride. A key consensus among these reformers was the need to learn from the West. Western sciences, mathematics, astrology, medicine, philosophy, psychology, in fact, every branch of Western knowledge were eagerly studied. Even Western forms of dress, customs, etiquette, and religion became popular and were marks of progress for those who adopted them. It was under such a condition that Western homophobia, piggybacked on Western science, finally and regrettably succeeded in infiltrating Chinese consciousness and began to take root.

China's intellectual and ruling classes went through a soul-searching period, trying to grapple with their defeat. They ended up translating copious amounts of Western scholarship in an effort to gain the knowledge of Western powers, including works by Western psychiatrists that pathologized homosexuality. "The transition was slow," Dr. Tan said in an interview, "and as late as the 1930s one could still find fairly un-self-conscious references to liaisons with song-boys." But as Western ideas and morality took hold in China, there was a reaction against the practice of same-sex love.

England imposed its homophobic laws on most of the countries it colonized, and China was no exception. Christian missionaries flooded in and further influenced the Chinese with Western values. China became increasingly closed-minded on the subject, and by the turn of the century the golden age of male same-sex love in China had come to an end. Homoerotic behavior in the early twentieth century was reclassified as a psychological disorder. The image of the effeminate homosexual men and song-boys fueled a desire to be rid of homosexuality, which was rapidly becoming stigmatized. The spirit of homophobia continued and accelerated, and by the time the Chinese Communist Party took over control of the government in 1949 most Chinese viewed same-sex love as deviant behavior.

No discussion of sex in China around the time of the late Qing Dynasty can be complete without mention of the Orientalist and linguist Sir Edmund Backhouse (20 October 1873 – 8 January 1944). A self-taught sinologist with an uncanny ability to learn new languages, Backhouse arrived in Beijing in 1898 and by 1903 was proficient enough in Chinese to work as a translator. He wrote two books with the help of British journalist J.O.P. Bland on life among the imperial family, *Annals and Memoirs of the Court of Peking* (1914) and *China Under the Empress Dowager* (1910), the latter of which would come to shape the Western world's impressions of Empress Dowager Cixi for much of the twentieth century. Backhouse provided the information and Bland wrote it up in an engaging style, and the two books quickly won critical acclaim; no others could match them for Backhouse's allegedly first-hand accounts of imperial life during the tumultuous last years of the Qing Dynasty.

In 1976, historian Sir Hugh Trevor-Roper in his book *Hermit of Peking, The Hidden Life of Sir Edmund Backhouse* exposed Backhouse, to his own satisfaction at least, as a con man who had based his writings on forged sources and who knowingly misled readers with stories pulled from his febrile imagination. Trevor-Roper methodically walks the reader through the sinologist's life, a tale of one fraud and swindle after another. Backhouse had a pattern of arranging fantastic business deals, each of which fell apart, usually leading to his running away. His life was so improbable it reads like pure fiction. Following Trevor-Roper's exposé practically no one took Backhouse seriously again, though some have argued there are enough grains of truth to his writings to make them a valuable resource. What was fact and fiction will never be fully known. (It is somewhat ironic that in 1983 Trevor-Roper's own reputation would be tarnished after he declared the forged "Hitler Diaries" to be authentic.)

Backhouse was a homosexual, and he wrote an erotic memoir, *Décadence Mandchoue*, which was only published in 2011 after nearly 70 years of neglect. It paints a graphic picture of homosexual life in Beijing. Backhouse makes extraordinary claims that strain the reader's credulity, describing how he had sex with such illustrious figures as Paul Verlaine, Oscar Wilde and, most notoriously, the Empress Dowager Cixi.

In the very first chapter the reader is drawn into the hidden world of a late Qing male brothel, where the owner is explaining to Backhouse how his business operates:

> The catamite's 'pudenda' (Ch'iao Tzu 巧子 or penis, "cunning tool"), testicles (Tan Tzu 蛋子), anal region, fundament and perineum are all delicately perfumed and, as goes without saying, kept most scrupulously clean: the pubic and anal hair is clean shaven like the face. Naturally, if the client desires intimate labial contact on his person, he will wish to perform appropriate ablution on his secret parts. An exquisite scent

from Java (or Borneo) is available for Taels 5 a bottle; so that the practical and aesthetic side of what might appear gross and physical (even filthy) be not neglected. However, you shall have everything for a fixed tariff of Taels 50, plus a fee for the "pleasuring" to him whom you deem worthy of your regard.

There were even special rates for those who wanted a catamite to hit them with a rod, or if they themselves wanted to hit the catamite, a process Backhouse describes in graphic detail. If the memoir is to be believed, Backhouse was nearly always engaging in sex in a wide variety of positions, be it with court eunuchs, nobility, celebrities or boy prostitutes. At one point he describes a young farm hand making love to a steer. Absolutely nothing is off limits. *Décadence Mandchoue*, for all its exaggeration, offers a valuable if shocking glimpse of gay life among China's nobility at the turn of the century. As its editor Derek Sandhaus wrote in his introduction, this is more than a sex diary: "This, his final work, is a eulogy to the Ch'ing Dynasty; an erotic love letter to a bygone era."

Sandhaus makes a strong argument that much of the book recounts actual events and that some of Trevor-Roper's criticisms are based on bias and the neglect of sources that could have corroborated much of Backhouse's story. In either case, the book stands on its literary merits, and offers a portrait of sex in late imperial China unlike any other.

The Twilight Years: Homosexuality under Mao and Deng

The ascension to power of Mao Zedong and the Communist Party in 1949 marked the beginning of the dark days for homosexuality in China. Homosexuality in any form was banned, as it was seen as a form of Western "spiritual pollution." For decades, China would deny that it was home to *any* homosexuals, since such deviants could only be the product of a corrupt and decadent Western society. The new communist government branded homosexuality as a kind of mental illness, and those who practiced it could be and often were arrested and tried for "hooliganism." There are no references to same-sex love in literature and art from the 1950s to the start of the 1980s. The notion of homosexuality was erased from public consciousness.

Homosexuals under Mao, and later under Deng Xiaoping, were forced underground, and most of them lived tortured lives, unable to be honest with anyone about who they really were. Those who tried to meet other gays in public parks or toilets ran a great risk of being arrested and even imprisoned. Although Mao did not launch any "strike hard" campaigns against gays in particular, many were persecuted mercilessly during the Cultural Revolution. Gay people were subject to criticism, and there are records of some being beaten to death, while others were simply interrogated. Since homosexuality was a form of spiritual pollution from the West, gays during this time were seen as pushing China backwards; many were branded as class enemies.

The law throughout these years, until 1997 when homosexuality was decriminalized, was vague and ambiguous. Sometimes consensual acts between adults of the same sex were treated as a crime, though often they just carried a warning. Gay men cruising in public parks and toilets were under constant risk of arrest by plainclothes policemen, but due to the lack of clear laws with standard penalties, punishment was usually meted out by local governments that handled homosexual acts of "hooliganism" in different ways. "Hooliganism" itself was a broad, amorphous term that could apply to any type of social offense. Gays were in a constant state of fear and confusion, not knowing the actual laws.

The most terrifying penalty homosexuals faced if they were caught having sex with another man in a public space was not abuse from the police, but administrative punishment from local officials. Since there were no clear laws about how to deal with this offense, local governments were free to handle it as they saw fit, leading to random and arbitrary penalties at the officials' whim. Administrative punishment often consisted of reporting the offense to the offender's *danwei*, or work unit. When those in the *danwei* found out, the offender was almost always stigmatized, and often they were demoted or thrown out of the *danwei* altogether. Sometimes families were notified. These penalties often ruined the offender's life, forcing them to live with nearly unbearable shame and isolation.

The Chinese simply had no understanding of homosexuality anymore, and they perceived it as a disease to be shunned. Even the homosexuals themselves had no understanding of why they were attracted to members of the same sex, and they, too, believed there was something wrong with them. Party members who were found to be having homosexual relations were often thrown out or given a demerit in their file, which meant their wages could be withheld and their chance of a promotion was slim. Some localities treated homosexuality as a mental illness, others as a crime of hooliganism, so penalties varied dramatically. There were also different penalties depending on sexual roles; the act of penetrating was more serious than being penetrated. Nearly all the records of arrests and administrative sanctions against homosexuals dealt with men having sex with other men. There are very few records of any such offenses involving lesbianism.

In 1985 a popular Chinese health magazine took the unprecedented step of publishing an article about how homosexuality exists in all cultures and nations, and arguing that gays should not be discriminated against. The article generated 60 letters from readers, mainly gay men, in which they described the misery in which they lived. The men, many of whom dared to use their actual names and geographic locations, expressed deep thanks to the author, Chinese sexologist Fang Fu Ruan, for having the courage to open a dialogue on what had become one of China's most taboo subjects. (No lesbians responded to the article, indicating they were even more closeted than gay men.)

In their letters, most of the men expressed deep sadness at

their inability to satisfy their wives and their need to live behind a lie. Others described the anguish of falling in love with a man and never being able to express their emotions. Some responders had been imprisoned for a gay encounter. The letters ache with despair and provide a rare microcosm of what it was like to live as a homosexual before China began to open up and liberalize. Several of the men described their thoughts of suicide.

While being gay in China today is for most men and women difficult and painful, during the time of Mao until the 1990s there was simply no hope and no support. A man had to get married and have children and keep his sexuality a closely guarded secret. Most Chinese had no idea of the country's illustrious history of homosexuality in times past. Millions of Chinese people still believe homosexuality was something imported to China from the West, and that traditional Chinese values would never have permitted the acceptance of homosexual sex. Just as Mao eradicated prostitution, so too did he eradicate all public records, all memory of China's gay history in literature and art. China's gay past is a heritage denied.

In a moving column in the *New York Times* in 1990, Nicholas Kristof tells of a gay man being subject to electric shock treatment and becoming suicidal. His description on the state of homosexuality in China at the time is insightful:

Homosexuality is rarely discussed in China's press or in routine conversations. Most Chinese assert that they have never known a homosexual and that there must be extremely few in Chinese society.

In large cities, particularly in the southern city of Canton, homosexuals meet in certain bars or parks. They sometimes refer to each other in the Cantonese dialect as *geilo*, or gay guy.

There are no advocacy groups for homosexuals in China. But if the nation lacks an outspoken gay community, it also lacks the invective and bitter hostility that is sometimes directed toward homosexuals in the West.

There are no common insults in Chinese related to sexual orientation.

HOMOSEXUALITY

Most Chinese frown on homosexuality, but characterize it as improper or in poor taste rather than as a sin.

While there was and is a great deal of stigmatization and discrimination against gays in China, the "gay bashing" that is common in Western nations, fueled by religious beliefs that gays are sinners and degenerates, scarcely exists in China. But as Kristof says, most Chinese during the Mao years did not believe homosexuality even existed because it was pushed so far underground. Gays at the time had no choice but to live in shame and secrecy, though the early 1990s began to show signs of increased tolerance, and gays in larger cities began frequenting China's new gay bars, the first of which opened in Beijing in 1993. The early bars kept a low profile and were sometimes closed down with no explanation, even as late as the mid-2000s, but they often reopened and were generally left alone.

The Cloud Lifts: Gays in Contemporary China

A major breakthrough occurred in 1997, when China decriminalized homosexuality. That same year the first gay hotline began operating in Beijing. Four years later homosexuality was removed from the list of mental illnesses. The days of Mao and Deng were over and China was in the midst of dramatic social reform. The country had opened up to foreigners, and Western influence was seeping in. China's sexual revolution had been progressing for years and people's outlooks on sex and homosexuality were changing, at least in the major cities.

In 1997, a 32 year-old gay man told a reporter from the *New York Times*, "No one bothers us anymore. As long as we're not disturbing anyone else, we can enjoy ourselves and the police will leave us alone . . . The government no longer has a problem with gays; it has problems with organizations. As long as you don't organize and speak out, you can do what you want." That may have been true in Beijing and Shanghai, but it is still difficult to be a homosexual in China if you live outside the international cities. Millions of gays continue to live like ghosts, hiding in a shadow world.

According to a 2007 survey by China's most vocal sexologist Li Yinhe 20 percent of Chinese people think there is nothing wrong with homosexuality. Of those surveyed, 30 percent believe it is "somewhat but not completely wrong," while 40 percent believe it is completely wrong. Surprisingly, when asked how they would react if a family member were homosexual, about 10 percent said they would be totally accepting and about 75 percent said they would tolerate it but hoped they would change over time. Li concluded that the Chinese seemed to be becoming more tolerant of homosexuality.

Based on population size, sex experts estimate there are between 30 and 40 million gays in China. Li Yinhe, who has carried out extensive research on the lives of gays in China, says the number could be as high as 46 million. Most gays in China remain highly closeted so gathering statistics about them is notoriously difficult, and any numbers include a degree of guesswork. Li estimates that about 80 percent of all gay men and women in China will get married. Sexologist Liu Dalin, now retired from the University of Shanghai, puts the number at 90 percent. Nearly all of those from previous generations, especially those born during the Cultural Revolution or earlier, are married today, and most gays will continue to marry. Filial piety and the pressure to have children remain intact, and for most gays, coming out is simply not viewed as a possibility.

As Chinese young people enter their mid-twenties, members of their family start pressing them on their plans to get married. Relatives will try to play matchmaker, and the topic never goes away until they announce their engagement. As they approach their 30s, both men and women who have not married are looked on with suspicion. A single woman over 30 is especially seen as a lost cause and people might well assume there is something wrong with her. She becomes a shame to her family, where face is such an important issue. So as they get older, parents and siblings up the pressure on them to find a spouse.

"I hate going back to my hometown, even for Chinese New Year, because all my relatives do is ask when I am getting married," said Larry Yang, a medical professional who moved to the United States from his small town in Shanxi province several years ago. He is 30 years old and gay, and has no plans to let his family know the truth. "You have to understand, my parents have never been to the big cities and they have no idea what a homosexual is," he said. "I could never explain to them that I'm gay. They would just look at me as if I were crazy. They never stop bothering me about getting married, and going to see them and my cousins and brothers is a nightmare. They are all married, and all they want to talk about is finding a girl for me."

The marriage of gay men and women to unknowing spouses who are straight is nothing less than a tragedy. In 2009, Li Yinhe wrote on her blog about a conference attended by several *tongqi*, or "homowives" – straight women married to gay men:

The condition for 'homowives' is extremely tragic. At the seminar, there were 'homowives' who burst into tears as they spoke, leading all of them to hug each other for a good cry. Most days, they wash their faces with tears. I heard what I considered the most shocking testimony that from a woman who told of how she even doubted her ability to attract men – why wouldn't her husband even want to look at her or touch her? Am I really that unworthy as a woman? She assumed that all men would treat her like that, not knowing that this is far from the truth. She did not dream that her husband would be gay. Under the circumstances, even the most beautiful and accomplished woman would not arouse him.

The story was widely reported in the Chinese media. Sexology and gay rights supporter Professor Zhang Beichuan estimates there are 16 million "homowives" in China. Such marriages are torture for both the wife and the gay husband. Neither has their needs fulfilled, and often the husband leads a double life. Lesbians are in much the same situation, and while they can at least more easily feign sexual pleasure, they, too, are trapped in loveless marriages. The *tongqi* who has no idea about her husband's sexuality will do all she can to stimulate him, often to no avail. She knows as he looks away that something is terribly wrong. A *tongqi* support group in Beijing offers moral support to women driven into deep depression because their husbands cannot have sex with them. They feel betrayed, and in a sense they are.

Chuang Wai, a 27 year-old magazine editor living in Xi'An, married her husband in 2007 and divorced him a year later after she learned he was gay. "When I first met my husband he was so polite, thoughtful and considerate," she says, but his lack of sexual interest in her was alarming, and she soon found him surfing gay websites.

"I tried to talk with him about his problem and our marriage but every time we started in a friendly atmosphere it ended with very bad results. I cannot remember how many times he used violence on me. There are four or five times when I was seriously injured. You cannot imagine that when I slept in bed he would use violence without any reason. I think it was because he didn't want to sleep with me. I still remember when he threw a kettle full of water at my belly. That was really a disaster. Before we married he was so nice and I felt truly loved."

They did not have sex on their honeymoon, and only tried to have sex five times during their one year of marriage, and her husband never ejaculated. Chuang says that many *tongqi* are reluctant to get a divorce because they already have children, or the woman is financially dependent on her husband. She also has advice for other *tongqi*: "Homowives should become financially and spiritually independent. They should love themselves. They should not give up on themselves even if their husband is cold and mistreats her. Never feel you are unattractive. Have self-confidence and make your own decisions for your future."

These relationships are as tragic for the gay husband as they are for the *tongqi*. Every weekend older gay men trapped in loveless marriages meet together at a rundown dance hall in Shanghai that reserves the weekend for them, and they dance together, one of their few opportunities to be who they really are. As described in a 2011 story in *Slate* magazine, watching these men who had to sacrifice a part of themselves to fulfill their family obligations dancing with and holding another man who made the same sacrifice is a scene of heartbreaking poignancy.

Since it is so hard for gay men and women to say no in the face of their parents' insistence that they marry, many have sought an innovative solution that has been gathering traction in recent years: Gay men marry gay women and pretend to be a happily married couple. Then they go off and stay with their same-sex partner. Of course, this compromise is still a form of a double life and living behind a lie, but there is no disappointment to either spouse over the other's lack of sexual interest, and they still fulfill their physical and emotional needs. Most importantly, the continuous pressure from the family to marry is alleviated.

A popular gay website in China in 2010 started to advertise "fake marriage markets" once a month in Shanghai. Scores of gay men and women meet at a yoga studio to try to find the right spouse to marry. Some say they just want a gay spouse for a couple of years followed by a divorce, just to show their parents that they respect their wishes. None of them feel they can come out to their parents, and this type of marriage is simply the last and least painful resort. The process of finding a spouse for such a marriage of convenience is not easy, especially for men. There are fewer women than men available, which gives women the power to set very high standards so they can win their parents' approval. They also must come to an agreement as to who owns what property and possessions, all of which is negotiated like a business contract. Often they sign prenuptial agreements to avoid future feuds.

Today homosexuality is generally tolerated in the international cities like Shanghai and Beijing, each of which has several gay bars and some of these are quite popular even with straight people. Visiting one of the better gay establishments in either city you might feel you were in a bar in New York or London. There, gay men and women are uninhibited and having fun. In front of the bars gay men stand on the sidewalk in groups and chat in plain sight, with no fear of discrimination or punishment. The thriving gay communities in these cities are supported by hotlines and web sites and LGBT (Lesbian, Gay, Bisexual and Transgendered) groups. Many gays here have come out to their friends and family, though the majority remains closeted. Gays refer to each other by the slang term *tongzhi*, or "comrade," a designation Sun Yat-sen brought into the common vernacular a century ago. *Tongzhi* connotes confidence, pride and solidarity.

It is a far cry from the early 2000s, when gay bars in the big cities were occasionally closed down with no explanation. Now these cities also have gay bathhouses that the police tend to leave alone. At the "gay parks," volunteers from HIV/AIDS prevention organizations hand out free condoms. Most larger cities like Chengdu and Chongqing, and even smaller cities like Kunming, have at least one gay bar as well as a gay bathhouse or two. Migrant workers living in these cities use the Internet to find out where the local gay-friendly bathhouses are, and that is their main vehicle for meeting other gays. The shift over the past 20 years from aggressive repression to an attitude of live and let live is unprecedented.

In 2005 Fudan University, China's third-largest university, began teaching a course on gay and lesbian studies that was so popular students were sitting on the floor. This class was the first in Chinese history to deal specifically with homosexuality and it received high praise in the Chinese and international media. *China Daily* trumpeted that it marked a new stage in China's open-mindedness, and concluded, "Our society needs to be taught to respect the diversity of the modern world. In the twenty-first century the Chinese mentality should include tolerance and acceptance." In 2006 Sun Yat-Sen University in Guangdong recognized the Rainbow Group, China's first legally registered LGBT student organization. These are giant steps forward.

This new-found openness does not mean gays can always do their own thing, even in Beijing and Shanghai. Before major events like the 2008 Olympics and the annual National People's Congress, the bathhouses are often closed. In 2011 a popular Shanghai bar featuring go-go boys was raided for its "pornographic" show and 60 patrons were arrested and held overnight. The incident lit up China's chief microblogging site, Weibo, with angry commenters condemning the government for arresting people who had committed no crime. In 2010, police converged on a park in Beijing popular with gays and arrested 80 men. In 2009 more than a hundred gay men were arrested during two separate raids of a similar park in Guangzhou; in August of 2009, there was a third raid and about one hundred gay men stood their ground and shouted at the police, who eventually left them alone. For poorer gays who cannot afford to go to bars, the parks offer their one place to meet. There are still no laws in China protecting the civil rights of gays. In nearly all cases, homosexual rape is not considered a crime.

Shanghai, probably home to more de-closeted homosexuals than any other city in China, broke new ground in 2009 when it held its first Gay Pride celebrations, with art exhibitions, drag shows, film festivals and get-togethers. They could only go so far, however; plans for a parade were canceled for fear police would stop it. Gay Pride is now an annual event in Shanghai. In Beijing in 2010, a highly publicized gay male beauty pageant was canceled minutes before it was scheduled to begin.

For gays in smaller cities and towns and in the countryside, options for expressing one's sexuality are far more limited: their only hope is to meet other gays over the Internet, though many in the countryside don't have the opportunity to go online. Many flee their hometowns for Shanghai and Beijing, where they can become part of the community and escape the daily pressure from their family to marry. But tens of millions of gay Chinese men and women who aren't so lucky continue to live in fear, loneliness and secrecy.

While the Chinese have become increasingly tolerant of homosexuality, this tolerance plummets when it comes to a member of their own family. Coming out remains next to impossible for most gays, especially those in less developed areas, where the pressure to marry is most acute. Even gays in the big cities face considerable pressure and most will end up marrying. Homosexuality remains a stigma in most parts of China, especially since it is so often associated with HIV/AIDS. Being homosexual and not having children goes directly against the Confucian concept of filial piety.

Nothing has transformed the gay and lesbian community in China more than the Internet. Unlike the dark period from Mao to the early 1990s, when millions of gays had no idea what to do with themselves and were unaware there was an entire population in China like them, millions of gays in Chinese towns and cities today belong to gay communities complete with support groups, publications and organized activities. These services are more available in the international cities, but for the first time in half a century young gay people anywhere in China can find and meet gay friends. Gay men and women can talk on chat sites and participate in online communities. Social networking brings together gays from all parts of China and helps them organize to support each other and the gay cause. Almost overnight gays had at their fingertips new resources to find love, friendship, advice and support.

The Internet is not, however, a panacea, and there are still no "gay rights" in China as there are in more developed regions such as Taiwan and Hong Kong. The government can still make life difficult for *tongzhi*. Dr. Lucetta Kam, a researcher specializing in sexual studies in China, said in 2010 that the struggle for equal rights would be an ongoing process:

The *tongzhi* movement is growing stronger. But it does not mean social pressure is decreasing. Government interventions are still prevalent in many forms. Gay websites, *tongzhi* organizations, publications and activities are still frequently intervened by the state, and stories of individuals being abused by the authorities are circulated in the community. It is still too early to say *tongzhi* will be accepted when ignorance, violence and prejudice against non-heterosexual people are still prevalent in society. But undoubtedly the achievements of the *tongzhi* movement, in such a short period of time, are unprecedented and inspiring to LGBT activists throughout the world.

Just as in ancient times, when Neo-Confucianism rubbed up against liberalism and Daoism with their very different attitudes toward sex, so too is contemporary China pulled by contradictory forces, sometimes highly encouraging to gays, sometimes threatening. The overall trend, however, appears positive. On Valentine's Day in 2009, a gay male couple held an outdoor "wedding ceremony" near Tiananmen Square in Beijing, complete with a "marriage certificate" created by the Beijing LGBT Center. The color photo of the couple embracing was splashed across the front page of China's largest English-language newspaper, *China Daily*. Several other public gay "weddings" have been held across the country since then, all covered approvingly by the Chinese media. At times China seems incredibly tolerant of homosexuality, at other times far less so. But the fact that stories like these can run on the front page of major Chinese newspapers indicates that homosexuality is moving, however slowly, into the mainstream.

China still has a very long way to go before discrimination improves significantly. In a 2008 survey of 1,259 gay men conducted by sexologist Zhang Beichuan, nine percent said they lost their jobs after employers learned they were homosexual. Twenty percent said they had suffered physical and verbal abuse, and about 35 percent said they had considered committing suicide. The majority, more than 60 percent, said they had never come out. Gays of all ages frequently seek medical help to change their sexual orientation. For all the progress, being gay in China is still an ordeal, and for millions it is nothing less than a tragedy.

Homosexuality remains a taboo subject in Chinese films, television programs and literature. The film *Brokeback Mountain* was banned in China. And yet the newspapers frequently publish stories about progress in gay rights and about discrimination against gays. The 2009 ShanghaiPride film festival featured a documentary, *Queer China*, on the history of gays in China directed by openly gay filmmaker Cui Zi'en. When "gay parks" were raided in 2009 and 2010, some newspapers, most of which are mouthpieces for the government, covered the story with a degree of sympathy for those arrested. As always, China seems to go back and forth, with no definitive policies or ideology regarding homosexuality.

Perhaps ironically, the outbreak of HIV/AIDS in China has drawn the gay community closer together and sparked educational campaigns that have helped many Chinese better understand homosexuality. Thousands of volunteers in AIDS prevention organizations have worked tirelessly to raise awareness of the disease and to fight the stigmatization of gays. There are now about three hundred such groups in China, many funded by international HIV/AIDS prevention organizations like the Global Fund. These grassroots groups carry out intervention programs even in remote towns and villages, where they provide support for Chinese gays who feel the most isolated. Unfortunately many less educated Chinese still associate homosexuality exclusively with HIV/AIDS, and public education must do much more to turn this idea around.

Lalas: China's Emerging Lesbian Community

Dr. Lucetta Kam has interviewed scores of lesbians in Shanghai for her research on sexuality on China. In a chapter of a book of essays, *As normal as possible: negotiating sexuality and gender in mainland China and Hong Kong,* she writes that even in Shanghai, China's largest and most urbane city, "lala girls" – slang for lesbians – feel strong pressure to conform to social norms and get married:

Many local Shanghai girls tell me they cannot move out of their parents' home until they get married and set up a family. As long as she is not married her personal life will be exposed to the scrutiny of others including neighbor, co-workers and friends . . . It is not unusual for them to demand the parents concerned take a more active role to find a suitable mate for their daughter.

The social stigma and shame of being an over-age unmarried woman will extend to her family, a key reason why so many lesbians in China feel they must get married. "Those who cannot fit in the dominant model can only survive as sexual deviants or inferior citizens with a lesser degree of resources and social respect," Dr. Kam writes. The pressure on women to conform and live a life similar to those around them remains intense, even in Shanghai.

In a recent interview, Dr. Kam said those lesbians who stay single for life usually have the resources to remain financially independent. For most who don't have such a luxury, the best they can hope for is a marriage of convenience with a gay man. Many of those who do leave home and choose to not marry go to Shanghai, where there is a thriving lesbian community, and where lesbians can enjoy a high degree of freedom and anonymity. In her writings she describes a series of interviews she held with twenty-five *lalas* in Shanghai, and found they all shared deep anxiety over the conflicts between family and the pressure to marry and their same-sex desires. Half of them were not from Shanghai, but moved there to work or study, and were attracted by the opportunity to live out their sexual desires in a relatively tolerant environment with a welcoming lesbian community.

Today lesbianism is thriving in the huge cities like Shanghai and Beijing, where *lalas* can express their sexual feelings while enjoying an invisibility they could never experience at home. They can be who they are without worrying that their family might learn of their sexual orientation. Most people in these cities display a high level of tolerance toward gays, as long as the gay person is not a member of their family. "I think people are more tolerant of female gays than male gays," said Li Yinhe in an interview with the *New York Times* in 2011. "China is a very patriarchal society, so people feel if a man is gay that's really shameful . . . Traditional society basically overlooks women in some ways, and there is a certain freedom in that."

The Internet has provided a relatively safe and easy way for lesbians in China to meet. In 2001, lesbian activist Xiangqi started China's first online lesbian community, Shanghai Nvai, which has more than 50,000 registered members. In a 2011 interview with the Singapore gay portal Fridae, Xiangqi said her group remains the only local Shanghai online lesbian gathering place that holds community events. "Our ongoing activities include speakers and salon discussions with the public," she said. "And right now, we're recording the oral history of lesbians in Shanghai. We record what their lives were like, what issues they faced, and how they overcame them."

More and more lesbians in Shanghai are coming out to their friends and colleagues, she says, but are still reluctant to tell their parents. Xiangqi herself has not come out to her family. Many are considering marrying a gay man to placate their parents and to have children. On a more practical level, they often want to marry for financial support, since Shanghai's cost of living is famously high.

China's first lesbian bar, the Maple Bar, opened in Beijing in 1999. The city now boasts five lesbian bars and several hangouts such as gay-friendly coffee shops and a lesbian community center, Lala Salon, that holds regular educational and social events and even offers an English corner for women. There are now three lesbian bars in Shanghai, and a popular straight club on the Bund made headlines in 2008 when it began to offer a "lesbian night" on Saturdays. Many *lalas* in both Beijing and Shanghai also hang out at predominantly gay male dance clubs.

Not all lesbians are closeted to their families. In 2011 more than 150 participants attended the "wedding ceremony" of two lesbians in Zhongshan, Guangdong Province, the province's first public lesbian wedding. Later in the year another female same-sex wedding was held in Wuhan in Hubei Province. But as encouraging as these developments are, the fact remains that it is still next to impossible for lesbians in China to come out to their families, and while they may enjoy their new-found freedom, nearly all of them suffer terrible stress hiding who they are from those they love. Lesbians in China's smaller towns and the countryside have it far less easy. Some of them only realize they are *lalas* after reading about lesbianism on the Internet. Before that, they simply believed they were abnormal. Nearly all of them get married except for the few with the means to move to the big cities. In 2011 the *New York Times* interviewed a 35 year-old unmarried woman, Xue Lian, from a small village in Hubei Province whose story illustrates the lack of information on homosexuality in much of China:

"I don't know a single woman around here who is 30 and unmarried," Ms. Xue said. "I'm nearly 40 and not married. It's a huge topic of discussion. I don't actually know a single other lesbian in Lichuan. I guess they all suppress it and marry. I couldn't do that. For me, it would be like rape."

. . . When she was in her 20s, she considered having a sex-change operation, "so I would be free to have a girlfriend here at home." She now thinks she won't. She learned from the Internet that she could be a lesbian and keep her body as it is, she said.

Her moment of revelation came while surfing the Internet in the summer of 2006. "I read about lesbians in Nanjing, who used to gather near a bridge," she recounted. With that, "I felt I had found a name for myself."

Although she longed to move to a big city where she could express her lesbianism openly, she decided to stay in the village to support her father, who remains deeply disappointed she never married. For now, lesbians who cannot leave the smaller towns and villages are guaranteed a life of extreme stress, loneliness and lack of fulfillment.

Like homosexuals, transsexuals, too, have a difficult time in China. The first male-to-female transsexual surgery was performed in 1983 at the Third Hospital of Beijing Medical University. But most transsexuals are turned down for the operation, and the number of those who undergo surgery is estimated at one thousand although more than three thousand apply each year. Applicants must undergo a battery of tests and psychiatric evaluations and "prove" they have wanted the operation for at least five years. Explaining their situation to parents and family is next to impossible, and that further dissuades many transsexuals from applying. Those who go ahead with the sex change usually leave their hometowns to avoid discrimination. The price, which can range from 57,000 yuan to 76,000 yuan ($9,000 to $12,000) is another deterrent.

China has the medical facilities to easily perform both male-to-female and female-to-male operations, but the problem is one of ideology. Like homosexuality, transsexualism is viewed by many as a form of spiritual pollution imported from the West. There is a profound lack of understanding about transsexualism and, subsequently, a lot of discrimination. One notable example of a transsexual who has been accepted by the Chinese people is the world-famous Jin Xing, born as a male to ethnic Korean parents in 1967 in the industrial city of Shenyang. A talented dancer, at the age of nine Jin joined the People's Liberation Army's dance troupe and rose up the ranks to become a colonel. From an early age Jin had felt she was a woman. After ten years of traveling around the world performing and teaching dance, she underwent a sex-change operation in 1996 at the age of 29. She now lives in Shanghai with her German husband and works as a choreographer and dance trainer.

Jin was brought to front pages around the world in the fall of 2011 when she was dropped as a judge of a Chinese reality TV show because she was transgendered. She spoke out to the Chinese media, condemning the prejudice of local officials in Zhejiang province who insisted she be thrown off the show. She is one of China's most renowned celebrities and is credited with giving a face to transsexualism and helping raise public acceptance of a person's right to undergo a sex change.

Gay Marriage and the Future of Homosexuality in China

Sexologist Li Yinhe has proposed legalizing gay marriage more than once at the National People's Congress, a motion that each time has been quickly defeated. Her proposals included changing the words "husband and wife" in the marriage code to "spouses." Li has acknowledged there is no hope for gay marriage in China at this time. This, coupled with her recommendations to decriminalize prostitution as well as wife swapping, has made her the most controversial sex expert in China. In 2007, she announced that due to pressure from the government she was being forced to "shut up" and would no longer grant interviews, and would reduce the number of papers she writes. As reported in several Chinese media, she refused to say exactly where this pressure was coming from:

I don't want to uphold any more of my social responsibility, because it's interfering with my life, and it's causing pressure on my higher-ups [at the China Academy of Social Sciences] . . . Gay marriage is not something that our country can accept at this stage of its cultural development. History will change when it must. And perhaps I will only be able to be a bystander when the change comes, rather than a participant.

Li's aggressive stance on gay marriage was obviously the key factor influencing her decision to hold her tongue, though despite her announcement, she has continued to do occasional interviews with foreign and domestic media. Her efforts have not gone unchallenged, and in 2011, Li Tie, editor of the Chinese journal *The Times Weekly*, argued that same-sex marriage would tear at the country's moral fiber, and claimed that legalizing it would pave the way to incest and pedophilia, a common argument from America's religious right. Li Tie, a graduate of Hong Kong Baptist University and a Christian, argued that China has had a moral vacuum and should embrace Christian ethics - including the refusal to accept same-sex marriage.

And yet, China has not reacted entirely negatively to gay marriage, at least not when it involves people outside of the family. The occasional symbolic "wedding ceremonies" of same-sex couples that have been held in different parts of the country since 2009 have received glowing coverage in the domestic media. And while there are no statistics available, young people, especially those in the larger cities, appear to be increasingly tolerant of homosexual men and women and would most likely have no problem with gays marrying.

With no religious call to denounce homosexuality as a sin, as is the case with Christianity, Judaism, Islam and other religions, the concept of gay bashing and active anti-gay discrimination is simply foreign to most Chinese people. There is still plenty of stigmatization and prejudice, and millions of Chinese people associate homosexuality with HIV/AIDS. But China's long period of coldness toward same-sex love is showing signs of thawing, and most signs indicate the country will become increasingly open minded toward alternative lifestyles.

Progress in terms of visibility, social acceptance and the official status of homosexuality has only increased since the China Psychiatric Association deleted homosexuality from its list of mental illnesses in 2001. The government has acknowledged the existence of millions of gay people. In 2011, China's online community called for a boycott of actress Lu Liping after she made homophobic slurs online, which resulted in state-run

China Central Television publicly condemning her.

Further proof of China's increased tolerance was seen in 2005, when Chinese literary editor Wu Youjian went on China Southern Network TV to publicly support her son Zheng Yuantao's decision to come out to his family six years earlier, when he was eighteen years old. This was a groundbreaking event; Wu had become the first mother in China to go on television to talk about her gay child. When Zheng first told her he was gay, instead of crying or condemning him, she gave him her total support. In 2007 she set up a website to help other gay and lesbian youth come out to their families. She soon became a folk hero to the gay community and in 2008 founded the support group Parents, Families, and Friends of Lesbians and Gays (PFLAG) China. She also launched a hotline to offer support and help to gays and frequently uses the Chinese microblogging site Weibo to express support of gay issues. In a 2010 interview she advised parents: "Having a gay child is not a bad thing; having a gay child is not an ugly thing; having a gay child is not wrong; and having a gay child really is nothing if you treat it that way." She has strongly endorsed gay marriage.

Zheng Yuantao himself went on to win international attention in 2010 with the publication of his Chinese translation of Mary Renault's novel *The Persian Boy*, a book in which male same-sex love plays an important role. It was remarkable that China's censors let it be. At the time of publication Zheng told the *New York Times*, "My goal was to translate a positive gay love story for Chinese people to see as a role model." In a later interview, Zheng offered a message to young people in China struggling with their homosexuality:

I know several kids who are 18 or 19. I envy them for their access to unlimited information of gay life on the Internet. There was no such thing when I was their age, and thus I felt very lonely. With the cyberspace and all its information out there, I think it's not as difficult as it used to be for the average gay youth to acquire self-acceptance.

But the paradox is that cyberspace not only connects, but also isolates people. Anonymous sex is easy to find; friendship and love somehow seem harder than before. And many gay youths think of themselves and others in a "top/bottom" dichotomy, associating bottoming with femininity, topping with masculinity, all such stupid labels. I feel concern, hoping that more gay youths can embrace their sexuality, and their humanity, in a fuller way.

Overall, China is still too orthodox and bound by the Confucian ideals of filial piety and the responsibility to bear children to approve of gay marriage anytime soon. And yet, judging by the lack of vilification directed at gays and their positive portrayal in the Chinese media, it does not seem impossible that one day China might at least consider legalizing same-sex marriage. True, China's current leadership has demonstrated it will not even consider *discussing* the subject, but that may change as younger generations replace the old. In a television interview in 2000, Li Yinhe said to the camera, "Tolerance does not cause the proportion of homosexuals to rise. Harshness does not make the number drop." Slowly but surely, it appears China is getting this message.

EDUCATION AND HEALTH

It is not surprising that a plague of sexually transmitted diseases (STDs) rose up in parallel with the sex industry in the early years of China's reform and opening up. As prostitution came roaring back at the end of the 1970s, and as the Chinese people slowly became more open-minded about sex, rates of gonorrhea, chlamydia, syphilis, and human papillomavirus (HPV) soared starting in the 1980s. HIV/AIDS began to reach epidemic proportions in the mid-1990s, and as of 2011, nearly 800,000 Chinese people are living with AIDS, according to China's National Center for AIDS/STD Control and Prevention. The AIDS epidemic started when marginalized rural Chinese in the 1980s sold plasma for money and became infected in the process, but now it is mainly sexually transmitted.

China's sex education has failed to teach young people about the threat of STDs and AIDS, and also left them in the dark about contraception. Millions of Chinese have an inadequate understanding of safe sex, and of how HIV/AIDS is transmitted. For HPV there is no nationwide organized screening program and no national vaccination program for girls. To make matters worse, about 30 percent of China's gay men are married, and many become infected with STDs when having sex with another man and then bring it home to infect their wives.

The blossoming sex industry provided a breeding ground for STDs and HIV/AIDS. The incidence of syphilis and chlamydia continues to rise to this day, especially in China's coastal region, where 16 percent of men and nearly 10 percent of women have been infected with chlamydia as of 2011. Syphilis, all but eradicated under Mao, is now the most commonly reported communicable disease in Shanghai, and nationwide China has seen syphilis rates increase tenfold over the past decade according to the medical journal *Lancet*. Based on 2010 numbers, a child infected with syphilis is born every hour in China – the fastest-growing rate of syphilis in the world. That means fifty-seven out of every 100,000 babies in China are born with syphilis.

STDs continue to spread from relatively localized groups such as injection drug users and sex workers into the mainstream population. Of the high-risk groups spreading STDs today, prostitutes are by far the leading source of transmission. The Chinese government has not shown itself capable of dealing with this crisis. The first step in eradicating venereal diseases is to prevent their transmission into the general population, which would require increased government control of the prostitution industry, a task in which the government has shown little interest.

China's Deadliest Scourge: HIV/AIDS

UNAIDS and the China Ministry of Health have estimated that by the end of 2011 more than 780,000 people will be living with HIV/AIDS on the mainland, 40,000 more than 2009. In 2012 the China Ministry of Health reported that in 2011 a total of 28,000 people died of HIV/AIDS in China, while another 48,000 were newly infected by the virus. AIDS has now become the country's most deadly infectious disease.

At first, the main cause of AIDS in China was not sexual transmission but contaminated needles, mainly those shared by injection drug users, but also needles used in unsanitary ways during paid plasma collection in the countryside. Now, however, sexual transmission is by far the largest contributor to HIV infection rates, with nearly 82 percent of the 48,000 new cases reported in 2011 transmitted through unprotected sexual intercourse, according to the Chinese Center for Disease Control and Prevention. About 30 percent of those cases involved men having sex with men. Surveys show that more than 80 percent of gay men in China marry, but still continue having sex with men, putting their wives at risk.

The start of the epidemic can be traced to rural Henan province in the 1990s, when hundreds of thousands of impoverished farmers became infected through unsupervised blood-selling schemes. In poorer parts of China, selling blood is a common way to earn extra money, especially for drug users and commercial sex workers. Many of the blood-collecting companies are unlicensed and illegal, and their use of contaminated needles has been a major factor in spreading the disease. Those who sell their blood to such companies are often in the most high-risk groups and have already been infected with HIV. Their blood was not tested, and was mixed into the blood pool and sold. Farmers who gave blood were infected by contaminated needles.

The epidemic is worse in provinces with a higher level of commercial sex and intravenous drug abuse such as Yunnan province. The most severely affected area is along China's southwest territory, bordering "The Golden Triangle" along the Myanmar, Laos and Thai borders, a region famous for its heavy trade in heroin, methamphetamines and other illegal drugs. In the northwest province of Xinjiang there has also been a massive outbreak due to prostitution, sharing of needles, and little to no awareness of AIDS and its prevention. Six provinces with the highest reported numbers of HIV/AIDS cases account for nearly 80 percent of the total number reported for all of China. These are, in descending order, Yunnan, Guangxi, Henan, Sichuan, Xinjiang and Guangdong.

One segment of the population that has seen a surprising jump in HIV has been Chinese men 60 and above. China's Center for Disease Control reported that the number of HIV-positive men for this demographic soared from 483 in 2005 to 3,031 in 2010, nearly nine percent of the total HIV cases in the country. The oldest patient the CDC tracked was a 94 year-old man in Guangzhou, who most likely was infected by unsafe sex. Authorities say the availability of cheap sex for sale combined with higher levels of disposable income and an increasingly active gay community are the main factors contributing to the epidemic among older men. AIDS activists have urged the government to roll out intervention campaigns targeting senior citizens to increase safe-sex awareness. Most current campaigns are focused on young people at college campuses and clubs.

AIDS in China has been a taboo topic for years, and to a large extent that has not changed. The Chinese culture's squeamishness toward open dialogue on sex and STDs has made it difficult to raise awareness, and many Chinese, especially in the countryside, are frightened to discuss sex-related topics. Their local governing officials often harbor the same fears. China has, however, made significant strides in improving services to people with HIV/AIDS. Through the late 1990s the government was slow to acknowledge the threat of AIDS, but since 2001 it has subsidized prevention programs, launched steps to offer universal access to anti-retroviral drugs, boosted awareness campaigns of the dangers of unprotected sex and initiated policies to curb discrimination. A 2011 study by China's National Centre for AIDS/STD Control and Prevention reported nearly 80 percent of those infected with HIV from the government-run plasma donation program were receiving free antiretroviral therapy.

Due to discrimination at Chinese hospitals, injection drug users, those infected sexually, and those underserved by the public health system such as migrant workers, the elderly, and minority groups, are at greater risk of not receiving treatment. Sixty-two percent of those infected through sex and 43 percent of those who acquired HIV by sharing drug needles were receiving antiretroviral therapy. Although the incidence of infection continues to rise, as of 2009 China had reduced its AIDS mortality rate by two-thirds since it began distributing free antiretroviral drugs in 2002. The Chinese government, after a slow start, appears committed to slowing the transmission of AIDS and increasing prevention and intervention services for at-risk populations.

Stigmatization against people with AIDS has been a serious issue since the first case of AIDS in China was reported in 1986. The taboo surrounding the disease is still very strong: People are ashamed to get tested or to ask for treatment. They are worried that if they test positive then they will be shunned by others. Prostitutes and intravenous drug users fear they may be punished. In rural areas, HIV/AIDS patients have been "outed" by local officials, and then scorned by their neighbors. The pain of the disease is doubled by fear and isolation. *The Global Times* in 2010 reported on how AIDS patients in the countryside are stigmatized:

"You know what, you got AIDS!" an unnamed official yelled at the 29-year-old farmer. A cluster of whispering villagers bunched together in front of Zhang's creaking door were suddenly shocked into silence.

"There were crowds of people. I was the last one to learn the fact," Zhang told the *Global Times*. "I felt as if I were a criminal." Zhang said he was so angered by this public humiliation that he briefly had thoughts of revenge, "spreading the virus to every person around me."

One week earlier, Zhang had accompanied his wife, who was seven months pregnant, for a routine medical test. The lab results would eventually show that both Zheng and his wife were infected with the AIDS virus. The farmer refuses to discuss how they might have contracted the deadly disease, spread through sex, blood, needles or birth. But the delight of soon becoming a father was ruined by the stigma of becoming an AIDS patient.

The news traveled to every corner of the county. Villagers dared not buy the fish Zhang and his wife sold. Local authorities forced his wife to abort the baby boy in her uterus. Like so many other AIDS patients in China, Zhang and his wife became instant outcasts in a society where the private suffering of AIDS patients is the worst kept secret shame.

China's Vice Minister of Health Huang Jiefu said in 2009 that the government had nearly eradicated the threat of HIV being transmitted through the sale of tainted blood, and that its next challenge was ending discrimination at the local level. But China's discriminatory attitude toward AIDS stems from the very top. China still bans foreigners infected with HIV/AIDS from entering the country.

"China's land is vast, and has great differences in local cultures, traditions and customs," Huang said. "So it will take a long time to raise levels of understanding among all the people and thoroughly eliminate discrimination toward AIDS patients." There are an estimated two million civil society organizations in China such as foreign NGOs, medical organizations and charity groups that have played a major role in reaching marginalized at-risk populations such as drug users, prostitutes and migrant workers and offering them contraceptive and prevention services. At parks where homosexuals gather in larger cities, members of domestic NGOs hand out condoms, lubricant and safe-sex literature. Other NGOs go deep into the countryside to offer services to farmers who may have never heard of AIDS.

Although NGOs are only supposed to operate jointly with the government, the AIDS epidemic has been growing so rapidly that local Chinese Centers for Disease Control have taken a pragmatic approach, working together with unregistered NGOs. Together they reach out to at-risk groups like frequenters of gay saunas and bars, injection drug users and sex workers, handing out condoms and helping them get tested. These domestic NGOs are severely under-funded, and there is intense rivalry between them since they all have to fight for operational funding. It is proving very difficult for NGOs and the government to cooperate.

The central government, all but silent on AIDS through the 1990s, has been working to destigmatize the disease and give a face to AIDS patients to convince people that those infected do not pose a danger to them. In recent years Premier Hu Jintao and other senior officials have made numerous high-profile visits to hospitals to meet with AIDS patients, shaking their hands and asking about their health. Basketball star Yao Ming appeared in a video urging Chinese citizens to stop the stigmatization of those living with HIV/AIDS. These people nevertheless continue to be pariahs, branded as untouchables. This discrimination can be turned around only when the government, in cooperation with China's hundreds of thousands of NGOs, charity groups and medical associations, launches an ongoing nationwide intervention and educational campaign, including standardized school programs teaching students that prejudice against those infected is wrong and only makes the situation worse by driving victims underground.

Men's Health: China's First Male Sex Clinic

Chen Wei is the head of the Shanghai Chengkai Male Sexual Rehabilitation and Treatment Center, founded by his father Chen Kai in 1988. Chen Wei is fourth in a line of doctors and grew up immersed in the world of medicine. He is 36, and says when he went to medical school sexual health was not in the curriculum. Doctors who wanted to specialize in andrology – male impotence and menopause, infertility, and other male sexual and reproductive disorders – basically had to learn by themselves through experience. "Andrology was not offered in medical school when I was there, but now it is," Chen explains. "It used to be a very minor branch under the urology or Traditional Chinese Medicine (TCM) department. The emergence of an andrology department is a new phenomenon." Chen's typical patients are men between 20 and 50 years old who want to improve their sex lives. The three main reasons for a visit are erectile dysfunction, problems with ejaculation, and infertility. As sex in China becomes more open and men increasingly let go of their inhibitions, business is booming and the clinic has had to move to larger quarters twice. They now have partner branches throughout China.

"We see all sorts of people here in terms of age, background and social status," Chen says. "We see university students and 90 year-old men, from government officials to migrant workers. Sex is related to everyone regardless of background. In the past people were under the misconception that sexual dysfunction wasn't a real problem requiring medical treatment. Now, with sex education and media promotion of sexual dysfunction treatments people are more accepting of clinics like ours. There are now many andrology clinics in China."

Chen Kai, Chen Wei's father, broke new ground in 1986 when he invented the Negative Pressure Suction Treatment Device, a special vacuum designed to improve circulation of blood through the penis, stimulating erectile tissue and helping the patient enjoy stronger, longer-lasting erections. The vacuum pressure also forces the prostate gland to open passively, sucking out inflammatory glandular secretions to make circulation smoother. Shortly after its invention the device won second place in China's National Science and Technology Progress Awards and won the endorsement of some of China's leading urologists. After many successful trials of the device, Chen Kai opened the clinic in 1988, and the device remains the treatment of choice for many of its patients.

Chen Kai's sex clinic was the first in China and it generated international attention. Along with profiles in the foreign media, the BBC produced a video in 2000 titled *Under the Sun: Dr. Chen's Sex Revolution*. Chen Kai also appeared on radio talk shows to answer call-in questions about male sexual issues. His name card was decorated with a drawing of an erect penis. According to his son, Chen Wei, the clinic has treated more than 300,000 men since 1988, and up to a hundred patients may visit in a single day. While Viagra may have eaten into their business, solving for many the problem of erectile dysfunction, Chen says patients still need device treatment and business is brisk, even though profits are not high. Viagra is prohibitively expensive for many Chinese, while a full treatment at the Chengkai clinic usually runs between 1,000-2,000 RMB.

Chen sees the clinic as a non-profit business for the public good. It works in cooperation with Shanghai's Changning District education board, for example, to provide free sexual check-ups for boys in primary and secondary schools. Some of these boys want to get circumcised, a service Chen's clinic offers at a very low price. They also have partnerships with several hospitals that send patients their way.

The clinic doesn't treat sexually transmitted diseases, focusing instead on sexual dysfunction. They do treat prostatitis, as it frequently causes sexual dysfunction. Prostatitis treatment, which is a relatively quick process, generates the biggest profits and helps subsidize the less-profitable dysfunction therapy, which requires many visits. The most typical problem they treat is ejaculation dysfunction, especially premature ejaculation. They usually treat it with TCM together with the vacuum device, but sometimes resort to surgery if the patient fails to respond. The operation consists of cutting some nerves on the glans to lower its sensitivity and prolong erections. The biggest draw of the clinic remains the vacuum, which Chen says is now used around the world, where it is sold as a "vacuum restrictive device."

"Our most competitive advantage is the treatment device, for both psychological and physical problems," Chen says. "It is non-invasive, it has no side effects and 50 to 80 percent of those who use it are satisfied with the treatment." Each treatment lasts for 20 minutes, and patients need to have one treatment per day for fifteen days to complete a course. Most patients need two or three courses, so a treatment cycle lasts 30 to 45 days.

The state of sexual education in China is a constant source of frustration for Chen Wei, and he laments that he's not permitted to talk about sex to very large audiences. "It's a kind of half-open environment in China and it's very annoying," he says. "The most essential issue in China is sex education. It should start from primary school so kids know how they are born, how mom got pregnant and how she gave birth to her kids."

One big change Chen has noticed in today's China is that as people live longer, their sex lives have been extended as well. Some of his patients seeking a better sex life are 80 and 90 years old. He says the next step he would like to see in the reproductive health industry is an appropriate treatment for women who experience low libido and frigidity. "Traditional Chinese women are more conservative toward sex and don't think it's important after they have children. For them, it's okay to stop having sex in their 40s. But today, females in the city have a demand for sex counseling. Girls want more knowledge of sex and a higher-quality sex life."

Sex Education -- and the Lack of It

As with so many China-related topics, one has to be cautious in speaking of Chinese sex education in absolutes. In many rural parts of contemporary China sex education scarcely exists, while in some of the more developed cities like Shanghai, Beijing and Chengdu, local governments have implemented experimental sex education curriculums that compare with the best in the world (though this is not across the board). For most of the country, however, sex education is inadequate, antiquated and ineffective.

While institutionalized mandatory sex education wasn't put into effect in China until 1988, the country has an interesting history of teaching young people about the art of lovemaking. The earliest recorded methods of sex education bear no resemblance to sex education today, and only began the day a couple got married. In ancient China it was believed that newlyweds needed at least a basic understanding of lovemaking, and a popular teaching guide was the "dowry painting," a series of erotic pictures showing several different ways to have sex. The bride's mother traditionally bought the woodblock prints before the wedding and put them in her daughter's dowry. On their wedding night, the bride would spread them out like postcards so the couple could use them as a sort of sexual guide. This practice dates back to the Han dynasty, and the paintings were affordable for average citizens.

If the mother could afford a more upscale, artistic sex manual she might have given her daughter a set of beautiful figurines made of fine China known as "bottom of the box" because they were traditionally placed at the bottom of a trunk given to the bride on her wedding day. These works of art displayed detailed illustrations of various sexual positions. Also popular were "Chinese love charms," an engraved coin displaying four positions the couple could use for their first night of sexual intercourse. Prior to their wedding, the bride's mother traditionally showed them to her daughter so she would know the basics before the couple's first night alone. The bride's sisters and midwife also frequently gave sexual pointers to the bride-to-be shortly before she tied the nuptial knot. There was no sex education for males or females before their marriage.

The world's oldest sexual how-to manual is Chinese and dates back to the mythical Emperor Huang-Ti (the "Yellow Emperor") about 5,000 years ago. His sexual handbook, which according to legend he wrote with the help of three female sex advisors, teaches the secrets of sexual ecstasy. It was believed that sexual energy was key to promoting a long, fulfilling life, and this astonishingly graphic manual teaches men how to engage in foreplay, how to properly thrust during intercourse and how to control premature ejaculation to give the woman more lasting pleasure. Such books were read only by the elite; the common people had to make do with what their parents taught them and what they learned from exploration and discovery. In a society founded on Confucian values of shame and morality, there was no place for formalized sex education, and sex was rarely talked about. Until the late 1980s, the masses in China were mainly on their own when it came to sex.

Under Mao, the topic of sex was shrouded in silence. Everyone wore the same drab, baggy, androgynous outfits and sex wasn't discussed until marriage. Sex was a matter of doing one's reproductive duty for the state. When China began to open up in the late 1970s and 80s, however, young people started to become more sexually active and most knew little or nothing about contraceptives. The abortion rate began to climb. Prostitution, banned under Mao, made a hasty recovery and was soon popular again all across the country. And sexually transmitted diseases, which fell to nearly zero under Mao, began to spread once again. Clearly the people of China needed to learn about sex, birth control and disease prevention.

In 1981, the first high school sex education courses were introduced in Shanghai, and five years later an experimental sex education course for co-eds was adopted by 40 Shanghai middle schools for 12 and 13 year-olds. These courses included lessons on physiology, anatomy and the changes brought on by puberty, as well as sexual hygiene and morality. The program was seen as a success, and by 1988 sex education classes had been implemented in more than 6,000 middle schools throughout China. That same year, the Ministry of Education announced that sex education courses would be established in all of China's middle schools.

Another factor that drove the government to recognize the importance of nationwide sex education was the implementation of the One-Child Policy in 1979. The policy implicitly required citizens to use effective birth control methods, and the government wanted people to understand their options. Part of the 1988 sex education charter was sexual morality, including educating adolescents about the dangers of premarital sex. While it acknowledged gender equality, it also advocated adherence to gender roles, such as the assertiveness of boys and the passivity of girls, and the notion that boys are better at abstract reasoning while girls are more commonsensical. One of its key themes was that students must be taught to resist "premature love," foregoing dating and denying their hormones and their growing interest in sexuality until at least 18 years of age. The thinking went that "premature love" carried with it temptations and dangers that would make it impossible for adolescent students to focus on their studies. In other words, adolescent sexuality was framed as a social problem that sex education was supposed to contain.

This ideological obsession, anchoring sexual morality in the traditions of Mao and the long line of Chinese rulers who sought to suppress sexuality, stemmed from a belief that sexual relations were a direct path to degeneracy and crime. Pre-marital sex, in the eyes of the Communists, was a product of Western decadence, another form of spiritual pollution that would upset China's stability. Sex education in China in the late 1980s took on distinctly Chinese characteristics, and was in many ways a tool for controlling adolescent sexuality with strict rules and threats of punishment. Abstinence until marriage was the cornerstone of sex education.

But something went wrong, and for many years sex education was almost completely ineffective and often didn't take place at all, despite the edict of mandatory sex classes. Millions of Chinese, especially in the smaller towns and villages but also in large cities, remain shockingly ignorant about sex. A 2009 article in *Slate* magazine interviewed a university student in Beijing:

The first time Hu Jing tried to have sex with her college boyfriend, there was a technical difficulty. "We knew we had to use a condom," she said. "But we didn't know how."

Faced with this conundrum, Hu and her boyfriend went looking for answers — he from his more experienced friends, she from the university library, where she combed through *Dream of the Red Chamber*, a literary classic from the Qing Dynasty.

The following week, they reconvened for a second try. This time, they managed to roll on the condom but then . . . well, where was the penis supposed to go? It took another week of research before they succeeded in doing the deed.

It is hard for well-educated, urbane people to believe college students would be mystified by a condom, but it is all too believable when you consider they grew up in a sex-ed vacuum in which the use of contraceptives was never mentioned, neither in the school nor at home. The institutionalized sexual education courses of the late 1980s were an important first step, but in most parts of China they were woefully inadequate. Many rural schools simply skipped that part of the curriculum, and the classes that were taught focused primarily on anatomy, physiology, biology and abstinence.

Stella, a white-collar worker who grew up in Shanghai, says she had no formal sex education. Sex was taught, very briefly, in biology class:

When I was eight or nine they explained conception in broad strokes, which resulted in giggles in the classroom. My classmates had more knowledge than the teacher and found it hilarious for a middle-aged lady to teach a bunch of kids these 'taboo subjects' out of obligation. There were only a few pages on sex in the biology textbook, and Chinese teachers tend to strictly follow the book, so contraception and other protective measure weren't taught.

Stella only learned about AIDS in college, at a Red Cross event that was mandatory for freshmen. Sex education in school, she said, was "totally worthless." Her parents never discussed sex-related issues with her. "They are the generation that went through the Cultural Revolution and were deeply influenced by Mao's ideologies. Even though my dad went to Australia in 1989 and stayed for three years, he remains very Chinese in many ways, including the exclusion of sexual topics at home."

There are many simple ways sex education in Chinese schools could be improved, Stella says. First, there should be a standardized curriculum that includes self-protection and contraception, along with discussions on sex in a cultural context, making students aware of how to refuse a sexual invitation and of the different courtship styles of Chinese and Western men. "China is more open now than before," she said, "but we largely lack the social skills or sophistication to deal with foreign cultures. The media in China often run stories on high school girls having abortions due to ignorance of protective measures, especially in rural areas. Things shouldn't happen that way. I am not advocating premarital sex, but I do feel that as Chinese, we should be honest with ourselves, reassess the sexual attitudes of younger generations, and create a system that rewards proper sex education."

Sex had become an increasingly taboo subject in Chinese culture since the Song Dynasty in the eleventh century, when the government began to control people's sexual lives and restrict sexual expression. (This attitude went back and forth, of course, with some periods far more liberal than others.) China's golden age of sexual openness under the Tang dynasty was over, and sex was increasingly thought of as dirty, as something that should not be talked about. Chinese people were embarrassed by any mention of sex, and were thus largely ignorant about the topic. This ignorance applies to many young Chinese growing up today as embarrassment over the topic of sex hampers their learning. Many parents were opposed to the teaching of sex in schools and believed their children were too young to learn about it. When their children asked questions they were evasive. Some told their children they found them on the street or that they popped out of a rock.

Since the 1980s adolescents have mainly been learning about sex through their peers or via media such as magazines and movies, and more recently the Internet. Many learned about it from watching pornography. These methods meant that much of what they "learned" was inaccurate. They knew nothing about preventing unwanted pregnancies or the right of a woman to refuse a sexual advance. They learned nothing about disease prevention or reproductive health.

In 2011, a new set of regulations mandated sexual and relationship psychology courses as part of China's compulsory university curriculum. The courses were designed to help students understand the psychology behind sex, and the psychology of love. Reporting on the new regulations, the Chinese newspaper *People's Daily* said that a 2011 survey of 2,060 Beijing college students about sexual knowledge revealed, "43 percent of college students are confused by sex-related thoughts."

Hu Zhen is head of the first sex education program administered by the AIDS Prevention Education Project for Chinese Youth. In 2009 she began setting up a pilot program to teach different sex-ed courses in 30 primary and secondary schools in Sichuan Province, including one for the children of migrant workers and another for members of ethnic minorities. Hu has created a unique curriculum that involves active participation by the parents. On the first day of the new semester, parents are invited to the classroom, where they are taught some of the basics of sexual education. But the main reason they are there is to put their minds at ease so they don't worry their children are being exposed to pornography. Hu's classes have proven to be incredibly popular, and headmasters have noticed that when the classes are over boys and girls treat each other with greater politeness and respect.

Hu said she has worked with kindergarten students whose parents have told them they were picked up from a rubbish bin or that they sprang up from pictures their parents drew. "Kids in kindergarten want to know where they came from, and we can't wait until they are in middle school to tell them," she said. "In middle school, there may be two or three pages in the biology textbook about the male and female reproductive system and a scientific explanation of puberty. In physical education class there's a chapter on physiological hygiene. Some high schools may have a course in psychological health that might mention AIDS prevention. But only the scientific knowledge about sex taught in biology and the physical hygiene class are compulsory in China."

She notes with some frustration that when she taught sex education to university students in Chengdu in 2000, many of them said they wished such knowledge had been available to them when they were younger. Sex education in China will never be exactly like what it is in the West, Hu says. With 560 million children, she explains, China has had to come up with sex education that fits in with its national culture. She estimates that 70 to 80 percent of the boys she teaches say they want their future wife to be a virgin, while the girls want to be the last girl their boyfriend ever dates before they marry. Hu asks,

If they all want to try sex now, where will the virgins be on their wedding night? A Chinese saying says the wedding night is like a thousand dollars. It is important for Chinese young people to know how sex, love, marriage and responsibility are all tied together. If you want to try sex, you have to think of the possible consequences for your body, your mind and your future. After you answer all these questions and you still insist on trying, the last thing you need to keep in mind is safe sex.

According to a 2006 study by the World Health Organization (WHO), Department of Reproductive Health and Research, sexual education in China lags far behind adolescents' attitudes toward sex. The study surveyed 688 students between 15 and 24 years of age and showed that while students learned about the biology of puberty from their teachers, the majority learned about sexuality and STDs from media and their peers. Only around 10 percent learned about these topics from their parents. Adolescents who had never had an intimate relationship were more likely to have obtained knowledge about sex from a teacher, while most of those who had experienced intimacy learned about sex from a book or magazine.

The study concluded that traditional Chinese cultural norms continue to influence parents and teachers who are reluctant to instruct their adolescent children about safe sex. Many Chinese parents worry that teaching their children about sex will make them more sexually active. The generational gap of young people's attitudes toward sex compared to their parents' also discourages them from talking openly about sex-related issues. These problems can only be turned around when parents and teachers overcome their own hang-ups about sex, but this will be a slow and difficult process. It may take a generation or two.

Discussion of STDs and AIDS in the media and in many classrooms has increased since the 1990s, but parents still decline to talk about them to their children. The more taboo the topic, such as sexuality and disease, the less adolescents learn from their teachers and parents. And outside of parents and teachers, young people have limited options for seeking help. A 2004 study conducted in several Chinese provinces indicated that most healthcare workers were unwilling to provide contraception education and services to unmarried young people, especially students in high school. Some local Chinese governments have tried to come up with their own innovative ways to teach young people about sex. In 2005 one city government in southern China opened a café offering free condoms and books about sexual health. It was a good idea in theory, but practically nobody came. Breaking the sex taboo is still a hard thing for Chinese people to do.

A hospital in Shanghai started a hotline for pregnant girls in 2006, and by 2011 it had received more than 50,000 calls. It offers sex consultation and advice on abortion and contraception, and before holidays like Valentine's Day it gets as many as one thousand calls a day. According to an article from 2011 in the *Shanghai Daily*, typical questions call-ins ask include, "Will I get pregnant if my boyfriend kisses me?" "Can I have another abortion after only one month?" and "Am I a bad girl/boy if I masturbate often?"

In 2011, Beijing took a radical step in ensuring young students learn about sex at an early age by introducing the first set of primary-school sex education textbooks. The first part of the book, for students aged between six and seven years-old, describes the act of intercourse and egg fertilization in detail and includes illustrations of a penis entering a woman's vagina. The book, created by experts at the Beijing Sex Health Education Research Association, goes on to teach about puberty, contraception, avoiding sexual abuse and speaking to one's parents about sex. Introduced to eighteen primary schools in Beijing as part of a pilot program, the new textbook immediately caused an outrage. Furious parents complained that the material was unsuitable for young children and the descriptions of the sex act too vivid, without the gentleness and humor of typical children's books. Some said it was simply pornography. Some thought it was an appropriate learning tool. Feng Zhihua, the deputy editor of a popular biological and medical website, told the *Xinhua* news agency, "Adults see dirty things in the book while students may not. They see things in a different way and we should not judge from our perspectives. The words 'penis' and 'vagina' will come to the students sooner or later. There is no need to avoid them in education."

In the same article, however, Wu Ou, a mother and deputy chief editor of a popular science website, said the material was simply too risqué and blunt for kids: "It's not wrong to describe sex in direct ways, but the sentences in the book are too rude, and it's even banned from our website." Parents expressed concern that the textbook would cause their children to go through puberty earlier than normal, and argued that children would try to reenact what they saw in the illustrations. In an online survey on China's biggest portal Sina, about 64 percent of 18,000 netizens supported the book as an effective tool for teaching children about sex, but 30 percent objected to the book's "inappropriate" illustrations and voted it unsuitable for children. A similar debate was triggered in September in central Henan Province, when a kindergarten used anatomically correct toys to teach children about sex.

Prior to the pilot program, sex education in Beijing began only in middle school. The debate over the appropriateness of the book brought back all the challenges of teaching sex to children in China, mainly the taboos that the older generation still harbors about sex, and the more progressive belief that children need to understand more about sex at an earlier age so they can avoid problems and later engage in it with knowledge, not ignorance. Later the same year, Shanghai introduced its own pilot program with the city's first sex education textbook for primary school children. It was far tamer than the Beijing textbook, substituting tadpoles for people in the illustrations. Objections to the books were nothing like what Beijing experienced.

Another study, published by the Shanghai Institute of Planned Parenthood Research and the WHO in 2006, offers potential hope that receiving courses on sex and sexuality over the Internet can enhance adolescents' knowledge of reproductive health. Based on a controlled experiment that sampled 624 students from two high schools and four college campuses, the study showed the Internet-based sex education program, which included online lessons, a bulletin board and instructional videos, significantly increased students' understanding of STDs, contraception and sexual morality. The control group that did not use the website saw far less improvement. The reason those using the website did so well was probably due to the privacy and confidentiality the Internet provides, so the students could learn about sex without embarrassment. A similar online sex program for middle school students was implemented successfully in Mao's home province of Hunan. These experiments could eventually point the way toward more effective sex education learning. It would be especially beneficial to students in remote areas of the country, where skilled sex-ed instructors are few and far between.

For adults, some of China's myriad sex shops serve in a way as sex-education centers. Many shop employees still wear lab coats and see themselves as sex instructors, not just salespeople, though this will not be the case in the seedier stores. Many of them are quite experienced in dealing with shy, nervous customers who may not be willing to talk directly about their issues. Good sex shop staff can help draw it out of them in order to find a solution that meets the customers' needs.

Perhaps the most unusual environment for learning all you ever wanted to know about sex in China but were afraid to ask is the Ancient Chinese Sex Museum in the beautiful town of Tongli on the outskirts of Shanghai. China's first sex museum, opened in 1999, displays more than 1,500 exhibits of sexual paraphernalia including coins and plates engraved with sexual imagery, sex toys, chastity belts, stone phalluses and erotic artwork from prehistoric times to the present. It used to be housed in the middle of Shanghai but the government wouldn't let it advertise and denied the request to make it an official tourist site. The museum was losing so much money it had to be moved to the countryside in 2003.

In Tongli, the exhibits are housed in different buildings, each with its own theme like sex in primitive society, women and marriage, sex in everyday life and unconventional sexual behavior. Sub-themes include autoerotic sex, prostitution, homosexuality and group sex. The museum, according to Liu Dalin, its 79 year-old founder and owner, is struggling, but the government has given him the space rent-free and it is doing better than when it was in Shanghai. Liu, a retired Shanghai University professor and sociologist, has made it his mission to reintroduce the Chinese people to their sexual heritage that was denied during the Mao years.

As usual, the Chinese government remains ambivalent about such projects. It allows the sex museum to operate but does its best to hide it away (in Shanghai Liu wasn't even allowed to put up a sign with the Chinese character for "sex" on it). In 2003, after giving approval to a "sex culture" exhibition in Beijing organized by the director of the Chinese Sexual Counseling and Therapy Committee, the government closed it down after its very first day, citing "safety concerns." The exhibition, featuring graphic sexual objects from China's dynastic past, drew so many visitors they had to be let in in small groups that could only view the displays for ten minutes. Within 24 hours of opening day it was closed. The exhibition disappeared for a year, and then was quietly reopened, but only to family planning specialists, not the general public.

Another sex museum, approved by the government in 2001, can be found in the scenic southern China tourist zone of Shaoguan, at Danxiashan national park. Surrounded by rocks that supposedly resemble the shape of human genitalia, the museum is smaller than the one in Tongli and displays ancient Chinese sex manuals, erotic carvings, dynastic sex toys and herbal aphrodisiacs. These museums provide yet another example of the sharp contrast between Chinese prudishness and openness. Their content would be controversial even in the developed West, but in China they are permitted to operate as long as their purpose is educational.

CHINA'S SHIFTING SEXUAL LANDSCAPE

In 2003 a 25-year-old female blogger and magazine feature writer in Guangzhou posting under the pen name Muzimei rocked the Chinese blogosphere with her descriptions of her very active sexual life, leaving nothing to the imagination. Her blog, started on June 19, had gone unnoticed until August, when she posted a detailed account of her one-night stand outside a bar with Guangzhou rock star Wang Lei, using his real name. She revealed how she lifted up her skirt so they could do it "doggy style." She wrote on her blog, "I live a very contented life. In addition to my work I have a very particular hobby – making love – and for making love I have lots of choices, lots of opportunity to change, those resources are endless. I don't need to be responsible for my lovers, and I don't need to get emotionally involved. It's like a CD, if you want to listen, you listen, if you don't, turn it off."

Blogging was still new to China, and suddenly Muzimei's blog, titled "Left-over Love Letters," was the most popular in the country, averaging 6,000 hits a day by October. Within a month her traffic soared to well over 100,000 hits a day and she had become the new face of China's sexual revolution at home and around the world. The *New York Times* and the *Washington Post* and *Time* magazine all wrote feature stories about "the Muzimei phenomenon." Never one to conceal her feelings, she told the *New York Times* in November 2003 that she was only seeking pleasure, not love or marriage: "I think my private life is very interesting. I do not oppose love, but I oppose loyalty. If love has to be based on loyalty, I will not choose love." As she was deluged with interview requests that month, she famously announced that anyone who wanted to interview her would have to sleep with her first. "The longer the sex, the longer the interview," she quipped.

Li Li (Muzimei's real name) told reporters that since she turned 21 years old she had slept with over 80 men, many of whom she hooked up with over the Internet. In her blog she described her penchant for orgies, and recounted her sexploits in graphic detail. She electrified China's blogs and message boards. The government-run newspaper *China Youth Daily* reported that only 10 percent of China's netizens supported Muzimei, while 90 percent disapproved. Nevertheless, the people's fascination never died down. In mid-November, less than three months after exploding onto the scene, Muzimei's blog was taken down, allegedly because it was crashing its host's servers, but this was most likely Chinese censorship as usual. She also lost her job, but soon found work as a consultant for a blog hosting company. She was about to publish her diary in book form at the end of 2003 when the Ministry of Propaganda banned it, and Chinese reporters were ordered to stop interviewing her. When her blog disappeared it had clocked more than 20 million visitors and had been the top search on Chinese search engines for months. The censorship only added to her notoriety, and foreign journalists again sought her out for interviews. "It seems like my government wants people to think of China as the traditional China with Confucian morality and blah, blah, blah," Li told the *Washington Post* soon after her blog was taken down. "We have these interminable meetings, talk a lot about morality, but when it's all over, people go home and return to their real lives. Most of the propaganda guys I know all have mistresses. Heh, I've even slept with some of them. That's why they're scared of my morality. I know their secrets."

Sexologist Li Yinhe, who said she had not read the blog, praised Muzimei for expanding sexual rights, particularly for women, at a time when only men felt they could talk openly about their sex lives. A columnist at *China Youth Daily* attacked Li Yinhe for her endorsement, charging that traditional Chinese values should not be forsaken in the name of open-mindedness and called for Muzimei's diary to be banned for violating China's obscenity laws. Muzimei's sex diary had pushed the envelope, daring to put into words what all the sex experts and survey takers knew – that millions of young Chinese in urban areas were having sex at a younger age and with multiple sex partners. Muzimei had rejected traditional morality and argued that sex, unlike love and loyalty, was a biological necessity.

The reactions to "the Muzimei phenomenon" revealed all the conflicting feelings of the Chinese people; the government still railed against vice and pornography at the same time China was clearly liberalizing and becoming more open about sex. Chinese psychiatrists wrote that Muzimei had a psychological disorder, others argued it was her critics who were mentally unbalanced. Many women took up her cause in blog comments and message boards for having the courage to talk about sexual desire the way men had done for centuries. When her blog was removed, Li Yinhe argued for its reinstatement for reasons of freedom of speech. When editorialists charged Li with seeking to license indecency she replied that most of the Chinese public had already been exposed to "indecent" materials and that it was hypocritical to censor what everyone already knew. *Sex in the City* was at this time one of the most popular shows in China (watched on pirated DVDs).

A national debate went on for weeks. Some argued that

while Muzimei had the right to keep a journal of her private life, she had crossed the line by "outing" her sex partners. Yet by doing so, she had changed the face of Chinese blogging forever. More and more young and even middle-aged women began posting diaries of their private lives online, some including racy photographs. Ordinary women felt empowered to express themselves sexually. The conversation about a woman's right to sexual pleasure was now public. Muzimei herself insisted she was never speaking for all women and felt no need of winning public tolerance or sympathy. She wrote for herself, she said, based on her whims, with no thought of leading a women's rights movement. Muzimei made headlines again in 2005, when she released a twenty-five-minute soundtrack of her making love with an excited male partner and ending with orgasmic groans and moans. It was available as a podcast. Once again, her popularity crashed the servers as more than 10,000 Internet users a day sought to download the sound files. (The podcast was later removed.) Muzimei now works as a columnist for the popular and relatively liberal Guangdong newspaper *Southern Metropolis Weekly*. She still writes about sex and love, but has toned down her style considerably, presumably to avoid further run-ins with authorities.

In the end, the significance of Muzimei is the debate she generated. Many of the online conversations about her remain on China's Internet even if her original diary does not. The praise and criticism of Muzimei offered a microcosm of contemporary Chinese beliefs about sex. Her supporters espoused relatively new notions of female sexual rights, the naturalness of sex and freedom of speech. In sharp contrast, her critics represented the Confucian mindset of propriety, righteousness and the place of women, not to mention the role the government should play in regulating people's private lives.

These forces continue to rub against each other as China struggles to come to terms with sex in the modern age and debates whether the government should serve as the gatekeepers of public morality. The fact that more and more Chinese people engage in pre-marital sex and have sex with more than one partner should indicate that the government cannot successfully bar the gate. To relinquish this role, however, would signal a weakening of its power, and that is something the Chinese Communist Party cannot tolerate. The policing of vice and the suppression of sexual advocates like Muzimei will continue, at least for the foreseeable future.

China's Love Affair with Sex Shops and Toys

Screenwriter and director Sam Voutas, whose groundbreaking 2010 film *Red Light Revolution* shed light on contemporary China's attitudes toward sex, remarked in 2011, "I've lived in China on and off for over 15 years, and one of the biggest changes at the street level has been this sudden emergence of sex shops. Back when they first opened in the 90s, it was like going to the pharmacy, with the employees wearing clinical white coats! That's all really changed with the growth in the Chinese economy, because the entrepreneur has become a big part of city life."

The first state-approved sex shop in China, named "Adam and Eve," opened in February of 1993 in Beijing. Like all of the early sex shops, Adam and Eve started off as an uninviting affair, run by women wearing white laboratory coats who mainly sold Traditional Chinese Medicine (TCM) potency pills to all-male customers. At this point, under the watchful regulation of the China Sexology Association, a body of academics and sex researchers, sex shops were only permitted to present themselves as offshoots of China's healthcare sector. Adam and Eve was a joint venture between the privately owned Beijing Life Guide Service Center and the People's Hospital. Little about it was erotic. There were no condoms to be bought, as at that time they were dispensed only by the government.

The Chinese government has made it clear that sex shops are okay – as long as they present their merchandise as being beneficial to the buyer's health and well being. The annual exhibition of sex merchandise in Shanghai is titled "China International Adult Toys and Reproductive Health Exhibition." The full name of the first sex shop is "Adam and Eve Health Care Centre." The government acknowledges the importance of enjoying a healthy sex life, and has no problem with citizens buying whatever sex toys or lingerie they desire to experience the true joys of sex. But the stores must serve a social and educational function; they exist to help people learn about sex and deal with dysfunctional sexuality. Or at least that is how the stores have to present themselves, even if it just means putting a plaque on the wall saying they are approved by the China Sexology Association.

While Adam and Eve began more as a TCM shop than a sex shop, it cautiously diversified its product line, offering more Western-style sexual aids, such as dildos and sexy clothing, all the while under government regulation. Soon the store was selling pleasure more than it was selling medicine. There was and is no pornography, though there are some graphic manuals on how to make love and improve sexual satisfaction. Even today, with much broader and racier product lines to suit nearly every type of fetish, sex shops in China must still serve – or appear to serve – as quasi-medical establishments that exist to improve public health. The staff, at least at the better stores, considers themselves sex counselors whose role is to help customers find the most suitable remedies for their sexual issues.

The day Adam and Eve opened it became international news. Its owner, Wen Jingfeng, quickly became a celebrity and in 2008 he published a book, *Forbidden Fruit 1993, My Sex Shop and I*. Keeping up with the times, Wen has since opened an online store and Adam and Eve is now a chain of three shops, including one in Beijing's busiest shopping mall. In a 2011 interview with *The Global Times*, Wen explained:

It'd be too obtrusive to have the word sex in the shop's name when we opened. Everything had to be done step by step . . . This business respects the Chinese law and has nothing to do with pornography, which deals with fantasies not objects . . . You should be open-minded, active and optimistic about sex. People should learn to perceive sex as physical, healthy and pleasurable, not as something dirty or a taboo.

Beijing is now home to more than 2,000 sex shops, and state media in 2010 reported there were approximately 200,000 shops throughout China with annual sales above 100 billion yuan ($14.7 billion). It is hard to walk very far in any big Chinese city and not run into at least one. Almost as prolific are the thousands of online sex shops that have opened for Chinese customers who would rather not be seen slipping into a shop on the street.

Competition ranges from elaborate, highly decorative retail establishments similar to what you might find in the West, to little walk-in cubicles operated in the tiniest of premises. Prices are unregulated, so profit margins can be tremendous. A pack of designer condoms that can be bought for three yuan wholesale can sell for 30 yuan at a sex shop in Beijing's Central Business District, while a competitor farther away from downtown might sell the same item for 15 yuan and still turn a handsome profit. While prices may vary from one part of town to the next, one thing is certain: items sold in sex shops are well beyond the means of the poor. Most of their clientele are open-minded members of the middle class and above.

Helen Zhou jumped on the sex shop bandwagon in Shanghai around 2007. At first she was quite nervous about it. This was a whole new world to her and she had very little support when she started out. Her friend Carol urged her on, telling her what merchandise to sell and how to display it to attract customers' eyes. Under Carol's guidance she modeled the shop after those in the US. At the time, sex shops in Shanghai were relatively few, catering mainly to men 40-to-50 years old who were interested in virility medicines. She stocked the shelves with a diversified product line that included lots of vibrators, dildos, sex toys, sexual lubricants, designer condoms, sexy underwear, handcuffs, blow-up dolls and role-playing costumes. Some of her most popular products are vibrators shaped like flowers or animals. Chinese people, she says, like products that let them act out their fantasies.

Business was very slow at first. People would lurk outside, looking in the windows, and when Helen stepped out and invited them to come in they would usually run away. After several depressing days, more and more customers began to trickle in, foreigners and Chinese. Word was slowly spreading. "Our first customer was a foreign girl," Helen recollects. "She bought stuff and then she rushed out. But this really gave me confidence that these products could sell."

Even though many of the products are for men, most of the customers doing the buying are women. About half the customers are couples, but women usually do the buying while her partner stays outside. Men, Helen says, tend to be embarrassed, and would insist they were buying the product "for my girlfriend." She says that women are more likely than men to talk with her about ways to improve their sex life. "Guys never talk about things like that." Helen has just begun advertising on the Internet, offering delivery service for customers who might be too shy to pick up the products in person. She's also considering starting an S&M club. Chinese people, she says, are curious about bondage and S&M but know little about it. Helen talks to them about it and gives them instructions. The store now welcomes between five and thirty customers a day, with business booming around holidays like Halloween and Valentine's Day.

Shanghai is also home to China's most spacious sex emporium, an unassuming four-story mall that sells sexual remedies and paraphernalia. The mall is located a bit off the beaten path and caters to every conceivable taste. Not surprisingly, it was closed during the Shanghai 2010 World Expo, like many sex establishments, but has since reopened.

The first three floors are crammed with small shops offering the usual TCM herbal remedies and aphrodisiacs: "African Superman" penis enlargement pills, ground deer, yak, wild wolf and dog penis, a special "penis pack" of various animal penises, and sheep's horn soaked in Baijiu, China's popular high-potency wine that foreigners compare to nail polish remover. The Chinese believe if a part of your body is ailing it is healthy to eat the same part of certain animals. If you are having issues with your muscles, you might eat beef muscle and tendons. If you are a man who wants more sex drive, deer, dog or ox penis might do the trick. You can buy an entire box of shriveled seal penis. Ground deer horn and desiccated snakeskin are also good sellers. As in most TCM shops, these items are displayed in large glass jars or open bins. There are also homeopathic pills that treat female frigidity and promise to make women's vaginas tighter. As you shop, 1980s pop music is piped over the loudspeakers, creating a surreal, uniquely Chinese atmosphere.

The entire fourth floor is dedicated to more contemporary sexual paraphernalia. It, too, is divided into small shops, each selling niche products. For instance, some stores sell lingerie and fantasy costumes, others sell dildos and vibrators, others S&M items like handcuffs, chains and whips. Condoms of all shapes, sizes, colors and flavors are sold everywhere, as is Viagra and Chinese herbal equivalents. Adventurous shoppers can purchase a long golden dildo or a female blowup doll with removable parts. A surprisingly wide variety of cock rings, including some that vibrate, are on display, as well as anal beads, pleasure balls for insertion into a woman's vagina, and a plethora of lubricants. Most of these items are relatively cheap (they are nearly all made in China) and some shops sell items in bulk at wholesale prices to other sex retailers.

One TCM shopkeeper on the first floor comes from China's northeast. When she first set up shop in the mall, her best seller was oil taken from the fallopian tubes of a particular breed of frog that can survive a cold winter. The frogs, also from northeast China, seem to be very hearty, so men buy capsules of the frog oil to make themselves strong and boost their sexual health. A box of the pills sells for 480 yuan ($70). Another best-seller is a type of lotus flower that grows in the snow mountains of Tibet and supposedly helps men with their blood flow, important for maintaining their erections.

Most of her male customers are middle-aged or older men interested in remedies for erectile dysfunction and premature ejaculation. Most of the women who come to the mall, she says, shop for dress-up costumes while the men buy TCM. Younger men, she says, are no longer interested in tonics and herbs. She also sells a vaginal spray peculiarly called "Britney Spears," which the shopkeeper says can make the vagina more springy and narrow. A key ingredient is Sichuan chili. The packaging features a drawing of Britney leaning against a doorframe wearing nothing but a pair of white pants.

Viagra is theoretically available in China only by prescription, but the sex mall, like nearly every other sex shop and pharmacy, offers it for sale over the counter (buyer beware: Viagra in China is often counterfeit). After thousands of years searching for the perfect sexual remedy for men, the Chinese look at Viagra as a miracle pill. Dog penis may soon be a thing of the past. Viagra has become a popular gift for the wealthy, replacing traditional gifts like expensive brandy and imported cigars. The Chinese name for Viagra is *"weige"* – "big brother."

China remains in many ways a prudish society, and sex remains a largely taboo subject, but that hasn't dented its interest in sexual aids and devices. The Chinese, with their fascination with sexual pleasure going back to ancient times, and with their disposable incomes rising, make an ideal target for sex shop vendors. A 2010 survey indicated that 93 percent of Chinese adults expressed a measure of approval for sex toys, and the number of sex shop customers bears this out. Some sex stores in good locations in Shanghai and Beijing are bringing in over $100,000 a month. About 70 percent of the world's sex toys are manufactured in China, mainly in Guangdong province in southern China, and about ten percent of those toys are sold domestically. Since the global recession started in 2008, orders from abroad declined as much as 30 percent, so tapping into the domestic market is more urgent than ever. While the shops have seen a slowdown, it is more than made up for by the success of their online businesses.

The Never-Ending War on Porn

China began censoring what it saw as obscene materials nearly a thousand years ago under the growing influence of orthodox Neo-Confucianists. China began to frown on any depiction of sex outside of monogamous heterosexual marriage and this wave of prudishness would continue, with many interruptions and exceptions, through the twentieth century. Early in the Ming Dynasty many erotic books were banned and burned, but toward the later years of the Ming there was a backlash against Neo-Confucian prudery, and erotic art and literature flourished. Incredibly graphic erotic art and fiction, including one of China's raciest novels, *The Plum in the Golden Vase*, thrived through the late years of the Ming. It was not until the Qing Dynasty that the government went into an anti-erotica frenzy and banned about 150 books. Censorship became routine, although it went back and forth; plenty of sexually graphic works of literature were written under the Qing.

Throughout most of the twentieth century the Chinese government's attitude toward pornography and "obscene" material saw little change. The Chinese Communist Party banned all pornography and erotic fiction as soon as it came to power in 1949. Anyone caught producing, distributing or buying books, photographs, magazines or any other material deemed obscene by the government faced serious penalties, including imprisonment. Any work of art that contained sexually graphic images was considered pornography. Just as he did with prostitution, Mao effectively wiped out all visible signs of erotica.

Nudity of any kind was considered obscene and was banned. Even nude models for art classes were prohibited. Mao's regime was the most prudish in Chinese history, every hint of eroticism being extinguished, the entire topic of sex being shrouded in silence.

The Communist Party was quick to force themselves into their citizens' private lives and demand that they conform because it believed social stability and harmony were essential for the party's existence, and that stability was closely linked to morality. Based on the Confucian ideal of the family as the "cell of society," if the government can ensure the stability of the family it could keep society in check and ensure its own longevity. Hence China's portrayal of itself under communist rule as morally superior and pure, cleansed of any element that could tear at the fabric of the family and of society, like adultery, prostitution and pornography.

This moral righteousness is also tied to political control. Cadres were called upon to police the virtue of their citizens and hold them in check. It was no accident that one of China's most massive, ruthless and tightly organized sweeps against pornography was launched five weeks after the Tiananmen Square crackdown on June 4, 1989. Nearly 70,000 police and state functionaries burst in on publishing houses, bookstores and book distribution centers and confiscated more than 10 million books and magazines. This kind of drastic action cuts off the flow of potentially "harmful" information while telling the public in no uncertain terms that it is not a good time to dissent or criticize the government. Two months later, *China Daily* quoted Li Ruihuan, a prominent member of the Communist Party's Standing Committee, as saying the assault on pornography was intended to combat "bourgeois liberalization." It is, and always has been, about holding onto power by ensuring stability at any cost. In 1957, a new article was added to the law making possession of "reactionary, obscene, or absurd books, periodicals, picture books, or pictures that have previously been repressed" punishable with up to ten days detention. Those selling and distributing such materials faced harsher penalties. The definitions were so broad, they could apply to practically anything.

During the Cultural Revolution there was no pornography per se, but young people passed around hand-copied scatological stories. The government cracked down and ordered all copies to be handed in to local officials under threat of severe punishment. Although the prohibition of pornography remains in effect today, as China opened up in the late 1970s and normalized relations with the West, "yellow" materials began to seep back into the country for sale through the underground market. Mao's successor Deng Xiaoping was alarmed and in 1980 the government launched an aggressive attack against "spiritual pollution," an amorphous term that let the government go after anything it perceived as threatening. All blame for the resurgence of erotica was placed on the decadent capitalist West.

But stamping out erotica was a difficult battle. Copies of "yellow videos" such as the American X-rated film *Deep Throat* proliferated on the black market, and small groups of Chinese were getting together to view them, paying a 5 to 10-yuan price of admission, a lot of money at a time when most Chinese took home less than 100 yuan a month. "Yellow" photographs and books were also making their way into the country on a regular basis from Hong Kong. In 1985, new anti-smut regulations were announced that went much further than those of 1957:

Pornography is very harmful, poisoning people's minds, inducing crimes . . . and must be severely banned. The items which must be severely banned include: any kind of videotape, audiotape, film, TV program, slide, photograph, painting, book, newspaper, magazine, and handcopied material which contains explicit descriptions of sexual behavior and/or erotic pictures; any kind of toy or article with instructions for use which were printed above erotic pictures; and any kind of aphrodisiacs and sex toys. The person who smuggled, produced, sold, or organized the showing of pornography, whether for sale or not, shall be punished according to the conditions, by imprisonment or administrative punishment.

But even this was not strict enough for Deng, who in 1988 was quoted in the Chinese media as saying some publishers of pornography should be put to death. A massive new campaign against pornography swept the nation and tens of thousands of erotic books and magazines were confiscated in city after city. In Shanghai, a railway employee received the death penalty for organizing nine separate parties during which he and four others played pornographic videos while having sex with female participants. The four others were handed lengthy prison sentences. Yet more anti-pornography regulations were signed into law at the 1988 National People's Congress, with higher fines and longer prison sentences. That same year one of China's greatest classic novels, *The Golden Lotus*, was banned, even after the publisher deleted all of the sexually explicit references.

The *"Sweeping the Yellow"* campaigns against pornography and vice continue today. A book like *Decadence Mandchoue*, the memoirs of Edmund Backhouse recounting his mostly homosexual adventures in Beijing in the early years of the twentieth century, could only be published in mainland China in Chinese in 2012 with all explicit descriptions of sexual activity expunged. The Internet is now the censors' number one target. Words relating to sex acts and erotica are blocked from China's search engines, as are most pornography sites. The government shuts down thousands of "lewd" websites every year, a catastrophe for legitimate discussion communities and gay and lesbian sites that get caught in the wide net cast by the censors. Dr. Katrien Jacobs, author of *People's Pornography: Sex and Surveillance on the Chinese Internet*, spoke in a 2011 interview about the draconian efforts to "strike hard" against Web pornography:

It seems as if sexual minorities, sex artists and activists are much more vulnerable than those involved in mainstream commercial porn, especially at this moment when film festivals are being shut down and human rights activists are being tortured and detained. These are the dark times of China's civil right and sexual creative outlet, but there is still so much porn and sex entertainment available that we can see it as a safer outlet . . . It seems indeed that porn cannot be banned and that the PRC government is perhaps even secretly letting it into the country. But besides their bombastic cleanup campaigns, they also censor web communities that stand for sexual freedom or queer identity.

Thousands of blogs have been deleted for content that the government deems harmful. Political blogs, especially those hinting at the benefits of democracy, are shut down or blocked. Phone-sex services have also been shut down, as have services that send out "dirty" text messages. On one of the nation's largest portals, Sohu.com, bloggers must agree to fourteen specific regulations, pledging not to "damage the nation's reputation or attack the party or government," "violate Chinese traditional virtues," or "damage social stability." China employs about 30,000 cyber police who scour the Internet looking for vice and political dissidence.

The Neo-Confucian mentality that the state must wipe out any self-expression that might threaten stability and harmony continues as vice is treated as an existential threat. So obsessed is the government with any hint of lewdness that in October of 2011 the State Administration of Radio, Film and Television (SARFT) sent out a circular banning sex-related content in television and radio advertisements. Tens of thousands of sites (no one knows the exact number), many pornographic or political, are simply blocked altogether by the filtering software known as the Great Firewall of China, though savvy netizens with a good proxy server can always get around the censors. Countless blogs are inaccessible, some of which consider themselves pro-China. And when a blogger is banned there is nothing they can do, no one to complain to. YouTube has been banned for years, replaced by Chinese video uploading sites that can easily be policed.

Facebook and Twitter, where users can speak freely and rally the masses to their cause as during the "Arab Spring," were blocked in the summer of 2009 and replaced by home-grown social media the government can keep in check (with limited success).

One of the Chinese government's chief justifications for "striking hard" is the claim that pornography leads to crime. Sexologist Pan Suiming has said publicly that this is nonsense, and that couples who watch pornography together actually enjoy a better sex life and are drawn closer to one another. Sexologist Li Yinhe has gone on the record saying pornography should be legal for adults who wish to see it, though parents should apply filtering software to keep it away from minors.

For all the fuss, pornography remains very easy to find in China. In 2010, according to the *Global Times*, Renmin University surveyed 7,200 people between the ages of 18 to 61, of whom more than 50 percent said they watched porn at least once over the past year. This was an increase of 12 percent since the university's last survey in 2000. Fifty percent of those between the ages of 14 and 17 said they had watched porn. The majority of viewers have college degrees and nearly half are white-collar workers. China's ban on pornography clearly is not working, especially not in urban areas.

Censorship in the new millennium often seems to have no rhyme or reason. China has been known to ban sites – even major news sites like the BBC – and then suddenly make them available again a few weeks or months later. A major Western pornography site that was banned years ago suddenly became accessible in 2010. One never knows. Many Chinese blogs include semi-nude images and can be very sexual, but they are allowed to remain while others are deleted. Censorship and anti-pornography crackdowns come in waves, and are especially aggressive before key dates like the anniversary of the Tiananmen Square Massacre and the annual National People's Congress.

Punishment, too, is erratic. In 2006 an operator of a porn site in China that drew 11 million hits was sentenced to life imprisonment, while others who made porn available on a smaller scale received a fine or a brief period of detention. In 2009 a popular voice actress who specialized in audiobooks, Ye Qiantong, was arrested for making voice recordings of pornographic novels that were sold to customers of Dongting China, the country's largest audiobooks producer. The business was shut down and she was sentenced to two years in prison, later reduced to two years probation. Two executives who ran the site were sentenced to three years in prison and fined 50,000 yuan ($7,900) each.

Li Yinhe, in a 2010 interview with the *UK Telegraph*, said that every time the censorship relaxes it soon tightens again: "I watched a television news report on a crackdown on pornographic organizations just a couple of days ago. Perhaps after a heavy period of suppression, they are relaxing their control for a little while. And perhaps their computers have been overwhelmed. The censorship will be back though, and will stay for as long as pornography is illegal."

There is plenty of irony here. While China is blocking websites and railing against the spiritual pollution brought on by pornography, the country is one of the world's biggest markets for sex toys. Prostitution is just a karaoke bar away. On talk radio programs callers phone in to discuss sexual techniques and problems, often in graphic terms. Anyone in China with a Web browser can download as much pornography as they want off of peer-to-peer and torrent sites, although the police will occasionally arrest a downloader and publicize their crime as a warning. Booksellers on the street often sell books the government bans as obscene, especially in the large cities. Expatriate bookstores openly sell English-language books that have been banned. Internet users can still use Google to find porn and sexual content, though only on sites run from outside China.

The battle against sex and political dissent can be closely intertwined. The anti-pornography campaigns are used to ramp up Internet filtering and censorship in general to crack down on political "cyber-dissidents." Ai Weiwei, a renowned artist and sharp critic of the Communist Party's censorship policies and the party's corruption, was investigated by the government for pornography in 2011 after he and some of his followers took nude photographs of themselves, which they posted to blogs and tweeted, trying to convince the government that nudity is not pornography. Hundreds of Ai's fans around the world posted nude photographs of themselves to a site titled "Ai Weiwei Fans – Nudity is not Pornography" (blocked in China, needless to say). Many believe that the pornography charges are simply a veiled attempt by the government to silence Ai, who remarked in an interview, "If they see nudity as pornography, then China is still in the Qing dynasty."

Yet the government's war on porn has some staunch supporters. Yang Shui is the manager of the anti-pornography website *haongo.com* and when asked by the *Global Times* whether banning erotica was stifling freedom of expression, she replied, "Define freedom. I think only people who are addicted to porn would agree [that it should be legalized]. Nobody has the right to give other people pain and trash." In the same article, a university student explained why he reported 32 porn sites to the authorities in one month, earning a 10,000-yuan reward: "He blamed the porn website for 'poisoning his pure heart' and causing him to fail school. 'I was always in the best class of the best school. My goal was to enter a really good university. After I became addicted to watching porn, I was only able to get into a junior college.'"

In 2010 Li Yinhe issued a blistering attack on China's "strike hard" campaigns against pornography, translated by the China Geeks blog:

In my opinion, citizens watching pornography in their homes and online is fairly equal to looking at pretty girls on the street: the degree of harm it causes to society and to other people is similar. It isn't necessary to see this as being like confronting a mortal enemy; the heavens will not collapse, there will not be chaos in society, and the stability of the regime and of society will not be threatened. Who knows, maybe it could make society more stable – if everyone were to concentrate their desires and passions into sexual happiness, they wouldn't be going out on the streets causing trouble, let alone thinking about overthrowing the regime. This [would be] a shared victory for the common people and the government.

For now, it appears the Chinese campaign against pornography will continue even though it is a losing battle. The prohibition is obviously unpopular and ineffective, and pornography is ubiquitous for anyone who wants to find it. All the government can do is tighten controls on the Internet, but so far users have proven adept at slipping past the Great Firewall. According to a 2010 poll by Sina, one of China's biggest portals, only about two percent of respondents are in favor of the prohibition. As China continues to liberalize the most likely scenario is that the government will keep rattling its saber over porn and continue to "sweep the yellow," while its citizens ignore the edicts and continue to enjoy pornography at their leisure. Like prostitution, pornography in China can be set back, but with its huge market demand it cannot be banned. The government today is constantly boasting of new crackdowns and arrests, but the campaign's chances of success do not look promising.

Getting Naked

Nudism has never been popular in China, as it has been in the West. While Confucius may not have looked at nudism as evil or immoral, it certainly would go against his ideals of propriety, righteousness and shame. In some periods in ancient China upper-class women did not disrobe when visiting a doctor, but instead pointed to an anatomically correct ivory statue to tell the doctor the location of their pain.

In the 1920s and '30s a few brave Chinese practiced nudism on some east and south China beaches, but it never caught on and by the 1940s the practice disappeared. Nudism in any form was completely banned under Mao who, as noted earlier, even banned the use of nude models at art classes. The Chinese are famously immodest when with the same sex in an environment like a sauna or segregated hot springs. However, co-ed nudity has always been considered off limits. In modern-day China nudism is still practically unheard of, though since the end of the Cultural Revolution China has become increasingly tolerant of the naked human body.

In 2002, one of China's only nudist colonies opened in Sichuan province at a secluded spot between two waterfalls. The Heaven Bodies Nude Bathing Center was soon a popular destination, but the government expressed its dissatisfaction shortly afterwards and the resort was shut down within a year. In 2009, *People's Daily* held an online poll in which more than 70 percent of readers said they wanted the bathing center to reopen, while 21 percent voted against it, citing the immorality of nudism. Remarkably, public pressure won out and the center was soon back in business after seven years and remains open today. There is also a popular nude bathing center to the north of Heaven Bodies in Chongqing, but it is for ladies only. A lavish nudist colony was planned for Hangzhou in 2004, when the builder received the necessary permits and spent half a million yuan to create two lavish pools surrounded by a bamboo forest. At the last minute the government nixed the project and it was never built.

The ban on nudes in art classes was lifted in 1978, when China began to liberalize, and in the next year paintings depicting nude women were shown publicly at the Beihai Park art gallery in Beijing, generating considerable media buzz. Most shocking was the unveiling of a huge mural at Beijing's new airport in 1979 that featured three nude women painted in a stylized, vaguely abstract fashion. The artist, Yuan Yunsheng, said later, "I was painting a bathing scene, so naturally people would not have any clothes on. In order to pass the official inspection, I painted extra lines in my sketch to make the women look like they were wearing clothes. I then erased those extra lines before finishing the painting. By the time the authorities found out, it was too late for them to do anything."

Thousands of Beijingers rushed to the airport to see the groundbreaking mural, but not everyone was delighted. Three months later, due to strong public opinion against the depiction of nudity, the three nude figures were covered with gauze. But despite the lingering prudishness, the thirst for nudity in art and photography was growing. The government formally approved of nudity in art in 1985, and three years later thousands stood on long lines in freezing weather to see the China Nude Art Painting exhibition at Beijing's National Art Gallery, made up of more than 100 candid works by students and teachers from China's Central Academy of Fine Arts. More than 200,000 visitors attended the exhibition's 18-day run. In 2001 thousands flocked to Hangzhou to attend China's first art exhibition of nude photography. The 117 photos were not provocative or steamy by Western standards, but they definitely signaled a seismic shift in the public's acceptance of the naked human body. Ever since, nudism in photography has been commonplace in China's galleries.

In the following years there have been many isolated incidents of public nudism, nearly always done in the name of the arts. For instance, on World Naturist Day in 2006 five artists from a "painter's village" at the border of Beijing and Hebei climbed up a sand peak nude and shouted, "Enjoy the sunshine!" That same year, in an incident that won huge media attention, an assistant professor of art at the Teachers' University of Technology in Changzhou, Jiangsu province, disrobed while giving a lecture on "nudity in the arts and human consciousness," shocking his 30 students and generating a mixed reaction from the public. In 2005 a writer named Li Suolun walked naked in front of a bookstore in the busy Xidan area of Beijing to promote a book he hoped would be published and was arrested. *People's Daily* reported that local residents thought the man's behavior was "indecent."

While nudity in art has been widely accepted, China remains largely priggish toward public nudity and even toward nudism practiced by private groups. Nudism websites have been routinely deleted by the Public Security Bureau, which likened them to pornography. The nudism community in China remains insignificant.

PARTING THOUGHTS

In January 2012, the Chinese government announced it was purging two thirds of prime time television programs including popular dating and variety shows. Two months earlier President Hu Jintao had warned senior Communist Party leaders that "hostile" foreign forces were seeking to "Westernize and divide" China. *The Associated Press* reported Hu as saying, "We should deeply understand the seriousness and complexity of the ideological struggle, always sound the alarms and remain vigilant, and take forceful measures to be on guard and respond."

Under the new regulations, from 7:30pm to 10:00pm Chinese broadcasters must offer at least two half-hour news shows, which tend to be lethally dull. No more than 90 minutes could be allocated for entertainment. The number of China's most popular shows such as game shows, dating competitions, soap operas, and American Idol copycats was slashed from more than 120 a week to fewer than 40. China's news agency *Xinhua* announced, "Satellite channels have started to broadcast programs that promote traditional virtues and socialist core values."

This was an echo of earlier calls by the government as far

back as the days of Mao and Deng to cleanse China of Western "spiritual pollution," and demonstrated the party's eagerness to continue serving as thought police. While personal freedoms are growing, the government seems more determined than ever to control what its people see and hear. Censorship of entertainment, Internet content and of social media, in particular China's popular microblogging site Weibo, is only getting more aggressive (though this censorship is at best only a mixed success).

Some shows that were not canceled were overhauled. One of the country's most popular reality dating programs, *If You Are the One*, crossed a line: Young people competing with each other for dates talked about taboo subjects like pre-marital sex and the One-Child Policy. Certain topics are not meant for public debate, especially when you are talking about a show with 50 million viewers. The censors knocked on their door, and now the show features some older contestants and a third host, a dowdy professor from a provincial Communist Party school. The show's producer said they were told to prohibit content that might have a "negative social impact."

Several media analysts said the replacement of popular television shows with those that promote the success of Chinese socialism was most likely part of the government's campaign to boost its soft power by instilling in the public a sense of patriotic sentiment. Many of these shows are watched by Chinese overseas and might reflect a view of China different from the party's line. No one can really say for sure, but there is no doubt it is part of an ongoing campaign to increase or at least maintain the Communist Party's grip on power by promoting "harmony" on the airwaves. Racy content and sex are still seen as destroyers of harmony.

So the eternal tug of war between social conservative prudes and a new generation of Western-influenced young people continues, and for now the powers that be have the upper hand; they can call the shots without any public debate. Whether this dynamic will change with the passing of the older generation is uncertain. Common sense says it has to, but with China one simply never knows.

It is safe to say, however, that no matter how hard the government tries to rein in people's thoughts, China's sexual revolution is not going away. It has already generated remarkable changes in how the Chinese see themselves and how they relate with one another and the world. This is a trend the government cannot reverse as long as there is an Internet and a population increasingly familiar with the outside world.

China's relatively newfound sexual freedoms and exposure to other cultures through the Internet and mass media have not only changed the way its people see themselves, but also have altered what people perceive beauty to be. It is a far cry from the unisex days of the Cultural Revolution, when people were taught to conform and dress alike, and when even thinking about making oneself more physically attractive through surgery would have been considered hopelessly selfish and politically incorrect. In fewer than thirty years, the very concept of beauty in China had been overhauled.

The sexual revolution, combined with increased disposable income and the ongoing influence of Western culture, has influenced how Chinese people dress, down to the watches they wear and the bags they carry. In every major Chinese city there are modern luxury shopping malls featuring the latest fashion from the likes of Armani and Gucci. If you sip coffee in a café in Shanghai's French Concession and gaze out the window you might think you were watching a fashion show from Paris. China's middle and upper classes, men and women, love Western fashion and big-name brands. Even in smaller cities you will see young Chinese keeping up with the latest fashions, though the brands they buy are more likely to be native Chinese.

But the Western influence on sex-conscious Chinese goes beyond clothing and appearance. For the past decade China has seen an incredible boom in plastic and cosmetic surgery that is closely tied to China's liberalized attitudes toward sex and beauty. In 2001, China's vice minister of health Ma Xiaowei said that plastic surgery had become the fourth most popular way to spend discretionary income in China. Only houses, cars and travel ranked higher, he told the *New York Times*. Plastic surgery was unknown in China until the 1980s. Now there are more than two million procedures performed each year, and most of the customers are young people in their twenties. Prior to reform and opening up in the 1980s, medical practitioners were only permitted to perform plastic surgery to correct physical deformities such as harelips. Doctors refused to put patients under the knife solely to improve their looks, as this would have been considered bourgeois.

Unlike in the West, most of the operations in China have nothing to do with aging, but with sculpting the face and jaw. The most popular procedure for women is adding a crease to their eyelids to create what is known as a "double eyelid." This look makes the eyes appear rounder and larger, and also more like Caucasians' eyes. Everywhere you look in Shanghai and Beijing there are signs and billboards featuring Western models, and for many young Chinese these Caucasian faces have become beauty icons. It should not be a surprise that many Chinese girls want to make themselves look more like these role models.

In 2009 Mattel opened its flagship Barbie doll store in Shanghai (which closed its doors two years later), but it offered only a few dolls with Asian faces because they sold poorly. For Chinese girls, the most beautiful Barbie was the one with blond hair, a slim, defined face and round blue eyes. Only in the past couple of years has the pendulum started to swing back, with more and more Chinese women seeking to emphasize their "Asianness" and turning to Korean pop stars and other Asian beauties as their models for plastic surgery. Many of these Asian role models, however, have had their own plastic surgeries, especially double eyelid procedures. After eyelid surgery, the next most popular operation is enhancing the bridge of the nose to make the face appear less flat. This is the opposite of the Western "nose job," which is usually performed to make the nose less prominent. Also much in demand are procedures to make the jaw line less square, sculpting it so it looks longer and slimmer. Breast enlargement and liposuction are also increasingly in vogue. And more and more young Chinese men are turning to plastic surgery, mainly to give them double eyelids, to reconstruct their nasal bridge or to diminish bags under the eyes. A large number of Chinese men have elected to have breast implants that make their pectoral muscles harder and more prominent, a procedure that costs about 9,500 yuan ($1,500).

In the 1980s and 1990s it was only the well off who could afford plastic and cosmetic surgery, but today it has become far more mainstream. There are thousands of stories of girls from small towns making the trip to Beijing or Shanghai with their savings to have their eyes made larger or their jaws streamlined. Clerks in high-end stores have been known to undergo plastic surgery because they believe the prettier they are the more they can sell. Many young Chinese women believe surgery will give them the extra edge they need to make themselves attractive to a wealthy man.

Only about half of the operations are performed for the sake of vanity. The other main reason is to look good for job interviews or promotions at work. There are many more applicants than there are jobs in China, and they want to do everything they can to tip the scale in their favor. The number of operations jumped after the start of the global financial crisis at the end of 2008 as jobs suddenly became more scarce. Ironically, the number of plastic surgery procedures in the United States at the same time dropped precipitously as Americans did all they could to conserve their disposable income.

In China, reshaping the jaw line can cost as much as 38,000 yuan ($6,000), and if you add reshaping of the cheekbones the tab can jump to 95,000 yuan ($15,000). Adding a fold to the eyelids only runs about 2,525 yuan ($400), while the average price for a nose job is 4,400 yuan ($700). Once they have one procedure, however, about thirty percent of the customers, liking what they see, decide they want another. Business is booming like never before. Plastic surgery is now so common and accepted in China that in 2004 Beijing hosted a "Miss Plastic Surgery" beauty contest. Nineteen finalists ranging in age from 17 to 62 years old, all of whom had their faces reconstructed at the hand of a plastic surgeon, faced off to win the prize. All a woman needed to do to enter was supply a certificate proving she had had her procedures at a legitimate plastic surgery clinic or hospital. The organizers came up with the idea after a Chinese contestant for the Miss Intercontinental Beauty Pageant was disqualified when it was revealed she had undergone more than 10 plastic surgeries.

Miss Plastic Surgery's stated goal was to give Chinese society a better understanding of cosmetic surgery and to accept women who chose to transform their looks. "Everybody should have the right to pursue beauty. And in fact, we all know that pretty women have more opportunities than others," one of the organizers said to *China Daily*. "Statistics have shown that those who are more beautiful than average are economically better off than others." The oldest contestant, 62 years old, had undergone eyelid surgery and a face-lift to make her skin wrinkle-free. "I want to send a message to society that the love of beauty is not limited by age," she said.

Unfortunately, there are many horror stories of botched plastic surgeries illegally performed in China's beauty parlors and private clinics. Over the past decade there have been more than 200,000 incidents of disfigurement caused by plastic surgery operations gone bad. Stories of serious infections following procedures performed at beauty parlors are commonplace. In 2010, doctor negligence during a plastic surgery procedure at a legitimate hospital led to the death of Wang Bei, the winner of Super Girl, China's singing contest based on American Idol. Wang was undergoing procedures for her cheekbones and lower jaw when bleeding from her jaw seeped into her trachea and suffocated her.

For all the dramatic changes in China's sexual landscape since the late 1970s, perhaps nothing will have a more dramatic effect than the looming gender imbalance, the consequences of which will be especially acute in the countryside and among migrant workers. These poorer, less educated men will have a hard time competing for brides who will have a disproportionately large pool of male suitors to choose from. Educated, financially secure men will have all the advantages.

Thanks to the One-Child Policy and the belief that having a son is necessary for continuing the family lineage, there are expected to be more than 24 million "bare branches" – men who cannot find a wife and will never have their own family tree – by 2020. For a society that values marriage, family and lineage above all else this is nothing less than a catastrophe. While India and South Korea also face gender imbalances, no other country approaches China's lopsided boy-to-girl ratio. And there is perhaps no greater fear a Chinese man can suffer than that of not being able to find a wife.

Prior to the implementation of the One-Child Policy, 106 boys were born for every 100 girls, numbers that tended to even out because men have a higher mortality rate than women. In 2010, according to a United Nations report, China's male-to-female sex ratio at birth was the highest in the world, at 120 boys for every 100 girls thanks to sex-selective abortions. In some rural areas where women are permitted a "second chance" if their first child is a girl, the imbalance soars to an astonishing 163 boys born for every 100 girls.

This phenomenon will affect practically every aspect of sex in China in the future, from prostitution to homosexuality to the way women choose their husbands to sex-related crimes to rates of sexually transmitted diseases. The One-Child Policy succeeded in preventing 400 million births and reining in China's unsustainable population growth, but it has left a demographic that is hopelessly skewed.

"Historically, societies in which men substantially outnumber women are not nice places to live," says Mara Hvistendahl, author of *Unnatural Selection*, a book about the preference for boys over girls in Asia and parts of Europe. "Often they are unstable. Sometimes they are violent." She points to times of violence such as the American frontier in the days of the "Wild West," when women were in very short supply, and attributes the atmosphere of violence at least in part to the dearth of females.

Statistical analysis has already shown that China's gender imbalance has led to a jump in crime and violence. Men who do not have their sexual needs fulfilled, and who have no family and the responsibilities that come with it, appear more likely to turn to crime, drugs and prostitutes. Those men who remain unmarried, most of whom will be poor and uneducated, tend to congregate together and often form criminal gangs. This could create a criminal subclass full of resentment, anger and frustration.

The "bare branches" phenomenon is a frequent discussion topic among men on China's online forums, and they make a lot of jokes about it, though they know it is no laughing matter. Chinese men are fully aware of their situation and understand that there will be stiff competition for brides. Men of means, skills and education will have a less difficult time finding a wife than will villagers and migrant workers. Many men are saving more than ever before hoping that their money will give them a competitive edge in the search for a bride. There is already a bride shortage in parts of the countryside, where desperate men have married "mail-order brides" trafficked from neighboring countries such as Vietnam, Laos and Myanmar. Male Chinese children, on the other hand, have been kidnapped and sold to families that would do anything to have a son. (These kidnappings have been especially frequent in southwestern cities like Kunming.) The government says that more than 2,000 children in China are abducted every year, and the number is probably higher. Forced marriages in the countryside are not uncommon, with women abducted from their villages and transported to another part of China against their will to marry men they had never met.

The Chinese government has launched a massive propaganda campaign urging parents to treasure their female child as much as a boy, but there is no indication it is working. It is difficult to undo a belief that has been ingrained in the Chinese psyche for thousands of years with posters that proclaim, "Caring for girls is caring for the future of our nation!" or "Times have changed! Boys and girls are the same!" This is too little too late. One can only wonder, did the architects of the One-Child Policy really not see the future gender imbalance, knowing that since ancient times the Chinese people have valued sons far more than daughters? How did China's leaders, who say they take a "scientific" approach to running the country, fail to take this into account? They most likely see it as an unfortunate but tolerable by-product of the One-Child Policy. The fact that the policy continues despite the acute gender imbalance indicates the government considers population control a higher priority than the sex ratio.

The options of bare branches when it comes to sex are severely limited. (On Internet message boards, young unmarried men have joked that their one recourse might be inflatable sex dolls.) Although no one can yet say for sure, the 24 million unmarried men will almost certainly create unprecedented demand for prostitution. Many single men will most likely live in "bachelor ghettos" where commercial sex will take off. Some Chinese sex experts predict this trend will be accompanied by a significant jump in rates of HIV/AIDS and other sexually transmitted diseases. Other experts predict that rates of STDs will actually go down because men will have far fewer opportunities to carry on affairs with multiple partners or to have pre-marital sex. No one really knows for sure. A 2010 study reported in the Journal of Health and Social Behavior concludes:

In contrast to pessimistic and often dire speculations regarding the possible impact of China's burgeoning deficit of women, our findings suggest a more guarded, and perhaps more optimistic, scenario. Consistent with these speculations, we find suggestive evidence that, when faced with an undersupply of women, men are more likely to engage in intercourse with commercial sex workers. But contrary to these pessimistic predictions, we also find that men who encounter comparatively few women in their local marriage market are less likely to have non-commercial premarital sex and, more importantly, are less likely to test positive for a sexually transmitted infection.

Many experts say just the opposite, since the men's chief option for sexual release will be commercial sex and the rate of STDs among sex workers is extremely high. Sociologists and healthcare professionals will be watching carefully to determine which scenario plays out.

A high male-to-female ratio increases the chances of a woman becoming pregnant before marriage. Studies have shown that when a woman has many men to choose from she is more likely to engage in pre-marital intercourse as well as extramarital affairs, boosting the odds of an unwanted pregnancy. Countries with a higher proportion of men tend to have higher rates of teen pregnancy. On the other hand, young men who fail to attract a female partner in the increasingly competitive marketplace will be unable to have non-commercial pre-marital sex. That leaves China with millions of unfulfilled young men and a major commercial opportunity in terms of prostitution.

One hypothesis put forward by some sex experts is that many of the 24 million bare branches will turn to homosexuality out of a lack of other options. There are those who believe homosexuality is either the product of genetics or social factors, or a mix of both. The social factor for millions of unmarried Chinese men is clear: Many will live much of their adult lives in the company of other unmarried men with neither wives nor children. Throughout history there are stories of men living in segregation from women turning to other men for sex. Whether this will hold true for the bare branches remains to be seen, as much of Chinese society remains intolerant of homosexuality, especially among the uneducated, and these men may not be willing to cross that line, which carries with it the risk of stigmatization.

In 2004 the Chinese government announced its ambition to balance the sex ratio in just a few years, but this will almost certainly take generations. One solution might be relaxing the One-Child Policy, or even encouraging multiple births, unlikely as that may seem at the moment. China now faces a doubling of its number of senior citizens and a dwindling number of younger working people. This will put severe economic strains on younger people who will feel it is their duty to support their aging parents. With few or no siblings to help, there will be even more hardship. Except for those who are lucky enough to eventually get married, bare branches will not have children to support them as they grow older and this will put a strain on China's welfare system.

A book published in 2005, *Bare Branches: The Security Implications of Asia's Surplus Male Population,* actually entertained the notion that China and India might consider going to war to help balance their high surplus of men. One of the book's authors, political science professor Valerie M. Hudson, said in a 2005 interview, "In 2020 it may seem to China that it would be worth it to have a very bloody battle in which a lot of their young men could die in some glorious cause."

While the One-Child Policy may have met China's goals for population control, it has opened a Pandora's box of demographic, social and economic challenges that seem impossible to solve. Perhaps as Confucian values slowly wear away, future generations of Chinese will let go of the notion that they must have a son at any cost even if it means resorting to female infanticide. There is no indication such a shift is coming anytime soon. For thousands of years China has been a country where change occurs slowly. That pattern changed in the late 1970s when China transformed seemingly overnight from an inward-focused backwater to manufacturing hub of the world. The sexual revolution that began shortly afterward has paralleled this spectacular trajectory, though with many fits and starts.

Where will it go from here? No one knows, but all trends point to increasing liberalization and tolerance. China's sexual revolution is real. Government intervention and thought policing may slow it down but it cannot halt the progress unless it wants to cut the country off the way Mao did. It is simply not possible for a nation to encourage greater economic freedom without allowing greater personal freedom, and that includes sexual freedom. In this regard, China is paralleling most other societies that have loosened their grip on their citizens – but with some important caveats.

While there have been rapid advances in sexual freedom, they are still largely on the government's terms, and that is key to understanding the difference between China's sexual revolution and the one that engulfed the West nearly half a century ago. The Chinese government has made a Faustian bargain with its people to give them freedom in their bedrooms and personal lives in exchange for a government with near-total political control.

In the West, the sexual revolution was about self-expression and the abandonment of inhibitions. Some of its hallmarks were multiple sex partners, the celebration of nudity, full sexual expression no matter one's sexuality and the rejection of all forms of censorship. China is not there yet. Nudity is all but forbidden, multiple partners are frowned upon and censorship is the law of the land, even if it often does not work. The Chinese are certainly expressing their sexuality far more freely, especially after sex bloggers like Muzimei opened a nationwide dialogue on sex for the sake of sex. But many Chinese remain sexually inhibited, especially those outside of the international cities. Change is being led by Shanghai and Beijing; rural areas lag far behind and always will.

No matter how much more freedom there is in China today, the government still draws the lines in the sand. When Li Yinhe pushed the envelope on gay marriage at the National People's Congress in 2007 she was told to "shut up" by the powers that be and the subject was closed. In 2010, a 53-year-old professor who ran wife-swapping parties in Nanjing was sentenced to three and a half years in prison for "group licentiousness." (This caused Li Yinhe to speak out, unsuccessfully, for legalizing wife swapping since it was a victimless crime.) That may seem harsh, but keep in mind that a similar wife-swapper arrested in the mid-1980s for organizing a sex party was sentenced to death. China's leaders have loosened the reins, but they still hold the reins.

"Sweeping the Yellow" campaigns continue to "strike hard" against pornography and prostitution. These efforts are erratic and ineffective, but they do happen regularly and they can be brutal. Gay parks are still raided and personal web sites that go too far, sexually or politically, can vanish overnight. The conservative forces within the government still have enormous sway.

China's past keeps pushing against its present. Even the most liberated young people in Beijing and Shanghai have a hard time escaping the influence of Confucius and his focus on filial piety, family and harmony. Young people everywhere in China still believe they must include their parents in their marriage plans. For nearly all of them, heterosexual and homosexual, not getting married is simply not an option. Most Chinese families still want a male heir to carry on the family lineage. And Chinese husbands still place a high premium on their wives' virginity.

All of this is changing. Most Chinese people now choose their own spouse, and most of them have premarital sex. It is now easier than ever for Chinese couples to get a divorce. Young people in China's cities are not afraid of public displays of affection. Gay men and women have resources for support and advice, and in the cities there are venues where they do not have to hide who they are. Bloggers can go surprisingly far writing about their love lives. The Internet, more than any other force, has opened the floodgates for sexual expression and exploration, and there is no going back.

Even politically, the people are gaining a bigger voice, routinely criticizing the government on blogs and social media – but usually within boundaries that are tacitly agreed upon. Certain topics like the Tiananmen Square troubles of 1989 and Taiwan independence remain off limits, but the government has been surprisingly tolerant of online discussions criticizing official corruption and ineptitude. As personal freedoms increase, there is no doubt people are going to demand more political freedoms and greater rule of law. Most Chinese people have not yet made these their highest priorities, but the seeds have been sown and the Chinese people will want a greater say in *all* aspects of their lives. Greater freedoms will come, albeit slowly, in a manner different from Western-style democracy; the Chinese will always have their own way of doing things.

The gender imbalance poses the most immediate threat to the sex lives of millions of Chinese. There is no simple solution. Chinese people are slowly shedding their Confucian traditions, and while many Chinese people are coming to view a female child as equally valuable as a male, statistics indicate the preference for a male child remains largely intact. It will be a slow evolution, but it can already be seen in the big cities. (A 2009 survey of 3,500 prospective parents conducted by Shanghai's family planning commission showed that a slight majority of couples in the city actually preferred their only child to be a girl.)

After years of dragging its feet, the Chinese government is now aggressively combating the spread of HIV/AIDS by launching awareness campaigns and providing antiretroviral drugs to many of those infected. They still have a lot of catching up to do, however, especially in the treatment of men who have sex with other men. Sex education remains woefully inadequate, but recent test programs in Beijing and Shanghai that teach sex to children at younger ages show promise. China knows that education is the key to preventing STDs and unwanted pregnancy, and perhaps future generations of teachers will be able to overcome their own squeamishness and inform students what they need to know about contraception and sexual health. Unfortunately, the countryside lags far behind when it comes to sex education, and the most one can hope for is that progress in the cities will eventually spread outward.

China's sexual revolution started in the 1980s, now more than thirty years ago, and will almost certainly continue until what was taboo just a few generations ago becomes the new normal. China still needs to overcome its stigmatization of gays and its Confucian attitudes toward women. And the government needs to get out of the business of sexual repression, unlikely as that is in the foreseeable future. But look at how far the country has come over so little time. There is still the potential for China to overcome past prejudices and to recognize sexual freedom as a fundamental human right. We may never see a society devoted to Daoist sex manuals and complete sexual liberation, but China does appear to be well on the course, however rocky, to greater sexual openness, tolerance and freedom. It is long overdue.

SELECTIVE
BIBLIOGRAPHY

Backhouse, Sir Edmund. *Décadence Mandchoue*. Ed. Derek Sandhaus. Hong Kong: Earnshaw Books, 2011.

Davis, Edward Lawrence. *Encyclopedia of Contemporary Chinese Culture*: Routledge, 2004.

Dougherty, Niklas. *Prostitution in China*. Master's thesis, Lund University, Sweden. 2006.

Fang Fu Ruan, *Sex in China: Studies in Sexology in Chinese Culture*: Plenum Press, 1991.

Francoeur, Robert T. , ed. *The International Encyclopedia of Sexuality: Volume I - IV 1997-2001*: Continuum Publishing Company, 2001.

Hans von Gulik, Robert. *Sexual Life in Ancient China: A Preliminary Survey of Chinese Sex and Society*: Brill Academic Publishers, 1964.

Hinsch, Bret. *Passions of the Cut Sleeve: The Male Homosexual Tradition in China*: University of California Press, 1992.

Honig, Emily. *Modern China, Vol. 29, No. 2*. "Socialist Sex: The Cultural Revolution Revisited": Sage Publications, 2003.

Hvistendahl, Mara. *Public Affairs*. "Unnatural Selection: Choosing Boys Over Girls, and the Consequences of a World Full of Men,": Perseus Books Group, 2011.

Jacobs, Katrien. *People's Pornography: Sex and Surveillance on the Chinese Internet*: Intellect Ltd., 2012.

Jeffreys, Elaine. *China, Sex and Prostitution:* Taylor & Francis, 2007.

SELECTIVE BIBLIOGRAPHY

Jeffreys, Elaine. *Sex and Sexuality in China*: Routledge, 2009.

Sang, Tze-lan Deborah. *The Emerging Lesbian: Female Same-sex Desire in Modern China*: University Of Chicago Press, 2003.

Shane, Kimberly. *Pleasures of the Bitten Peach: An Exploration of Gender & Sexuality in Late Imperial China*. Honors Thesis, University Of Vermont, 2009.

Sommer, Matthew H. *Sex, Law and Society in Late Imperial China*: Stanford University Press, 2000.

Dr Tan Chong Kee. "Same-sex Love in Ancient and Modern Chinese History", Internet. www.fridae.asia. 2007

Wu, Cuncun. *Homoerotic Sensibilities in Late Imperial China*: Routledge Curzon, 2004.

Yau Ching, ed. *As Normal as Possible: Negotiating Sexuality and Gender in Mainland China and Hong Kong*: Hong Kong University Press, 2010.

FOOTSORE 3

WALKS AND HIKES AROUND PUGET SOUND

SECOND EDITION

By Harvey & Penny Manning/Photos by Bob & Ira Spring
Maps by Gary Rands/The Mountaineers: Seattle

Footsore 3

Walks & Hikes Around Puget Sound

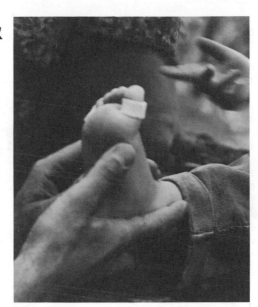

Second
Edition

By Harvey and Penny Manning/Photos
by Bob & Ira Spring/Maps by Gary Rands

Whulge Trail — Everett to Bellingham •
Stillaguamish River • Skagit River •
The Western Isles • The Northern Isles •
North Kitsap and Olympic Peninsulas

THE MOUNTAINEERS

Organized 1906

"...to explore, study, preserve, and enjoy the natural beauty of the Northwest."

Published by The Mountaineers
1011 S.W. Klickitat Way, Suite 107, Seattle WA 98134
Published simultaneously in Canada by Douglas & McIntyre, Ltd.,
1615 Venables Street, Vancouver, B.C. V5L 2H1
Published simultaneously in Great Britain by Cordee,
3a DeMontfort Street, Leicester, England LE1 7HD

Manufactured in the United States of America
Edited by Barbara Chasen
Maps by Gary Rands
Cover photograph: Driftwood on the shore of the Strait of Juan de Fuca
Book layout by Nick Gregoric

Library of Congress Cataloging-in-Publication Data
(Revised for volume 3)

Manning, Harvey.
    Footsore 3: walks & hikes around Puget Sound.

    Includes indexes.
    1. Hiking—Washington (State—Puget Sound Region—Guide-books. 2. Puget Sound Region (Wash.)—Description and travel—Guide-books. I. Title.
GV199.42.W22P835   1982   917.97'79   82-2100
ISBN 0-89886-156-X (v. 1)
ISBN 0-89886-187-X (v. 3)

INTRODUCTION 3

Footsore being a single book, though in four volumes, it would be wasteful of time and paper to repeat the same introductory information over and over again. Each of the four volumes therefore specializes. Here, the subject is beachwalking. *Footsore 4* summarizes the maps indispensable or helpful to the walker. *Footsore 2* describes the operation of a commercial tree farm and how to be reasonably content there.

Introduction 1 to *Footsore 1* is basic to the series. The data-coding system is explained, the Two-Hour Rule, and the Ten Essentials. The Trespasser's Code (briefly summarized later in these pages) lays out the commandments for behavior on those private lands (notably tree farms) where the owners have a "pass through" policy, or "tolerated trespassing." *Footsore 1*'s introduction to the Whulge Trail summarizes what was considered the law of the beach, explaining why owners of waterfront property think their rights extend out over tidelands. Students of the common law always have known they are wrong; statute law now confirms it. In 1987 the Washington State Supreme Court, in *Caminiti v. Boyle*, ruled that the Public Trust Doctrine gives the public certain inalienable rights on so-called "private" beaches. Among these is the right of passage on foot. (Note: the doctrine *does not* give the right to cross private uplands to get to the beach.)

Please, dear reader, never ever tell an irate beach "owner" that "the *book* says we can walk here." Read *Footsore 1*'s several introductions and help keep us out of nuisance lawsuits. If told to go away, do so, smiling; at most politely saying, "*Caminiti v. Boyle*, State Supreme Court, 1987." Then *run*.

Much Footsore country is in such flux that a guidebook cannot give a moneyback guarantee. No sooner does a new edition come out praising the wild solitude of a certain beach than a wealthy Privatizer erects a castle there and sics his dogs and lawyer on us. Nature, too, has a hand in land management. This volume was fully surveyed—every described route was walked —in 1977-78. In 1981 and 1983 the more popular and vulnerable routes were revisited. In early 1988 the surveyors, now two in number (not counting the photographer, who also served), conducted a front-to-back revision. Every trailhead was checked. Trips were thrown out that had been trashed or Privatized beyond redemption. Exciting new trips were discovered and walked. Old trips that needed close looks also were walked. (In some cases they were surveyed by eyeball from a distance; if no disruption was seen, the previous description was repeated. Joyous as it would be to walk every one of the trips every year or two, that is not economically practical. Happily, long stretches of beach see little significant change in 10 years, or 10,000.) Current information supplied by trustworthy native guides was embodied, and bless their hearts. The text is candid when fire or snow or other impediment prevented the walking or rewalking of a trip.

Should you find a situation not as we describe, check the date on the copyright page. Reflect on how much growth the trees have put on since then. How many houses have been built, forests shipped overseas. But please do complain—your cards and letters are a welcome help in keeping the book current.

Whulge: The Saltwater We Know

Vancouver, in 1792, placed "Puget's Sound" south of "The Narrows," where it remained while the Hudson's Bay Company established a post there and the first Americans settled nearby. Later arrivals, some farmers, some loggers, some fishermen, more real estate speculators, found the good sites on Puget Sound already platted and had to look for opportunities to the north. But town-boomers had to have Eastern money to make a big noise, and Easterners hadn't heard of any waters except Puget Sound. Boomers therefore claimed their plats were on Puget Sound; by saying so they made it so. Puget Sound expanded north to Whidbey Island.

That has been a done deed for a century and it would be pointless to try to convince Seattleites they live on Admiralty Inlet. But Puget Sound didn't stop growing. People in the young city of Seattle, newly in from the East and with a dim view north, and people in the middle-aged city of Seattle, newly in from the East and with no notion where they are, have pushed Puget Sound steadily toward Canada, the ocean.

They are more to be pitied than censured. As they gain rudimentary orientation, they discover innumerable saltwaterways, each with a name, but no umbrella name to plainly state the self-evident truth that they are a unity, parts of a whole. Vancouver saw this straight off and called them collectively, "Gulph of Georgia." Though his personal popularity survived America's Manifest Destiny, not so that of King George III; the "Gulph" was deported to Canada. Japan had had an "Inland Sea" for centuries; there wasn't room on the globe for another. No other candidate came to mind, and so it was that Puget Sound began moving toward encompassing everything wet except rain and root beer. The more thoughtful of the new arrivals began to feel uneasy about calling the San Juans, as one magazine did, "Islands in the Sound"; they took to speaking of "Greater Puget Sound" and "North Puget Sound." The one falls on the ear as sweetly as "Greater Seattle." The other is what old settlers call the waters off Edmonds.

Walking north on the shores of Possession Sound, Port Susan, Skagit Bay, Padilla Bay, Samish Bay, Chuckanut Bay, Bellingham Bay, and the rest, the surveyors of this book grew increasingly discontented with the umbrella of Peter Puget. They became consumed by the waters' needs—and their own needs—for a Big Name. An authentic name. A name with deep roots and meaning. Their route passed the present or former homes of people who had lived by this water for a dozen thousand years. Did they have a name?

Indeed they did. Rendered in English as whulge, whulj, whulch, whole-itch, and khwulch, it means "sea, ocean, sound, saltwater, any and all saltwater where Lushootseed-speakers live." The language of the Salish peoples from Olympia to the Skagit River is Lushootseed. For thousands of years the saltwater of their homes has been Whulge.

Much time must pass before the hundreds of governmental agencies and citizen groups can be convinced to buy new letterhead. Indeed, the surveyors and their publisher are not, in this edition, quite ready to change the name to "Walks and Hikes Around the Whulge." Next time.

What That Old Glacier Did

Four *glaciations* by the Juan de Fuca and Puget Lobes of the Cordilleran Ice Sheet, which in the Pleistocene Epoch invaded from Canada, have been identified in Western Washington lowlands. First were the Orting and Stuck Glaciations, of unknown dates (but less than 2-3 million years ago); their handiwork has been obscured by successors. The Salmon Springs Glaciation culminated prior to 38,000 years ago with a maximum reach 15-20 miles south of Olympia. After the Olympia Interglaciation came the Fraser Glaciation, with three *stades* (intervals of advance). Between 15,000 and 13,500 years ago, during the second, the Vashon Stade, Seattle was under 3300-4000 feet of ice. (Maximum ice depth in the Bellingham area was about 5250-7000 feet; Olympia, about 1200-1400 feet; the terminus 100 feet). The glacier pushed beyond the Nisqually River but stayed only briefly in its southernmost extension and Vashon drifts thus are scanty there. The Everson Interstade was succeeded by the Sumas Stade of 11,000 years ago; this time the Canadian ice barely got over the border.

Only in several areas does hard rock outcrop on *Footsore* shores, which mainly are of *glacial drift*, a term inclusive of all materials transported by the ice. An *erratic* is a boulder that rode the glacier until ultimately dumped. *Till* is an unsorted mixture of particles of every size from clay to boulders; the concrete-like "hardpan" characteristically erodes into vertical walls. Most drift has been sorted by meltwater,

Rosario Strait from Juniper Point

sand and *gravel* deposited by water of lesser or greater velocity in river beds or deltas, *clay* settling out in lakes from ice-milled rock milk. Drift overridden by the glacier during its advance was compressed and hardened. Organic materials from trees and plants that grew during the glacial lulls were sealed up by clay, preserved from total oxidation and rot, and became blackish layers of *peat*.

Fraser-Vashon drift, the most abundant, is relatively unconsolidated and new-looking when it dates from the retreat, quite compact if from the advance. Whether a lay walker can readily distinguish the older Vashon drifts from the Salmon Springs is debatable. However, he will frequently observe old-looking drift, more compacted (by weight of later ice) or even folded or faulted, often somewhat cemented by yellow-orange iron oxides, getting along toward becoming mudstones, shales, sandstones, and conglomerates; cliffs of this "nearly rock" may be quite tall and vertical.

The walker also sees peat beds containing branches and logs, cedar bark and fir cones, that appear to have come from the woods mere months ago.

A surveyor of the mountain front cannot comprehend the terrain ("island" peaks, riverless valleys) without knowing there once was a Really Big River, maybe two or three times the volume of today's Columbia, the sum of all the mountain rivers thwarted from direct seaward courses by the northern wall of ice stretching across the Puget Trough from Olympics to Cascades. Forced southward along the ice margin, Really Big eventually attained the ocean via the valley of today's Chehalis.

Similarly, a surveyor of Whulge beaches must realize that the glacier caused ups and downs of the water surface and thus the shore location. First, the ice wall from range to range dammed freshwater Lake Russell, which to empty south to the Chehalis River had to fill to a height substantially above the modern Whulge. The trained eye discerns, at various levels above today's beaches, representing various levels of the old lake, the flats of old bay floors/lakebeds, the steeps of wave-cut cliffs.

5

Sandpipers searching for food on Dungeness Spit

Then, when the ice front retreated north and let the salt flow in, there wasn't as much water as now, much of the world's supply being locked up in continental glaciers. As these melted, sea level rose some 200 (or 300?) feet from the Pleistocene minimum, reaching today's approximate level about 5000-6000 years ago. Above the beachwalker may be one or more fossil shores; below, unseen under water, may be a drowned shore.

Finally, the land, released from its burden of ice, has risen, in recent millennia, enough for old beaches to be elevated several feet above today's beaches. During postglacial earthquakes certain former beaches have been bumped up 20 feet or more above sea level.

But it's not all that simple (?). Sea level and land surface rose simultaneously, at different rates. Sea level is still slowly rising. Maybe the land surface, too.

How Beaches Get How They Are

The *coast* is an indefinite strip landward from shore. The *shore* is the narrow zone between low-tide shoreline and high-tide shoreline. The *shoreline* is the intersection of water and land.

The chief agents in eroding the shore are wind-generated *waves* that carve *wave-cut cliffs* whose debris forms *beaches* of gravel (cobbles, pebbles, and granules), sand (coarse to fine), and mud (silt and clay). Waves that strike the shore obliquely have a component of motion along the shore; the resulting *longshore currents* transport materials, depositing some on beaches, using some to build *spits* and *bars*. In any locality the orientation of spits and bars is determined by the direction of the dominant longshore current, a resultant of the dominant winds and the orientation of the shore. (*Tidal currents* go back and forth and accomplish relatively little constructive.)

As waves erode inland the beach widens. The retreating cliff leaves behind a *wave-cut bench*, a platform of rock (or, in most of our area, drift) usually covered with sand and gravel that gradually are moved seaward by the *undertow* and dumped in deep water, forming a *wave-built terrace*, at whose outer edge is the dropoff that wading children are warned against.

Width of the bench and terrace and thus the beach they constitute depends partly on how long the waves have been at it; Whulge isn't old enough for much erosion of the hard-rock shores and that's why there's so little beachwalking in such places as the San Juan Islands and the west side of Hood Canal.

Beach width also depends on vigor of the waves, which depends on strength of the wind. Weather shores (in our area, mainly south and west) tend to have the wider beaches, lee shores (north and east) the narrower; in fiordlike estuaries the wave action on all shores may be so feeble the beach is mere inches wide. Beaches of protected shores with meek waves are uncleanly green; trees typically lean horizontally far and over and close to the beach; fallen logs are not churned around and abraded to splinters or floated away, they just lie placidly where they fall, growing seaweed and barnacles. Walking such beaches, narrow and perhaps steep, cobbles weed-slimy, can be a misery of slithering and brushfighting and log-crawling and pulling seaweed out of your hair.

Beach width also depends on the vigor of longshore currents; where these are very strong they sweep away the materials from the bluff, drastically slimming the beach.

Not all shores have beaches. Rock cliffs may plunge directly into deep water. Delta and estuary *salt marshes* may merge with bay-bottom *tideflats*; some of these vast low-tide expanses of sand or mud, also found in shallow bays perhaps rimmed by skinny beaches, can be walked a long way from shore, far out in birdland.

As wave-cut bench plus wave-built terrace grow, the widening beach may become *"complete."* Above regularly washed sands and gravels a *driftwood line* of logs is thrown up by big storms and remains untouched by ordinary high tides, perhaps jostled once or twice a decade. Behind the driftwood is a sand ridge rising above the high-tide shoreline, a *dune line* of particles blown from sun-dried beach. Though usually not resembling the classic marching dunes of deserts, being mostly vegetation anchored, the sand ridge encloses a shallow *lagoon*; this may be freshwater, fed by a creek or seepage, may be dry in summer, may be partly freshwater marsh; or it may be tidal, connected to the sea by a channel, may be sometimes tideflat, may be partly saltmarsh; normally a lagoon holds a raft of old, bleached driftwood cast up by big storms.

A longshore current picks up material when it hits the shore, drops material when it runs out in deep water and loses momentum. When a current manages to fill an offshore area, creating a shallows, breaking waves then build an *offshore bar* that may be raised above the normal high-tide line by storm tides and ultimately connected to the shore, enclosing a lagoon—another route to a complete beach.

Longshore currents work to straighten out shores, by this process: When the shore bulges abruptly out or curves abruptly in, the currents tend to keep going straight, soon losing momentum in deep water and dropping loads. Thus *spits* are built. When one terminates in open water, it forms a *point*. When it connects mainland to an island, the latter becomes a *tombolo*. When a spit reaches across the mouth of a bay and nearly or completely closes it off, it's called a *baymouth bar*—here are the great big lagoons, marshes, dredged boat basins, fancy yacht-and-mansion subdivisions, ecological disasters. A delta pushed out into open water and subjected to the spit-building process typically becomes a *cuspate* hybrid.

Why the Tide Waits Not

Understanding the mechanism of tides is not essential to beachwalking; caused by the moon (most important) and sun (very helpful), they are shaped by some 250 factors only digestible by a computer. But the habits of tides are easily observed—and jolly well had better be if a walker doesn't care to become an involuntary surfer or cliff-clamberer.

Of the several types that occur around the world, our Whulge has a *mixed tide*, with two high-low cycles in a period of approximately 24 hours and 50 minutes (so, each day the tides are about 50 minutes later than the day before); alternate highs are nearly equal and lows very unequal, or vice versa.

INTRODUCTION

A tide is not, as commonly imagined, a ridge of water dogging the moon around the globe, but an up-and-down, thus in-and-out, motion in a tide basin, in our case the Pacific Ocean. The tide enters and leaves the Whulge mainly through the Strait of Juan de Fuca, to a minor extent through the Strait of Georgia. The tides thus are earlier near the ocean. The tide table for Seattle, published in the daily newspapers along with moon phases, is the reference for *Footsore* walkers; to correct for other areas, subtract 30 minutes for Dungeness Spit, 20 minutes for Quimper Peninsula and Whidbey Island's west coast, 10 minutes for Everett; add 6 minutes for Tacoma, 35 minutes for Steilacoom.

The difference on the open ocean between *high water*, the highest level of a tide cycle, and *low water*, the lowest, is much less than on the Whulge, where narrowing shores constrict the tidal current and "pile up" the water. At the mouth of Admiralty Inlet the *mean tide range* (the year's mean of the vertical differences between daily high and low waters) is a meager 4 feet; at Olympia it's a whopping 10.5 feet. At Seattle the daily tide range builds to around 16 feet in June and January, in May and October-November dwindles to as little as 1.7 feet.

Highs and lows vary a lot, depending on the mix of those 250 factors. In a recent year, Seattle's highest forecast highs (14 feet) came in December-January (and slightly less in June-July, the lowest high (7.4) in May (nearly matched in fall). The lowest lows (-3.3) were in June and January, the highest lows (7.2) in December-January-February. As can be seen, some highs are virtually the same as some lows. At Seattle, during a month the highs may vary up or down 4 feet or more, the lows 8 feet or more.

The greatest difference between high and low comes on a *spring tide*, which has nothing to do with the season but occurs twice every month, near new moon and full moon, when sun, moon, and earth are in line. The tide range at Seattle is then as much as 16 feet (a whole lot). The least difference is in a *neap tide*, near the first and last quarters of the moon, when the heavenly bodies are farthest out of line. The tide range at Seattle is then less than 2 feet (hardly anything).

Okay, those are the numbers. Which affect a beachwalk?

First is the *height of the high water*. Since that's how beaches are made, at the highest highs the waves are pummeling the cliff and anybody who gets in the way. Generally, then, when the high forecast for Seattle is 13 or 14 feet, there is going to be dang little beach anywhere on the Whulge. (Note: The forecast tides published in tide tables are the *astronomical tides* created by moon and sun and etc. The actual tides usually are to some extent *meteorological tides*, responding to differences in atmospheric pressure and force of winds and perhaps to a glut of water from flooding rivers; in *"sunshine tides"* with high atmospheric pressure, levels are under the forecast; in *storm tides* the levels may be several feet over the forecast. surprising the heck out of beachdwellers and delta farmers and marina operators and ferryboat captains.) With a forecast of 10 or 11 feet, and good weather, considerable stretches of beach will be easy-open at the high—but will be skinny and have many obstacles, such as bulkheads and fallen trees and pieces of slid-down bluff. With a forecast of 9 feet or less, most beaches will be mostly negotiable, though some obstacles may remain until the tide ebbs to 7 or 6 feet or less. Except on feeble-wave beaches, at that level the main obstacle may be human constructions.

Second is the *height of the low water*. Feeble-wave beaches are best walked at quite a low level to avoid a brushfight; however, an adjoining exposed mudflat can be a boot-sucking snare and delusion. (Note: The mudflat immediately adjoining the beach commonly is a soupy quickmud, due to the underground drainage of freshwater from the upland, while outside the narrow belt the mud/sand is wet and sticky but solid and easy-walking.) Strong-wave beaches may be most effortlessly walked on the wide, firm sands of a wave-built terrace exposed at a very low tide, much easier going than a sloping gravel beach.

Third is the *time of the high water*. In a neap tide the high may be so low there's nothing to worry about. In a spring tide, look out—some of those so-and-so's flood

Baywater Bay and Hood Head

scarily fast and practically climb the cliffs. When it is suspected the beach may be wiped out by the day's high, the better part of valor is to schedule the trip for an outgoing tide. If the high is around 8-10 in the morning, a person can set out then or soon after, and though perhaps forced to clamber the bank a little or crawl over logs or wait a while at obstacles, can journey relaxed and comfortable in the knowledge the beach will grow steadily until evening; the return will be a cinch. Walking on an incoming tide can be nervous business but is not irrational if the high is low, if the beach will be left well before the high, or if an escape is available leading to a decent overland return.

What do you do if there's no daytime neap or afternoon low? Head for the all-tides-walkable "complete beaches" of benches-terraces, baymouth bars, spits. Or hie yourself to a delta dike or a handy shoreside railroad trail.

Where To Find a Beach For Your Feet

Thanks to easily eroded glacial drift, most of the Whulge is beach shored. And thanks to the hiker's pal, that lovely and nearly omnipresent drift cliff, hundreds of miles of beach are "wild" — that is, "owners" are kept at a respectful distance from the water by walls of till and gravel and sand or, even better, clay that is ever on the move, dragging down trees and bushes and houses.

A bluff of 200 feet and more usually is just about a perfect guardian; houses may be atop but probably can't be seen and the residents rarely toil to and from the water. With lower bluffs the owners, though still normally out of sight on high, safely back from the unstable brink, maintain contact with the beach. Studying their means of doing so adds interest to a stroll. There are spiffy electric cablecars, cog railways, tramways, and inclined elevators; two-and-four-storey-tall timber stairways, masterpieces of engineering and carpentry; well-maintained, railing-protected, switchbacking trails; toboggan-slide mudchute paths; decrepit old staircases missing critical pieces and ending in air, the bottoms torn apart by storm waves; spooky ladders fit only for daring young fools; and even – heaven help us! – rope ladders dangled down overhangs. As the bluff lowers, houses approach the water, but even a bank of a mere dozen feet may shelter the stealthy beachwalker from picture-window eyes. It's when the bluff dwindles to naught that civilization uncomfortably crowds the waves. Near Puget Sound City, few indeed are the unbuilt-on spits and benches, and often bulkheads extend the flats along the bases of bluffs; these are the beach-destroying villains that compel an inland detour, a bulkhead scramble, a wade, or a wait for low tide.

If a walker can somehow get on a wild beach he's home free, often for miles. As with kayaking, it's the "put-in" that's the problem. (Unlike a kayaker, a walker isn't too concerned about the "take-out"; infrequently will residents muster with cutlasses to repel boarders.)

What's a good put-in? First, there must be someplace to park. This needn't be near the beach — after all, if you're going to be walking a few miles, another 1/4 or 1/2 mile is no sweat. Second, there must be access from road to beach without climbing a fence or walking through somebody's garden.

Contrary to the opinion of the masses, public parks are not necessarily good put-ins; in heavily populated areas, on summer Sundays the neighbors may be up to here with crowds swarming off the ends of public beaches, they may shout a lot, and gripe to park rangers, and call the police, who are uniformly unaware of Caminiti v. Boyle.

Sometimes a put-in can be made where there is no public access. Examples are a private community boat-launch or swimming beach and a subdivision with as-yet-vacant beach lots. The key to using these is to park a goodly distance — if necessary, 1/2 mile or more—away. A major agony of beach communities is slobby, thoughtless invaders leaving cars any old place, blocking driveways, clogging narrow streets. If the car is placed considerately and distant, an alien often can walk a private community road to a private boat-launch and onto a beach with no greeting from the locals but hospitable smiles — if even aware of the alien's presence, they'll usually assume he's some resident's guest.

This, of course, is thought by beach "owners" who haven't kept up with the court decisions to be trespassing, and for quite some while ought to be treated as such by the walking public. Such "trespassing" on beaches is best not done except where tolerated. And where is that? Well, in walking hundreds of miles of Whulge beaches the surveyors rarely were challenged. The reason, aside from niceness of beach residents, is that were "No Trespassing" to be enforced, not even locals could walk far, each property owner condemned to forever pace only his petty plot. (In many a beach community there is, in fact, a curmudgeon whose single purpose in a curdled life is to keep neighbors' feet off his sand.)

There definitely is a "toleration season." It cannot be precisely defined, differs from place to place, and must be sensed on the spot, but the elements are clear enough: Toleration is least on a sunny summer Sunday, near major population centers, on heavily built-up beaches; it's greatest in bad weather, on weekdays, in winter, at a goodly distance from the masses, on mostly wild beaches.

During put-in and take-out, and also while passing a row of water-close homes in the course of walking an otherwise wild beach, a person must adhere faithfully to the Trespasser's Code: travel not in mobs but in small groups, the smaller the better; leave the dogs home and also the kiddies if they can't be taught to stifle childish shrieks; be quiet; leave no trash and commit no offenses against sanitation; dig no clams and pick no oysters and gather no souvenirs; build no fires; do not picnic near homes; walk by houses quickly; do not stop to stare at the houses, the boats, the flowers, the sunbathers; walk as far from houses as the waves allow; under no circumstances walk through a yard, even if the tide is high and you must otherwise wade or turn back; if challenged, humbly apologize, say *"Caminiti v. Boyle,"* and go find another beach — there are plenty around.

Yes, beach people are mostly nice. And yes, respectful, discreet trespassers are accepted lots of places the loud-mouthed rowdies aren't. Still, the sanest, kindest, most generous and hospitable of beach folks will turn surly if too much imposed upon. Any "private" beach has a "carrying capacity" for "trespassers;" if the capacity is exceeded, the beach will be "destroyed" — defended against all alien walkers in all seasons, Supreme Court or no Supreme Court. Therefore, should you come to a planned put-in and observe others already trespassing, switch to another put-in, another beach.

Privates and Publics and the Conjunction of Four

When the older surveyor and the photographer were little boys, there was no such thing on the Whulge as a "private" beach. In the years after World War II, however, the region was invaded by people from the inland who did not know the common law. Assured by their lawyers that they "own" the beach, they seek to suppress the freedom which has prevailed on the Whulge for some 12,000 years.

Readers seeking a happy walk do well not to argue with the Privatizers. Don't start civil war on the beaches. Instead, sympathize with the folks who were swindled into building on spits and bars and terraces, in or near the driftwood.

The morning of December 16, 1977, the older surveyor's father looked out the window of his home on Hood Canal and was confounded to see that his large, sturdy dock had disappeared. There had been no storm, no night of howling winds. The water, in fact, was glassy calm. As he watched, his dock reappeared in the ebbing of a 14.63-foot (Seattle) tide, the highest on record (equalled on January 27, 1983). He was witnessing a Conjunction of Three: (1) a spring tide (a twice-monthly event); (2) heavy, warm, snow-melting rains in the mountains that caused rivers to dump more water in the Whulge than it could quickly flush to the ocean (which happens two or three times in a normal winter); and (3) a deep storm centered offshore in the Pacific, its extremely low pressure extending inland over the Whulge (an event of every other winter or so).

This Conjunction of Three (C/3) carried driftwood onto the porches of spit houses and into the privies of public parks, flowed over the tops of Skagit delta dikes, and set the more thoughtful of beach residents to brooding over what would have happened had that deep storm not remained in the Pacific but moved in on the Whulge. They knew the glassy water would have been stirred to furious waves pounding the spits and dikes. They realized that over the centuries the Conjunction of Four had occurred many many times and would again. Next winter, or the winter after. With a probability verging on certainty, within the lifetimes of people now living on the spits.

The National Weather Service has begun issuing "high tide warnings." The press has the subject permanently on its tickler calendar. Thankfully, therefore, few if any lives will be lost in the next C/4. In its wake, however, there surely will come a new public policy for "private" tidelands.

People laughed when the first edition of this book said Hood Canal Floating Bridge was temporary. The book was scarcely in the stores when, on February 13, 1979, Bridge I went to the bottom. When these surveyors make a prediction, you better listen.

Harvey and Penny Manning
Cougar Mountain

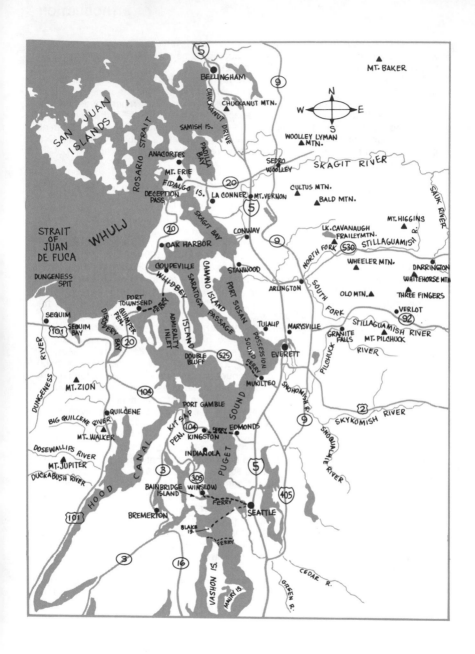

CONTENTS

TABLE OF CONTENTS

Safety Considerations

Safety is an important concern in all outdoor activities. No guidebook can alert you to every hazard or anticipate the limitations of every reader, so the descriptions in this book are not representations that a particular trip is safe for your party. When you take a trip, you assume responsibility for your own safety. Some of the trips described in this book may require you to do no more than look both ways before crossing the street; on others, more attention to safety may be required due to terrain, traffic, weather, the capabilities of your party, or other factors. Keeping informed on current conditions and exercising common sense are the keys to a safe, enjoyable outing.

The Mountaineers

WHULGE TRAIL –
EVERETT TO BELLINGHAM

The segment of the Whulge Trail described in these pages begins with the Everett waterfront. Once entirely logs and mills, the scene recently has added a variety of other attractions: shoppes and eateries, enormous fleets of stinkpots, a (proposed) museum display of obsolete ships of the U.S. Navy, and the best — easy ferry access to the sea lions on Jetty Island.

Next north is the estuary of the second-largest river to enter the American portion of Whulge, the Snohomish. Disdained for a century as mucky, stinky, and ugly, fit only for a log dump, garbage dump, and sewage dump, only now is it widely recognized as a prodigiously rich wildlife habitat, a wilderness treasure within the city of Everett-Marysville. Presently the pedestrian must be content with distant views. However, nothing bars him from borrowing or renting a boat. About once a month, Everett Park Department leads canoe trips to explore the estuary. For information call (206) 259-0300.

At Priest Point the estuary ends and Possession Sound beaches begin. From there to the head of Port Susan, the faithful bluff of glacial drift stands between homes and waves, wilderness interrupted only intermittently and briefly. Here is the most pristine mainland shore between Olympia and Bellingham.

Then commences the crossing of the deltas. The reader who wishes to learn "what it's really like (or was)" is referred to *Walking the Beach to Bellingham*, the story of how the older surveyor got from Seattle to Fairhaven in the late 1970s. Do not attempt to use that volume as a guidebook. The barb-wire fences have been strung tighter and higher.

In these pages the bad delta walking is excised, the good retained. The first of the deltas is that of the Stillaguamish River. Next is the South Delta of the Skagit, mainly composed of Fir Island, enclosed between the South Fork and North Fork distributaries of the Skagit; in modern times it has been on this delta that the Skagit has emptied mountain water into Skagit Bay.

The Middle Delta is bounded on the south by "captured islands" of the San Juan Archipelago, on the north by Pleasant Ridge "Island," a heap of glacial moraine, and on the west by Swinomish Channel, which cuts off Fidalgo into islandhood and connects Skagit Bay and Padilla Bay; in the 19th century the dikers halted most of the Skagit River overflows through the Middle Delta to the bays. The North Delta, from Pleasant Ridge "Island" to Elephant Mountain (Blanchard Hill), hasn't seen the big river in ages, only seepage and dribbles emptying to Padilla Bay and Samish Bay.

For the first edition of this book the older surveyor walked virtually every foot of the delta front, hoping to so publicize the route as to hasten its formal establishment as a trail. The immediate consequence was to the contrary. Paths where once the alien pedestrian was tolerated are now closed off by houses, fences, mean-it "No Trespassing" signs, and shotguns, even. Eventually the delta crossing *must* be opened to the Publics, not monopolized by Privatizers whose great-grandparents displaced the Samish, Skagit, ducks, and geese and who now sell the shooting rights to wealthy duckbusters.–"Must"—but not with this edition. The frontier (and still prevailing) law says dikes are the property of the abutting owner. There is some justice to this, since the owners, organized into diking districts, have largely built and maintained the dikes. Comes a wet disaster, though, as one does every several years, and they are not too proud to accept public funds for sandbags, doughnuts, and hot coffee. Come the C/4 in one grand "whoosh" returning the wetlands to the status of 1870, and government will be petitioned to rebuild the dikes. Government likely should and will do so—but at that time it must require trail easements.

The crossing of the deltas is unique among pedestrian routes of the West (and probably the East and South and North). Most walkers are drawn initially by the fleets of waterfowl sailing, mobs of shorebirds hustling, raptors patrolling, songbirds chirping. So famous is the birding that fans often fail to mention the panoramas over marshes and bays to islands and Olympics, over fields of corn and cabbage and tulips and cows to Cascades. Never are the mountains so dramatic as when seen from "at sea" in the overwhelming horizontality, where a walker feels so conspicuously vertical as almost to want to get down in the muck and wiggle.

History is central to the delta experience. Agriculture started even before the 1860s, when dikers began claiming (farmers and engineers insist on calling it "reclaiming," as if they were here first and Nature were the intruder) the riparian and tidal marshes. Hamlets founded in that era remain, charming antiques more or less hale, and everywhere are wonderful old barns and three-storey farmhouses replete with chimneys and gingerbread. The 19th century lives! And dies: there also are derelict houses sagging in the silt, rotten boats moldering in sloughs, decaying pilings thrust out in bays, and names on old maps marking the sites of vanished villages.

Not to be scorned is the walking of delta roads; the barnwatching is the best, as well as the savoring of the ripe aroma of manure, as characteristic of the delta as pulpmill perfume of Everett. The survey followed the boundary dike between crops on one side and tidal marsh or tideflat on the other. That no longer is feasible—rationally speaking, it wasn't feasible *then*. However, remember that at lower-than-middling tides there is walkable marsh and sandflat *outside the dikes.* The farmer-gunner may claim these tidelands are Private. The rule is to never argue with a red-faced, hollering man who is brandishing a shotgun.

The conclusion of the Trail is as unique as the delta. After sitting far back from saltwater in all its length from California, here the Cascade Range juts out to the shore and from the loftiness of Chuckanut Mountain plummets to the beach. Except there's darn little beach. Just rock cliffs. Never fear. To the rescue of the hiker comes his old friend from the south, the familiar pair of shining steel rails leading onward from Samish Bay to Chuckanut Bay to Bellingham Bay and the triumphant denouement of the Whulge Trail. Fairhaven Historic District, that is.

USGS maps: Everett, Marysville, Tulalip, Stanwood, Juniper Beach, Utsalady, Conway, La Conner, Deception Pass, Bow, Anacortes, Bellingham South Walkable all year

Mile 0–6¹/₂: Everett Waterfront-Snohomish River-Marysville (map—page 20)

When last heard from (*Footsore 1*) the Whulge Trail had skinnied along the railroad tracks between the shore bluff and two Weyerhaeuser pulpmills, one dying and the other sick, to the Everett Amtrak station. Both mills are now extinct, replaced by Port of Everett facilities, but the tracks still proceed north. Another way to the Amtrak station is to drive I-5 to Exit 192, go west on Broadway to Hewitt, turn left 1 mile to Bond Street, and left again to plentiful parking.

The Trail sets out north beside the railroad tracks, soon passing the site of the Everett Massacre, where on "Bloody Sunday," November 5, 1916, some 17 Wobblies and 2 special deputy sheriffs were killed, and 47 from both forces wounded, as the steamer *Verona* attempted to unload its free-speech passengers. The surveyors were unable to find a memorial to Milltown's most dramatic moment.

The next point of interest is the Scott sulphite (white paper) pulpmill, whose stack gases are now so thoroughly scrubbed as to emit little but water vapor; when atmospheric conditions are right, the stack sends a tall white plume skyward, marking the position of Everett for travelers at a distance on seas or on mountains. The walking route turns away from the tracks, up California to West Marine View Drive and thence north.

Immediately north of the Scott complex is the U.S. Navy Home Port for aircraft carriers, cruisers, destroyers, and frigates, a basic battle group that in time might be expanded to 20 ships or decreased to zero. Critics in Congress and the U.S. Navy itself comment that carriers are as obsolete in 1988 as battleships were in 1941.

Pulpmill at mouth of Snohomish River in Everett

Jetty Island ferry leaving Everett

At 1 ¼ miles from the Amtrak station is the big business for the sightseeing walker, Marina Village. At the entrance is a gabled, Tudor-style building constructed in 1927 as local headquarters for Weyerhaeuser, moved in 1938 from the location of the company's first sawmill, at the foot of Pacific Avenue, to the sawmill-pulpmill complex on the Snohomish River east of Highway 99, and in 1984 to a third location, where it serves as quarters for the Chamber of Commerce. Weyerhaeuser's pulpmills on the waterfront were dismantled in the early 1980s. The sawmill on the Snohomish River, built in 1915, was closed in 1979 and burnt in 1982. Mill E, built in 1971, was closed in 1984—Everett's last sawmill. Though Milltown retains small processing mills and two pulpmills, it now mainly is Logtown — lakes of logs, seas of logs, oceans of logs floating in waterways, mountains of logs piled on reclaimed tideflats, waiting for shipment overseas, so that America can afford to import dirtbikes, ATVs, and ORVs.

Marina Village offers restaurants, inns, knicknack shoppes, and free parking. A walkway around the outer rim gives view of 2000-odd play boats in slips and a number of millions of logs in the bay. At the south end of the village is the *Equator*, a two-masted schooner built in 1888, in California, as a South Seas trader and mail boat. Robert Louis Stevenson chartered her to cruise the South Pacific and is said to have written *Treasure Island* while aboard.

Jetty Island. Now for something really excellent. Thursdays through Sundays, from mid-July through the first week of September, a passenger ferry carries visitors from the Marina to Jetty Island, the breakwater which encloses Everett's harbor. The ferry runs from 10 A.M. to 6 P.M., every half-hour or so; the fare is $1 for adults (1988), free under 17.

Heaped up from dredging spoils at the turn of the century, the manmade "spit" has developed beaches and dunes and marine vegetation, just as if it were a real spit. The birds and sea creatures love it. So do the sea lions. The whole 2 miles, from Snohomish River to Home Port, are open to walking (allow 5 hours for a round trip). The route, including a nature trail that samples the life systems from the lug worms to the dune grass where the voles hide, was not surveyed for this guide because the survey was done during the off-season. The next edition will include a fitting rhapsody.

The ferry is small and the island popular. It is advisable to make reservations with the Everett Park Department (259-0311). Rangers lead natural-history walks twice a day.

North from Marina Village at 10 Street, 1 ³/₄ miles from Amtrak, is the jutting fill of an enormous Port of Everett boat-launch; plentiful parking and a jolly good viewpoint of logs rafted in Port Gardner, protected by Jetty Island from stormy winds that blow, and the Olympics beyond.

The next ³/₄ mile along West Marine View Drive is on the shore walkway by gardens, parking areas, and grand views, of Port Gardner Bay South View and North View Parks.

Where mills resume, West Marine View Drive (formerly Norton Avenue) climbs the bluff to join Alverson Boulevard. A mandatory sidetrip is the ¹/₂-mile walk up the viaduct to Legion Memorial Park and its blufftop viewpoint. Tremendous. Down Possession Sound to the pastel oil tanks of Mukilteo, over to little Gedney (Hat) Island and long Whidbey Island and the Olympics, to Camano Head and Port Susan, north over the Snohomish estuary to Wheeler, Frailey, Devils, Cultus, Baker.

Back down by the water, the Trail returns to railroad for a mile, rounds Preston Point to banks of the Snohomish River, passes Weyerhaeuser's stupendous hissing rumbling steaming kraft (brown-bag) pulpmill to Delta Junction, beside the twin bridges of old Highway 99.

Scramble up the embankment to old 99. There's nothing for it — the 2 ³/₄ miles to Marysville are all road-walking. But definitely worth it. In succession are crossed: Snohomish River (views downstream to the kraftmill, source of the other Everett-identifying steam plume); Smith Island (a huge log dump and sawdust mountain); Union Slough and a nameless island (nice boatyard); Steamboat Slough (another pair of drawbridges, for a total of five bridges over the slough; more views to the Cascades); a large island on the Tulalip Indian Reservation; Ebey Slough (be careful before crossing it to go left on 99); Marysville and a final batch of ducks, boatworks, and mills.

(Happy note: In 1988 the DNR sold the City of Everett 97 acres on Smith Island for a park. Watch for it).

Mile 6 ¹/₂—9 ¹/₂: Snohomish Estuary (map—page 20)

These 3 miles of the "Trail" are not walkable; the pilgrim in quest of Bellingham must detour inland on Marine Drive or hitch a ride on a passing inner tube. The banks of Ebey Slough are not gently sloping gravel but steep mud. The final tributary of the Snohomish, Quilceda Creek, comes to the confluence through a fine, wild, tidal marsh. When open beach begins, it is clogged by broken boats, rotten fragments of mills, and a miscellany of Everett debris washed up by a century of southwesterlies. (Opened in 1988 too late to be surveyed for this edition, Riverfront Park provides 1 mile of Snohomish riverbank for walking. From I-5 northbound, follow signs from Exit 195; southbound, from Exit 198.)

However, there is much to think about and see—1900 acres of the estuary of the second-largest river (after the Skagit) to enter the Whulge. In 1884 there were 12,000 acres. Industry, highways, the Everett sewage lagoon, log mountains, and other appurtenances of civilization have consumed most of the primeval estuary. The remainder nevertheless deserves the name, The Great Marsh. The labyrinth of sloughs and deadend channels, the archipelago of islands, remind of Mississippi bayous. It makes a walker want to be a boater. Still, the chief argument for

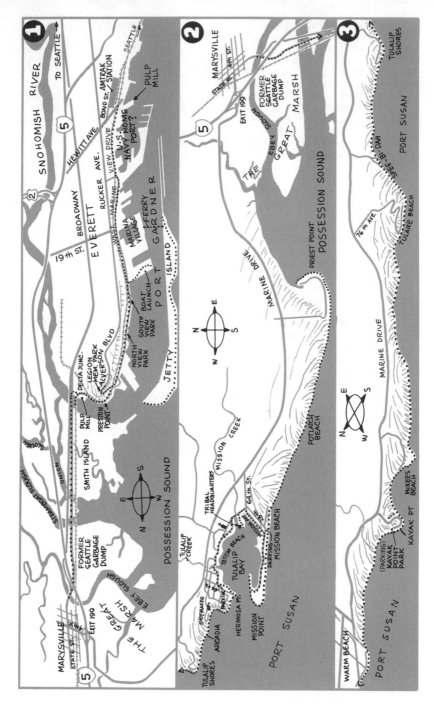

preservation of the remaining estuary, an urban wilderness that is half water, half wetland, is not the pleasure of humans but the habitat of wildlife.

The goal of the Snohomish Wetlands Alliance is to purchase the Quilceda Marsh, most of Smith Island, and much of the wetlands along Ebey Slough, Steamboat Slough, and Union Slough upstream to the tip of Ebey Island. Clean up a century of junk, perhaps brush out a few dike paths for birders afoot, and leave wetlands and waters to the birds and the beasts and such quiet human friends as come to pay respects. That's the plan for the Snohomish estuary.

Mile 12 ½–9 ½: Mission Beach-Priest Point (map—page 20)

At Priest Point the Snohomish estuary ends and Whulge beaches begin, miles of Possession Sound shores guarded from human intrusion by a bluff as high as 200 feet and for most of its length formidably vertical.

At Priest Point (site of a Catholic mission in 1858; the bell is now in St. Anne's Church, Tulalip) true beach resumes. However, getting on the beach through the solid row of homes is chancy. A wild-eyed (but polite) pedestrian bearing a strange device ("Bellingham or Bust") might be let through; most folks had better do this as a 3-mile walk from the north.

Drive Marine Drive north from I-5 (Exit 199), turn left on 64 Street (signed "Mission Beach, Tulalip Bay, Tribal Center") a scant 0.5 mile to a Y. Go left on 28 Avenue 0.5 mile. Just across the street from the fire station, note a turnout atop the low bluff and a roadway down to old pilings of the vanished Mission Beach Boathouse. Do not park here. Instead, drive back up the county road to any handy turnout that is not posted and walk back down to this beach access.

Below-bluff, trail-access-only cottages of Mission Beach quickly end and for 1 mile the beach is wonderfully lonesome under the naked bluff topped by an overhanging tangle of forest. Staircases down from homes of Potlatch Beach begin, and continue 1 mile, but the houses stay up where they belong. Then the bluff yields to the spit of Priest Point, ¾ mile of hip-to-hip houses waiting for the C/4. A person must debate whether or not to round the point to the salvage-tug dock in the angle between river slough and bay beach, where used to be the lagoon outlet.

The view is grand over Possession Sound to Jetty Island, guarding Port Gardner harbor, to pulpmill plumes, to oil tanks and ferry of Mukilteo, to ships at anchor and ships underway, to rotting old hulks — all in all, the best middle-distance perspective on Milltown. Also look to Gedney (Hat) and Whidbey Islands, to Cascades from Three Fingers to Index. Hear the drone of Everett, savor the rich aroma of pulp.

Mile 12 ½–16 ½: Mission Beach-Tulalip Bay (map— page 20)

The feature is picturesque little Tulalip Bay, and a cozy spot it is, with a ton of history, much of it painful. Here are headquarters of the Tulalip Reservation to which Governor Stevens and the U.S. Army herded the Snohomish, Stillaguamish, Snoqualmie, and Sammamish peoples.

From Mission Beach the Trail goes 1 mile north on fine under-the-bluff beach to "Mission Point," whose long arm enwraps Tulalip Bay on the southwest. On the bay side a long sandspit invites a sidetrip out in the middle of the bay for close looks at the hamlets of Tulalip, Totem Beach, and Mission Beach. At low tide walkers can then get off the beach onto public road, Mission Beach Drive, and loop back past a fleet of pleasure craft floating, and a fleet sunken, so many moldering wrecks the waters appear to have been the scene of a miniature Pearl Harbor.

Just before the fire station, turn north on Mission Avenue. Joining 28 Avenue at 64 Street, the way passes a broad flat on a stubby peninsula, former site of a village, then of the Indian Agency Office, and now the business and social center of the peoples.

Crossing Mission Creek and passing through Totem Beach, the road passes below pretty and historic St. Anne's Church. From there a new road rounds the bay but the old road, blocked off, can be walked to Tulalip Creek, dammed for a salmon-rearing pond from which the Tulalips have released some 5,000,000 juvenile salmon since

Sunken Boats in Tulalip Bay

1970. A detour to the beach gets around the closed-off bridge. In a scant ½ mile more the road is joined by 44 Avenue and reaches a gap in houses, a mass of logs and pilings, and a large, undeveloped, public parking area, base for hikes south and north.

To reach this parking area, from Marine Drive turn westerly on 44 Avenue, signed "Hermosa Point," and drop 0.2 mile to the water.

Mile 16 ½–24: Tulalip Bay-Kayak Point Park (map— page 20)

When nominating sections of the Trail for the Best Walks Award, don't omit this beauty. At a half-dozen spots roads have crept down the treacherous bluffs, but these are brief interruptions; there are three 1-mile wild stretches and three shorter ones, and more than half the length is utterly lonesome. The only public accesses are at the ends of the strip.

The way rounds Hermosa Point, with views south to pulpmill plumes, to mountains from Si to Rainier to Olympics. North of the point ¾ mile is the last piling-protected boathouse (of Arcadia) and the start of the first wild bit, 1 ¼ miles long. From beneath the noble bluff, largely sand with blue-clay cliffs, up to 200 feet tall, the views south to Whidbey Island begin to yield to Camano Head and Island, across the mouth of Port Susan.

A bulge is rounded, views of Tulalip Bay are lost, and homes of Tulalip Shores occupy ¼ mile of a narrow sand flat. A scant ½ mile of empty beach leads to the wide valley and cute old community of Spee-Bi-Dah, one-time summer cottages clinging to forest hillsides above the green vale. In 1 mile more of wildness another bulge is rounded to another inhabited beach bench beneath an imposing 400-foot bluff. This ⅓ mile of Tulare Beach is followed by a ¼-mile wild bit, a lesser bulge, behind which is Sunny Shores, the homes mostly up on the hill. Then comes 1 mile of wild beach — though with several trails down the 300-foot bluff from unseen houses. Now comes McKees Beach, ½ mile of homes on a sandy-flat point. A final ⅓ mile of wild-bluff beach leads to Kayak Point Park.

Mile 24–30 ½: Kayak Point Park-Warm Beach-Hat Slough (map—page 20, 24)

It's ending, it is, the "typical Whulge beach." Here is the Trail's final offering, a last wild beauty before entering the Something Else of the deltas.

Go off I-5 on Exit 199 and proceed left on Marine Drive, following "Tulalip" signs 13 miles to Kayak Point (Snohomish County) Park. Turn left 0.5 mile down to the beach parking lot.

Though presently (1988) in a state of disrepair, as is the entire Snohomish County park system, Kayak Point Park is a glory of the Whulge. The history is long. Not to mention the 12,000 years or so of earlier chapters, in 1909 a developer sought to capitalize on that year's Alaska-Yukon-Pacific Exposition by offering sternwheeler tourist service from Seattle and the chance to buy 5-acre parcels for $750 each. Sons of a purchaser developed a resort, put two Eskimo kayaks on display, and thus the name. In the 1960s an oil company bought up the land for a refinery but aroused Port Susan citizens chased the oil tankers north to a more compliant (then) county, opening the way for Snohomish County to buy the land in 1972, when federal and state funds were available, as they scarcely are in 1988.

Poverty has deferred grand plans for a trail system in the park and for a Kayak Point-to-Cascade Crest Trail. However, a short path from near the ranger station descends to the beach; passing an enormous Douglas fir. From the south-end shelter on the beach the Bluff Trail follows the fence ¼ mile up to the blufftop campground. Combining wildwoods and saltwater, the 670-acre park, 3300 feet of public beach, is notable for bald eagles that visit almost daily, mobs of great blue herons, bold coyotes, and sea lions—the last commonly hang out just off the end of the park's 300-foot pier, which the park brochure quaintly imagines "extends into Puget Sound."

But, to the Trail. Once past several homes, the first 2 miles are mostly wild, houses kept respectfully distant from water by the bluff, up to 180 feet high, of till and blue clay and much-played-on sand cliffs. Views are over Port Susan to Camano Island and Olympics.

A point is rounded and the view opens north to the head of Port Susan, to the Stillaguamish delta, to Chuckanut Mountain. And cheek-by-jowl homes line the beach for the next 1 ½ miles. This is Warm Beach, where the older surveyor swam 50 yards, long ago, to become a First Class Scout. The once-enormously-popular public beach now is entirely private, not so much as a street-end access.

Old pilings are passed, views begin north to Cultus and Twin Sisters and Baker, and habitations are left behind. So too is "dry land" as the bluff retreats inland, the beach yields to mudflat bordered by delta saltmarsh and tanglewood swamp. At medium tides the tidal channels can be hopped over to reach the dike.

Fields and cows on one side, saltgrass on the other ("meadows" and then mudflats that in low tide can be wandered far out in the bay), the dike twists and turns 1 mile to Hat Slough, at this moment in history the chief distributary of the Stillaguamish River, which makes the head of Port Susan largely a freshwater bay (and that's why, to the amazement of the surveyor on a frigid winter day, it was partly frozen over).

In 1-½ more miles beside or near the slough river, passing low-tide sandbars, horses, crabapple trees, cornfields, and a grand barn, the dike comes to Marine Drive a few steps south of the bridge over Hat Slough.

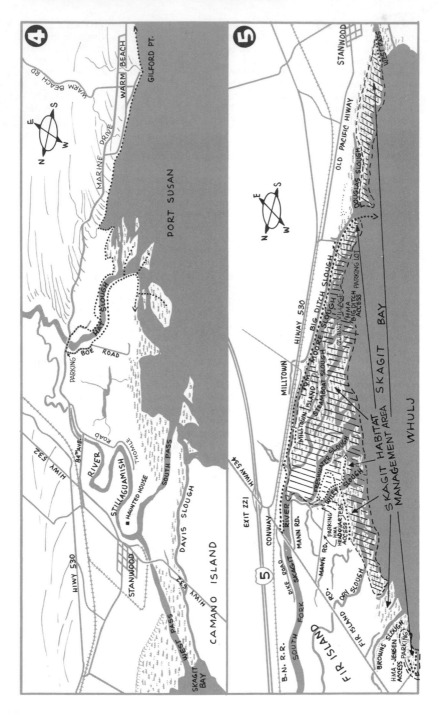

Beach at Kayak Point (Snohomish County) Park

Mile 30 ¹/₂–39 ¹/₂: Hat Slough-South Pass-Stillaguamish River-Stanwood (map—page 24)

The Long March over the deltas begins; not for many a mile, now, will the stranger with the strange device see more than scraps of true beach. Mostly there is the heaped-up mud and sand of the dikes.

This opening section is not to be undertaken lightheartedly. At two points the older surveyor risked grievous injury on barbs. He never was challenged by sentries, but the weather was of the sort when birds were drowning in midflight. A part of the way, though, is open and easy and splendid.

Go off I-5 on Exit 212 and drive Highway 532 to the east edge of Stanwood. Just past the bridge over the railroad turn south on Marine Drive, signed "Warm Beach," 2.5 miles to Boe Road, also signed 236th. Park at the "Public Fishing" area on the left side of Boe Road, a short way from the bridge.

Walk Boe Road west ¹/₂ mile; where it goes straight, climb atop the dike along Hat Slough. In 1 ¹/₂ miles more the dike reaches the slough mouth and turns north. To the right are fields and mountain views, to the left are marshes and open water (or vast mudflats) of Port Susan, beyond which is Camano Island. The thing to do here, at the proper tide, is to strike off from the dike out into saltmarshes of Port Susan, out into tideflats, out among the birds. And make that the trip.

The walker determined to venture farther should be prepared to turn back at any mean-lt fence, sign, or frown. Should he proceed, in 1 mile more he would find the dike turning inland to the end of Boe Road (no parking), there passing farmhouses where smiles must be hoped for, and bending north a winding 1 ³/₄ miles to the mouth of South Pass.

Emptying into Port Susan, this distributary of the Stillaguamish River connects to another, West Pass, that empties into Skagit Bay, the two providing boats a passage through; the passes also make Camano an Island, here a clam-toss away.

For the record let it be noted that in the next 1 mile the dike comes to the division of the Stillaguamish into passes and turns east along the river. The tall smokestack of Hamilton Lumber's long-gone mill marks the location of Stanwood — a location that swings all over the compass as the river meanders east, south, even southwest, then southeast, north, and so on. Cow paths lead to a haunted farmhouse, three storeys, three chimneys, tilted in delta mud, hellberry-overgrown, upstairs windows framing faces of Charles Addams characters.

The next scant 1½ miles continue on the dike, passing across-the-river Stanwood and its industrial cluster, then a line of fishing boats; the dike becomes impassable; the farm lane carries on, passing headquarters of industrial-farm Twin City Food, Inc.

Here begins public Thomle Road. In a scant ¾ mile Thomle leaves the river at the northward meander and cuts across the neck, in ¼ mile returning to the river.

In ⅓ mile more on Thomle is a bridge, left on 84 Avenue NW, over the river. The Trail crosses the river to Marine Drive, passes under Highway 532, and after a final scant 1 mile from Thomle reaches the main drag of Stanwood.

Mile 39 ½–44 ¼: Stanwood-West Pass-HMA Big Ditch Access (map—page 24)

The Stillaguamish delta is polished off and the Skagit delta begun. Now the view is over Skagit Bay to the north end of Camano Island and to Whidbey Island, to peaklet islands of Ika and Goat, and to Mt. Erie on Fidalgo Island. Vistas open to more San Juan Islands and over the delta to Little, Devils, Cultus, Wickersham-Woolley-Lyman, Chuckanut, Baker.

However, skip this stretch. The natives are not friendly. Judging from the fences, they don't even like each other very much. No great loss. At the end of the segment is the joy of public property.

Mile 44 ¼–47 ¾: HMA Big Ditch Access-Tom Moore Slough-Milltown (map—page 24)

Hurrah for the State Wildlife Department and its Skagit Habitat Management Area! Here is the first stretch of mainland dike open to Public feet in sunshine and on weekends. Here, too, is one of the greatest delta walks.

From the east edge of Stanwood drive north on Highway 530. In 2.2 miles, where 530 drops from the hill to meet railroad tracks and Old Pacific Highway, turn left on the latter, then immediately right on the narrow road signed "Skagit Habitat Management Area, Big Ditch Access," leading 0.7 mile to the parking area. (Note: To park here a car must display either a hunting license or a conservation license.)

Cross Big Ditch Slough. On the far side a sidetrip goes left on a spur dike 1/2 mile to the slough mouth; at low tide a person can sortie a mile or more out in the vast sandflat-mudflat, out amid the peep that whirl around the walker's head by the hundreds, and scurry across the sand—peeping, peeping, peeping. *This* is the trip.

However, to forge northward, turn right on the grassy dike between Big Ditch (a manmade drainage slough) on the right and cattails on the left. Out left is a 2-mile-long line of ancient pilings in the mudflats north of Tom Moore Slough. These mark a "training dike" built by the Army Engineers in 1911, part of a complex project to permit paddlewheel steamboats to navigate upstream to Mount Vernon.

In 1 mile of strolling in broad views over Skagit Bay to islands, over Skagit delta to mountains, is a delightful surprise. On stilts beside Tom Moore Slough is a village of "duck shacks" ingeniously constructed—largely in the 1930s and earlier—of driftwood and salvaged lumber. Each little house has its own perilous plank walkway from the dike, on the way passing a littler house; trips to these littler houses from the little houses, during the midnight celebrations that inevitably follow the daytime birdbusting, are the subject of innumerable hilarious anecdotes.

The grassy dike path yields to a semi-tunnel through hellberries, passing another village; taking pains not to meddle, walk out to the bank of Tom Moore Slough; upstream at the toe of Milltown Island it is joined by Steamboat Slough, onetime route of the sternwheelers.

Beyond this second village a final 1 mile of dike leads to Milltown.

Mile 47 ³/₄–49 ¹/₄: Milltown-Conway (map—page 24)

This segment used to feature a sidetrip that was one of the most intriguing parts of the Trail. Milltown Island, diked early in the century to keep out Tom Moore and Steamboat Sloughs, at last was abandoned by the farmer and bought by the State Wildlife Department. The pedestrian used to be able, in low tide and river run, to circle the island on dikes to Steamboat Slough—a scene removed from the modern world, safely still in the primeval. However, the bridge across Tom Moore Slough was permitted to collapse, and shame on somebody for that. The Milltown Access of the Skagit Habitat Management Area is now boat-access only. But, there is still the mainland dike.

Leave I-5 on Exit 221 and drive Highway 530 a scant 2 miles to no mill, but a solitary domicile announcing itself as "Milltown."

The dike goes pleasantly a scant 1 mile to the splitting of waters into the two sloughs at the head of Milltown Island. Use the railroad to cross a ditch, return to the dike, now a pasture, and in 1 ¹/₂ more miles, where the South Fork Skagit splits into Steamboat and Freshwater Sloughs, hit Fir Island Road. To the right is Conway, whose chief industry is antiques, and among whose gracefully old, well-kept houses is gracefully old, well-kept "Conway Tavern 1932." (How many of you kids have heard of "Repeal"?)

Mile 49 ¹/₂–51 ³/₄: Conway-Fir Island-Skagit HMA Headquarters Access (map—page 24)

Don't walk, drive. A bridge over the Skagit River leads to Fir Island, enclosed by the two main distributary forks of the river. Just below the bridge the South Fork splits into Freshwater and Steamboat Sloughs, each of which splits again, the river splintering into a maze of distributaries, a wet wildland that makes a hiker yearn for a boat.

The appealing dike along Freshwater Slough is inhabited. Proceed on wheels to the Skagit Habitat Management Area Headquarters Access.

Skagit Habitat Management Area Headquarters Access (map—page 24)

Encompassing sloughs and islands, tideflats, swampy woods, marshes of saltgrass, cattails, and sedge-bulrush, and farm fields and dikes, the 12,761-acre Skagit Habitat Management Area is the most important waterfowl area in Western Washington; wintering or nesting, 26 species of ducks are found here and three of geese, and brant and whistling swan and sandhill cranes. There are also 200 species of songbirds, plus harbor seal, river otter, mink, deer, and beaver. The 20,000-35,000 snow geese that winter are the superstars, but if a walker misses their show, he won't fail of other bird experiences, ranging from flitters in the bushes to great blue herons to clouds of sandpipers wheeling and diving in tight formation.

Offering all this, and on a hassle-free easy-strolling route, the Skagit HMA Headquarters Access is far and away the most popular walk on the delta. Eventually there will be a wildlife interpretive center, viewing "blinds," and additional trails.

From Conway drive Fir Island Road. Taking the east entry to Mann Road (the west entry also leads there) drive 2.2 miles to where Mann Road turns sharp right. Go left, signed "Skagit HMA Headquarters," 0.2 mile and turn left on the dike road to the large parking area. (Note: To park here a car must display either a hunting license or a conservation license.)

Snow geese in Skagit Wildlife Recreation Area

The walk is a loop, with sidetrips, around a nameless island between Wiley and Freshwater Sloughs. From the parking area walk the dike downstream along Freshwater Slough, tanglewood swamp left and drainage ditch right, at a couple points crossed by footlogs permitting roving in the fields. The dike bends right and in 1 mile crosses the marsh island to Wiley Slough. Here is an intersection. To the right is the dike leading back 1 mile to the parking lot, completing the basic 2-mile loop.

For the full treatment, first go left. Pass a causeway right, over Wiley Slough (for a sidetrip off the sidetrip, take the causeway and proceed ½ mile, until halted by a mean-it fence). Hundreds of weathered tree roots in the marsh speak of past floods. As do rotten rowboats sunk in the reeds. The dike ends in ½ mile at the mouth of Freshwater Slough, a supreme viewpoint over the waters. — Or mud: at low tide one can wander the sandflats. Seeking a mystical experience? On a crystalline winter day when the sun is bright and the breezes brisk, watch for a low low tide and roam far out on the wet sands mirroring the sky. The thousands of whirling, diving, running, peeping sandpipers will accept you as part of the scene. When they run across your boots and a gull perches on your head, you've got it.

The original intent of the land (and water) acquisition by the (then) State Game Department was to provide public hunting. However, the sport has gone steadily downhill since the 1930s, when the shooting was so good that had it continued at that rate another decade would have seen entire species eliminated from the delta. Conservation has helped spoil the fun. So has overpopulation by shooters. A few birdbusters persist in believing the basic fault is the birdwatchers, who now far outnumber the busters. They are accused of frightening birds away with the tromp-

tromp of their feet on the dikes and the click-click-whir of cameras. However, considerable credit for the bad hunting must be given to smarter birds. For the smashing finale of a walk during hunting season, wait until 15 minutes after the close of legal shooting hours and see the thousands of fowl fly in from the bay, where they have safely been sitting out the day, watching the clock.

Complete dike tour 4 miles, allow 3 hours

Mile 51 3/4–55: HMA Headquarters Access-HMA Jensen Access (map—page 24)
At 1/2 mile from the Wiley Slough causeway the dike is blocked by mean-it fence and signs crying "Private!" Here as elsewhere on the delta, hunting rights have been purchased from farmers by a gun club. Members are hostile to Public birdshooters, absolutely choleric about birdwatchers. Don't walk, drive.

Mile 55-57: HMA Jensen Access-HMA North Fork Access (map–page 31)
Jensen Access is not a good put-in for dike-walking. A short way southerly are mean-it fences. In the other direction the hostility commences right at the access. However, from 1/2 mile south of Jensen Access all the way to the North Fork Access and on out to the mouth of the North Fork Skagit the tidelands—marshes and sandflats—are purely Public. At low tide, therefore, a person knowledgeable in the tricks of the marshes can walk (and partly wade) the entire distance outside the Private dikes.

Drive north on Mann Road, then west on Fir Island Road, crossing Dry Slough and Browns Slough. Where Browns Slough Road turns north, go straight ahead on Maupin Road, in 0.5 mile reaching the turnoff, left, to HMA Jensen Access. (Note: To park here a car must display either a hunting license or a conservation license.)

On a lonesome winter weekday the older surveyor climbed from parking lot to diketop—and a white cloud rose from the waters lapping the dike—thousands of snow geese. It was high tide. On another day, another high tide, the photographer and wife carried their canoe over the dike. Hours later they paddled in from the bay, amid the fleets of snow geese and friends—and a half-mile from the dike, ran out of water. However, at low tide, with no canoe to lug, all that marsh and mud and sand can be a pedestrian heaven.

Skagit Habitat Management Area North Fork Access: North Fork Mouth, Craft Island (map—page 31)

More of the same—and something completely different—a couple things. Unlike the many-sloughed South Fork, the North Fork hugely flows to the bay in a single surge. And here the flatness of delta bumps against hard rock and startling eminences of peaklets of the San Juan Islands.

Drive Fir Island Road to just south of the bridge over the North Fork and turn west on Rawlins Road, perhaps signed "HMA North Fork Access" or maybe only "Blake's Skagit Resort." In 1.7 miles the road ends at the dike; park on the shoulder. Don't forget your conservation license.

A full, rich day can be spent here. At high tide walk south on public dikes totalling nearly 3 round-trip miles, burrowing through dike-top thickets and baldhip roses, the hips appearing in winter to be millions of cherry tomatoes. Two spur dikes permit sidetrips up to 1/4 mile out in the water—or marshes. At low tide the sea-meadow and sandflat roaming is limitless.

From the road-end, walk the dike 1/4 mile to the North Fork—broad, deep, swift, impressive. Turn downstream through a sand-floored alder forest to meadows. Across the river are startling cliffs of "Fish Town Island." In 1/2 mile on the bank is an

29

Mouth of Skagit River and a half-mile-wide tideland from Craft Island

indistinct Y of paths. Both are essential. (For an alternative approach to the Y, from the road-end cross the dike and follow the obvious path out through the meadows.)

The right fork continues on the banks in grass hummocks and bulrushes; across the river are clifftop cow pastures, then the bizarre village of Fish Town. At $1/2$ mile from the Y the river at last splits. Bend left a final $1/2$ mile to the mouth of the south distributary. A genuine mouth of the Skagit! Views are superb of incredible Ika Island, a mountain rising 450 feet abrupt as a cinder cone.

The left fork crosses wet-foot meadows $1/3$ mile to the fairyland of Craft Island. Clamber up a bit of rock and spend hours (but watch the tides, in order not to spend a whole lot more hours) poking around green benches of moss and lichen and grass, in masses of ferns, miniature forests of small cedar and juniper, fir and madrona, thickets of snowberry and rose. The knobby algae-colorful walls of conglomerate are eroded by tides into weird textures. In spring it's all flower garden.

Though only 75 feet high, amid such flatness of delta and water the "mountain" seems enormously taller. The view is from Rainier to Canada, Olympics to Baker, and all around to the green delta and the island-dotted waters. On one survey, some 30 herons were spotted perched on logs and roots, pretending to be part of the woodwork. Beware of gulls dropping clams on the rocky island to break them open; the shell fragments show it's a popular sport here.

Round trip, all tours, 7 $1/2$ miles, allow 5 hours

Mile 57–66 $3/4$: HMA North Fork Access-North Fork Skagit Bridge-Dodge Valley-Landing Road-Quarry Mountain-La Conner (map—page 31)
Here is another lacuna in the pedestrian route. Quarry Mountain, Fish Town, and other objectives described in previous editions are not here.

Drive from I-5 or Highway 20 to La Conner and park on First Street where it and Morris Street (the in-town name of Chilberg Road) meet.

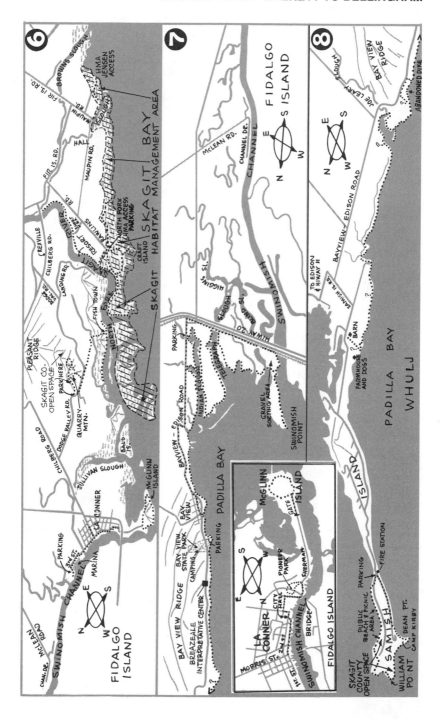

La Conner is a town worth a walk. Located where the San Juan Islands "come ashore" in the Skagit delta, beside Swinomish Channel which connects Skagit and Padilla Bays and makes Fidalgo an island, the old fishing-farming-trading village become artist colony has much geographical and historical and cultural interest.

From the Magnus Anderson log cabin, built in 1869 on the North Fork Skagit and moved here in 1952, walk south on First by shoppes and old houses and museums, by fishing boats and pleasure craft and tugs towing log rafts, with views over to the Swinomish Reservation, to which Governor Stevens assigned the Skagit and "South" Indians. Where First enters an industrial concern, jog left on Commercial, then right on Second, by the City Hall (1886) and the La Conner House (1878). At Moore Clark's business turn left on (unsigned) Caldonia, then go straight on Third to Sherman, then right at the foot of "Pioneer Park Mountain." Leave the street and climb the trail into the forested park (camping permitted) dedicated "In memory of Louisa A. Conner, for whom La Conner was named in 1870." Pass the High Orange Bridge to Fidalgo Island (but first walk out on it for the view up and down the channel) and drop back to Sherman at Schenk Seafoods, a scant 1 mile from Morris Street. Return north along the channel, admiring the work boats, looking over the waters to the play boats stinking up a onetime marsh on Fidalgo, pausing to appreciate the arts and crafts of the Fish Towners who display their works here, and to have a progressive lunch at the string of fooderies.

McGlinn Island (map—page 31)

From the south end of La Conner a tideflat neck hitches "Pioneer Mountain Island" to "McGlinn Island Mountain." At about 1 mile from Schenk Seafoods the public road

South entrance to Swinomish Channel from McGlinn Island

Swinomish Channel, La Conner, and Mt. Baker

ends at an old quarry. Unsigned but obvious trails lead up and around the "Mountain." For the best start, go east a few feet to a turnaround and find a big trail into the forest of fir and madrona.

The ¼ x ½-mile "McGlinn Mountain" towers 125 quite vertical feet above saltwater and marshes. The interlacing paths require no guidance. Poke around and find a little sandy-beached cove at the mouth of Swinomish Channel, and another cove harboring a houseboat. Other paths open to grassy brinks of alarming 100-foot cliffs dropping sheer to the water. Look over the jetties guarding the channel entrance, the enormous rafts of logs, to the towering 450-foot peak of Ika Island, and to Goat and Bald and Craft Islands, and over Skagit Bay and delta to Three Fingers and Pilchuck. From another spot, look over the delta to the white cone of Baker. Note large granite erratics dropped by the glacier that gouged the cliff-walled outlet of Swinomish Channel.

—Now, the shocker. This jewel of the delta, this joy of the Public pedestrian for better than a century, is claimed to be Private! As of 1988 the road from La Conner is gated and signs forbid "CRIMINAL TRESPASS."

Let it be noted that a 1988 survey witnessed many acts of "criminal trespass." It seemed, indeed, to be the La Conner town sport. The surveyors don't know what this all means.

Loop trip up to 2 miles, allow 2 hours

Mile 66 ¾–72 ¼: La Conner–Swinomish Channel (map—page 31)

Another lacuna. Another greedy gulp by the Privatizers. The only way to get to the water around here is by boat. The Port of Skagit County Marina can still be enjoyed, if that is the emotion occasioned by googols of superpowered fun boats, the same ones that on summer weekends make the San Juan Islands an uproar. From the large parking lot a scant 1 mile from Morris Street, the surveyor walked north by boats boats boats, birds birds birds, in views to Canada and Baker, south to Pilchuck, by a junction of Higgins, Telegraph, and Blind Sloughs, to Highway 20. But that was way back in the good old days of the late 1970s. A decade later the Privates were living on the dike and scowling at the Publics.

Swinomish Point (map—page 31)

Clouds of dunlins dipping beaks in mud, fleets of ducks sailing, "Christmas trees" of Marsh Point oil refineries, a stunning panorama of San Juan Islands from Fidalgo (Mt. Erie) to Hat to Guemes to Cypress to Orcas (Mt. Constitution) to Samish to Lummi, peaks in Canada, Chuckanut, Skagit valley and Baker and Shuksan. All from a saltmarsh peninsula, enlarged by sand dredged from the Swinomish Channel, thrusting far out in Padilla Bay.

Drive Highway 20 west from I-5 (Exit 230) to about 0.3 mile short of the bridge over Swinomish Channel. Spot a paved, one-way, single-lane road diverging right. Drive it to parking space on the shoulder near the channel.

Cross the railroad tracks and skirt the edge of a gravel factory to the beginning of the spoils-dumping area. Inland, the sands are sorted by winds and driven by winds, though prevented from forming classic dunes by the intrusions of wheels. Seagrasses have established themselves — and birds. In $^3/_4$ mile, on a medium tide the walking ends at low mounds of recently dredged bay bottom. At low tide the route extends far out on the undredged bay bottom.

Round trip 2 $^1/_2$ miles, allow 2 hours

Mile 72 $^1/_4$–83: Swinomish Point-Bay View State Park

The dike-walking around the south end of Padilla Bay is the best. A series of sloughs (birdways) are crossed, the peninsulas between them reaching out in the bay to broad views of refineries and San Juan Islands and supertankers, delta and "come ashore" islands, Cascades and Olympics. There also are grand homes built at the turn of the century and lovingly preserved by sons and daughters of the diker pioneers. As of 1988 the residents tend to display an olden-time tolerance of wayfaring strangers. That, of course, can change in a minute; no Private dike can be guaranteed. But there *is* a definitely Public dike.

Because of public highways at both ends and three spots in the middle, this segment of the Trail lends itself to loops, using public roads for shortcut returns after twisty-turny stretches of dike. (Note: A put-in that is posted may, in a loop, serve neatly as a take-out.)

The first put-in is the parking place for Swinomish Point. Tall grass on the diketop makes for harder walking than the sand-mud beach; a middling-to-low tide is recommended. The dike bends out to a little point of salt meadow, a marvelous vista of birds and horizons, then south over the mouth of Blind Slough, now mostly converted to cornfields. Detour by hellberry thickets via dike-base meadows to improving dike path. Pass more peninsulas, marsh islands, concrete-box duck blinds where hunters lie in ambush; again, the dike becomes so overgrown the only passage is along the base, at a medium tide. The way bends southerly up Telegraph Slough, full of ducks and peep, and at 2 $^1/_4$ miles from the Swinomish Channel comes to railroad tracks and Highway 20, either of which can be walked back for a 3 $^1/_4$-mile loop.

From here the Short Trail goes east from Telegraph Slough 1 mile on railroad tracks and north $^1/_4$ mile on Bayview-Edison Road to Indian Slough. The Long Trail is a splendid 3 $^1/_2$ miles on dikes, partly open, partly tangled (the slopes walkable), around the magnificent peninsula between Telegraph and Indian Sloughs. The two trails combine for a neat loop.

Telephoto of Whitehorse Mountain (left) and Three Fingers (right) from Indian Slough dike

Just short of the bridge over Indian Slough is parking for several cars, a good start for walks in either direction.

Easy dike goes down Indian Slough to a point at the mouth of a nameless slough, across which is an old dock, interesting junk, and a handsome farmhouse, and then up Nameless Slough to the highway, this tour covering 1 1/2 miles, hitting the highway 1/2 mile from the previous parking place. (Here is parking for a couple cars on the shoulder.) The 2-mile loop is among the best short dike walks on the whole Trail.

The next 2 miles, to the dike end, are also terrific. Having come up one side of Nameless Slough, the Trail now goes down its twists and turns on the other side a long 1/2 mile to Indian Slough, turns north by a grand white farmhouse, uninhabited, then a couple inhabited houses—blind-eyed if one is walking beside the water at low tide. The way is then clear the 3/4 mile to the mouth of Indian Slough, where marsh islands and points are foreground for Padilla Bay, 120,000-ton supertankers anchored off March Point, and San Juans. The final 3/4 mile is along bay shore, by a long line of pilings; sea-meadow isles decorate the bay, hawks patrol the fields, views are tremendous. Now the dike ends, the Trail bumping against the rise of "Bay View Ridge Island."

Gloryosky! The last 2 1/2 miles of this stretch of the Whulge Trail are the Padilla Bay Diketop Trail — fully public, balm for the nerves of walkers afraid to trespass, tolerated or not. Eventually there will be more such friendly miles.

To complete a dandy 4 1/2-mile loop, climb from the dike to the Bayview-Edison Road and walk it south 2 1/4 miles, in fine bay views, from the island heights, then over delta flats, to Indian Slough.

35

To proceed north, at high tide walk the highway north 1 mile to Bay View State Park; at low, take the beach, detouring up to the highway briefly to get around docks at the hamlet of Bay View.

Padilla Bay National Estuarine Research Reserve (map—page 31)

For nigh onto 13,000 years the Skagit River has been pushing its delta out through its one-time fiord (which originally extended 20 miles into the Cascades) into the Whulge. Left to itself another millenium or so, it would have finished filling Padilla Bay —as it very nearly did before the main outlet shifted south to Skagit Bay. In 1859 European settlers arrived to take up the assault on the bay where the Skagit had (temporarily) left off, and by the 1890s had diked off most of the semi-land of the saltmarsh, establishing the artificial shores of today's bay. Over the years this "unused" remainder kept exploiters busy with schemes: oyster-ranching, a nuclear plant, a log-export port, more oil refineries, a magnesium smelter, a lime plant, a concrete plant, a plan to fill the whole thing to grow turnips for gasohol. The acme was a grandiose notion to create a "Venice" of 30,000 people living on 90 miles of artificial peninsulas built by the spoils from dredging channels that would lead stinkpots to front yards. "Even the Army Corps of Engineers had a hard time keeping a straight face...." (The hiker is hereby commanded to hie to a library for the Summer 1987 issue of *Living Wilderness* and read "Fecund Mysteries," by Phillip Johnson.) Starting in 1963 the Orion Corporation bought up much of the bay bottom (yes, Virginia, that is possible under our laws!) and has been pressing its reducto ad absurdum claims. Early in 1988 the state Supreme Court ruled against Orion's attempt to extort an inflated price for the bay from the public agencies seeking to buy it. The matter will linger in the courts a few more years, or so it may be hoped: the longer the exploiters receive publicity for their scheme, the more support will be obtained for rationalizing the boundary between Private and Public.

The opposition to the Orion scheme was organized by Edna Breazeale, who had lived on Padilla Bay since 1901. Having aroused the public and donated the family farm, in 1982, at the age of 87, she was the star of the ceremonies dedicating the Padilla Bay National Estuarine Research Reserve. By the time of her death in 19 J7 her dream was coming true, her home valued across the state and nation.

The 4000-acre reserve has shortcomings. It is not large enough and must be enlarged to at least 11,600 acres to forestall continuing attempts to "use" the bay. (If all the proposed marinas were built, the bay would be nigh onto clogged by stinkpots.) Further, a "research reserve" is not a sanctuary. Despite federal auspices and state management, the protection is less than perfect even within the present boundaries.

The species of plants and wildlife will not be enumerated here; the visitor will want to make a first stop at the Breazeale Interpretive Center, just north of Bay View on the 64 donated acres of the Breazeale farm. In addition to permanent displays, the center offers a year-round program of lectures and walks; to be placed on the mailing list for the quarterly announcement calendar, write Breazeale Center, 1043 Bayview-Edison Road, Mt. Vernon 98273.

A ¾-mile nature trail explores upland woods and touches on bay beaches, A 7-mile shore trail has been proposed.

Mile 83–89 ¼: Bay View State Park–Samish Island

Bay View State Park has a campground in the forest on the uphill side of the highway and a picnic area on a fill jutting out from the shore bluff. Modest eminences provide climax views of March Point refineries and supertankers and steam plumes, and glorious perspectives on the San Juan Islands, of which long long Samish now grows prominent.

Drive Highway 20 west from I-5 (Exit 230) and turn north on Bayview-Edison Road to the park.

San Juan Islands from beach at Bay View State Park

As a base for shore walks, the park is a future, not a present, attraction. To the north is a skinny strip of beach beneath the shore bluff, then a narrow strip of saltgrass, yielding to saltmarsh where the dikes have been abandoned, letting Nature flood to the foot of the bluff and ebb to uncover vastnesses of bay-floor mud. In 2 ¼ miles is Joe Leary Slough, bounding the north foot of "Bay View Ridge Island" and opening out to the northernmost of the three segments of the Skagit delta. However, the publicity surrounding establishment of the reserve and opening of the interpretive center has attracted so many Publics that formerly tolerant Privates have grown testy. Until easements are acquired, shore-walking cannot be advised.

Samish Island (map—page 31)

A celebration is in order. This de facto public park, a treasure of the Skagit delta, was bought up by Snohomish County PUD for a nuclear power plant that would employ the saltwater for cooling the furnace. The technology for doing this proved even more impossible than other pipe dreams of the WHOOPS mentality. The PUD then rigged a deal to sell the land to a developer. Skagit County, its citizens at last rising to protest, threw in a monkey wrench. PUD sued Skagit County. At that point the older surveyor went away from the scene wailing in rage and despair, assuming the game to be over and lost. His brain reeled in 1988 to find a sign had been erected: "This property is designated as OPEN SPACE under Skagit County open-space agreement No. 5782 and is available for public access for recreational purposes. Motor vehicles, fires, camping, firearms, and gathering of wildlife or shellfish prohibited."

Actually two islands joined by a sand neck, and now really a peninsula, Samish Island is a trip to sea. Miles and miles it reaches out from the delta, dividing Padilla Bay from Samish Bay, seemingly striving to escape the mainland and join companions of the archipelago. Views are spectacular from the San Juan-typical grass-moss balds, flowers and Douglas firs and madronas atop, rock cliffs and deep water beneath.

Drive I-5 to Exit 231 and go off west on Highway 11, Chuckanut Drive. In 6.5 miles, at Bow Post Office, turn left 1 mile to Edison. South of that quaint village a scant 0.5 mile, turn west on Bayview-Edison Road. In a long 1.5 miles, where that road turns left to Bay View State Park, go straight, then turn and twist, to Samish Island. Beaches of the first island and the sand neck are elbow-to-elbow Private, a total loss. Just where the neck connects to the second island is a junction, identified by the fire station on the left.

Two routes may be used to explore the outer island. For one, turn right and drive 0.3 mile along the north shore to Samish Island Public Beach and Picnic Site. Utilizing 1500 feet of public tidelands and a bit of upland donated by local folk in 1960, the state DNR was first to save a portion of Samish for the public. Descend the staircase to the beach (at high tide there is none), guarded from houses by a bluff of glacial drift. in ³/₄ mile there is no beach at any tide, cliffs of metamorphic rock thrusting out in deep water. The cliffs are easily climbed on obvious scramble paths to the flattish island top, elevation 100-150 feet. Paths crisscross and fade but by trying this and that, trending inland from the bluff edge, a walker shortly emerges on an old woods road through a field and orchard, by a collapsed farmhouse, to an old quarry.

From the quarry several paths lead northward to "North Point." From a clifftop sea meadow the views are grand to Guemes, Cypress, Orcas, Vendovi, Sinclair, Eliza, and Lummi Islands—the latter revealing its amazing 1500-foot summit-to-beach western precipice. Only a scattering of distant houses is visible, the San Juan Islands seem a wilderness, and this point part of it.

After a certain amount of trial-and-error probing, the correct path can be found southward from the quarry area to William Point, site of a beacon light atop another sea-meadow bluff. Now the views are southerly. A short way from the point a path switchbacks down cliffs to beach that extends onward to Camp Kirby, property of the Samish Council of Camp Fire Girls. Public access to this beach is strictly on the basis of toleration, usually automatic on stormy winter weekdays (the most exciting times) but actively discouraged in high-use summer periods.

At 1 wonderful mile from William Point is the tip of the long spit of Dean Point, where a person stands far out in the waters, swept by winds, the cross-chopping waves a foreground for views over Padilla Bay to Guemes and Jack and Hat and Fidalgo Islands, refineries on March Point, supertankers at anchor and supertankers underway north to Cherry Point refineries; south over the Skagit delta are Cultus and Devils.

Proceed ¹/₃ mile along the south side of the spit to the bluff and find a steep path up the jungled cliff to the public road, attained near and outside the entrance to Camp Kirby. Walk the road a scant 1 mile back by the fire station to the start.

Full exploration 5 miles, allow 4 hours

Mile 96 ³/₄–89 ¹/₄: Blanchard–Samish Island (map—page 40)

The last of the delta is some of the best. Dikes round the shores of Samish Bay. Samish Island bounds the view south, perspectives change on the San Juans; drawing very near, now, are Chuckanut Mountain, with its steep dun slopes of sandstone-banded brush dating from the mid-1960s forest fire, and the great canyon of Oyster Creek.

However, to say it that way is to say it backwards. Starting at Edison is not practical due to "No Trespassing" signs.

But every dike has two ends. So, start at Blanchard. Go off I-5 on Exit 231 and

Samish Bay south of Larrabee State Park

follow Highway 11, Chuckanut Drive, over the delta to the foot of Blanchard Hill. At Legg Road turn left then right to parking at the mouth of Colony Creek.

The easy-strolling dike rounds little peninsulas and little bays, passes rotting-away pilings reminding of frontier forts, and duck blinds where gunners crouch, making noises they think sound like ducks. The ducks mostly think otherwise and stay out of range. See mallards and bufflehead and goldeneyes, brant and snow geese, herons and gulls and hawks, plovers and peep. In 3 1/4 miles the dike gets into hostile territory, so turn back.

Mile 96 3/4–102 1/2: Blanchard–Larrabee State Park (map—page 40)

Now for something completely different. Sacre bleu! Who'd have thought the old Earth had so much elevation in it? After days and miles of delta, viewing the abrupt verticality of Elephant and Chuckanut, this precipitous plunge of the Cascades to saltwater, gives a neckache. Yet, surely, it's entertaining after sand and mud to slice cliffs of sandstone, conglomerate, shale, coal, and fossil beds. Differential erosion by waves sculpts odd knobs, scoops, rock filigrees. Views change of beaches, points, bays, San Juan Islands, and barges, tugs, sailboats, oyster dredges, and super-tankers.

The trail is plainly marked by two parallel steel rails, infrequently traveled by the choo-choos, yet often enough that a person must watch his back. The shore is always close below, just steps away, but there is very little beach. Close above is Chuckanut Drive, providing frequent accesses for short walks.

Go off I-5 on Exit 231 and follow Highway 11, Chuckanut Drive, over the delta to the foot of the Elephant (Blanchard Hill). At Legg Road turn right to park in the heart of moldering (1885) Blanchard.

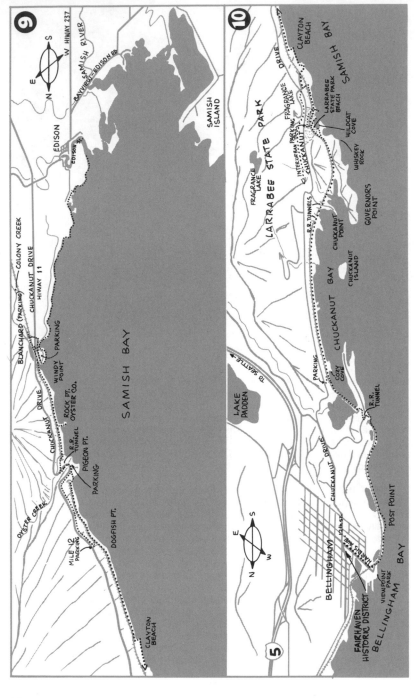

40

The railroad tracks cross the mouth of Colony Creek and thereafter are beside the water, passing Windy Point, views over Samish Bay to Samish and other San Juan Islands, Olympics and all. Ahead are the striking barrens of the mid-1960s Chuckanut Burn.

At 1 1/4 miles is the Rock Point Oyster Company, selling fresh oysters. The family-run operation is open to examination from the dredge to the oyster-sorting room to the retail store. No parking except for customers.

Just north are the siding of Samish, the mouth of Oyster Creek, and Pigeon Point, bored through by a 1/4-mile tunnel too dangerous to walk. So, at the mouth turn off on a path to the Rock Point access road, climbing to Chuckanut Drive. A few yards north, past Milepost 11, is a parking area atop Pigeon Point, 2 1/4 miles from Blanchard and a good spot to hike south or north from.

A little road-trail drops back to the tracks north of the tunnel. The way goes 1 mile by a huge heap of ivy-overgrown oyster shells to a pretty waterfall; here a trail climbs easily to the highway, attained just north of Milepost 12. At the parking area here, find the trail on the water side of two large firs with leaning trunks that form a V.

In 1/2 mile the Trail rounds Dogfish Point, whose impressive sandstone cliffs are fenced by a wire mesh that catches small rocks and has a sensor wire to warn trains of big rocks fallen, and the bodies of idiots who try to come down here from the highway. A grass-topped sandstone point is a nice spot to sit and look south over the Skagit to Cultus and beyond, north to the tall bulk of Lummi Island.

Lovely madronas hang over the water. Blackened fir trunks tell that the Chuckanut Burn came down to the very shore. At 1 mile north of Dogfish Point the tracks are separated from the beach by a sand terrace; go onto it, or onto Clayton Beach, marked by stubs of old pilings — relics of the Mount Vernon-Bellingham Interurban Railway.

In 1/4 mile sand ends at sandstone and the best part of the whole Blanchard-Bellingham segment of the Trail. There is sand, sand, sand. And moth-eaten sandstone with lenses of conglomerate forms buttresses enclosing tiny coves. Late in 1988 Clayton Beach was purchased for the State Park; development plans remain to be made. From the beach a trail goes inland to the tracks.

For the shortest access to this glory spot, drive Chuckanut Drive to Milepost 14, enter Whatcom County, and pass the unsigned south entry to Fragrance Lake Road; just beyond is a sign, "Emergency Phone 1/4 mile," and then on the left are three white concrete posts and a sizable parking turnout. From here a trail reverse-turns south, following the grade of the old interurban railway down through lovely woods, over a nice creek, to reach the tracks in 1/2 mile, a short bit from Clayton Beach.

From the beach the tracks go inland; paths lead out through the sandstone knolls to lovely coves. In 3/4 mile is the main developed section of Larrabee State Park. (The inland and upland portion of the park is discussed in the Skagit River chapter.)

Mile 102 1/2–106: Larrabee State Park-Chuckanut Bay (map—page 40)

The park is the big business of this segment, which aside from that has nice parts but is mostly cut off from the shore by private property.

Just south of Milepost 15 on Chuckanut Drive take either entry down into Larrabee State Park, park at any lot, and take any path down to the tracks and the shore. Only about 1/3 mile presently is public. But good, but good. The beach of cute Wildcat Cove is a delight, as are sandstone cliffs of points south and north and of nearby Whiskey Rock.

Bellingham calls. Proceed north, crossing public roads sternly signed, "No Beach Access." Thus pass Governors Point and Pleasant Bay and Chuckanut Point, total losses. The way is now along Chuckanut Bay, little Chuckanut Island a foreground grace note to looming Lummi. The tracks traverse two short tunnels dated 1912, cross two wild ravines, pass waterside houses and also blufftop houses, until the cliff rises too high and steep. Great tilted slabs, 200 feet high, suggest fantastic rollerskate runs, one to a customer. The way enters the north arm of Chuckanut Bay, enclosed on the

Terminal Building built in 1888 in Fairhaven

west by a long point with sprawling mansions of the beautiful people at the rocky tip. Then, just past a private road down to a beach home, is a little rock point, a white all-shell beach on one side, a cozy cove scooped in the other. A wondrous spot. And wild, because here the steep, forested slope rises 200 feet to Chuckanut Drive. Note railroad gravel sloping into bushes, marking a trail outlet.

To use this access to the Trail, drive Chuckanut Drive to just south of Milepost 18. By the sign, "Entering Bellingham," is a turnout on the inland shoulder with room for several cars. The obvious trail sidehills south in marvelous big firs up to 4 feet in diameter, then drops—clay-slick but safe— to the tracks at Cozy Cove.

Mile 106–109: Chuckanut Bay-Marine Park-Fairhaven Historic District (map—40)

Though Cozy Cove is a convenient access to the south end of the home stretch, more popular starts are in the middle and on the north; these will be noted as the story winds down.

42

The Trail shortcuts across the head of Chuckanut Bay on a causeway of granite blocks. The west shore is a stone fantasy, ribs of sedimentary rock pushing out in the bay, their walls pocked with cavelets eroded in the softer or more soluble components. The tracks enter a tunnel dated 1913. Daring youths enjoy laughing and shouting their way through the long, curving, dreadful night. Not the surveyors, no sir.

No need. A fine trail has been built up the steep slopes of the tunnel ridge. At the parking area on top is a joyous sign: "OPEN SPACE REGULATIONS. Designated trail areas are open space area with access limited to pedestrians only during daylight hours. . . . No fires, camping, firearms, being naughty. Bellingham Parks and Recreation."

To drive to this two-way trailhead, turn left from Chuckanut Drive on Viewcrest Road 0.7 mile. Turn left on Fieldston Road through a ritzy subdivision to the road-end atop the tunnel.

Behind the Open Space sign the north-side trail follows powerlines a short way. The main trail bends left. Spot a sidetrail on the right, descending to the tracks. But first walk out on the main trail to a rocky-mossy point with panoramas over Bellingham Bay, the destination of most walkers.

The way north passes a series of lagoons impounded behind the track causeway. Wild woods on the bluff yield to homes. At 1 long mile north of the tunnel is Post Point. Ah, joy. Slabs shelf into water, separating private sitting nooks. Two trees on the grassy point pose prettily for the camera. The view over the broad reaches of Bellingham Bay is dominated by the massive bulk of Lummi Island and the long thrust of Lummi Peninsula, but there are still Orcas, Constitution close enough to see the summit tower, and Cypress, Guemes, Samish, and Fidalgo with its hump of Erie and steam plumes of refineries. And there are more plumes north, beyond now-appearing Bellingham.

At $1/2$ mile from Post Point is a sewage-treatment plant and then the superb viewpoint of Marine Park. To start walks here, follow Chuckanut Drive into Bellingham; past Fairhaven Park and Bridge it becomes 12 Street. At the second stoplight turn west and descend Harris Avenue to Marine Park.

Having devoted all this effort to getting to Bellingham, the walker ought to see a bit of the city. The old city, that is. From Marine Park ascend Harris Avenue a long $1/4$ mile to Fairhaven Historic District. The red brick buildings dating from the 1880s have been restored to house such modern enterprises as the 1890 Marketplace, the Monahan Building (the saloon transformed into the Picture Show Theater), two bookstores, the Colophon Cafe and other eateries and etc. shops. Good coffee. Good ice cream. Good soup and sandwiches. Just what the hiker needs who has newly arrived from Everett. Or is just setting out for Seattle.

STILLAGUAMISH RIVER

Of all the rivers within the close ken (an easy day's round-trip drive) of Puget Sound City, the Stillaguamish is the most varied. At Stanwood it meanders among cows into the Whulge, the first stream north of the Nisqually to meet tidewater in pastoral rather than industrial mode. In the headwaters it flows from glaciers that hang high above farms, strikingly Alpine-like.

Between the two forks and their geometrically fenced floodplains lies the Boulder River Wilderness, established in 1984. Less known to hikers is the thrust of highlands west from the wilderness to tree-farming (and tree-mining) country. The heights of Olo, Blue, and Wheeler have been scalped almost to the last huckleberry bush and will not see chainsaws again until some century after the 21st. The broad views over the lowlands from near the Cascade front therefore will last almost that long. Not surveyed for this book was the absolute front, 1770-foot Ebey Hill and 2240-foot Jordan Mountain. Clearcut in the late 1980s, the scarp has become a favorite family drive for picnicking and sunset-watching. (See the February 1989 *Signpost* for driving directions.)

This lowland-invading peninsula of high country is paralleled by two others. South of the South Fork Stillaguamish is the ridge climaxing in Mt. Pilchuck. The grand old "Nanga" might be supposed to be totally tramped by boots. Yet the south slopes above the Pilchuck River (the River not the Creek; "pilchuck" is Chinook jargon for "red water," or as we call it, "mountain tea," and there's a lot of it around) are neglected. Why has no government agency been smart enough to reopen the south-slope summit trail, free of white slop months before the north-side trail is suitable for genteel travel?

North of the North Fork the highland peninsula splits in two, divided by the odd valley that accommodates Deer Creek, flowing south, and Lake Cavanaugh-Pilchuck Creek (the Creek not the River) flowing westerly. The valley cuts off an "island" of peaks — Frailey, Washington, and Stimson—a marvelous opportunity for a city-close, mountain-edge, all-year trail system. North of the Cavanaugh valley are the Cultus Mountains, where logging long ago obliterated the trails, but to whose abandoned logging roads the boots are returning for snowline-probing and bush-roaming.

The sensitive hiker duly honors the birds and beasts, the flowers and trees, and is interested by the perspectives on man's reshaping of the landscape. He should not overlook the reshaping by Nature. To comprehend the landscape, visualize the Canadian ice overtopping peaks as high as 4000 feet, pushing from the lowlands up such valleys as those of Lake Cavanaugh and Jim Creek, and up the Stillaguamish North Fork nearly to Whitehorse, and up the South Fork far past Pilchuck, dumping all that gravel and clay and till. The observer also must visualize the Big River, carrying as much water as today's Columbia, fed by all the streams of the North Cascades, flowing along the ice margin, dodging this way and that, trying to find a way to Aberdeen.

USGS maps: Stanwood, Arlington West, Arlington East, Lake Stevens, Granite Falls, Silverton, Clear Lake, Oso, Fortson, Darrington

Stillaguamish River: From Whulge to the Forks (map—page 46)

During the first bull market for new lowland trails, in the 1960s-1970s, everyone was excited about routes from the saltwater to the glacier snouts. Citizens, then Snohomish County Parks, proposed trails from Port Susan and Skagit Bay to the

Mount Rainier from near summit of Mt. Pilchuck

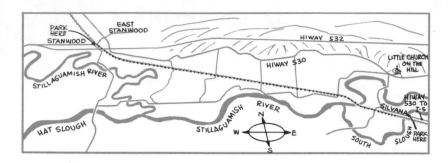

Cascade Crest. Stanwood would be the Whulge trailhead for the segment extending east to Arlington. There two branches would diverge, up the North Fork and South Fork (see below).

Stanwood to Silvana (map—page 46)

The 2-mile-wide floodplain features meanders and sloughs and oxbows, cows in green pastures, handsome old farmhouses and barns. The rustic scene is traversed by an excellent trail marked by two parallel steel rails.

Leave I-5 on Exit 208 and drive Highway 530 west. Just before Silvana is a bridge crossing the river, parallel to a railroad bridge. On the far side is a sign, "Silvana River Access. Snohomish County Parks." Park here, elevation 29 feet, and hit the tracks west. Or, continue driving (pausing to visit the Little White Church on the Hill) to Stanwood, elevation 7 feet; park and hit the tracks east. For shorter walks, a half-dozen country lanes off 530 cross the tracks.

Except when the infrequent train passes, the dominant sounds out there in the middle of the plain are birds singing in creek tanglewoods, cows mooing, plows plowing, grass growing.

Round trip up to 11 miles, allow up to 7 hours
High point 29 feet, minor elevation gain
All year

The Island (map—page 46)

A water-side path on pasture edges and river bars readily could be established the 8 river miles from Silvana to Arlington, but at present the route is cluttered by barbed-wire fences and brush. However, easements purchased by the State Wildlife Department make possible an easy, fairly lengthy walk that samples the section known as The Island, enclosed between the present river channel on the north side of the floodplain and an old one, now occupied by Portage Creek, on the south side.

From Exit 208 on I-5 drive Highway 530 west ¾ mile and turn north on 7th Avenue N.E. (Gulhaugen Road) 1 mile to the end by the river (beside Exit 208), elevation 40 feet.

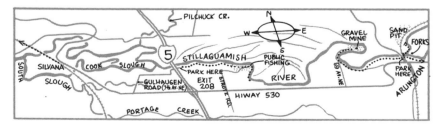

Stillaguamish River near Blue Stilly Park

The path begins in willow woods, drops to a gravel bar, climbs to a pasture edge. Occasional fences (to keep cows in, not people out) are simply stepped over. On the bluff across the river is a wildwood from which bears emerge to go fishing. According to a camper met by the older surveyor, the place is infested by sasquatches, red eyes burning in the black night, nostrils steaming, B.O. sending dogs into hysterics. The broad, green-brown river sweeps along between steep bluff and farmers' riprap, dividing around an island of cotton-woods.

In 1 long mile is private (public camping) Blue Stilly Park and a second Wildlife Department access (from Highway 530 via Strotz Road, also signed 27th Avenue N.E., 1/2 mile east of Exit 208). Gravel bars and pastures lead around a bend a final 1/4 mile to a mean-it fence marking the end of easement.

Round trip 3 miles, allow 1 1/2 hours
High point 40 feet, no elevation gain

47

The Forks (map—page 48)
The magnificent sandbar is thronged in season with kiddies building castles, bigger folks swimming in the deep, brown-green, silt-murky pools, and by fishermen.

Drive Highway 9 north in Arlington to the town edge and Haller Bridge Park, elevation 60 feet.

In high water the rush of the river around the loop is exciting to see—from a dry distance.

At medium-low water the big bar is walkable downstream ³/₄ mile. The Dike Road can be walked another 1 mile to a boggling-huge gravel mine.

In low-enough water one can mosey up the South Fork a ways, and also cross the river and poke around a bit on the North Fork. River forks are geographically significant and ever-amusing.

Round trip 2-4 miles, allow 1 ¹/₂-2 ¹/₂ hours
High point 60 feet, no elevation gain

River Meadows Regional Park (map—page 48)

Someday there will be a trail the entire 15 miles from Arlington to Granite Falls, tying to the Monte Cristo Railroad. Perhaps only the Green River and its gorge surpass this stretch of the Stillaguamish for wild excitement. A 200-acre Snohomish County Park samples the scene.

Drive Highway 530 east about 0.5 mile from the Arlington town-edge bridge and turn right on Jordan Road ("Granite Falls"). In 0.8 mile more turn right again, again on Jordan Road. In some 2.5 miles more cross Jim Creek; 0.7 mile beyond is the park entrance, signed "River Meadows." The entry road descends four alluvial terraces representing four river eras. From the highway on the topmost level, 209 feet, the way drops to a terrace featuring a barn and orchard, then to a forest flat, and then a broad field very fit for cows. At the field edge, 0.5 mile from the highway, the road ends at the last step down, to the water. Park, elevation 100 feet.

The park was acquired in the 1970s when funds were still flowing from the federals, when Snohomish County Parks was alive and well. A new administration in D.C. cut off the money. As of 1988 the park is undeveloped; a deteriorating picnic area and rude campground speak of past plans. However, the walking needs no improvement.

For the introduction, walk downstream past the picnic tables into alder-cottonwood forest. The closed-to-vehicles road ends in ¹/₂ mile on a river bar across from a 200-foot wall of glacial clay and till. A fishermen's path proceeds another ¹/₂ mile, nearly to Jim Creek; where the terrace pinches out, a rude path ascends to the next level and a good trail leading to the highway.

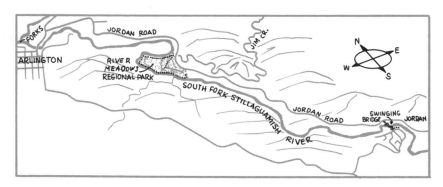

Jordan Bridge and South Fork Stillaguamish River

Now go upstream, close by the river in the narrowing pasture, ½ mile to the terrace end and park boundary. It's all wild, just trees and water and birds. A path continues and might be walkable another 2 miles or so. Or might not.

If, after this introduction, further exercise is desired, by no means ignore the gravel bars.

Introductory round trip 3 miles, allow 2 hours
High point 100 feet, no elevation gain
All year

While in the vicinity, don't overlook another prize offered by Snohomish County Parks. Continue upriver on Jordan Road a scant 3 miles to Jordan General Store. Park in the space provided and cross the Jordan Bridge, a swinging footbridge built in 1977 to replace the rotted-out historic structure. The span gives a bouncing walk (don't run) and fine river views; a path leads to a picnic-type gravel bar.

Pilchuck Vista (map—page 50)

When the summit trail on the north side of Nanga Pilchuck is up to your hiking shorts in snow, as is normally the case until July, why fight it? Come to the sunny south side of the mountain, where the undrivable old logging road melts out in April, perhaps even March, and climbs to views across the Pilchuck River valley to the Skykomish and on south to Seattle, and out west to Granite Falls and Everett and Port Susan and Whidbey Island, and much more too.

From Highway 2 at Monroe drive north on Woods Creek Road (part of the way signed Yeager Road) 11 miles to a Y where the left goes to Snohomish. Turn right, and in a couple hundred feet right again, following signs for Lake Roesiger Park. Continue 4 miles to the north end of the lake and at the junction there proceed straight. In 2-1/4 more miles, a long 17 from Monroe, gravel road SL-P-SP-500 makes a reverse turn right. (This spot also can be reached by driving the Monroe highway south 4.7 miles from Granite Falls; see Littler Pilchuck.) The (unsigned) "Sultan Basin Road," as some maps call it, follows the Pilchuck River upstream. At 4 miles from the blacktop is a Y, 706 feet; go left, uphill, climbing very steeply from the river, on P-5100. In 1.7 miles is a Y; make the reverse turn right, climbing even more steeply. In 0.4 mile, a total 6 miles from the highway, is a Y. Park here, elevation 1600 feet.

A newer road (SL-P-519) climbs left. The older, narrow road contouring right, SL-P-SP-510, is the hiking route. At no great distance from the Y the grade is washed out by a snowmelt creek; the crossing is easily walkable but not razzable.

The way ascends eastward across steep slopes of Pilchuck. In a scant 1/2 mile is the first joy—the 60-foot waterfall, in a narrow slot, of West Fork Kelly Creek, a cool corner on a warm day, stirring thoughts of showerbaths. Windows in the second-growth open to valley and lowland vistas. In 1 mile more, at 2150 feet, just past a road-obliterating blowout, is dandy East Fork Kelly Creek; a logging spur crosses, but a hundred feet short of the stream, switchback west into a bit of nice virgin forest, recross the blowout, switchback east and west and east again, emerging from greenery into a poorly restocked clearcut of the early 1950s and the start of wide views. At 2750 feet the road crosses East Fork Kelly Creek, brawling down granite boulders, and climbs to another creek; just before it, switchback west; views become nearly continuous. At 3200 feet is the final switchback, under a granite wall. Going east from here, the way crosses a small marshy flat below a basinlet and ascends to an end on a promontory,

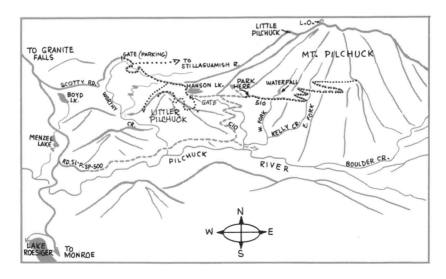

Water cascading down on the Monte Cristo Railroad

3525 feet, 4-¹/₂ miles from the car. Climb a few yards up the clearcut to a knoll, marveling at how little the shrubby trees have grown in a third of a century. This ain't farming, this was a cellulose mine.

From Knoll 3550, close to the uppermost limit of the clearcut, above the gulch of loud Boulder Creek, admire the panorama. Virgin forests rise steeply to the 5324-foot summit; from near here a trail used to go to the top, and ought to be reopened. Below is the Pilchuck River. Across is the amazing plateau where sits Echo Lake, and beyond are Woods Creek valley, Skykomish valley, Monroe, High Rock Hills, Mt. Sultan, Seattle. Leftward are Pilchuck headwaters and, across the unseen Sultan River, Blue. Rightward are Lake Roesiger, Lake Stevens, Farm and hamlets, Everett pulpmills, the Olympics.

Round trip 9 miles, allow 6 hours
High point 3550 feet, elevation gain 2000 feet
April-November

Littler Pilchuck (map—page 50)

On the absolute westernmost edge of the Cascades, snuggled at the foot of Pilchuck's subsummit, Little Pilchuck, boldly stands the jaunty footstool peaklet of "Littler Pilchuck." Prominent from miles around, the trimming of some of the greenery from the summit area has given it popularity as a viewpoint open to the boots when the high country is unpleasantly white and sloppy. The stroll has other amenities, including the marsh-meadow shores of Hanson Lake.

Drive Highway 92 to the east edge of Granite Falls. At the stoplight there, turn right on Alder. In three blocks turn left on the backroad highway to Monroe. At a Y in 2 miles, go left on Scotty Road. In 1.3 miles pavement ends at a sign, "Primitive Road. No Warning Signs." In 0.3 mile is a Y; go left. In 1.3 miles is another Y; continue straight ahead, right. In 0.3 more mile, 1.6 miles from the "Primitive" sign, is a gate, elevation 720 feet. (Even if the gate is open, do not drive on—you may get locked in. But don't complain about the gate; the exclusion of public vehicles is what makes this a quiet footroad, the peace broken only by an occasional logging truck.)

At the Y just beyond the gate go right, across the wide lake-meadow valley of Worthy Creek. On the far side go right. Climb in young plantations by a noble waterfall, cross and recross and recross Worthy Creek, and emerge into big skies of the tiny-tree plateau. Ahead leaps up the imposing bulk of Pilchuck. Also leaping up, less ambitiously, is 2350-foot Littler Pilchuck.

At all the many junctions stick with the obvious main road, steering toward Littler. Pass below its cliffs, along the denuded shores of Hanson Lake, 1400 feet. At the lake head, 3-3/4 miles from the gate, is a fork, 1480 feet. Turn right and up 1/8 mile to a gate. Proceed on by, avoiding spurs. The forest is mainly hemlock—spurned, so far, by the loggers. Small waterfalls splash. If the trip is done to take advantage of a foot or so of fresh snow, it will be enlivened by myriad tracks of dogs and cats (coyote and bob) and Littler critters.

At 1840 feet, 1/2 mile from the second gate, a landing gives views up to Big and Little Pilchuck. The road forks in another 3/4 mile, 2240 feet; go left 1/8 mile to the main summit, 2320 feet, cleared for a tower, two huge discs, and a noisy generator. Here and nearby and on the ascent are views to pulpmill plumes of Everett, shining waters of Possession Sound, Hat Island, Whidbey Island, Jordan and Blue and Olo and Green.

There's a lot more exploring to do on sideroads up the Pilchuck scarp, to an overlook of Lake Julia, and elsewhere. And for an entirely different trip, after crossing the meadow-lake valley bottom of Worthy Creek, take the left fork. From it, spurs lead to other peaklet viewpoints. It is also possible, if not entirely pleasant, to descend precipitously (but perhaps safely) into the Stillaguamish gorge and look across to the Monte Cristo Railroad.

Round trip to summit 10-3/8 miles, allow 6 hours
High point 2320 feet, elevation gain 1600 feet
All year

Monte Cristo Railroad (map—page 53)

White water churning through a wild green gorge at the edge of the lowlands, close to Puget Sound City, open to walking the whole year. That's the South Fork Stillaguamish River.

Plus history! To bring out gold and silver and other goodies, "as rich as Monte Cristo," the incredible railway was built through canyon and forest, reaching Granite Falls in October 1892 and Monte Cristo in August 1893. That winter floods tore out the grade, as other floods did other winters. Rebuilt in 1902, when only the most vacant-eyed dreamers still persisted in burrowing away at Monte Cristo, the line was operated with a gasoline-engine car (the "Galloping Goose") through the 1920s, largely for

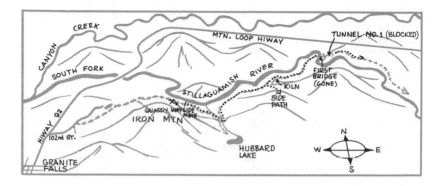

tourist excursions. A flood in 1930 ended that, and in 1936 the track was dismantled, and in 1942 an auto road was completed to Monte Cristo, occupying most of the grade from Verlot upvalley.

However, the 12 miles of rail grade from Granite Falls to Verlot have been partly left alone by man, partly not obliterated by Nature. Artifacts of the engineering feat—dating halfway back to inception of the Industrial Revolution—compete with scenery. Snohomish County Parks had a grand plan for preservation and respectful recreation; a change in the administration at Washington,D.C. cut off federal funds and pretty well put County Parks out of business. Does State Parks have a plan? Does anybody care? Yes indeed. Even now, when the sole guardian is Divine Providence, the route is prowled by history buffs and wildland fans. Some of the walks are very easy. Others are beastly.

Wayside Mine to First Bridge (map—page 53)

Consider this stretch to be "in the bank," awaiting a more settled future and a government that cares. As of 1988, walking is not absolutely forbidden but can be extremely dangerous. Go to a library to consult previous editions of this book to find out what you're missing.

First Bridge to Blocked Tunnel (map—page 53)

From First Bridge upstream 2 1/2 miles to Tunnel No. 3 no trail ever has been provided by benefactors. Explorers must be sturdy and indefatigable. Much of a rainy, drippy-brush, salmonberry-slashing, slippery-muck day the older surveyor suffered pain, frustration, and humiliation here. He has no guidance to offer.

Blocked Tunnel to Old Robe (map—page 53)

Here is everybody's favorite tour, the long-tamed classic. Tunnels and masonry vividly preserve memories of the railroad. And the reason for the tunnels is that here the river is its most exciting, a white turmoil in a slot gorge of black cliffs and green

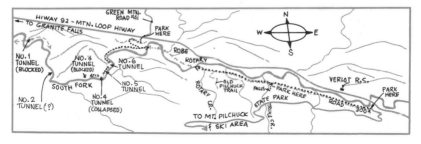

jungles. In miles the walk is short, but the sometime roughness and the archaeological riches make for a long day. Scott Paper (the former land owner) has logged slopes above with care to leave the gorge undisturbed.

Drive Highway 92 east from beautiful downtown Granite Falls 7 miles to where road No. 41 ("Tupso Pass") veers off left. Park on the wide highway shoulder, elevation 1000 feet.

David Ripperger, Eagle Scout of Troop 43, has erected a handsome brick-and-log sign, "Old Robe," to mark the trailhead. Signed "Tunnel 6 1.6 miles, Tunnel 5 1.8 miles," the trail crosses the plantation and descends a forested hillside to an alluvial terrace, at 1/4 mile intersecting a woods road. Turn right and follow the road as it drops to a lower terrace, makes a U-turn upvalley, then a U-turn downvalley. (Here the old rail grade is joined. A grownover lane goes upvalley a short bit to a sidechannel of the river. In low water a person might wade to a causeway—but to little purpose, since Robe Valley starts here and the 1 mile upstream to the site of the Rotary Bridge is built up and PRIVATE KEEP OUT.)

At 1 mile from the highway the woods road ends on the riverbank and the trail proceeds downstream along the edge of a wide, marshy alder bottom. In 1/3 mile the bottom ends and the grade slices the canyon wall. (Here a sidetrail climbs to rotten boards, a chimney, and a trail to a logging road, an alternative approach from the highway.)

Now the fun! The river enters a gorge and turns crazy white. Here began the engineering feats, the blasting and concreting, the hole-digging and wall-building. At 1/4 mile from the alder bottom is Tunnel No. 6, a spooky cavern 30 feet high and about as wide, 300 feet long, littered with old timbers, ties still set in rock slots.

Returning to daylight, a walker finds the river a tumult of cataracts, the grade narrow, the gorge wild, the ghosts pushy. A bit farther is Tunnel No. 5, 100 feet long, the downstream mouth partly blocked. The grade enters a deep cut blocked by a heap of debris (Tunnel No. 4, collapsed) over which the path clambers. Then comes a single concrete span arched over a rock chute plunging to the river, and a decent place to halt, at 800 feet, 1/2 mile from Tunnel No. 6. The chute demands a couple steps most folks won't care to dare. And anyhow, a few yards on is Tunnel No. 3, blocked, no way through and the exposed trail over the top of the ridge not something to discuss in polite society.

Round trip 4 1/2 miles, allow 5 hours
High point 1000 feet, elevation gain 400 feet
All year

Rotary Bridge to Verlot (map—page 53)

Across the river from the highway the grade parallels the stream in great green woods, passes beaver marshes and waterfalls, and joy would reign supreme—except that 2 miles of the way have been made into a road. Still, when the road quits there remains a superb stretch of wheelfree walking, so tangled at the end, indeed, as to become virtually free of feet.

Drive Highway 92 to the east end of Verlot and turn right on the Mt. Pilchuck road. Almost immediately turn right again on the Monte Cristo Grade Road. For the longest possible walk, park here, elevation 999 feet.

When crowds of machines aren't razzing by, the road is a grand stroll, close by the river, past a fine waterfall of a nameless creek, a noble rock wall, the stub of the old bridge over to the Verlot Campground. Then edging inland, the way goes through silvery alders by a marshy pond fed by waterfalls of Heather Creek. More gorgeous forest, another beavery pond, and at 2 miles, where a sideroad leads right to private lots by the river, the road abruptly narrows. If you've been driving, quit now, elevation 900 feet.

Tunnel No. 6 on the old Monte Cristo Railroad

In a few steps is Triple Creek, the bridge a mass of collapsed timbers but the crossing generally a simple hippetty-hop involving naught worse than wet ankles.

(Before crossing, admire the waterfall. Then take the trail uphill 200 feet to an even more admirable falls. Amid intense green of the mossy big-tree underworld, the whiteness of the 40-foot falls dazzles.)

Machetes wielded by Scouts once trenched the salmonberry thickets 1/2 mile beyond Triple Creek. There the way returns to the river, then thrusts into a great swamp (beavers at work) where are heard the falls of nearby Hawthorn Creek. But as of 1978 (and 1981 and doubtless 1988) the machetes had quit and so did the surveyor.

May the benefactors return with cold steel to finish the slaughter of the brambles. In the scant 1 mile downstream from the swamp will then be added these items of interest: Hawthorn Creek; the short sideroad uphill to what was in 1940 the start of the trail to the summit of Pilchuck; Rotary Creek; the site of the railroad bridge to old Rotary.

Round trip 1 or 3 or 7 miles, allow 1-5 hours
High point 999 feet, minor elevation gain
All year

Heather Lake (map—page 57)

The trees are the superstars here, the lake merely an extra added attraction—prettiest, indeed, when you can't see it, all covered with snow beneath cirque cliffs dribbling (or thundering) avalanches. Bright are the blossoms of summer but dumbfounding in all seasons are the giants of the forest primeval. The trail is popular with snowline-probers and, in early winter, after hard freezes but before deep snows, ice-skaters. There's probably no weekend of the year that hikers don't visit the lake, so the route generally is boot-beaten and evident. But to repeat, if snow grows too deep or slippery, forget the lake—the trees are what it's all about anyhow.

Drive Highway 92 to the east edge of Verlot and turn right, over the river, on the Mt. Pilchuck road. At 1.2 miles is a large parking area for the Heather Lake trail. Elevation, 1350 feet.

The hiker-only path follows a logging road of the late 1940s up through tall second-growth. Nearing Heather Creek, in views down to the valley and across to Green and Olo and Three Fingers, the trail quits the old road and switchbacks steeply upward, leaving trees 30 years old for those centuries ancient, leaving the young forest for a system that is, aside from the ages of individual members, 10,000 years old. What a change in mood! The young forest is claustrophobic dense-lush. The old forest is an open, airy, green-light chamber under the canopy of high-arching branches. Confronted by cedars 7 feet in diameter, one feels the urge to drop to the knees.

The cathedral of cedars and hemlocks continues upward to the lip of the cirque, where the way flattens amid subalpine trees. Commonly the snowline is met here. Proceed, if desired, to the shore. Watch the skaters. Or the avalanches. Or the flying snowballs. Or the water ouzels. Or whatever is happening. Clamber onto a shoreside boulder for lunch. Circle the shore, in proper season sniffing the pretty flowers.

Round trip 4 miles, allow 3 hours
High point 2450 feet, elevation gain 1100 feet
June-November (for the forest, March-December)

Mount Pilchuck (map—page 57)

From Chuckanut Mountain to the Bald Hills, up and down the length of the Cascade front, the *Footsore* series spotlights dozens of mountain-edge viewpoints. However, undisputed monarch of them all is Nanga Pilchuck. Pushing an abrupt and imposing vertical mile above farms and villages, jutting so far out in lowlands that from the top you can practically see fish jump in saltwater bays, it provides a panorama beyond praise. Towers of downtown Seattle, pulpmill plumes of Everett and Port Townsend, oil-refinery plumes of Anacortes. The Whulge from Puget Sound to Possession Sound and Strait of Juan de Fuca and Skagit Bay. Olympic Mountains and San Juan Islands and Vancouver Island. Volcanoes from Baker to Glacier to Rainier. Near and far, a couple thousand Cascade peaks. There's too much for one trip, you must keep returning, again and again.

Drive Highway 92 to the east edge of Verlot and turn right, over the river, on the Mt. Pilchuck road. Ascend 7 miles to Rotary Creek and the trailhead, elevation 3100 feet.

When the trail started down by the Stillaguamish River (see Monte Cristo Railroad) this area, 5 miles from the road, was called Cedar Flats and was the standard camp for summit climbers. Logging in the late 1940s and early 1950s obliterated the lower trail, until then among the most popular in the state. Much of the upper portion was devastated to develop a portion of 1975-acre Mt. Pilchuck State Park as a fifth-rate ski area; this was abandoned in the late 1970s.

Skirting desolation, the trail ascends in virgin forest, passing glades bright with flowers in season, bushes blue with berries in season. At the cliffy base of Little Pilchuck the way sidehills to the site of the upper lift terminal at 4300 feet. Then, leaving all this nonsense behind and below, the path enters a garden of ice-polished-

A shoulder of Mt. Pilchuck overlooking Heather Lake

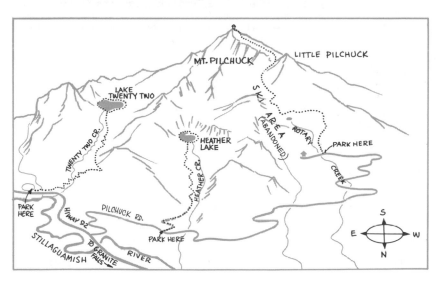

and-scratched granite slabs, heather and alpine shrubs, flowers and creeks. And the view north grows. At 4600 feet the Little Pilchuck saddle is topped. Now the view south begins. Climbing steeply along granite walls of the final peak, the trail swings around on south slopes into clumps of storm-sculptured mountain hemlocks, then switchbacks and scrambles to the granite-jumble summit, where short ladders lead to the old fire lookout, 5324 feet.

The cabin offers some shelter from freezing blasts but no solace for the giddy, hanging as it does above the northern precipice. If the ocean of air doesn't make you dizzy, the 360-degree view very well may, what with swinging the head around and around.

Round trip 4 miles, allow 4 hours
High point 5324 feet, elevation gain 2300 feet
July-October

Lake Twenty Two (map—page 57)

A daughter of the surveyor was much impressed, at a certain age, by white-foaming torrents plunging down cliffs—as she called them, "wow-fows." The climb to Lake Twenty Two ends in a cirque where waters ripple and cliffs beetle, and that's all very pretty. But this really is a walk to exclaim at the wowfows. And the wow trees. Set aside in 1947 to permit comparison of virgin systems with managed (logged) ones, the 790-acre Lake Twenty Two Research Natural Area is among the most-visited, most-loved wilderness forests in the Cascades. (No camping, no fires, walk softly).

Drive Highway 92 east 0.6 mile from the Mt. Pilchuck road and turn right to the trailhead parking area, elevation 1100 feet.

The trail begins in an arboretum of giant trees and tiny flowers, gently ascends the forest slope downvalley ⅓ mile to a junction with the old trail. The loitering ends here, the way is now straight up the hill. Tree-gawking continues, the crown canopy of 3-foot hemlocks and 9-foot cedars high above the steep slopes of moss and ferns. In ¼ mile, at 1400 feet, is a bridge over Twentytwo Creek and the first of the wonderful falls; particularly on hot summer days, many walkers never proceed past the green pools and chill spray. But a bit farther is a sidepath to a truly sensational falls, and soon another. Now the way leaves the creek and ascends an avalanche slope with views over the valley to Green, Liberty, and the tip of Three Fingers, and up the valley to Big Four. Also in sight are clay banks—silt deposited in the lake dammed by the Canadian glacier, from which the Big River flowed over the divide east of Pilchuck (see Twin Falls Lake).

Switchbacking over the top of the avalanche slope and a rockslide, the trail reenters big-tree forest, crosses any number of sipping creeks, passes another terrific falls, and at last flattens in a little valley to the lakeshore. A solemn spot, avalanche snow lingering most of most summers beneath the cirque headwall. But if snow prevents reaching it, as it well may in spring at the avalanche slope, the trip is still a huge success at the third wowfow. Or second. Or first.

Round trip 4 miles, allow 3 hours
High point 2450 feet, elevation gain 1400 feet
June-November (to the wowfows, March)

Bear Lake and Pinnacle Lake (map—page 61)

Excellent old lichen-decorated trees, valley views, a forest lake minutes from the car, and a subalpine lake a good sweat distant.

Drive Highway 92 east 4.6 miles from the Verlot Public Service Center (nee Ranger Station) and just before Schweitzer Creek turn right on road No. 4020, "Bald Mtn.

Twenty Two Creek beside the lake trail

Ashland Lakes. Twin Falls Lake. Trailhead 5 miles." Avoid obviously lesser spurs and stay on the main road, climbing to views over the Stillaguamish valley to Three Fingers. At 2.6 miles is a junction. Road No. 4020 goes ahead to Boardman Lake. Turn right on No. 4021, signed "Bear Lake—Pinnacle Lake." In 1.4 miles is a Y, the uphill left signed "4021-016—Trailhead." Go right on a contour, cross Black Creek, dodge spurs, and in about 1.5 more miles cross Bear Creek to the trailhead parking area, elevation 2650 feet.

The graveled turnpike trail (hikers only—peace, it's wonderful!) ascends in hemlock-cedar forest a short bit to a Y. The right fork offers in passing a broad view down to the valley and the source of the Stillaguamish River's murkiness, a bank of blue clay (deposited in a lake dammed by the Canadian glacier). A few feet onward is forest-ringed Bear Lake, 2775 feet.

Back at the Y, the left fork soon loses the fancy gravel and becomes a staircase of roots and rocks switchbacking up and up to a ridge crest. From there the way swings into the valley of Black Creek, passes little ponds in little subalpine gardens, and drops a bit to the shores of Pinnacle Lake, 2 miles, 3800 feet.

Presumably a pinnacle is in the vicinity? Cliffs, at least, and in season there surely are pretty flowers, and the trees are pleasing. What else? Golly knows, maybe bears. All the older surveyor can testify to is a bowl of milk, a homogeneous blur of fog and snow, some of the latter so flat it doubtless was the lake. But that sort of scene is nothing to sneeze at, not with pointy-top trees in Japanese-etching silhouette, and a varied thrush trilling.

Round trip 4 miles, allow 3 hours
High point 3800 feet, elevation gain 1300 feet
May-November

Boardwalk on the Ashland Lakes trail

Ashland Lakes and Twin Falls Lake
(map—page 61)

Behind the ice dam of the Canadian glacier a huge lake filled, fed by the Skagit and Suiattle and Sauk and Stillaguamish Rivers. The level rose to overtop the ridge east of Pilchuck and the Big River flowed over the granite spine, waterfalling to join the Skykomish River. Ice and Big River have been gone these 15,000 years but the waterfalls remain, though now only Wilson Creek tumbles down the granite walls. Between upper and lower falls is the pothole of tiny Twin Falls Lake, which might be called "Plunge Basin Lake," or "Falls-In-Falls-Out Lake." This final feature of the trip is the show-stopper, but for shorter hikes or early in spring there are three delightful subalpine meadow-marsh lakes on the way.

Drive as for Bear Lake (which see) to the Y at 4 miles. Go left, uphill, on the lesser road signed "4021-015—Trailhead." In a few hundred feet is the trailhead, signed "Bald Mtn. Trail" on the left and "Ashland Lakes Trailhead" on the right. Park on a turnout just beyond the signs. Elevation, about 2400 feet.

Note the broad valley westward, below Pilchuck. Here, where Black Creek now flows, the Big River crossed the ridge. At the far end of the trough is Twin Falls Lake; the trail, however, takes a roundabout route via Ashland Lakes.

The trail begins on a logging road closed to wheels. After 1 mile of 1960s clearcut the way enters virgin forest of lichen-hung hemlocks and big old half-alive cedars. Built by the state Department of Natural Resources in 1972-75, the trail is novel, interesting, and a bit controversial. A few call it costly and obtrusive; most call it meadow-preserving, mud-avoiding, wheel-excluding, and environmentally sensitive. Much of the length consists of plank walks, parts are puncheon, others are cedar-round "stepping blocks," and still others are granite staircases. Fun. By the 1980s the planks were getting slippery; the DNR then installed miles of non-skid "hardware cloth." Good thinking.

In 1 3/4 miles a sidetrail drops left to Beaver Plant Lake, 2880 feet, a shallow meadow-bog-pond ringed by plank walks, permitting a circling of the shores without stomping them to black muck. Campsites here.

At the far end of the lake is a Y in the puncheon. The left is to Bald Mountain (see *100 Hikes in the Glacier Peak Region*); go right. In a short bit is another Y, the two paths (the right is shortest) going around opposite shores of Upper Ashland Lake on plank walks, rejoining at the outlet, 2860 feet. More camps.

Now the trail drops a bit, following the lake outlet, Wilson Creek, switchbacking. In a long 1/4 mile a sidetrail goes left, dropping a bit to Lower Ashland Lake, 2700 feet, 3 miles from the trailhead. Another shore-circling loop in meadows and forests. More camps.

The way starts down for real, first crossing Wilson Creek. (Incorrectly shown by the USGS map, this creek actually flows to the waterfalls of the Big River.) Contouring and switchbacking, dodging through granite cliffs, twice via bridges built to avoid having to blast rock, the trail comes in view of the lower waterfall and a vista out the Pilchuck River valley, sidehills to the lip of the lower waterfall, which flows from a pool of foam-flecked weak tea beneath a marvelous granite wall. A few steps more lead to the plunge basin of the upper falls, 2300 feet, 1 1/2 miles from Lower Ashland Lakes, 4 1/2 miles from the trailhead.

Sit by the shore (or on a summer day swim the waters) and admire the upper waterfall dropping 125 feet down the granite. In mind's eye see, here, the Big River, maybe as big as today's Columbia. Horrors.

For views, visit the privies on a rock outcrop above the camp. Look to the 400-foot falls below the lake and south over the valley of Pilchuck River to the lowlands.

Round trip to Twin Falls Lake 9 miles, allow 6 hours
High point 2900 feet, elevation gain 1300 feet
May-November

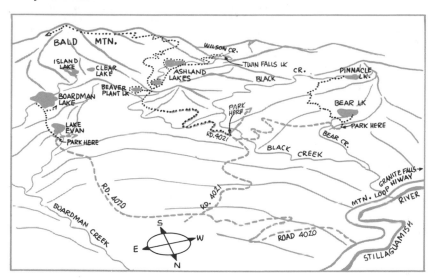

Trout Lake and Olo Mountain (map—page 62)

Saunter along a (usually) wheelfree footroad in lovely woods, by cattail marshes, to a beautiful lake deep in a valley. Or sturdily climb high and see cirques (sometimes) on the side of Pilchuck, smoke curling from cabins by the Stillaguamish, radio towers of the Navy, plumes from Everett pulpmills, and the Mukilteo ferry. Thanks to a company gate, see it all with no (well, almost) racketing razzers to jar the contemplative spirit. The route is excellent for snowline-probing; it starts by the highway, crosses numerous creeks never prettier than when snowmelt-fat, and at several elevations reaches contenting-view turnarounds, satisfaction guaranteed.

Drive Highway 92 east from beautiful downtown Granite Falls 4.5 miles to a sign, "Masonic Park." Of the two roads off the highway left, take the first, going a couple hundred feet to a gate. Most of the year this gate is closed and public wheels of all kinds are banned from the road; at such time park here, elevation 601 feet.

In fishing season, from spring to fall, the gate is open and perhaps signed "Trout Lake." Drive the highball-wide logging road as it drops 0.3 mile to Canyon Creek and a Y just beyond the bridge. Park here, elevation 500 feet.

The left, road No. 100, leads to Trout Lake, or Mud Lake as some maps rudely slander the pretty thing. The gate is open on fishing-season weekends, so don't do the walk then, for gosh sake. But on fishing-season weekdays, or weekends the rest of the year, come enjoy. The trip has special attraction on winter days when the snowline is down close to the highway.

In the first mile the pleasant road crosses the creek, climbs by a clearcut, and levels off beside a cattail marsh (the old Johnson Dean Millpond). The way is then in mossy maple forest, over little streams, to the lake—a true gem, not the least muddy—tucked in the second-growth-forested hills. Continue 1/4 mile more to a rocky point which the photographer, who surveyed this trip but is sort of new at it, having worn out only about 50-odd pairs of boots, recommends as a great spot to soak sore feet.

Round trip from second gate 5 miles, allow 3 hours
High point 665 feet, elevation gain 200 feet
All year

Now for the highlands. (They were not resurveyed in 1988, but as viewed from the valley seem unchanged by man. As for Nature, the reader-hiker is requested to file a report with the surveyors.) Even when the highway-side and road No. 100 gates are open, the right fork at the Canyon Creek Y, road No. 200, is gated shut, always closed to public wheels. Olo is ever-lonesome.

Go right 3/4 mile on road No. 200, through a frog city, to a Y. The major road left climbs high on Blue Mountain; go right on lesser road No. 201. In 1/3 mile is a bridge

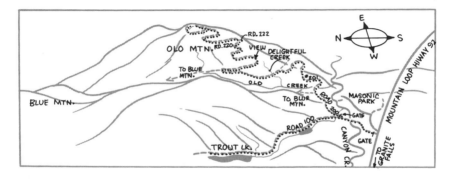

over lovely Olo Creek and the end of flatwalking. Switchback up and up in second-growth from 1940s logging, by windows over Canyon Creek to the lakebed-flat ridge dividing it from the Stillaguamish River. Topping the moraine ridge, the road starts up a rock-hearted ridge. At 1 ³/₄ miles from Olo Creek bridge is a Y, 1400 feet; go left on the lesser road, over a delightful creek, by roadcuts in black metamorphic rock decorated with moss gardens. A series of creeks climaxes in a waterfall down a quarry. Just beyond, 1 mile from Delightful Creek, is a junction with a better road from the Blue Mountain network; switchback right onto this road No. 220. See the Navy towers on Wheeler.

At 2500 feet, ³/₄ mile from Quarry Junction, 5 miles from the highway, pow, a view that demands a long halt (and if snow is deepening, a turnaround). To the trip's best view of Pilchuck are added Big Four, Rainier, Issaquah Alps, Everett, and Olympics.

In ³/₄ mile more, at 2800 feet, is a Y; go left on lesser road No. 220, cut in outcrops of red jasper, and pass a serpentine quarry. Now second-growth from the 1960s screens a wide world. Where a sideroad goes left to a 1970s clearcut, climb right to the ridge crest. The summit is close. Good grief but there's a lot of air around, an enormous sky. At 1 ½ miles from the 2800-foot Y is the last Y. Both forks must be walked.

For the East-South Vista, go right a few yards, until at 3350 feet the road starts down toward on-going (1970s) logging. Sit on a stump of a clearcut and wow away an hour; the near headwaters of Canyon Creek, the finger of Liberty, the brilliant glacier on Three Fingers, and Pilchuck, Si, Tiger. Contrast the total scalping of Olo done by Scott Paper with the Forest Service cutting of small patches on Green, across the valley.

For the West-North Vista, from the Y go left ½ mile to the road-end at 3400 feet, just below the 3451-foot summit, cluttered with rotting heaps of 1977 slash. Along the road and at the end: Seattle towers beside Elliott Bay, Possession Point on Whidbey Island, Strait of Juan de Fuca, Port Townsend pulpmill plume, Ika and Erie and Constitution in the San Juans, Devils and Cultus, Twin Sisters and Baker. And close by, Blue and massive Wheeler, and between them the six Navy radio antennae stretched over Jim Creek.

Round trip from highway 15 miles, allow 9 hours
High point 3400 feet, elevation gain 3000 feet
March-November

Wheeler Mountain (map—page 65)

Tired of the everyday world? Want to get away from it all? We offer you—*escape*. Magnificent views, yes, every step (all 42,000 or so) of the trip. But more—the prickling at the back of the neck as you darkly suspect you have walked right out of the world and never will get home again, not in this lifetime.

Drive Highway 92 east from Granite Falls 7 miles and turn north on road No. 41, signed "Tupso Pass." Follow the "main" road (No. 41, then No. 4110), about 9 miles to the crossing of Canyon Creek. Proceed west about 4.7 miles more from the crossing to a Y. Go left about 3.2 miles, crossing Meadow Creek from slopes of Meadow Mountain to those of Ditney Mountain; beyond a large, nameless creek is a Y, 16 or 17 miles from the highway. Park here, elevation 2100 feet.

Walk the unmaintained and undrivable left fork, contouring and then descending 2 miles to a T at 1691 feet with the private road; the road is normally gated miles and miles away at Highway 92. Go right, round a corner, climb and dip, 1 ½ miles to the crossing of Big Jim Creek at 1950 feet. The route at last touches the base of Wheeler.

At the Y beyond the crossing turn left, downvalley, and climb to a promontory and an extension of the views south to Rainier. The road switchbacks up the ridge spine to a Y at 2720 feet, 1 ½ miles from Big Jim Creek; go left. (The right climbs to the top of, and all over, 3450-foot East Peak of Wheeler, with views, a plateau of lakelets, and no

Wheeler Mountain road

doubt plenty of fun; West Peak, however, gave the older surveyor all the fun he could handle in one day.)

Prominently in view much of the way have been the six wires draped 1-½ miles through the air over Jim Creek from towers on Blue and Wheeler. Presumably because of them, when passing creeks the surveyor felt a strong urge to jump in, shouting "Dive! Dive!" Informed of this, a Navy security officer said it was nonsense; the Jim Creek messages to submarines around the world are, of course, in code. He did warn that hikers illegally snooping too near the towers are liable to burst into flame.

From the Y a contouring 1 ¼ miles into and up the valley of Little Jim Creek lead to a two-creek gulch on the side of East Peak. Just beyond are the first confusing junctions of the day. At a first Y, go right, uphill. At a second, go left, contouring ¾ mile to the crossing of Little Jim Creek, 2800 feet. A couple minutes upstream, in the headwaters basin, is a surprising little lake, the shores a meadow-marsh skunk-cabbage farm.

Now for the final assault; beyond the creek looms mighty West Peak. Swing around the valley, climbing to a Y; take the left, downvalley fork. Excitement impels weary legs as horizons grow in every direction across the rolling, shrub-dotted ridges, uncannily Scottish-moorlike. At 3300 feet, 1 mile from Little Jim, the road completes a sweeping switchback to the right near the ridge crest; at a Y here, go right. A bit beyond is another Y; both forks are mandatory.

First take the right, contouring a scant 1 mile to Whammo Landing, 3400 feet, 9 miles from the car. WHAMMO! This is what you came for: the straight-down view to cows in green pastures, to meandering river and bug-infested highway; east over skinned-brown East Peak to virgin-green Ditney and white Whitehorse and Three Fingers; a long arc of the North Cascades; the flat strata, faultline, and dipping strata of Higgins; Frailey, Cultus, and Baker. And do not miss the lakebed-flat moraines of the Canadian glacier at the mouth of Boulder River valley. Gosh. The same glacier rode over the top of Wheeler, flattening the summit terrain. The ridgetop valleys of Big Jim and Little Jim are the work not of those present-day piddles, but rivers gushing from the ice front.

But save some gasps, return to the previous Y, and take the left. In a few feet is another Y; go right, and at the next two Ys also right, and at the next, left. This isn't really confusing because the summit is near and impossible to miss; in ¾ mile from Whammo Landing Junction the way curves around onto the absolute tippy-top of West Peak Wheeler at 3700 feet. Whee. Added to an inferior but still stunning version of the Whammo panorama is the west view: San Juan Islands, Whidbey, Camano, and silver-shining Whulge waterways from Skagit Bay to Puget Sound. On the way back, a spur offers a south view: Blue, Olo, Pilchuck, Everett, Issaquah Alps, Seattle.

But in case you hadn't noticed, the sun is sinking in the west and the coyotes are howling and it's time to run for home. Hope you make it.

Round trip 20 miles, allow 12 hours
High point 3700 feet, elevation gain 2800 feet
April-November

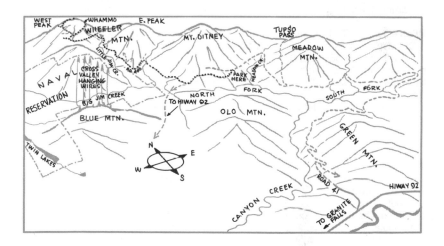

North Fork Stillaguamish River Trail (map—page 67)

Walk from Whulge plain far into the Cascades, partly on banks of wild river in a fine green frenzy of forest, partly in pretty pastoral scenes right out of Old America. The trail is occasionally traversed by iron horses, but as of 1991, Burlington-Northern was planning to abandon the line. The Snohomish-Arlington Trails Coalition is working with Snohomish County Parks to perpetuate the best long-distance, low-elevation path in the county.

The route may well be much-tramped in future years by backpackers—who even now can find pleasant camps, conveniently spaced. The older surveyor made the journey with two one-way walks on separate days, each time thumbing back to his stashed car. The main use, of course, will be for day hikes, Highway 530 providing any number of access points.

Mile 0–4 ³/₄: Arlington to Trafton Fishing Hole (one-way walk 4 ³/₄ miles)

Arguably the very best part of the whole trail, the more glorious for its nearness to Whulge City.

Drive Highway 9 to the north edge of Arlington and park at Haller Bridge Park, elevation 40 feet.

Walk north over the highway bridge, just below the union of the river's two forks, climb the embankment to the railroad grade, and turn left the short bit to the Y of Arlington Junction; go right. After an unprepossessing initial 1 mile past an enormous, motorcycle-infested sand pit, joy begins. For much of a long 2 miles the trail is sliced in hanging-garden walls of rotten sandstone and conglomerate dropping to green pools and white rapids of the wild river, the bird avenue nearly arched over by alders and maples. Wildwoods-wild water end at a river bridge, a logical turnaround for a short walk (6 miles round trip); picnic on any of several secluded gravel bars-swimming beaches.

Now is introduced the route's second major mode, the pastoral, which henceforth alternates with the wild. Beyond fields abruptly rises the front of the Cascades—Washington, Stimson, and "Little Ridge" north, Ebey Hill south. From here on the cows in pastures and herons in sloughs of cutoff meanders are too frequent to be noted. Splendid old wooden barns (they don't build 'em no more). Graceful old farmhouses with full-length verandas where many a generation has spent summer evenings in "front porch" swings.

Suddenly the river is again beside the tracks; as it diverges leftward, hikers can drop to a streambank woods road for the final ¹/₂ mile to an unsigned State Wildlife Department fishing access on a gravel bar of the wild river flowing through wildwoods.

Miles 4 ³/₄–7 ¹/₄: Trafton Fishing Hole to Cicero Bridge (one-way walk 2-¹/₂ miles)

Of lesser interest, but featuring vast pastures with nice barns.

Drive Highway 530 east 0.3 mile from Trafton Road (Jim Creek Road) and turn north on Lime Road, which in 0.5 mile crosses the railroad tracks. Just beyond on the left is the unsigned Wildlife Department public fishing access. Park here, elevation 98 feet.

Wild river is briefly touched, a slough crossed, and the trail heads out for the middle of the floodplain fields. Now the route is definitely leaving lowlands, passing between the portal peaks of Stimson and Ebey. The rails cross the highway and parallel it a last ¹/₄ mile to side-by-side highway and railroad bridges at Cicero.

Mile 7 ¹/₄–10 ³/₄: Cicero Bridge to Oso (one-way walk 3 miles)

More visions of America Past, including rotting artifacts of a lumber mill.

Drive Highway 530 east 3.5 miles from Trafton and park by or near Cicero Bridge, 125 feet. (Two parking options: just before the bridge, between highway and railroad; or turn right before the bridge on Monty Road to "Public Fishing." The gravel bar here is a popular swimming beach.

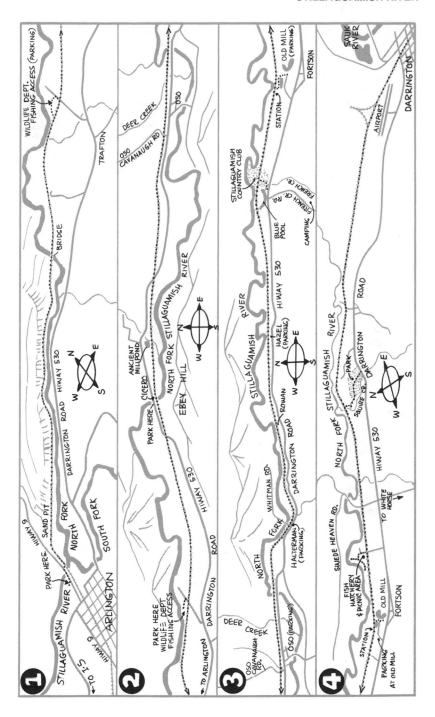

The trail briefly touches the river, then swings away past a large slough with mossy concrete footings and old pilings and a collapsing wooden bridge; presumably this was a millpond. Frailey now dominates the view north. Big-tree forest leads to another touch of the river, across which is a hideaway farm with a gorgeous old barn.

Highway 530 is crossed (parking available) to the route's only significant sally into civilization. With the tracks close by the highway, an old millpond is passed, then the historic, picturesque Oso School. The trail crosses the paved Oso-Cavanaugh Road and river-size Deer Creek, the bridge embellished with such graffiti as "Welcome to Oso, Partytown USA." Wheeler now dominates the view south, but up the valley can be glimpsed glaciers. Frailey falls to the rear on the north and ramparts of Higgins come in sight ahead.

Mile 10 ³/₄–16 ³/₄: Oso to Hazel (one-way walk 6 miles)

The dominant mode shifts from the pastoral toward the wild, the alpine. The geology gets great.

Drive Highway 530 to the major metropolis between Arlington and Darrington, quaint old Oso, elevation 200 feet.

The trail passes a shake mill, community chapel, and fire station, and crosses the river. The valley-bottom flat, previously 2 miles wide, narrows to less than 1 mile. The way hits the river and follows it to Halterman, where Whitman Road (parking) is crossed, 2 miles from Oso.

Wheeler walls the valley on the south. But to the north, now, a central feature of the trail dominates: the geology-textbook folding and faulting of Higgins north, horizontal strata divided by a faultline from folded, dipping strata, one of which forms the great naked slab known as the Roller Rink.

The pastures diminish to occasional openings in woods. For a long stretch the tracks are beside or very near the stream, the river wild, the forest noble.

Note hereabouts terminal moraines of the Canadian glacier, identifiable by exposures of gravel in hillocks.

Decrepit shacks of Rowan Station are passed, and then comes the longest highway-side piece, ameliorated at Hazel by a return to the river.

Mile 16 ³/₄–20 ¹/₂: Hazel to Fortson Mill (one-way walk 3-3/4 miles)

Farms yield to woods, farmhouses to stumpranch cabins and summer homes.

Drive Highway 530 east from Oso 6.2 miles to 310 Street NE (Hazel Road, a section of old highway replaced by a cutoff), which leads to riverside parking, 300 feet.

At every pasture opening in the woods, Higgins grows more impressive. Boulder River is crossed. The trail again follows wild river a long way, passes the long slough called Blue Pool, where fields open on the vista to Whitehorse. In deep woods are cabins of Stillaguamish Country Club, where the tracks cross French Creek, Mingled fields and woods lead to an old train station and millpond.

Mile 20 ¹/₂–27 ¹/₂: Fortson Mill to Darrington (one-way walk 7 miles)

Lots of folks spend the whole day prowling Fortson Mill, surely among the route's top attractions. But also the alpine views climax, and the solitude.

Drive Highway 530 east 9.5 miles from Oso. Just after passing a powerline swath, turn left on Fortson Mill Road to a huge paved circle, around which are artifacts of the vanished mill. Turn right at the circle and drive a woods road by the millpond to a parking area at the east end, elevation 400 feet.

Find a road-path by the pond, cross its outlet on a plank bridge, and proceed along the pond to the tracks near Fortson Station of yore. (However, do not neglect the mill—poke around concrete structures, ax-hewn timbers, rotting pilings, and mysteries; try to figure out what all these vanished structures were for.)

But to proceed east: Highway 530 from now on is distant, making this the longest lonesome stretch of the route. The bad news is that the river is also mostly distant. And pastures become few, meaning forests block the view just as the most impressive

Mt. Higgins and North Fork Stillaguamish River

part of Whitehorse is passed; this gasper of a mountain thus is better admired from the highway than the trail.

Nevertheless, there is another highlight near Fortson. At a long ¹/₂ mile from the station a road from Highway 530 (here ¹/₂ mile south) leads to ponds and picnic areas of a public fish hatchery in a bulge of forest enclosed by a river meander. A sidetrip to hatchery and river can fill up what's left of a day after polishing off Fortson Mill.

To proceed east: In ¹/₂ mile is Swede Heaven Road (crossed ¹/₂ mile from Whitehorse Store on Highway 530), giving great views of Higgins and Whitehorse. For an interesting sidetrip, walk north on this road, over the Stillaguamish, to fields of barns and terrific Whitehorse-Higgins views at the old community of Swede Heaven.

In lonesome woods the trail crosses Squire Creek; less than ¹/₂ mile upstream via rude paths is Squire Creek County Park. The next big event is a succession of decks of logs and rail spurs off left to mills which are the chief reason the railroad still runs.

The mainline tracks bend south to the Darrington Airport (stupendous views of Jumbo and Whitehorse glaciers) and to beautiful downtown Darrington, elevation 549 feet.

One-way trip 27 ¹/₂ miles
High point 549 feet, elevation gain 500 feet
All year

Catkins on alder tree

Boulder River (map—page 71)

How could so gorgeous a wilderness woodland survive at such low elevation, so near cities and sawmills? A miracle? Sort of. Canyon walls too expensive to gouge for tracks saved the valley from railroad loggers. Then, as modern engineers were cranking up to bulldoze roads over the ridges and haul away the juicy giants, the preservation spirit rode to the rescue and in 1984 the Washington Wilderness Act established the Boulder River Wilderness. Virgin forest, wild river, white waterfalls on green-mossy canyon walls.

From Arlington drive Highway 530 east 20.5 miles and just past Milepost 41 turn south on French Creek Road, signed "Road 2010." Pass French Creek Campground and at 3.7 miles from the highway reach a Y. Park here, elevation 948 feet.

The Boulder River trail takes the right fork, straight ahead on the olden-day railroad grade, which was briefly opened in 1952 for a gypo logging show and since has reverted to foot path. In big second-growth the grade contours the sidehill steeply above the Boulder River, cutting through ferny rock walls. At ¾ mile valley and trail turn sharp left. Here are sidepaths down to camps by the river, and up a short ridge to terrifying (but poor) looks straight down to Boulder River Falls and out over the

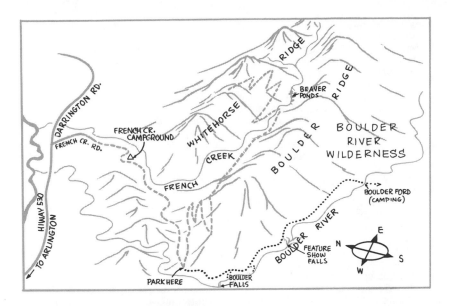

Stillaguamish valley to the strata of Higgins.

Back on the main route, a cliff marks the end of old railroad and start of pure trail, and the transition from great second-growth to awesome virgin forest. In ½ mile is the central extravaganza of the trip. Most parties end the hike here, 1 ¼ miles from the car, and many camp overnight to enjoy the scene: huge boulders in the river, sandbars for wading edges of wide green pools, just a bit milky from stone-grinding of Three Fingers Glacier, and (gasp) the 200-foot vertical wall inscribed with lacework of white foam. Upstream a bit is the show-stopper—a much larger falls down the same precipice.

Enough, certainly. But there's more. Beyond is still another fine falls. And let us now praise the forest, so saturated in this dank valley that trees and rocks and loitering hikers are covered with moss. Cedars grow to 8 feet thick and firs nearly that diameter and hemlocks also do themselves proud. Going up and down, passing a series of delicious creeks, in a scant 3 miles more, 4 miles total from the road, the trail reaches Boulder Ford. A footlog (sometimes) crosses the river but this is the logical turnaround and lunch spot, with just the tiniest windows upvalley to glaciered headwater peaks.

Round trip to ford 8 miles, allow 6 hours
High point 1550 feet, elevation gain 1000 feet
February-December

The Lost Alexander Range (map—page 72)

In 1977 the older surveyor set out to explore the group of Cascade-front peaks cut off from Frailey Mountain by another of those old channels of the Canadian glacier. The USGS Clear Lake quadrangle, 1956 edition (but much of the information dating from 1947-48 and even 1941) showed a "jeep trail" to the summit of 2850-foot Stimson Hill, a "Mt. Washington Trail" winding around the peak's 2705-foot summit, a "Spar Tree Trail" connecting the latter to the "Frailey Mountain Truck Trail" and the "Alexander Trail," this last climbing from the North Fork Stillaguamish River.

The Frailey Mountain "truck trail" is described in this book. Stimson Hill was in the first edition and in 1988 is still easy; close by Rock Creek on Cedarvale Road, 6 miles east of Highway 9, the old "jeep trail" (become service road) takes off from an elevation of 700 feet and climbs 3 ½ miles to the summit. A nice exercise in winter. Window views. Omitted from this edition because the mountain is in that awkward stage: the forest too young to be richly complex, yet not young enough for really big views of the clearcut variety.

> ("If seven gypos, with seven saws,
> Logged here half a day,
> Do you suppose," the Walrus asked,
> "That they could make 'er pay?"
> "No chance," replied the Carpenter,
> "But then we'd see the bay.")

Mt. Washington proved as inaccessible as Mt. Everest used to be. Later, a local Mountaineer smirked while telling the surveyor how he ran up Washington all the time, via an old logging road that climbs the northwest side via an offshoot of an offshoot of Cedarvale. Doing an eyeball scan from below, the surveyor decided not to run. As of 1988 the summit is still hairy, though reputedly with views along the way.

Alexander, aye there's a tale . . . In the words of the first edition:

"Who was Alexander? Why and when was a trail of that name built? And why so bloody steep? And why, after striking so bravely upward into a great wildland forest, does it abruptly come to naught?"

In 1977 the older surveyor walked the old logging railroad grade that started (and still does in 1988) 1 ¼ miles south of Rock Creek on Cedarvale. In 2 miles he was stunned to see a large, old wooden sign, "Alexander Trail, SNF." Why so big and elaborate a sign? The business smacked of the CCC. In the words of 1977:

". . . at the brink of a gully the trail turns left and becomes for-sure-never-anything-but-foot-trail. Pause here to wonder at a moss-and-fern-covered boulder big as a two-storey house. Now address the slope and proceed straight up. In roughly ¾ mile old Alexander gains about 1200 feet beside the aforementioned gully. . . . Amid large Douglas firs grown up since logging of the 1920s or so are several huge old-growth specimens . . . the entertainments are mainly those of a chanterelle sort of forest. At ¾ mile, about 1800 feet, the Alexander, in excellent shape despite 40 years of zero maintenance, simply fades away like an old soldier . . ."

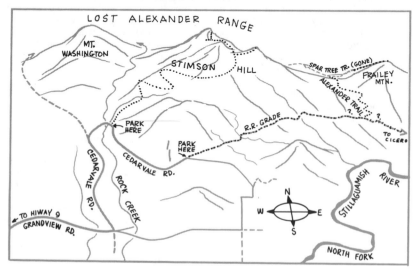

In 1977 the surveyor could find no "Spar Tree Trail" continuing to Mt. Frailey. Also in 1977, exploring from the Mt. Frailey side, he could find no evidence of human presence except logging artifacts.

In 1988 the same surveyor left the Arlington-Darrington highway at Cicero Bridge, drove Grant Creek Road, then the old railroad grade 2.4 miles to a washout, and walked the scant 1/2 mile to where the Alexander should have been. The sign was gone; one hopes it was hauled off to a museum, not chopped to kindling wood. The trail had vanished in swordfern and moss. Yet the Alexander has to be there someplace because as of 1988 the loggers haven't headed up the creek. However, the walk is recommended only for those with a taste for woodland history. Mystery. And chanterelles.

Though not explicated in this edition, the Lost Alexander Range is spotlighted because of its potential future. At the Cascade front, low elevation, close to cities. Open to boots all year.—And of the 9 square miles of the range, some 7 or 8 are public land—DNR land. Designate it as a tree-farm hiking area, a State Forest? Spend a few dollars to sign trailheads and flag routes which volunteers then could improve?

In the early 1980s the surveyors heard a rumor that the DNR "Motorcycle Club" was noodling an ATV Park.

Frailey Mountain (map—page 75)

Frailey is a long mountain, for better than 7 miles forming the divide between Stillaguamish and Lake Cavanaugh valleys, and in some good future might be the entry to a whole system of Cascades-edge trails. The standard route to the summit lookout tower used to be from the Stillaguamish side; the logging road is still there, 1/2 mile west from the Arlington Fish Hatchery, but the state never obtained an easement and the homeowners have discontinued their former hospitality and the signs say "Private Keep Out" and mean it.

Fortunately, there is the other side of the mountain, with a road that also leads to the summit. The ascent is similar but with more ghosts. The lookout tower is gone but the looking-out is as goggling as ever. Below south are green fields of the North Fork Stillaguamish, the right angles of human geometry contrasting with the sweeping curves of river geometry. Out the valley west are saltwaterways, and east are glaciered towers of Whitehorse and Three Fingers. And below north, in spitting distance, is remote, tucked-away Lake Cavanaugh.

From Highway 9 just north of Milepost 44, at the south end of Big Lake, make an acute turn south onto Lake Cavanaugh Road. A short bit past Milepost 10 is a Y; go right on South Shore Road 0.9 mile; as the road bends sharp left, spot an old, obscure, boulder-blocked sideroad right. Park here, elevation 1020 feet.

The first 1/4 mile is over the valley bottom, through a splendid swamp, by huge cedar stumps from the 1920s railroad logging. Then comes the largest of several creeks oozing from one swamp to another. Is a plank bridge already jury-rigged? If not, do it yourself or get your ankles wet. Perhaps your knees. The old road now climbs a little onto the sidehill. At 3/4 mile it is joined by a newer road connecting to Second Wave clearcuts and the Cavanaugh Road, where it is firmly gated. But not always, and the trip may thus be marred by fun wheels. Proceeding by marshes and creek-access paths, the road passes spurs to clearcuts. At 1-1/2 miles it switchbacks left and starts a steady climb.

Ferns drape rock walls. Small creeks splash. Windows open to modest views to "Bumpy Ridge" on Cultus and the freaky rock dome of Bald. At 1 mile from the start of the uphill is the Big U-Turn around the west end of Frailey.

About those ghosts. Nowadays it hardly seems possible, but in olden days this was a railroad grade. Bits of rotting trestles remain. A large landing is passed that for one summer a half-century ago was a noisy scene, donkeys steaming, whistlepunks whistling, engines going choo-choo and hiss-hiss. Rusting in the brush is all manner

Lake Cavanaugh from Frailey Mountain

of good junk to kick at and wonder about. Across the valley on Stimson Hill is a gigantic landing, probably in use several years. So massive was the soil disturbance that even now only alder grows there, its reddish-brown (winter) or light green (summer) contrasting with darker green of surrounding second-growth conifers. From the landing radiate alder lines, marking the spider-web pattern of old railway grades and skidways. On this side of Frailey the ghosts compete with the views.

Speaking of views, after screened preliminaries they climax at Window Point, 2250 feet, 3 miles from the Big U-Turn, 5 ½ miles from the start. All this final way is a lovely stroll by creeks and cliffs on a footroad so narrow and exposed and so prone to washouts in glacial till as to daunt the saner of the wheelers. Look east to close Whitehorse and Three Fingers and distant Pugh, south across valley farms to Wheeler and Blue and the U.S. Navy wires stretched across Jim Creek, to Pilchuck and Rainier, west past Stimson to Arlington and Possession Sound, sloughs of the

Snohomish estuary and pulpmills of Everett. Ships on the Whulge, Olympics, Seattle.

To rest is not to conquer. It's 1 ½ miles from Window Point to the 2450-foot junction with the road from the Stillaguamish and ½ mile more to the summit, 2666 feet. On the way is another wow vista, Glacier Peak emerging from behind Whitehorse. Swing into a saddle and climb to the summit, 2666 feet, 7 ½ miles from the start.

Actually, the view from the lookout site is no better than those had before, so the summit isn't worth it for that. However, a couple hundred feet before reaching the top, spot a path left through woods to a cliff-edge. This is worth it. Below is Lake Cavanaugh, in that odd valley that makes Frailey-Stimson-Washington an "island" of peaks cut off from the main Cascades. Hear the dogs bark, the cabin owners chopping wood, whistling while they work. Beyond the odd valley are the weird Cultus Mountains, featuring queer Bald and "Bumpy Ridge," and Haystack, Talc, Iron, and Coal, and Big Deer and Little Deer, and Gee Point, and Higgins.

The old USGS map shows trails from Frailey into the "Lost Alexander Range." The older surveyor spent hours wandering, following imaginary paths. But he found kitchen middens, broken saws, rusty cables. Check it out, pot-hunters.

Round trip to Window Point 11 miles, allow 8 hours
High point 2250 feet, elevation gain 1300 feet
February-December

At day's end, driving home, the surveyor ceased checking his odometer and altimeter. Following is a rude outline of the quickest and easiest way up Frailey:

From Oso on the North Fork Stillaguamish, drive the (other) Lake Cavanaugh road. Up and up. At the first (and only) switchback that has a grand view down to farms and out to Whitehorse, Bullon, Three Fingers, and Wheeler, spot an abandoned, gated sideroad going off west. Park here, something like 1500 feet. In about 2 miles the undrivable road joins the south-side road which ascends to the 2450-foot junction. The round-trip distance to the summit must be about 7 miles, elevation gain some 1200 feet. Views, yes indeed. In 1977, when a mile of the route was surveyed from the west end, there even was some virgin forest.

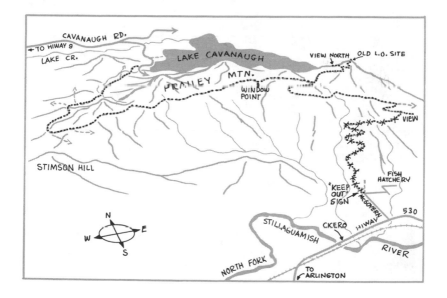

Split Rock Meadows (map—page 77)

The southwest salient of the Cultus Mountains, jutting into the angle between the graben of Big Lake and the trough of Pilchuck Creek–Lake Cavanaugh, has enough curiosities to choke a geomorphologist: Big Hole, Devils Garden, Bald Mountain, Table Mountain, "Bumpy Ridge." Most features are explained by the glacier from Canada riding over the Cultus crest, smoothing here, plucking there, dumping everywhere. But certain chunks and clefts seem to speak of fault blocks and earthquakes and cataclysms. What about Split Rock?

The pity is that this unique museum gets no respect. Geology means nothing to the wheelers who burn rubber and sling mud on the logging roads. They don't know where they are, really, and don't care so long as they can keep their wheels spinning. Nor would we stop them. We would leave them 99 percent of the Cultus Mountains for

Split Rock

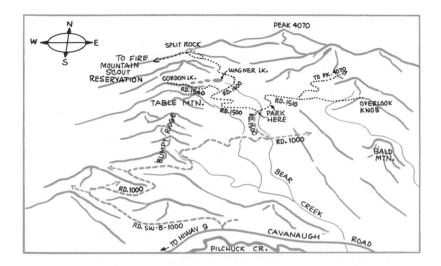

their sport, hundreds of miles of roads. But we would ask that a Foot-Only Zone be set aside on the dozen miles of old logging roads between the Fire Mountain Scout Reservation and the south slopes of Table Mountain. The DNR, the major land manager, established the Walker Valley ATV "Park" to afflict the Nookachamps and the Cavanaugh "Trail" to noise up that side of the mountain. For conscience sake, couldn't it do something nice for the Quiet Americans, the Silent Majority?

Here we describe two routes to Split Rock because both belong in the Foot-Only Zone which does not (1988) exist. Be warned. Come on a weekday. Or in early spring when snowbanks halt wheels but not feet.

Nookachamps Route

Begin from the Fire Mountain Scout Reservation (see Donkey Vista), elevation 400 feet. The route—road, then trail—climbs 3 1/4 miles to 1800 feet. The trail rejoins the road and continues upward 3 1/2 miles, along and sometimes near Nookachamps Creek, to the top of the divide. There sits Split Rock, a great naked hunk that doesn't grow out of the mountain but alienly sits atop, split by giant cracks, feeding a talus of huge boulders. Its 150-foot wall rises vertically from a bog-meadow 1/4 mile long, coursed by a creek flowing from one tea-dark, spookily deep pool to another. In spring (June) the bog flowers bloom. For the best views scramble up the forested backside to the summit, 3260 feet.

The Scouts have neat sidetrips to creek-side camps, other summits. But they presently also have a plague of DNR-sponsored motorcycles and jeeps. Gates could be installed (and defended) to make this a foot route.

Round trip 13 1/2 miles, allow 9 hours
High point 3260 feet, elevation gain 2900 feet
March-November

Cavanaugh Route

From Highway 9 just north of Milepost 44, at the south end of Big Lake, make an acute-angle turn south onto Lake Cavanaugh Road. At 7.2 miles turn off left on SW-B-1000, main entry to a DNR/Georgia Pacific road system which penetrates deep into the innards of the Cultus Mountains. Usually the only sign marking this junction, elevation 800 feet, is "Truck Crossing."

The explorer who ventures farther should be equipped with compass, altimeter, USGS maps, and innate canniness. Though the older surveyor got through the maze in 1978, on two attempts early in 1988 he (and the younger she) were halted by snow. However, since in 1978 the loggers were shaving the crests of the ridges and getting ready to go away for 400 years to await the next crop, not much has changed on high, we think.

Along the way will be seen DNR signs pointing to "Cavanaugh Trail" and the like. Ignore. Better spend Halloween in a Chamber of Horrors than set foot on any of them.

A few yards from Cavanaugh Road is a Y; go left on road No. 1000, probably unsigned (as, probably, are all or most other junctions, though the numbers will be given here just in case signs have survived or been replaced). At 2.3 miles is a Y, 1200 feet; go left (straight ahead). At 3 miles, 1350 feet, the road (old logging railroad grade) makes a sweeping switchback from west to east. At 3.2 miles is a Y, 1400 feet; go right on 1000. At 4.4 miles, 1800 feet, is a Y; go right on 1000.

The road this far is in a green trench of second-growth that in the near future will be shorn, opening views and confusing the route. Not far past the 1800-foot Y the snows of 1988 were too deep for wheels and, after a while, for Shelties. The following is basically from 1978:

At 7 1/4 miles is a Y, 2100 feet. The logging here is more recent and big views begin. On a February Monday after an overnight snowfall sufficient to give Shelties their fill of white candy, a walk this far will be most entertaining. Unfortunately, snowline-probing cannot be recommended on weekends; for 4x4s this is more fun than mud.

From the 2100-foot Y, road No. 1000 contours east (right) to overviews of Bald Mountain, a wart erupting from the hillside for no apparent reason. Instead go left on No. 1500 to a Y at 2400 feet, 7 3/4 miles from Cavanaugh Road.

For a sidetrip (that is, not to Split Rock) go right on No. 1510 across Bear Creek, then another piece of Bear Creek with a lovely waterfall and a splendid rock buttress. Park here (probably), elevation 2500 feet. The steep, rough road is drivable beyond but the views are such you risk crashing and burning. Ascending, then contouring, in 1 mile the way comes to a triple-fork Y, 2900 feet. The left climbs to Peak 4070, the scalping finished early in the 1980s; the right contours to Knobb 2950, clearcut and burned in the mid-1970s.

From either, look. Directly below is ridiculous Bald. Farther down is summerhome-ringed Lake Cavanaugh, the source of Pilchuck Creek. Above it is the long ridge of Frailey, which connects to Washington, which connects to Stimson, the three forming an "island" cut off from the main range by the Deer Creek valley flowing to the Stillaguamish. Southward are Jumbo, Whitehorse, Three Fingers, Pugh, Glacier. And sprawling Wheeler, and Olo and Blue, Pilchuck and Rainier. Westward are "Bumpy Ridge" and Table Mountain, the Stillaguamish delta, many fingers of the Whulge, Camano and Whidbey Islands, the Olympics. Ponder this strange valley and its mysteriously muddled drainages. In mind's eye see the Canadian glacier pushing up the valley and over the peaks, and the Big River flowing around the ice front, at different times both to the west and the east of Frailey.

But this is not the way to Split Rock. From the 2400-foot Y take the left fork, No. 1500. Here or hereabouts we recommend the (gated) boundary of the Foot-Only Zone; in 1978 the road was such that only the most violent wheels ventured much higher. The views are too enormous to be wasted wrestling a steering wheel. So, walk. In 3/4 mile begin switchbacks, the views bigger by the switch. At 1 1/2 miles is a Y, 2900 feet.

First go left on No. 1540. Across the gulch of a Bear Creek tributary is "Bumpy Ridge," the series of knobs on a crest descending from Table Mountain. The highest knob, 3200 feet, is on the map next to the words, "Table Mountain." But it's no table, it's a cleaver, so precipitous it hasn't been logged; if it were, the view would be fantastic. The road ends on a narrow ridge nearly as high, 3125 feet, no table either. Logged clean in 1976, it lies between a saddle separating it from Peak 3200 and another saddle containing the little Gordon Lakes, ringed by subalpine meadow-

Under side of devil's club leaf

marshes. Here, $^3/_4$ mile from the Y, are views northward over the Nookachamps valley to Hugeview Corner on Cultus, down to Big Lake, Devils, Little, Ika and Goat Islands in Skagit Bay, Erie, San Juans, and the Skagit River meandering to Mount Vernon. Where's the table?

This is *still* not the way to Split Rock. From the 2900-foot Y go right on No. 1500 and abruptly emerge from stumps of 1976 logging to subalpine meadows in a 3100-foot plateau-saddle-pass. Proceed through parkland, by ponds. (Is *this* the table?) Good grief! What's that ahead? Split Rock!

Round trip to Split Rock from 2400-foot Y 5 miles, allow 4 hours
High point 3260 feet, elevation gain 900 feet
April-November

SKAGIT RIVER

Draining a third of the north-south length of the Washington Cascades plus a chunk of Canada, the Skagit is far and away the largest stream of the Whulge region. It's a big river and a big country—to walkers from homelands of cozier dimensions, overwhelming. The present survey strives humbly to cope, first, by treating only the delta and mountain front. Second, since the distance from Puget Sound City bends the Two-Hour Rule, the province is not exhaustively mined but only high graded; the described trips are strictly A material, good enough to justify the extra highway time for hikers who live south of Everett.

Glories are many: the plain so vast a walker feels at sea in the green; the come-ashore San Juan Islands, islands of rock amid delta alluvium; the fault-block mountains and valleys; the handiwork of the Canadian glacier, nowhere so awesome as here near sources of the ice, where lobes widened and deepened the valleys, rode over the highest summits of the mountain front; and finally the startling bulge of the Cascades west to saltwater.

The province is virtually total farm: down low, fields of corn and cows and cabbages, hay and tulips; up high, trees on state (DNR) and private lands, dominantly Georgia-Pacific. But there is also one of the state's largest wildland preserves outside the alpine mountains, Larrabee State Park. Ranging from sea level to 4000 feet, the province offers walking the whole year: valley flats are particularly popular in winter when clouds of wildfowl are on vacation here from the frozen North; enormous-view heights, appealing for snowline-probes, are dependably open in fall and late spring.

Most distinctive of the subprovinces is, of course, the delta-floodplain, far and away largest in the region. To be duly impressed by the river, one ought to stroll the dikes in floodtime. Stroll or wade. On second thought, scratch that idea. Let the river subside a respectable bit down the dikes that, beginning a century ago, bit by bit claimed this agricultural treasure house from primeval tidal marshes and floodplain swamps. A person doesn't walk here long without becoming a connoisseur of 19th century three-storey farmhouses and majestic old barns. The proposed Pacific Northwest National Scenic Trail would pass through on the way to Montana; that plan aside, certainly there should be a Skagit Trail extending from the Whulge Trail to—to where? Well, how about the Fraser River?

South of the valley, forming not the true front of the Cascades but a false front, is the fault block of the Devils Range, isolated by the block valley (former glacier trough) now occupied by a string of lakes. Rising sharply from the delta, the 25 square miles of second-growth forests, peaks, and secluded-nook lakes are an amazing wildland at the edge of pastoral civilization. Sadly, thanks to Privatizers, this province has been omitted from this edition.

The true front is Cultus Mountain, south portal of the Skagit valley, a bully of a peak hulking 4000 steep feet above the barns. Its 100-odd square miles of tree-farm wildlands are well known to loggers but terra incognita to all but a handful of hikers, few of whom even know the name. Too bad. The views drop you to your knees. And there's the funny stuff—the Big Hole and the Devil's Garden.

Finally, north of the delta is the big push of the Cascades to their terminal plunge to the beaches. This section of the range is unique for that, but also for being split by the north-south valleys (faults, glacier troughs) of Oyster Creek, Friday Creek-Samish Lake, Lake Whatcom-Samish River, and South Fork Nooksack River-Jones Creek, these valleys separating the "island" mountains of Chuckanut, Elephant, Anderson, Lookout, and—the north portal of the Skagit valley, making a pair with Cultus—Wickersham-Woolley-Lyman. Again, loggers know the area best. However, the 10,000 combined acres of Larrabee State Park and the DNR wildlands on Chuckanut

Skagit River at the mountain front

and Elephant one day will be very famous among hikers. From some of these heights the views of the delta and the San Juan Islands are sensational. From others the close-ups of the Great White Watcher are scary. Though geologists and journalists ran off to St. Helens when it blew, the steam continues to leak from Baker's crater.

USGS maps: Conway, Mount Vernon, Clear Lake, Wickersham, Alger, Bow, Bellingham South

Skagit River Banks (map—page 84)

It's a big river and takes a lot of learning. The lesson for today is the transition from the outer delta (see Whulge Trail) to the Cascade front. There is the monster stream to study, fascinated and—in high-water season—a bit nervous or a whole lot frightened. Views of mountains are mingled with views of crops and barns. And steelhead fishermen.

At present it is not possible to walk straight through on either side of the river; much of the route is on dikes where trespassing is tolerated but some fences are of the mean-it variety—the barrier of barbed wire and the array of "Keep Out" signs show the folks aren't fooling. However, walks on one bank or the other sample the river's sinuous length between Conway and Burlington.

Round trip total, all hikes, 23 1/2 miles
High point 43 feet, minor elevation gain
All year

Fir Island-Skagit City

Between the distributary forks of the Skagit is Fir Island, reeking of agriculture and history.

Drive I-5 to Exit 221 and go off through Conway and over the South Fork Skagit River. Immediately turn right on Skagit City Road and park near the little white church. Elevation, 15 feet.

The diketop strolling is easy, only a few easy-over fences (for keeping stock in, not people out). Should the situation change and mean-it fences arise, the country lane is close for detouring. The view west is to wonderful old barns and the cultivated plain, east over the river to Little, Devils, Scott, Cultus, Baker.

In 2 miles is Moore Road. Walk west 1/4 mile to Skagit City School, closed in 1940, maintained by local history buffs. You can't do without a photo. To go with the one you took of the church.

Round trip 4 miles, allow 3 hours

The dike is easy-open north 3/4 mile from the Moore Road access to a "Public Fishing" sign. The fences then become mean-it.

A marvelous sandbar thrusts into the angle between the North Fork and the South Fork. This, the wilderness tip of Fir Island, is a grand spot to sit and look. Ought to be a park.

Here was Skagit City, which from a campsite in 1856 and trading post in 1869 grew to the metropolis of the delta, the head of navigation. But in 1879 the giant logjams that made it so were removed, Mount Vernon grew, and Skagit City died. Not a trace remains. A park would at least provide a place to muse. Legally.

Edgewater Park-Youngs Bar-Mount Vernon

Sandbars and public parks make the walking free and easy.

Drive I-5 to Exit 226 and follow Highway 536 west through Mount Vernon and over the Skagit River. Just nicely across, turn left on Baker Road and proceed around

Mt. Baker and Skagit River from site of Skagit City

Edgewater Park 1 scant mile. Where Baker, here atop the dike, hits the river, park in the wide flat by the bank.

Walk upstream on the splendid broad sandbar to the end. Detour by brushy banks on tire tracks in a flood-open woods being considered for an enlargement of Edgewater Park, which is quickly reached. A Wildlife Department access here. Interesting perspectives over the river to beautiful downtown Mount Vernon, dominated by the noble old Hotel President.

At park's end a detour on streets is necessary. Follow Ball north over Division (Highway 536); beyond a trailer court regain the river on Youngs Bar, a beauty, enormous, and with a Wildlife Department access. The river now bends west away from the city. The grassy dike goes 1/2 mile more by fields and barns to a house and mean-it fence.

Round trip 4 miles, allow 3 hours

Mount Vernon-Big Bend

Overlapping the previous walk is this one on the other side of the river.

Park in Mount Vernon—a suggested spot is the Lions Club-Kiwanis Parks beside the river on Freeway Drive on the north edge of town.

Walk the shoulder of Freeway north 1/4 mile and just short of River Bend Road go left on a woods road and climb onto the lawn-kempt dike. Stroll from city to farms, from freeway to Yolk Haven, hobnobbing with fishermen and ducks. The panorama north and east over the delta is grand to Blanchard, Anderson, Wickersham-Woolley-Lyman, Cultus, Little, and Devils. Here is the waterworks for Anacortes, which purifies a piece of the river and pipes it west to refine oil.

The dike rounds the Big Bend and heads east toward I-5, but that's going too far.

Round trip 6 miles, allow 4 hours

Big Bend-Burlington Sewage Plant

Recross the river. Now there is a definite feel of moving from delta to mountain-walled floodplain. Devils presses close from the south, Cultus nears to the east; northward the delta "sea" is dotted by the "islands" of Burlington Hill and Sterling Hill.

Drive I-5 to Exit 227 and go off east on Highway 538. In 0.2 mile turn north on old Highway 99, cross the Skagit, and turn west on (unsigned) Whitmarsh Road. In 1 mile, where the road turns north to become Pulver, park on the shoulder.

The diketop view extends over to Mount Vernon, up the valley, out to the San Juans. The sky is vast, there's an infinity of air around. The way goes beneath I-5 and old 99 and the mainline railroad bridge. Construction of I-5 without a drawbridge moved the

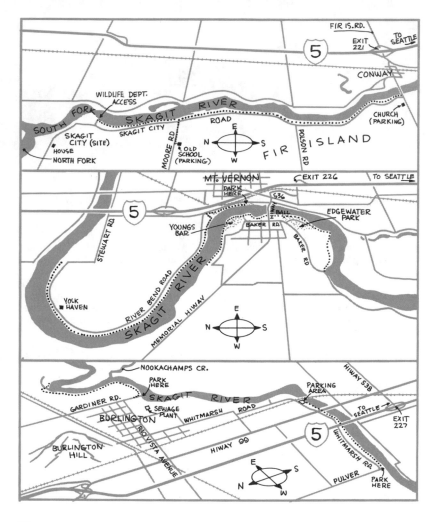

Skagit River near Burlington

Skagit head of navigation downstream to here (though at very low water sternwheelers might get under).

At 1 ½ miles, by the railroad bridge, is a public parking area. Here the river bends north and the dike diverges; the walking route is on a two-wheeler, three-wheeler, four-wheeler "mud run" ½ mile to another large public parking area accessible from Whitmarsh Road.

Beyond here Diking District No. 12 jealously protects its dikes with mean-it fences. A pity. The walking used to be pleasant, the stock fences all easy-over or easy-around. Across the river was a long stretch of wildwoods, a lovely sandbar (how do you get there?). A boat moorage harbored a row of those charmingly graceless boxes-on-rafts characteristic of the Skagit fleet.

The best route shifted to the cow-cropped diketop. The mountain front loomed closer, taller. To the left was the sewage plant of nearby Burlington. A pair of mean-it fences discouraged further progress.

Former round trip 6 ½ miles, allow 4 hours
Current round trip 1 mile, allow ½ hour

Burlington-Dike's End

Immediately over the two mean-it fences of Diking District No. 12 begins the final walk.

Drive north on Whitmarsh Road into Burlington, turn east on Rio Vista Avenue 0.7 mile, and then south on Gardner Road several hundred feet to the dike. Park on a shoulder, or, if not daunted by mudholes, continue over the dike on the playboys' fun road, past some mysterious old structures, to the riverside sandbar.

Walk upstream on the sandbar. Where it ends, push into woods, skirt a stock fence via riverbank riprap, and proceed in pleasant pastures below the dike. Look across the river to the mouth of Nookachamps Creek; in winter watch for the flocks of swans that frequent close-by Barney Lake.

The river turns east to the end of the dikes that began at saltwater, to the head of boot navigation. In low water a little slough can be hopped over to a fine sandbar at the top of the meander, a lovely wild spot, no houses visible, tanglewoods around. Beyond, progress is possible only for critters that slink through brush or those that swim or fly. Peaks of the Cascade front hang heavy, heavy over thy head. Listen to the swans bark.

Round trip 3 miles, allow 2 hours

Little Mountain (map—page 87)

If the mountain is little the view is anything but. Lifting abruptly from flat delta, high enough for a broad panorama but not so high as to lose intimacy, the summit is unsurpassed for studying the geometry of green squares (black after the rich soil is plowed). Bring maps and spend hours tracing bends of the Skagit River, peaks of the drowned mountain range of the San Juan Islands, bumps of the Cascade front. Bring binoculars and watch the grass grow in the fields through which I-5 roars.

Drive I-5 to Exit 224, go off east, then north on Cedarvale, and turn east on Hickox Road. In 1 mile, spot on the left a plank and a post marking the trailhead, elevation 60 feet. No parking is possible here so continue a bit. In less than 0.2 mile, just past Stackpole Road going right and then Pamela Street going left, is a Y; the left goes a couple hundred feet to an archery range where parking seems tolerated; if the situation changes, find room on a shoulder south of Stackpole Road 0.2 mile.

The trailhead is a ditch plank red-and-white lettered "Do Not Remove. Little Mountain Trail Head." Information on the post: "Hiker Trail Only. Permission for use revokable at any time; first ¹/₂ mile is private property." The maintenance is the contribution of local philanthropists.

Marked at the start by plastic ribbons, the path crosses a field and enters woods and climbs the steep slope. In 1 mile is an intersection; proceed straight ahead and up. (The right goes several steps to the 610-foot switchback on Little Mountain Road; the left was not surveyed.) In a final ¹/₂ mile the trail climbs by view windows (gasp and rave) and contours westward in dense summit forest to the Highway Patrol microwave tower. A few steps beyond over glacier-polished slabs of sandstone and conglomerate is the road-end parking area, 934 feet. But there are 50 more feet to climb, up steps of the observation tower that is the center of this Mount Vernon city park.

The view? Words fail. It's a 250-degree sweep, only the arc east to Cultus and Baker blocked by trees. Homes and farms of the emerald plain, silver meanders of Skagit distributaries, Skagit Bay and Padilla Bay and Samish Bay, Camano and Whidbey and Fidalgo and Guemes and Cypress and Orcas Islands, the Olympics.

Bring a flashlight to allow a night descent and stay for the gaudy sunset and the dazzling electrical show.

Round trip 3 miles, allow 2 hours
High point 980 feet, elevation gain 950 feet
All year

Should the trail ever be closed (as of 1988 it's been open at least a dozen years) the Little Mountain Road provides assured access to the city park.

Drive I-5 to Exit 225, go off east a short bit on Anderson Road, and turn north on Blodgett. In a long 0.5 mile turn east on Blackburn Road, which in 1 mile bends south and becomes Little Mountain Road. Park here, elevation 370 feet, or drive 0.7 mile to the first big switchback right, 610 feet. Here is a small parking area and an official city-park "Hiker Only" sign marking the trail that leads in ¹/₂ mile to the top.

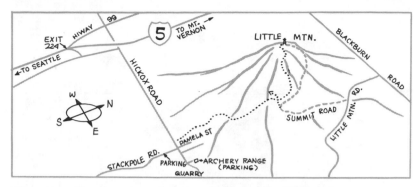

The Devils Garden (map—page 87, 90)

Residents of hot lands envision Hell as a furnace, and cold-land folk as an icebox. It follows that for Whulgers the lair of the Devil is gray, twilight-gloomy, green-oozy, dank and clammy, slimy and slippery. Yet if it is to be the Enemy's garden, it must suit infernal notions of beauty, which is to say it must be frightening as Hell.

Well, something bloody awful happened here. The ranger speculates a gas explosion—a burp from His furnace beneath. The surveyor hypothesized a cataclysmic landslide, a huge piece of Cultus busting loose. The entire mountainside clear down to Walker Valley is littered with monster boulders, mostly hidden by trees. Here in the Garden they are nakedly open, some 50 to 100 acres of rocks as big as houses—a chaos—a catastrophe frozen in the moment of its conclusion. The chilling fact is, this was no slow talus growth of millennia, this happened all at once, in minutes—and not in the remote past but, as geologists measure time, just a tick ago of Earth's clock. When the surveyor climbed above, seeking an absence matching the presence of the landslide, none was to be found. Louis Reed put forth a speculation that solves the puzzle. Not far north is the Big Hole in the side of Cultus. It seems almost self-evident that when the Canadian glacier was slowing down, melting down, its surface lowered from the summit (and then some) of Cultus nearly to the foot. A chunk of ice-oversteepened mountain collapsed onto the glacier, which still maintained some motion south even as the front was melting north. The landslide got only this far before the glacier stagnated, then melted away beneath the boulders.

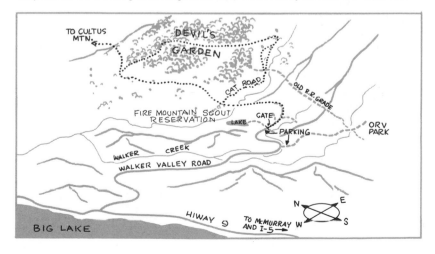

Devils Garden

Drive I-5 to Exit 221 and go off east on Highway 534 to Highway 9. Turn north to Big Lake and at Milepost 46 turn east on Walker Valley Road. Drive the blacktop a twisting 2.2 miles through pastures and woods to a gravel sideroad right, signed "ORV Park 1-¼ miles." Continue ahead on the county road 0.5 mile to the end, elevation 400 feet. The road beyond is private, entry to the Fire Mountain Scout Reservation. Opposite the ranger's residence is a shoulder with space for two or three cars. If it's full, drive back to the ORV Park road and park on a shoulder of it—not of the county road, which must be kept freely open for Scout use.

Passage through the Scout reservation is entirely dependent on hospitality. This depends on the manners of guests. Were hikers to get in the habit of parking in such manner as to clog the road, the Scouts would have no alternative except to cease permitting the public to cross their land. The hike was very hesitantly included in the first edition of this book, not knowing how the relationship would stand the test of time. Happy to report, as of 1988, after a decade of mutual courtesy, the ranger says the hikers have been no problem whatsoever; he feels *Footsore* has improved the local environment; the Scouts enjoy the company. The only problem of this decade has been the mounting snarl and roar from the ORV Park, distinctly no enhancement of the wilderness-edge peace of the Scout reservation. Why the DNR chose to inflict this on the Scouts (and on the pedestrian public) has not been satisfactorily explained.

To begin, obtain permission from the ranger, granted in most friendly fashion except in fire season, when no entry can be allowed. Then, where the driveway goes right to the ranger's house, and a gated road left to the camp, take the gated road straight ahead. In about 250 steps is a Y; the right is NO TRESPASSING; go left on the main road, along the edge of a pasture adjoining the reservation. At the far end, elevation 500 feet, as the road is starting an ascent into forest, note on the right a cat road partly blocked by a heap of gravel. Just before this cat road is a cropped-off cedar. Just beyond the cat road is a wood sign on a fir tree, "Devils Garden"—poorly placed, impossible to see except when descending the main road. So watch where you're going. Hikers chattering back and forth walk right on by and then complain to the surveyors.

Turn right, uphill, on the cat road. At an elevation of 750 feet cross an ancient railroad grade. The cat trail here splits in two pieces which later rejoin. For simplicity, take the left and proceed up through a swale. At about 925 feet, $3/4$ mile from the pasture, spot a flagged trail taking off left.

The Alpine Scramblers first (?) flagged the route in 1976, marking the way to "toulders" (tower-boulders) they named Whalehead, Church Tower, Camelback, Blockhouse, etc. However, the 1988 survey found no flags beyond the first boulder field and no evident route. The surveyor of 1988, as had the surveyor of 1978, crossed a hump from the first boulders to—horrors! The Garden! How to describe it? With a catch in the breath, a prickling of the skin. Extending some $1/4$ mile ahead along the slope, and nearly that much up and down, is a "talus"—but no cliff in sight above, just forest all around. Boulders the size of watermelons, and suitcases, and bales of hay, and Volkswagens, and Winnebagos, and summer cottages, and apartment houses, strewn in disorderly ridges of rocks separated by valleys of rocks, 50-foot towers adored by cragsmen thrusting above black clefts only a caver could love.

Progress is less walking than scrambling, using the hands and the seat of the britches, bewaring of moss-and-lichen slip-and-slide disasters. How far to go? How much time to spend? A person easily could devote a day to exploring trogs and pinnacles. Or could be content to spread a picnic lunch on the green moss table of a boulder and admire the devilishness.

Purely for the Intrepids—and not for them on wet and slippery days—is a crossing of the Garden. The surveyor(s) adventured out to the middle of the boulders, watching for boot tread; this vanished with the flags. A dodging, clambering, zigging up and zagging down way was taken toward the biggest boulder in the lower part of the Garden and below this Big One into the woods. Only then were ribbons found, leading down past more monster boulders to the main lower road about $1/4$ mile from where it was left at pasture's end.

In some opinion this "escape route" is the easiest entry. To do it, walk the $1/4$ mile or so from the pasture. When gigantic boulders appear in the woods, watch for a meager path and ribbons lingering from the last (?) visit of the Alpine Scramblers.

Loop trip 3 miles, allow 4 hours
High point 950 feet, elevation gain 700 feet
All year

Donkey Vista (map—page 90)

Eye-widening, breath-stopping views from Seattle to the Olympics to the San Juan Islands. To be sure, only a prelude to the brain-spinning panorama from Hugeview Corner. But this route also features a donkey engine peacefully rusting at the landing where the logger walked away from it a quarter-century ago, plus a visit to the Big Hole.

Drive to Fire Mountain Scout Reservation (see Devils Garden). From the reservation entrance at 400 feet set out as for Devils Garden but where that sideroad turns off, continue on the main road. Ahead is the goal, Cultus, Chinook jargon for "useless"; however, the Skagit Indian name translates as "Fire Mountain," and thus the name of the Scout reservation. Note the forests of bleached snags from the fires that earned the name.

Passing a sideroad to Scout cabins, in a scant 2 miles the way levels at 900 feet. Ahead a loud creek is heard and in bushes to the right is a white survey post. To save walking a long way around, here take a Scout-built shortcut trail that links old cat tracks and climbs steeply, crossing a branch of Nookachamps Creek, and in 1 1/4 miles

SKAGIT RIVER

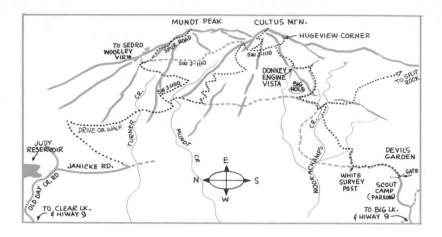

Donkey Vista

1950-or-so forest fire on Cultus Mountain (originally called "Fire Mountain")

rejoins the road at 1800 feet.

To the right, the road leads 3½ miles to Split Rock Meadows (which see), or in about the same distance to a 3970-foot peak of Cultus. For the trip here in hand, go left, lose 100 feet to a plank bridge over tumbling Nookachamps Creek, then contour to a Y at ½ mile from the shortcut trail. The road left is the long-way-around-home; go right, climbing again. At a junction in ½ mile the main road proceeds straight ahead. Take a sidetrip along it the short bit to the Big Hole, where an enormous chunk of mountain slid out, creating this scoop prominent from the lowlands—and also creating Devils Garden.

Returned, turn right on grassy-grown SW-J-1000. Impassable to wheels, the old road ascends eastward in mostly alder forest screening a very big picture. In 1 mile, at 2400 feet, a grade obscurely continues ahead; instead, switchback left a final ½ mile to glory. At 5 ½ miles from the start, at 2758 feet, the road emerges from alders on a landing. Zounds.

The vista is plenty to keep you wheeing and wowing through lunch. But buffs of logging history will be equally enchanted by the donkey engine left here in 1954 or so by Toughy Boyd when he finished salvage-logging and snag-falling after still another of Fire Mountain's fires.

Round trip 11 miles, allow 8 hours
High point 2758 feet, elevation gain 2500 feet
April-November

On a day when the brush is dry and you're feeling nimble, try the Scout "trail" upward. Just before the landing, note ribbons leading up a cat track. When the track ends at a draw, a rude path continues in a vertical gymnasium, a snarl of fallen logs and a jungle of young greenery, fun for limber youths but very rude indeed to middle-aged trail-trampers. The acrobatic log-walking and clambering soon yield to easier going and in 1/2 mile, at 3400 feet, the higher road is reached that leads in 1/4 mile to Hugeview Corner. Having fainted and fallen down and revived and gotten up, while the echoes of your bleats reverberate, sit and gaze: South—to Stimson and Frailey beyond Pilchuck Creek, Wheeler beyond the North Fork Stillaguamish, Pilchuck beyond the South Fork, Sultan and Si beyond the Skykomish, Rattlesnake and Issaquah Alps beyond the Snoqualmie, and Seattle and Rainier. Southwest and west—down to the Scout camp and green pastures of Walker Valley, Big Lake and Lake McMurray, Devils and Little, Everett and Possession Sound, Camano and Whidbey Islands, Port Townsend and the Olympics. Northwest—the shining Skagit winding through green floodplain and delta, Craft and Ika Islands in Skagit Bay, Erie on Fidalgo Island, the other San Juan Islands, Vancouver Island, Strait of Juan de Fuca, Whulge. East—over headwaters of Nookachamps Creek into the maze of the Cultus Mountains. Sometime, bring overnight gear and camp, adding dimensions of the night, the lights of civilization and outer space.

Wickersham-Woolley-Lyman Mountain (map—page 92)

The trough abandoned 12,000-15,000 years ago by the Canadian glacier and now employed by the South Fork Nooksack River in one stretch and Jones Creek in another forms the hypotenuse of a right triangle whose legs are the Samish River and

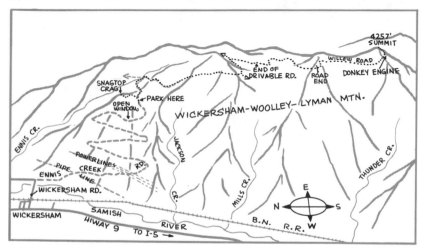

Mt. Baker from Wickersham-Wooley-Lyman Mountain

the Skagit River. The triangle encompasses 50 square miles of a single mountain mass, a behemoth that lumps 4257 feet above floodplains barely higher than sea level. The mountain has no name on maps. The surveyors thus have given the mountain the name(s) of the communities it overpowers: Sedro Woolley (56 feet), Lyman (87 feet), and Wickersham (314 feet). (A name emerged in 1992 from a geology report: "Lyman Hill." Nowhere near as elegant as ours.)

Were a Seattle located at the base, the mountain would have a trail system in the hundreds of miles. Once upon a time, it did have trails. The logging railroads wiped them out. Doubtless there are locals who do know where they are and have walked those grades of a half-century ago, as well as truck roads so faded in the brush they have the look of game traces, and the newer roads that have the look of pig wallows. The surveyors have managed to find two ways to the summit. Enough for a start.

From Wickersham

Drive Highway 9 north from Sedro Woolley 10 miles to Wickersham and turn east on Wickersham Road. In 0.4 mile, just after crossing the Samish River, the main road bends left. Go off right on (unsigned) Ennis Creek Road, which appears to be merely the driveway to a stumpranch — until logging trucks bigger than the road come juggernauting down. Just beyond the stumpranch the road is gated, elevation 300 feet. On the survey day early in 1988 the gate was open, but the trucks were juggernauting and the higher, safe roads were deep white. There's more news, worse still. In 1991 a reader was menaced by a pack of hostile dogs and their owner. The owner let the reader and his fellow hikers through — whereupon they got totally baffled by a maze of new roads. They attained the summit, somehow; the dog-owner told them there were plenty of other no-dog roads they could have taken. So what do *we* know? The best we can do is repeat, verbatim, the 1978 survey (and suggest that the Lyman route be considered):

Narrow and often steep but solid and safe (except when washed out), the road climbs through old second-growth and new clearcuts, starting off southward, switchbacking north, south, north, and, at 2050 feet, a scant 4.5 miles from the highway, south. At 5 miles, 2350 feet, hurrah, an open window! Brace yourself—green pastures of the Samish are precipitously below, the bulk of Anderson is huge to the west, and out the slot south is the Skagit and out the slot north is Lake Whatcom. For a snowline-prober starting in Wickersham, ascending the pleasant footroad, this is a dandy turnaround.

It's getting about time to stop driving and start walking. the suggested spot is Snagtop Junction, 2450 feet, 5.5 miles. (Note: In case the gate at 0.5 mile from the highway happens to be closed, here is a satisfying destination. And also for a snowline-probe.)

Even if you vote to drive farther for the main hike, pause here to ascend Snagtop Crag, 2550 feet, several minutes away via an old quarry road. From bald slabs of a greenish metamorphic rock among silvered snags, on the brink of an alarming, overhanging, 180-foot cliff, look to the green checkerboard of the Samish and Nooksack valleys, Lake Whatcom, Anderson, and Skagit valley.

For the main feature, onward. The road swings around the head of Ennis Creek, crossing it; at a Y in 1/3 mile from Snagtop Junction, go right. Climb from the Ennis valley around a shoulder onto the main ridge of the mountain; little windows grow larger, eliciting gee whizzes and wowees, but you ain't seen nothing yet. At 3200 feet, 1 1/2 miles from the Ennis Y, where a lesser road goes straight, switchback left, north. In another 1/2 mile, at 3500 feet, where a lesser road goes straight, switchback right. If you've not already changed from wheels to boots, do it soon—shortly the road is slid out and unmaintained.

Now in continuous stunning views, the way contours the mountainside just below the ridge crest. The airy, open slopes clearcut in the 1960s or so have only modest shrubbery amid the silvering slash, the splashing creeks. Around a corner the 4257-foot summit appears and then, at 3800 feet, 3 1/2 miles from Snagtop Junction, the road withers away and dies.

A party electing to stop here would not be disappointed; the views are eyeball-bulging, head-spinning. But golly, the summit is close, why quit? You may think of

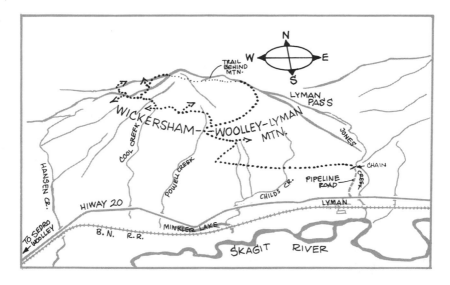

Skagit delta and Olympic Mountains from the Cascade front

reasons in the next bit, angling uphill from the road-end through slash and marsh marigolds and 12-foot silver firs, but in no more than a couple dozen groans and dirty words, voilà, at 3950 feet, hit the Willow Road, a thicket of whips but better than slash. Follow it right ¼ mile and receive your reward—a donkey engine resting on skids, the wooden roof snow-crushed and the ironware rusty and willow-encumbered, but virtually intact; in the boiler furnace the ashes of its last fire (when? 1960ish?) look as if they might still be warm. Worth the trip in itself.

But don't quit now. A couple hundred feet beyond the donkey leave Willow Road and proceed straight up, partly following open alleys, partly thrusting through young trees. The schisty, stumpy summit appears. And in perhaps ¾ mile and 1-¼ hours from where the road ended and the silly stuff started, see a huge granite erratic (the Canadian glacier was here!) and (curses!) a road.

But never mind. Several steps up the road is the top, and here you cannot be bitter. To list a tenth of the sights would require a chapter. But demanding mention are: Skagit valley and delta, and Stillaguamish delta too, from Chuckanut Mountain to Camano Island, Sedro Woolley to La Conner; San Juan Islands and Whidbey Island and Everett pulpmills; Cultus and Three Fingers and Glacier; Sauk Mountain and Eldorado; Lake Whatcom and Bellingham Bay and Garibaldi; fresh clearcuts dropping east to Jones Creek-South Fork Nooksack valley, skinned slopes of the 4100-foot summit just north, beautifully desolate; iron-red crags of Twin Sisters; five (5, count them, 5) mountain ranges—a great sweep of North Cascades, the Olympics, the San Juan Islands range, Vancouver Island Mountains, and white giants of the British Columbia Coast Range.

Don't forget the Great White Watcher. Watch it. If it happens to be steaming the day you're here, keep your boots on.

Round trip from Snagtop Junction 8 ½ miles, allow 7 hours
High point 4257 feet, elevation gain 1800 feet
May-November

From Lyman

That new road the older surveyor discovered on the summit in 1978 preyed on his mind through the years. Often, driving up the Skagit, he was tempted to forswear the cheap and easy pleasures of the North Cascades to revel in the stumps and slash and beer cans, at last to solve the puzzle of where the road came from. When at length he organized his Shelties into a sleuthing expedition, the season was deep winter. Though unable to walk out the route to the top, he did determine the beginning; the trip plan sketched here is not for freshmen or remedial students but should be a cinch for doctoral candidates.

Drive Highway 20 east from Sedro Woolley to the Whistlepunk Cafe and the turnoff to beautiful downtown Lyman. In 0.2 mile more turn left on Pipeline Road, which ascends through a stumpranch suburb of Lyman. In 1 mile, at the last house, is a Y. Go right 0.2 mile to the end of maintained road. A chain bars progress onto the withering, brushing-in logging road shown on the USGS map of 1951, still shown on the map of 1973—but *not* that of 1976, presumably because by then the alder canopy had blinded the camera in the sky. Elevation, 400 feet.

(Note: To the right of the chained road the slope falls off into the valley of Jones Creek, in 1951 the route of the major logging road to Soundview Logging Camp 17 at Lyman Pass, and in 1988 the route of the major logging road of Scott Paper Company. This private road requires a permit to drive to Lyman Pass and/or the summit of W-W-L Mountain. So forget it and return to the chain.)

As eyeballed from the Skagit valley, the route lies in old second-growth alternating with new clearcuts, at a certain elevation (the limit of tree-farming, the start of tree-mining) yielding to old clearcuts that never again will produce a commercial crop. Views begin at no great distance. The map shows three perennial streams; in spring the number likely is in the dozens. The map shows the old road going west 2 miles, then switchbacking east ¾ mile to join, at 1500 feet, the spur road from Scott's Jones Creek road. From there it is perhaps 6-odd miles to the summit road that probably rarely sees legal wheels; the traveler must decide for himself at each of the junctions which is the way up through the maze.

The walk from the valley to the summit obviously is a good workout. In springtime a person doing half or less of the route surely will be transported by the snowmelt cataracts, the flowers that bloom, and the ever-growing views over Skagit valley and Whulge.

Round trip to summit about 18 miles, allow 1 day or (with backpack) 2
High point 4257 feet, elevation gain 3800 feet
March-November

Snowline-probing round trips as short as whiteness and energy dictate

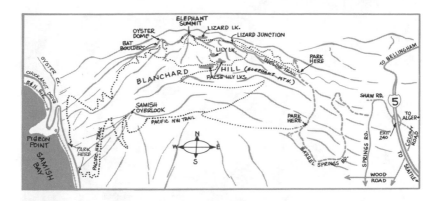

Elephant Mountain and Oyster Dome
(map—page 97)

Lift eyes from the Samish section of the Skagit delta and see the elephant. Why government mapmakers ignored the flavorful local name in favor of innocuous "Blanchard Hill" is not known. So far as the Oyster Dome is concerned, nobody seems to have felt the inevitability of the name until the surveyor, recently returned from Yosemite domes, happened by. As the elephant is the dominant feature of the landscape from below, the dome is the supreme feature on high.

"Hill," even "mountain," fails to do justice; more properly it's a range that rises abruptly from the north edge of the Skagit-Samish delta and sprawls over a dozen square miles between the glacier troughs of Oyster Creek and Friday Creek-Samish Lake. Railroad-logged in the 1920s-30s (or 1911?), in the 1980s it's a spacious second-growth wilderness. A second clearcutting has begun on the 8000 acres held by the DNR, but provision is being made to preserve foot trails. Adjoining, across Oyster valley, are the 2300 acres of Larrabee State Park; lands of Whatcom County parks are contiguous. When the interagency trails plan is completed and implemented, the pedestrian will be able to walk from the Whulge to two summits, to Cedar and Pine Lakes as well as those described in this book, to old-growth Douglas fir forest and to scenic overlooks, and also right into downtown Fairhaven.

As for Elephant Mountain, a trail from the east is the shortest. The shortest way to Oyster Dome is a trail from the west. The two trails are the same one, actually, but are best described separately.

East Trail: to Elephant Mountain

Drive I-5 to Exit 240 (Alger) and go west on (unsigned) Alger Road 0.5 mile. Turn left on Barrel Springs Road, signed "Blanchard Hill Trail." In 0.6 mile turn right on a gravel-mud logging road also signed for the trail. At a junction in 1.6 miles go straight ahead (right). Just beyond on the left is the trailhead, signed "Lily Lake-Lizard Lake-4 miles." Continue a short bit to a parking turnout signed "Blanchard Hill Trailhead—DNR." Elevation, 800 feet.

(Another 0.9 mile up the road is the start of the Incline Trail, which follows a logging railroad incline 1/2 mile straight up the slope to 1770 feet. The only superiority of this route is history—the rusted kitchen pots and broken machinery of an old logging camp. The rail grade goes left to join the newer trail.)

The newer trail begins in second-growth above a parallel log-haul road which is clearing the ground for third-growth. In 1/4 mile cross a pretty creek flowing over bedrock slabs. Now the path diverges from the road. At 1 mile, 1150 feet, is the first switchback.

Lily Lake on Blanchard Hill (Elephant Mountain)

At 1 ¼ miles is a junction. The left is signed "Pacific Northwest Trail—Samish Overlook—Under Construction." This trail is described in the PNWT guidebook as contouring westward 1 ½ miles and descending five switchbacks to an old sawmill site. The vicinity—"Samish Bay Overlook"—has the same sort of views, though not as broad, as Elephant Mountain and Oyster Dome. At 4 ¼ miles from the junction the PNWT hits Chuckanut Drive a short distance north of Windy Point (see Whulge Trail).

At the 1 ¼-miles junction go right (unsigned), recrossing the pretty rock-slab creek, ascending moderately to wet-footed woods and a boggy pond, into cedar groves, up a hillock, through an old burn, into a choked forest, dark and spooky. Upon emerging to brighterness, at 2 ¾ miles, 2000 feet, is the intersection with the old rail grade which contours the mountain this way and that. The right is signed "Incline Trail–Lizard Lake"; the left, "Lily Lake."

The right, a lovely stroll in the deep green, contours steep hillside about 1 mile to a Y. The right fork is the Incline Trail. The left leads ¼ mile to the bowl of 1862-foot Lizard Lake, a stump-and-snag-and-log-littered pond only a duck could love. The best feature is a three-storey boulder and a trog camp it provides. (The PNWT guide says a new trail has been built from Lizard "1 mile to North Butte, 2200 feet . . . and another mile to Lily Lake." The route was not surveyed or confirmed for this guide. The location of "North Butte" is not given by the PNWT guide.

At Lily Lake junction, go left, through a rock slot into a forest bowl, by the stumpy frog-wallow of False Lily Lake. At 3 ¼ miles from the trailhead is True Lily Lake, 2010 feet, a clean droplet ringed by boggy meadows at the foot of the final rise to the summit of the Elephant. Signs point right to "Lily Lake Camp Horse Facilities" and left to "Hiker Camp."

Go left along the lakeshore (note the thickets of aromatic Labrador tea) to the north end of the lake and up to the hiker camp. A boot-beaten path sets out north, fades and disappears, succeeded by flagging to the summit, 2225 feet, 4 miles from the trailhead.

Sit atop huge boulders and look west over the Oyster Dome to Chuckanut Mountain, to the San Juan Islands. Great! From an open rock below the summit, see Twin Sisters and Mt. Baker. Greater!

Round trip 8 miles, allow 6 hours
High point 2225 feet, elevation gain 1425 feet
February-December

Now, back at the Lily Lake junction. Behind the sign, spot a trail. In ½ mile along ponds of Lily Creek it leaves the rail grade and drops a bit to an unsigned junction. The fork down left is to the Bat Boulders and Chuckanut Drive, discussed below. The right is to the summit of Oyster Dome, also saved up for description below.

West Trail: to Oyster Dome

On Chuckanut Drive 1 mile north of Chuckanut Manor Inn, 0.3 mile north of Oyster Bar, just past a highway turnout, look right for a gully and an obscure, unsigned trailhead. Just beyond the gully is another turnout. If you come to Oyster Creek bridge you've overshot; go back to the first turnout and park. Elevation, 200 feet.

The trail ascends the gully ¼ mile to a woods road. Turn left on it to where a sign, "Trail," points to the right. Elevation 475 feet.

The way climbs steeply a scant ½ mile and at 625 feet levels out to an alder bottom. From here, up up up you go, ½ mile to a lovely rock-slab waterfall at 900 feet; at 1125 feet, cross. In another ¼ mile, at 1325 feet, hit a ridge top, leave alders for big cedar, fir, and hemlock. Hearing a gurgle, sidehill to cross the creek. Looking up through the treetops, see a looming cliff. Continue climbing, listening to Lily Creek on the left, dodging paths that go there.

At a scant 2 miles, 1825 feet, the major sidetrail (look for a fir tree with orange arrow) crosses Lily Creek and its waterfalls to the heap of gigantic boulders at the foot of the slabs, trogs, ribs, cracks, and chimneys rising vertically to the top of Oyster Dome. The Bat (talus) Caves appeal to some tastes—though apparently not to bats, which haven't been seen in recent years. Neither have the domestic goats which in the early 1980s were released here—to become coyote suppers? Rock climbers are abundant, slithering about the treacherous boulders amid perilous pits.

The best is yet to come. Return to the main trail and climb a steep ¼ mile to the junction at the leveling-out, 2000 feet. Lily Lake lies ahead. Turn left, cross Lily Creek, cascading over rock outcrops, and ascend ¼ mile on a path through scraggly trees and mossy boulders to the great, glacier-polished slab of Oyster Dome, 2025 feet.

Gasp! Walk carefully! The slab is slippery when wet and the brink hangs a giddy 350 feet above the Bat Boulders. Wind-tortured pines and hemlocks and a picturesque weathered snag cling to the edge. The views? Skagit delta, Skagit Bay, San Juan Islands, Olympics, Rainier, China.

Round trip 4 miles, allow 3 hours
High point 2025 feet, elevation gain 1625 feet
February-December

Larrabee State Park (map—page 100, 102)

In the hundreds of miles from California through Oregon and Washington the Cascade Mountains sit far back from saltwater. But here at the north edge of the Skagit delta the range juts to the very shore and dives to the beaches. Spectacular. Maybe a geologist would say these aren't the Cascades at all, but an extension of the drowned range that forms the San Juan Islands. Certainly here is the most dazzling view of that archipelago.

Put this splendid lump of mountain—Chuckanut Mountain—together with lakes fragrant of wildness, lakes lost behind the ranges, wave-swept shores of the Whulge, and what have you got? Larrabee State Park, some 2500 acres of glacier troughs and glacier-streamlined ridges, deep forests and sky-open, wide-view rock balds, and saltwater beaches. Put that together with some 8000 acres of adjoining DNR lands and you've got—well, something very, very good. Something unique.

Several walks sample the park. One is on the shore—the Whulge Trail. Another climbs to big views and a secluded lake. Two others go higher on the mountain, to bigger views. A last goes over the mountain to no views except those into the heart of solitude.

Fragrance Lake (map—page 100, 102)

When all roads are loud with machines, all beaches hectic with childish laughter, when all Larrabee State Park seems groaning under weight of deserved popularity, there is yet a haven, a foot-only trail through marvelous forest to a gem of a lake in a quiet green bowl. And on the way is a superb view over Samish Bay to the San Juan archipelago. What's the fragrance? Peace, it's wonderful.

Drive Highway 11, Chuckanut Drive, to Larrabee State Park. A bit north of the highway-side garages and ranger's house is a parking area and trail sign, "Viewpoint 0.9 mile, Fragrance Lake 1.9 miles." Park here, elevation 130 feet.

Switchback steeply a short bit up to a powerline-woods road on the grade of the old Mount Vernon-Bellingham Interurban Railway. (Under development, partly complete and fully walkable in 1988, is the 6-mile Whatcom County Interurban "Trail," linking Larrabee State Park to Fairhaven City Park in Bellingham. The route is a joint endeavor of Whatcom County, Bellingham Parks, and State Parks. A nice bikeway/backyard stroll it is; hikers coming from Puget Sound City, though, will pass it up in favor of more exciting park paths.)

Turn right a few steps to a resumption of trail. The good trees begin—and get better. The trail switchbacks up through noble specimens 3/4 mile to a saddle. The trail ahead is "Fragrance Lake, 1.1 miles."

First turn left to "Viewpoint 0.2 mile." In gorgeous forest, firs up to 5 feet thick, proceed to a railing-guarded cliff brink. At an elevation of 650 feet survey the horizon of islands and waters from refineries of March Point on Fidalgo to Guemes and

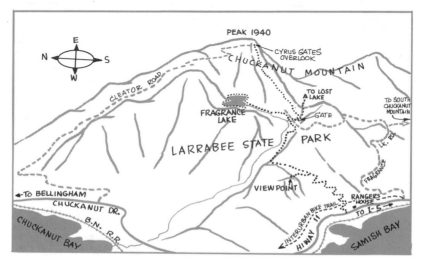

Fragrance Lake

Cypress and Orcas and Samish and Lummi and the rest. And look straight down to the highway and the shores of Wildcat Cove.

Return to the junction, follow a creeklet down, then again switchback steeply up to another saddle. Here a sidetrail climbs right a few steps to Fragrance Lake Road—the short route to the lake. The main trail drops gently ¼ mile along a small vale in tall-tree forest of cedar and hemlock, a lush understory, to the lake, 1030 feet.

Good-to-meager path circles the lake, over creeks, through groves of 8-foot cedars and 6-foot spruces, under gray rock walls half-hidden in greenery. All is silence. Then—"splash!"—a fish leaps. The fragrance? Sniff and sniff and you'll inhale many fragrances, but not the "Fragrance," which is how local Anglo-Saxons misheard the name of a foreign feller who had a cabin at the lake.

Round trip 4 miles, allow 3 hours
High point 1100 feet, elevation gain 1000 feet
All year

South Chuckanut Mountain (map—page 102)

Each vista point has a variation. Some look so straight down it seems a thrown rock would miss highway and railroad and hit the water. South over the Skagit delta are Devils and Cultus and Rainier, and even the Issaquah Alps and Seattle. Southwest over myriad islands and waterways is the backdrop of the Olympics. But it's the San Juans that enthrall. There is Fidalgo with the hump of Erie, the plumes of refineries.

Then low-profile (mostly) Guemes, then high, double-humped, wild-wooded Cypress. Below, enclosing Samish Bay, is the long hook of Samish Island. West on big Orcas is the high peak (see the summit lookout tower) of Constitution. Mostly hidden, San Juan. North is the tall cleaver of Lummi Peak on Lummi Island. And Vendovia and Eliza and Hat and Sinclair and Lopez and—well, counting islands is the sport. How many can be seen? About 20, 25? Would you accept 35?

Let it be noted that though Chuckanut has summits as high as 1940 feet, these are forested and rather viewless and not worth an effort—unless virgin forest of trees too wind-tortured to interest loggers is to your taste. When trails are built (some old scraps do exist) to tour these trees, they will indeed be worth it. Until then, the views are the draw and those are best from South Chuckanut Mountain.

On Chuckanut Drive 0.5 mile north of Milepost 12, park at the vista atop Dogfish Point, elevation 190 feet.

Across the highway spot the narrow woods road switchbacking southward. The road becomes undrivable trail, switchbacks steeply upward in forest, sidehilling north beneath wonderful sandstone cliffs, weirdly weathered, and ascends a gully. An old cat track clambers the crest of a little ridge, an airy skyway, at 1 mile from the road hitting the end of a meager road, atop a promontory, 860 feet.

The views! Far enough!

Yet this sweet and short afternoon picnic-walk can be enlarged to an all-day exploration. A person even could get lost. The special quality is that this slope of the mountain was cleared of greenery by the Chuckanut Burn of the mid-1960's— the Burn plus the salvage logging, which opened up the balds of the sandstone cliffs plucked and polished by the Canadian glacier. The geology is fascinating— the north-south channels of ice and meltwater running sideways across the slope, the little valleylets enclosed by little ribs of sandstone.

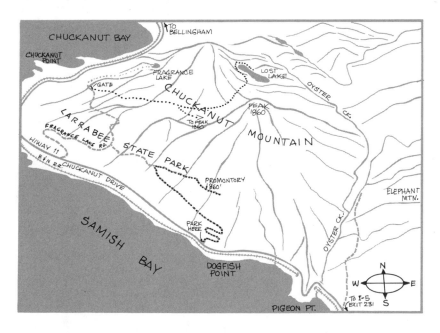

Telephoto of refineries at Anacortes and Olympic Mountains from Chuckanut Mountain

Round trip to Promontory 860 2 miles, allow 2 hours
High point 860 feet, elevation gain 700 feet
All year

Cyrus Gates Overlook

Cleator Road permits the carbound to achieve the views. They are better, of course, when attained by footpower.

On Chuckanut Drive 0.2 mile north of Milepost 14, Fragrance Lake Road takes off right from a broad gravel turnout, elevation 170 feet. The sign reads "Larrabee State Park. Fragrance Lake Road. South Logging Road 1 mile. Lost Lake Trail 2.1 miles. Fragrance Lake Trail 2.2 miles. Road end 2.2 miles." The white gate is open all year, from 6:30 A.M. to dusk.

In 1 mile, 657 feet, the (unsigned) South Logging Road goes off right, in 0.7 mile intersecting the hike described above. The route having been newly obtained for the park through an exchange with the DNR, logging will cease and the trail will become a reality any hiker can follow. Meanwhile, it's four-wheeler razzerland and will be until the state park's tidy white gate shuts off the wheels.

At 2.1 miles, 1050 feet, is the gated sideroad, right, to Lost Lake. A hippety-hop farther along is the end of the road and the short trail down to Fragrance Lake. The

103

Skagit delta from Chuckanut Mountain

proper way to do this hike, therefore, is from Chuckanut Drive to the lake, and thence to Lost Lake road-trail.

The 1-mile Overlook trail climbs left from the gate to a ridge and drops a bit to Cyrus Gates Overlook, 1800 feet, on the side of (North) Chuckanut, 1940 feet. Views? Yes, indeed, though frankly not as grand as from South Chuckanut. The trail is the trip.

**Round trip from Lost Lake gate 2 miles, allow 1 ¹/₂ hours
High point 1800 feet, elevation gain 750 feet
February-December**

Lost Lake (map—page 102)

Lonesomeness is the attraction of the over-the-hill province of the park. Lonesomeness and geology. The sedimentary structures strike northwest-southeast, dictating alignment of valleys and ridges, and the shales-sandstones-conglomerates differ so greatly in resistance to erosion as to form prominent trenches and ribs and cliffs with the same orientation. Here in the second-growth wilderness myriad ponds and lakes and marshes dribble together to form Oyster Creek, which exploits a line of weakness to cut between Chuckanut Mountain and Elephant Mountain (Blanchard Hill) to saltwater. Occupying one trench in the rocks is Lost Lake. And lost a walker may well feel in these faraway depths where once the Canadian glacier gouged.

Drive Fragrance Lake Road to the gated Lost Lake road-trail (see above), elevation 1050 feet.

In big-fir, maybe-virgin forest, then alders, passing a great window to the San Juan Islands, Skagit delta and Olympics, at 1 long mile from Fragrance Lake Road the way reaches a 1577-foot saddle in the ridge of Chuckanut Mountain. Here is a T. The right, incompletely surveyed, goes out of the park to logging shows on Peak 1860. The left is the way to Lost Lake. Descend an aldery ravine, with looks over Oyster Creek to 1870-foot "Cedar Peak" and 2300-foot Elephant, and I-5 and Samish Lake, and Cascades beyond.

The road bottoms and levels beneath an imposing cliff. Lost Lake is glimpsed below in big firs. At 1 long mile from the saddle is a T. The left used to be the razzers' mudrun, now is gated shut. Take the right a few yards to a mucky trail which proceeds ¹/₄ mile to the head of the black-bottomed, weak-tea lake. Ducks take off, scaring a walker half to death. Bald eagles nest hereabouts. They perch in snags, often scaring the ducks all the way to death. Where a shore trail goes right, turn left up rocks and follow the sandstone-hearted rib downlake to an excellent mossy slab tilted steeply into the lake, elevation 1182 feet. This is the lunch spot. (But no camping. And please, no fires.) By all means continue a bit farther to where lake water pours over a rock sill and sheets foaming-white down black cliffs. Skid down a path for close looks. Below is a beaver pond in another long valley, contained by another long rock rib. The ranger once saw six beavers in a day. The bottom of the Oyster valley is still a couple hundred feet below, with more lakes, marshes, and a maze of old logging roads. You could get lost, okay.

**Round trip from Fragrance Lake Road 5 miles, allow 4 hours
High point 1577 feet, elevation gain 1000 feet
February-December**

THE WESTERN ISLES—
BAINBRIDGE, VASHON, MAURY, BLAKE

Any Puget Sounder who was around when the Model T yielded to the Model A, and that magnificent machine to the V-8, recalls how the water once set apart the Western Isles. Even then, however, the car ferries were converting independent villages to little suburblets of Puget Sound City. After World War II, as the combine of transportation engineers, land-developers, and tax-hungry bureaucrats became rampant and triumphant, Bellevue clones grew feasible, more or less, on the islands. To the extent that they have *not*, there is room for the walker. "Beachwalker," that is. What else is an island for?

Bainbridge Island has been de-islanded on one side by the Agate Pass bridge. On the other, the jumbo ferries are so huge and swift they are not so different from the mainland freeways. The older surveyor, who in his parents' memories if not his own vividly recalls the first Model A on the island, and how the entire population took turns flinging it about the washboard-and-rut roads, circled the shore—again—in 1988. Glad to report, though the only Model A's to be seen are fakes, the hoods concealing Volkswagen engines, and though Privatizers have been busy, a surprising number of beaches are open to Publics.

Vashon is even better. The sole water supply is the sky, barely sufficient for the present population; there often may be seen, running away from local posses, the advance agents of developers. Further, the ferry services are neither jumbo nor truly super, and when you do manage to get from the island to the mainland, where are you? West Seattle! Point Defiance! Southworth! You can't get anywhere from there. Nevertheless, a scattering of Privatizers stand guard; clever Publics easily outflank them.

Sharing Vashon's permanent water problems, Maury has the added advantage of being a longer drive to the ferry lines. Little of the shore is developed; that of the Gravel Coast is beneath bluffs so tall they scarcely have trails down from the houses.

Then, Blake Island. Blake Island *State Park*. The *entire island* is a *park*. On the 4 1/2-mile beach no Public ever will be chased by a Private brandishing hedge clippers. Never will a clearcut let daylight into the green vaults of the forest. Additionally, visitors do not arrive here via car and car ferry. They voyage on the *Good Time* fleet, modern mosquitoes. The Blake experience is less like 1988 than 1888, 1688.

USGS maps: Duwamish Head, Vashon, Tacoma North, Gig Harbor, Olalla, Bremerton East, Suquamish, Shilshole Bay

Bainbridge Island (map—page 110)

From any spot in Seattle between Alki Point and Carkeek Park, look due west across the Whulge and the land you see is Bainbridge Island, 10 miles north-south long and 4 miles east-west wide. The island is partly a suburb of Bremerton, mostly of Seattle, connected to the central city—and cut off from it—by the ferry. But as the century ends the central city itself is becoming an island, cut off by gridlock. Indeed, Seattle and Tacoma and Bellevue and Kent and the rest are incipiently an archipelago of islands separated by concrete. Bainbridge has, instead, water.

A walk on the island begins with a voyage over water—liberating, in absolute contrast to journeys on concrete. However, Privatizers are so numerous that Publics are advised to go elsewhere for long walks on the beach. For short walks, though, the closeness to Seattle is attractive. The rules are: (1) Never come in summer; (2) Never come on weekends; (3) Never come when the sun is shining. That's a slight exaggeration. As will be seen, certain of the trips are easy-open on a brilliant midsummer Sunday; bring a book for the long wait while the ferries come—and go without you. The surveyor's favorite scheme is to choose a February Tuesday of

Bald eagle on snag overlooking beach

Eagle Harbor from Winslow City Park

decent but not spectacular weather and circle the shore, piecing together short walks and their varied views in a good, long day. Enjoy the sunset from the ferry on the way home, arriving in Seattle after the evening commute is over. In these pages the entire shore is sampled, starting and ending at Winslow.

Eagle Harbor

Park the car on the Seattle waterfront and walk on the ferry, paying only the foot-passenger fare (cheap).

Walk off the ferry, turn right, circling the terminal building, and between the parking-lot fence and the ferry ramp find a rude path down boulders to the beach. On a medium-low tide (in that winter midweek), the beach can be walked 1 mile, nearly to the battlements of Wing Point. In the beach gravel are rusted artifacts of a century of industry. Views are excellent to the continuing industry: the creosote plant, the shipyard, and the home port of Washington State Ferries. Ferry-watching is superb.

In the other direction from the ferry dock, walk the neat main street of (New) Winslow and turn left, downhill, to Eagle Harbor Waterfront Park. A shore path gives close looks at the shipyard, where may be seen at close range the likes of *Amfish* and *Aleutian Bounty*. Return to the main street, proceed west, then sharply downhill, to (Old) Winslow. You wouldn't know that's where you are unless this book told you. On the survey for the first edition the pilings and even some plankings remained of the Winslow Dock, where the older surveyor and parents used to catch the steamer

Winslow to Seattle. A marina is there now. On that survey in 1978 the Galbraith warehouse was intact, complete with the holes accidentally shot in the wall by the surveyor's father and pals during rat hunts. The sheet-metal walls have been painted green and the birdshot holes plugged up. The structure, however, is basically intact— as much so as that of its parent across the waters, the Galbraith Dock, the dock that was used by the *Winslow* and other steamers of the White Collar Line. Ivar's now sells steamers there—buckets of them.

Both round trips 3 ¹/₂ miles, allow about 4-6 hours

Manitou Beach
Views to Main Street ship traffic, West Point sewage plant, towers of downtown Seattle, Alki Point.
From the Winslow stoplight drive Highway 305 to a stoplight at 2 miles. Turn right and immediately park in the "Free Parking" lot. There is no parking at Manitou Beach.
Walk a few feet along the road to a Y and continue straight ahead ¹/₄ mile to the beach. The way west is to the estuary head of Murden Cove, east to Skiff Point and views north along Rolling Bay, and perhaps past the ¹/₂ mile of beach homes to the nearly 2 bluff-wild miles of Rolling Bay.

Round trip 2-7 miles, allow 2-5 hours

Fay Bainbridge State Park
The 17-acre park has ¹/₃ mile of public beach wedged between rows of homes. South is downtown Seattle, across the Sound are West Point and Shilshole Bay, and north over Port Madison and the Sound are Richmond Beach, Edmonds, and Glacier Peak.
Drive Highway 305 for 4 miles, turn right at the sign for the state park, and follow signs 3.2 miles to the beach.
The militia that patrols both ends of the park when alien invasions are expected relaxes its vigilance enough during storms that a person can skulk north past a row of houses waiting for the Conjunction of Four to reconstitute the stinkpot-ravaged lagoon. From Point Monroe look across Port Madison to the excellent drift bluffs of Indianola (there's the long beach walk).
Immediately south of the park are houses, a solid ¹/₂ mile. But beyond lie some 2 mostly wild, beneath-the-bluff miles south on Rolling Bay.

Round trips ²/₃-7 miles, allow 1-5 hours

Port Madison County Park
Aha! Another bit of incontestably Public beach. The trick is finding it. To foil off-islanders—and new-islanders—the old-islanders remove signs. To their credit, they also pick up the garbage strewn by jolly boys who come roistering in the middle of the night.
Drive Highway 305 for 5.8 miles and turn right on West Port Madison Road, which in 0.9 mile, at a sharp bend right, becomes County Park Road. A hundred feet short of Gordon Road, spot a woods road-trail on the left. A few feet short of that is a turnout with parking for two cars.
Walk the road-trail about ¹/₈ mile through 13 acres (seems like hundreds) of old-growth Douglas fir and associates, past dilapidated picnic shelters. Sit on the bluff brink and gaze across Port Madison to Suquamish and Indianola and Three Fingers. Peace. Big trees. Quiet views. One of the choicest spots on the island.
The bluff isn't high, the beach is close, but the short path down is mean, though not very dangerous. Note the big slabs of hard peat, sloughed off the bluff along with a mass of clay and a number of living alders. The beach easterly rounds to Hidden Cove, a cute estuary which harbors hundreds of stinkpots. The seals make sure to be

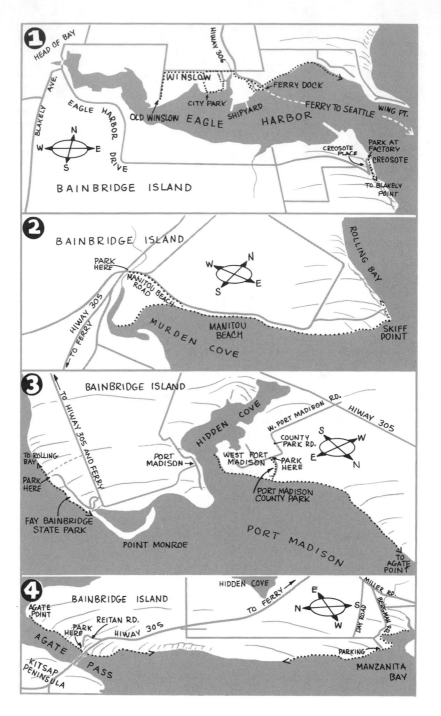

1 HEAD OF BAY

HIWAY 305

WINSLOW

FERRY DOCK

CITY PARK

OLD WINSLOW

EAGLE SHIPYARD

EAGLE HARBOR

FERRY TO SEATTLE

WING PT.

PARK AT FACTORY

CREOSOTE PLACE

CREOSOTE

TO BLAKELY POINT

BLAKELY AVE.

EAGLE HARBOR DRIVE

N W E S

BAINBRIDGE ISLAND

2 BAINBRIDGE ISLAND

ROLLING BAY

PARK HERE

MANITOU BEACH ROAD

HIWAY 305

TO FERRY

MURDEN COVE

MANITOU BEACH

N W E S

SKIFF POINT

3 BAINBRIDGE ISLAND

HIDDEN COVE

W. PORT MADISON RD.

HIWAY 305

TO HIWAY 305 AND FERRY

PORT MADISON

WEST PORT MADISON

COUNTY PARK RD.

PARK HERE

S W E N

TO ROLLING BAY

PARK HERE

FAY BAINBRIDGE STATE PARK

PORT MADISON COUNTY PARK

POINT MONROE

PORT MADISON

TO AGATE POINT

4 HIDDEN COVE

TO FERRY

MILLER RD.

BAINBRIDGE ISLAND

AGATE POINT

PARK HERE

REITAN RD.

HIWAY 305

E N S W

BERGMAN RD.

LAFE RD.

PARKING

AGATE PASS

KITSAP PENINSULA

MANZANITA BAY

110

Agate Pass Bridge

elsewhere on Sunday. In the other direction, 1 ¼ miles distant, is Agate Point, the entry to Agate Pass.

Round trips ¼-5miles, allow 1-3 hours

Agate Pass

Boat-watching is notably excellent on beaches of the narrow pass, where at the turn of the tide craft get either an assist or a tussle from the swift current.

Drive Highway 305 nearly to Agate Pass Bridge and turn right on Reitan Road. In 0.3 mile, at a powerline tower, are a turnaround and parking area and good trail dropping to the beach.

The walk north 1 mile to Agate Point, views opening over the water to Suquamish and Port Madison and Indianola, is by a row of near-beach houses.

South, beyond a couple houses up on the bank, the tanglewood bluff rears up 100 feet and the beach is houseless and wild more than 1 mile and virtually empty the whole 2 ¾ miles to Manzanita. On the way, Agate Pass widens into Port Orchard. Views open around Point Bolin to the Navy installation at Keyport and south into Manzanita Bay and to Battle Point. On the Kitsap Peninsula rise the peaks of Green and Gold; beyond are Constance and Warrior.

Round trip up to 7 miles, allow up to 5 hours

Suquamish (map—page 112)

Not on Bainbridge Island, to be sure. But since the bridge was built, the island hasn't truly been one, not on this side. Not so very long ago, islands didn't really exist—waters were not an obstruction to travel, they were the travel routes. Today cars whiz over Agate Pass high in the air and motorboats squall through from Port Orchard to Port Madison. Just beyond the memory of people now alive the waters were plied by dugout cedar canoes of the Suquamish people headquartered here under their leader, Sealth.

For the first of four beach accesses, drive Highway 305 to the west end of Agate Pass Bridge and turn off right to a parking area. A path drops through woods to the beach, lonesome-wild under the protective bluff for ¼ mile in either direction. To the north, front-yard beach continues 1 mile to Old Man House (see below). To the south the clusters of houses are widely scattered and mostly up on a high bank the 2 miles past Sandy Hook to Point Bolin, at the mouth of Liberty Bay.

For the second, shortly after crossing the bridge turn right on Suquamish Highway 1.2 miles and just beyond a shopping center go right on Division Street, then left on McKinstry, in 0.4 mile from the highway arriving at Old Man House State Historic Site. Parking space for perhaps two cars.

An interpretive shelter tells the tale. On a fossil-beach terrace elevated barely above high tide was the largest known longhouse, 500 feet long, up to 60 feet wide. Construction began about 1800, at the instance of Sealth's father, and was completed under Sealth. In 1870, after his death, the U.S. Army burnt the ruins.

The beach south goes under the Agate Pass Bridge and onward. The beach north comes in ½ mile to Suquamish Dock.

For the third, continue on the highway into Suquamish to parking for the Suquamish Dock. Walk on out for views down Agate Pass, across Port Madison to Agate Point and Point Monroe, across the Whulge to Shilshole Bay. North 1 mile on the beach is the entry to Miller Bay, and a look across to the spit that was supposed to become a state park, but didn't. While in Suquamish visit the Memorial Cemetery, where rests Sealth (1786-1866), who signed the 1855 Treaty of Point Elliott which "gave" his Suquamish and Duwamish peoples the 1375-acre (reduced from a former 8000 acres) Port Madison Reservation.

For the fourth and best, drive Highway 305 beyond Suquamish Highway 0.4 mile, turn left at the sign, "Suquamish Museum and Tribal Center," in another 0.4 mile turn left again, down to the parking area. The museum and tribal headquarters, built in the early 1980s, have given the original settlers an organizational focus.

Spend half a day in the museum. The other half, walk the nature trail looping through the woods by the museum, then the beach. A staircase drops to the beach, which goes this way to Agate Pass Bridge and that way to Suquamish.

Round trips ½-16 miles, allow 2 hours-2 days

Manzanita Bay

The cozy little bay beguiles. Views are fine over Port Orchard to Keyport. The Olympic skyline shines from Zion to Walker to Turner.

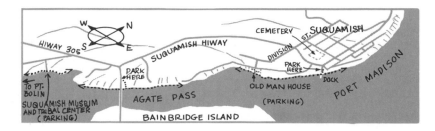

Canada jays (gray jays or camprobbers) scavenging bread crumbs on Mt. Walker. Mt. Constance in distance.

Drive Highway 305 for 4 miles, to where the road to Fay Bainbridge State Park goes off right, and go off left at the sign for "Manzanita." Immediately go right (straight) at a Y, on Day Road. In 1.1 miles turn left on Manzanita Way. On the right, spot white concrete posts that mark a public street-end. Parking space for a car or two.

North, beyond a handful of houses, the beach leads to wildness and, in 2-3/4 miles, Agate Pass Bridge. South, no houses, it's 1/2 mile around the bay to the inlet estuary oozing muckily out of green forest.

Round trips 1-5 1/2 miles, allow 1-3 hours

Battle Point

A lagoon-enclosing spit thrusting out in Port Orchard, a light at the tip. Views north to Agate Pass, south to Fletcher's Bay and suburbs of Bremerton, and across to Keyport. Heavy water traffic, recreational and Navy. But: Is the beach access private? If so, why no houses on it? No forbidding signs? Is it public, being held for a park? The neighbors never will tell. In fact, some of them don't know who owns the property. After 1988, what?

Drive Fletcher Bay Road (see Fletcher's Bay) to Island Center. Continue straight on Miller Road 0.5 mile and turn left on Battle Point Drive. In 1.7 miles turn left on Skinner Road 0.2 mile, down to beach level and a farm; at a left bend the road becomes Ollalie Lane. On the right is a wide field grown up in grass and scotchbroom. Park on the shoulder and walk the path the several hundred feet to the beach.

Northwest 1 mile is Arrow Point at the mouth of Manzanita Bay.

Southwest 1/2 mile is the tip of the Battle Point sandspit, no houses near the water. The 1 1/2 miles south from there to Fletcher's Bay are partly populated.

If you've got to have a battle, this appears a decent spot for it. Who did the fighting?

Round trip to Battle Point 1 mile, allow 1 hour

Fletcher's Bay

Another of the fiord-like coves for which Bainbridge is noted. The harbor is half plugged with boats, dinghy to million-dollar yacht. Views along Port Orchard to Keyport, and of Olympics from Constance to Jupiter to The Brothers.

Drive Highway 305 for 1 mile and turn left at the stoplight on High School Road. In 2 miles turn right on Fletcher Bay Road about 0.5 mile to Island Center. Turn left on Fletcher Bay Road 0.3 mile and turn left on Foster Road. In 0.3 mile is a T with Hansen Road. Go right a short bit, then left on Fletcher Landing Road. Parking for two cars at most.

The public street-end has been fenced. But the gate cannot legally be locked. Open it, walk through. The Privatizers try to daunt you but they cannot forbid you to walk to where the ferry used to cross Port Orchard to Brownsville, the route to Bremerton.

The beach leads north to the spit at the bay mouth, once the harbor for rowboats and naphtha launches bringing folks to trip the light fantastic at Ma and Pa Foster's dancehall. The older surveyor's father, when his battlewagon was in the Bremerton Navy Yard, had the use of a cabin on the spit owned by a retired veteran of the Great White Fleet. The beach leads south beneath a steep forest where all-year residences have replaced the summer cabins once served by steamers from Seattle. The surveyor's mother summered here with her mother and sister. At a beachfire here the surveyor's parents met, so he danged well ain't going to be hollered off by modern Privatizers. Down the beach some 2 miles, wild then populated, is Crystal Springs.

Round trips up to 4 miles, allow up to 3 hours

Point White-Crystal Springs

Views north up Port Orchard. Views across the narrows of Rich Passage, through which hurtle the Seattle-Bremerton ferry and the U.S. Navy.

Debarking from the ferry at Winslow, at the stoplight in town turn left at the sign, "City Center." Turn right on Madison Avenue, left on Wyatt Way, to "Head of Bay." Bend left on Bucklin Hill Road to a Y; go right on Blakely Avenue, signed "Lynwood Center." Following Lynwood signs, take a right turn, and at a Y go left. At the junction in Lynwood Center turn right 2.2 miles, passing Point White, to a public dock at Crystal Springs.

Walk out on the dock for the views. Then follow the beach ³/₄ mile to Point White in one direction and 3-odd miles the other way to Fletcher's Bay.

Round trip 3-4 miles, allow 2-6 hours

Fort Ward State Park

A beauty of a forest. A shore that can be walked on the dandy beach or paralleled atop the above-tides wave-cut bench. And mountings of the old gun batteries, strategically located to batter such Spaniards as got this far. Established in 1891, in 1958 the fort was surplused. Tragically, of the 480 acres only 137 were obtained for park.

Drive to Lynwood Center (see Point White) and continue straight on Pleasant Beach Road. At the Y in 0.6 mile keep right, in another 0.6 mile coming to the park gate and in a few yards more the parking area.

The park presently is undeveloped; that, of course, is the best kind for walking. A loop samples the varied entertainments. From the parking area walk the ³/₄ mile of beach, featuring sandstone outcrops, ferries rocketing through Rich Passage so close you can see the hamburgers being gulped, views of the Kitsap shore and The Brothers, Jupiter, Constance. (Also featured are masses of poison oak, so beware!) At high tide, walk the closed-to-vehicles road. A small gun emplacement is all that's war-like remaining, but here in War II were stretched the anti-sub nets that slowed each ferry trip by a quarter-hour as nets were opened. (After the war it was discovered a Japanese sub had gotten through to take periscope photos of the Navy Yard. Very

Point White

simple. Just follow the ferry in and out.) The park ends at the site of Timber Lodge, in previous incarnations an Army recreation center, then Sunset Lodge, then an amusement park.

Now for the woods. Backtrack from the park boundary to the gun battery and spot an old road-trail climbing a scant ¼ mile to the blufftop at 150 feet. Hit an old blacktop road and follow it left past two three-storey Army mansions. At blacktop end a woods road-path continues in the woods, first young alder and then splendid big firs, cedars, hemlocks, and maples. Ignore a sidepath that drops left to a deadend at a pump house and proceed straight, at ¾ green-shadow big-tree mile from the blacktop reaching the boundary fence. Here the road-trail descends left, passing an ivy-overgrown gun battery, to hit the park entry road just north of the parking area.

Loop trip 2 miles, allow 1 ½ hours

Port Blakely
Started in the Civil War, what once was the largest lumber mill in the world completely occupied shores of Port Blakely; sailing ships carried Washington wood from here around the planet. There were three mills in succession; the first two burned, in 1888 and 1907, and the third was closed in 1914 and dismantled in 1923. Lumber schooners remained moored in nearby Eagle Harbor long after; the older surveyor attended a birthday party on one. In 1937 the Black Ball Line moved its ferry landing from here to Winslow, previously a stop only for vessels of the White Collar Line steamers, and Port Blakely was left to quietly marinate in memories.

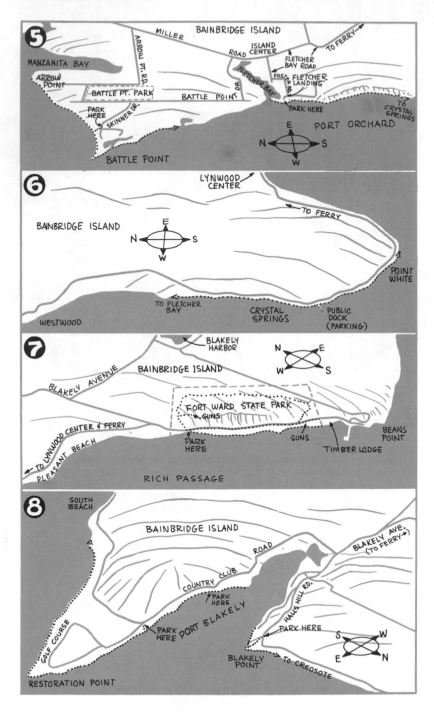

Debarking from the ferry at Winslow, at the stoplight in town turn left at the sign, "City Center," then right on Madison and left on Wyatt, following "Head of Bay" signs. Bend left on Bucklin Hill Road to a Y. Go right on Blakely Avenue to the head of Blakely Harbor. Turn right on Country Club Road, which in 1 mile touches the beach. Park on the wide shoulder.

Drop off the low bank and walk the beach 1/4 mile west. Look out the harbor mouth to Seattle. Look around the harbor to a few old pilings, hulk of a wrecked ship, a couple remodeled houses recognizable as dating from the mill era, remnant pilings of the ferry dock. In mind's eye reconstruct the mill and docks and piles of lumber, the ships filling the harbor, the ferry shuttling in and out, the bustling town.

Round trip 1/2 mile, allow 1/2 hour

Restoration Point
Named by Vancouver to celebrate restoration of the British monarchy, and at the time of his visit the site of an Indian village, this striking peninsula is the most spectacular natural feature on Bainbridge. Until such time as it is (as it must be) acquired for a public park, exploration demands the utmost in courtesy and discretion.

From the parking place for Port Blakely (which see) continue on Country Club Road (or better, walk the beach) 1/2 mile to a Y where Upper Farms Road goes right. Park here if not before.

Walk the banktop on the grownover previous route of Country Club Road. When there's beach, walk that. However, there's not always beach, for this is the center of the only extensive area on shores of Puget Sound where hard rock outcrops through glacial drift. From here to Fort Ward, and also across Rich Passage, sandstones, shales, and conglomerates often make buttresses and walls rather than beaches.

In 1/4 mile is the edge of the country club. Views are fine to Eagle Harbor, the ferry scurrying in and out, and over the Sound to Seattle.

On stormy winter weekdays, a quiet, respectful, humble walker may proceed to the point. Sandstone-pavement beaches are ribbed and knobbed with protruding strata and nodules of harder rock. Here and there are pockets of dazzling-white shell beach. Above, on the former-island (tombolo) hill are mansions built by some of the oldest money in the Northwest. Around the foot of the forested hill curves the onetime golf course, greensward rolling over an old wave-cut bench to the edge of the sandstone wall that drops a dozen feet to the beach, at low tide providing good cover for a walker who keeps head and voice down.

The views! This way bustles the ferry to Winslow. That way hustles the ferry to Bremerton. And there's where they come from and go to, Elliott Bay, enclosed by West Seattle and Magnolia Bluff. Far off south, beyond Blake Island, is still another ferry, from Fauntleroy to Vashon Island. Up the Sound is the shore from Alki to Tacoma. Rainier. Down the Sound, past Blakely Rock, is West Point.

Round trip to Point 2 miles, allow 1 1/2 hours

Blakely Point
Across the mouth of Port Blakely from Restoration Point is a companion jut of rock. As of 1988, no houses block access, no signs seek to affright Publics.

Drive Blakely Avenue to the head of Port Blakely and continue straight. Where four roads go off—left and right, up and down—split the middle, ascending 3-T (Halls Hill) Road to the top, attained in 0.6 mile from the confusion. Park on the turnout.

Beyond a barricade of brush and logs erected to prevent youths from driving to a spot where they might ingest controlled substances, a road-trail skids straight down clay to the beach. A path leads out on the tip of Blakely Point, a fantasy of conglomerate pillars and clefts. The views extend from West Point to Alki Point, over Seattle to the Issaquah Alps and Cascades. Ferries race every which way.

Immediately north of the point are houses without a break a long 1 mile to Creosote at the mouth of Eagle Harbor.

On the Port Blakely side the shore rocks can be clambered from one pocket beach to another. Or, in high tide, a person can stroll the trail along the grade of the ancient shore road, beneath conglomerate walls; madronas and firs lean over the conglomerate bank to the water. In 1/3 mile the old road comes to a house and the walk ends.

Round trip 1-3 miles, allow 1-2 hours

Vashon Island (map—page 120)

A 1983 study commissioned by King County found that rainfall was the sole source of the groundwater that the 7300-odd residents of Vashon Island drank, that a relatively small population increase would quickly deplete and even more quickly pollute the groundwater, and that therefore development should be strictly limited. We'll see. The scene strikes a visitor as rural, most settlements modest expansions of farming crossroads or summer colonies. But the expansions go on, and on. Longtime residents say, via bumper stickers, "Vashon is Sinking."

The attitude toward visitors may be characterized as a genial xenophobia. Recreational visits tend to be discouraged—there is no tourist industry, no system of regional parks, and virtually all beaches are "private." Nevertheless, except in the summer season and other times when large numbers of residents are actively using their beaches, trespassing by small groups of quiet, clean, polite foreigners is generally tolerated—so long as they lay off the clams and don't picnic in somebody's front yard. Few are the signs saying "Keep Off"; many say something firm but courteous such as "Private Beach—Do Not Loiter," or "No Clamming," or "No Fires." Leave your dog home, haul away your garbage, and eat your lunch on the long wild stretches. Behave so and your meetings with locals are likely to be pleasant—they'll tell you about island history, give information on that classic beach walk, the 35-mile around-the-island loop.

Precisely because it is so centrally located, so quick of access from Tacoma, Seattle, and Bremerton, Vashon "belongs" to a great many people, whether or not they ever so much as visit. The existence of islandness is potential opportunity enriching all of us. Those walkers who do visit must perforce become active Defenders of Vashon. And one way to do that is by not contaminating the island any more than necessary with your personal wheels. Take the bus. And/or one of the two ferries. Proceed then by shanks' mare.

East Shore

Walk the entire east shore, miles of wildness, in ever-changing views across Main Street traffic to Seattle shores and mountains beyond, on a beach that is easy-open at all but the highest tides.

The bus enables the ingenuity. The destination on Vashon Island, the "trailhead," is Ellisport. Metro bus 118 leaves 8th and Blanchard in Seattle at 6:35 A.M. weekdays, ferries to the island, and proceeds to Ellisport, arriving 9:04. (Saturday: leave 2nd and Pike at 8:32 A.M., arrive Ellisport 9:38.) The alternative is to drive to the Fauntleroy ferry terminal and park (lots of luck). Walk on the ferry. At the Vashon terminal catch buses at 6:35 A.M. (Ellisport, 6:53), 8:45 A.M. (9:04). This is the schedule for summer 1988. Consult current bus and ferry schedules. They change frequently.

Should the water be too high on your arrival for the beach to be easy, the first 3/4 mile can be walked on public road climbing above the shore, then dropping to cross the lagoon onto the Point Heyer spit; aside from the KVI radio tower the spit is in a natural state of lagoon, dune, driftwood. Much time can be whiled away amid waves and gulls, looking to Rainier, watching jets land and take off at Sea-Tac Airport. When the water has lowered to 10 feet or so, head north.

Dalco Passage from Vashon Island

The 2 ³/₄ miles to Dilworth Point (Point Beals) are virtually all wild beneath a tanglewood bluff as high as 300 feet. The cozy trail-access cottages of Klahanie briefly interrupt, and a mansion at ancient Vashon Landing, and cottages in the valley-cove just north, but mainly the people are atop the bluff with not even trails down. Creeks flow from jungle over gravels—which by the unusual abundance of red-brick pebbles and cobbles tell of a past when the island had nine or more brickyards. Across Puget Sound is the thrust of Three Tree Point.

Dilworth Point (where in the 1930s, while swimming, the older surveyor watched an airplane fly over, carrying Wiley Post and Will Rogers to Alaska and eternity) is a logical turnaround; it's 3 ¹/₂ miles back to Ellisport, where any of five afternoon buses can be taken to the ferry dock. No time or energy is saved by turning back here, but more of the day is spent in wildness, because Dilworth itself is densely populated, as is the entire shore for a mile north.

In good toleration season, though, the next 3 ¹/₂ miles to Dolphin Point have much interest. The architectural tastes of beachdwellers entertain, especially in those constructions dependent not on tons of money but on beachcombing, scavenging, and do-it-yourself handicrafting. At 1 ³/₄ miles from Dilworth wildness resumes for nearly 1 mile; then, at Cowley's Landing, is a vision of the past—a nearly intact dock and gangplank from the era of the mosquito fleet. Just beyond, on beach-invading riprap, is a short stretch that at above 7 feet of water cannot be passed without wading—the only such obstacle on the route.

Dolphin Point, thoroughly habitated, is yet a marvelous viewpoint. Ferries shuttle to Fauntleroy, Southworth, Bremerton, Winslow. Look south on the Sound to where you

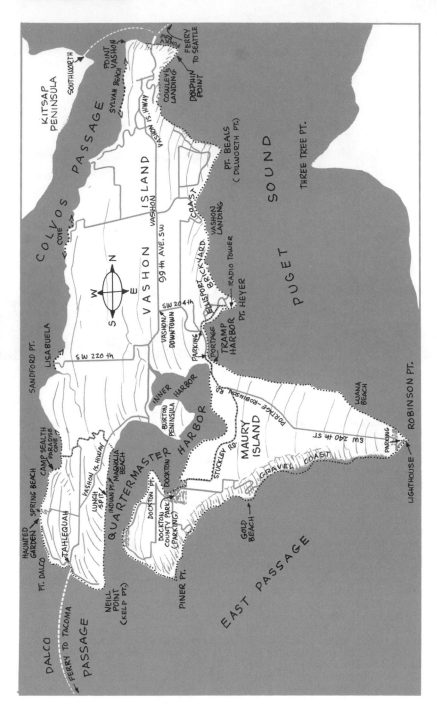

came from. And north to Blake and Bainbridge Islands—and Whidbey. The Seattle shore is distinguished by the Green Mile of Lincoln Park.

The final ¹/₂ mile is quaint along cabins-cottages, home-made and homey. The escape from the beach is blocked by their bulkheads and requires less than 7 feet of water: walk easily off the beach on a ramp to a restaurant parking area.

One-way trip 7 ¹/₂ miles, allow 7 hours

Northwest Shore

In some opinion the northwest shore is the best of Vashon. Colvos Passage is so much narrower than East Passage that you can't miss the gray whales swimming by, and the view is not to Puget Sound City but such lesser megalopolises as Olalla and Fragaria. The beach seems lonesomer, the bluff taller and greener. The shore was not surveyed for the first edition except by eyeball from across Colvos Passage; the succession of wild delights was seen to be interrupted only intermittently by tidy little villages. The shortcoming is that the Metro bus routes are such they would require a deal of road-walking to do a vehicle-free tour. However, should a person be willing to walk the roads, or should dare on a midweek winter day to intrude his vehicle onto the island, several beach accesses permit walks. All take off from the main island highway.

For Sylvan Beach, drive the highway from the ferry to the top of the hill, past the fire station, and go right on "Corbin Beach Drive-Sylvan Beach." In 0.1 mile is a junction. Park on a shoulder hereabouts; there is no room farther down, and certainly not at the beach. Go right and walk the ¹/₄ mile from the junction, down the narrow, winding, steep road, to the road-end, signed "Limited Beach Access."

For the next access, at Cove, drive the highway to just before beautiful downtown Vashon. Turn west on Cove Road about 2.5 miles and go south on 131 Avenue SW, Tahlequah Road, to 0.5 mile south of Crescent Drive SW. Turn west on SW 172 Street 0.1 mile, go right on a one-lane road, past three-storey Cove Motel, to the water. This is a cable crossing; parking is easy; nobody hollers at you; feel free. To the south are walk-in cabins. To the north the beach is beneath a steep and ever-sliding bluff overhung with alder; except at low tide expect to have to scramble over chunks of former bluff.

The next access south is Lisabuela, on a spit of driftwood and sandy beach poking out in the cove to which drains lovely Judd Creek. In 1906 the community sought to secede from King County, next year tried to join Pierce County, and in 1912 almost got the legislature to establish Vashon County. It is not clear what was bugging them, or whether it still is. As of 1988 the public can reach the beach but the plague of realtor signs bodes ill. A couple attempts have been made to get this beach/land for the public, but so far the public hasn't been willing to pay for it. Check it out. At the Center stoplight south of downtown Vashon turn west from the highway on SW 196 Street (Cemetery Road). Follow the twists (don't give up when it becomes 131st SW) and turn right on SW 220th, which makes a sharp left, becomes 142nd SW, and drops to the water. On the way down note the waterfall of Judd Creek. Pretty!

Paradise Cove is reached from the highway via 131st (Orchards Road) and Bates Road. See the next trip description.

Mind you, the tolerance Vashon Islanders traditionally have had for beachwalkers cannot be guaranteed. The doctrine of "private" is spreading. The island population is liable to grow by 50 percent before the wells run dry. Thirst will make the residents testy. They are testy now when they spot an alien car probing for a way to the beach. They fear the car may be a prospective new resident.

South-End Loop

Of all the beach walks in this book, here perhaps is the richest in combining solitude of wild beach beneath green-jungle glacial-drift bluff, views over busy waterways to the metropolis of Second City, and poignant memories of the grand old days of the mosquito fleet.

Tahlequah ferry dock

Drive (or take the Point Defiance bus from downtown Tacoma) to Point Defiance Park. Walk on the nice little ferry for the 15-minute voyage over Dalco Passage to Tahlequah, an old village in and around the valley of Tahlequah Creek, the weathered houses grown comfortably into the landscape.

To loop is not compulsory. A person can stroll up the west shore, along Colvos Passage; Camp Sealth at 3 miles is a good turnaround. Or the other way around Neill Point to Quartermaster Harbor; "Lunch Spit" at 3 miles is a fine goal. For each of these round trips, 6 miles each, allow 4 hours.

The loop is the classic if time, tides, and energy permit. To do it clockwise, walk off the ferry dock, turn left to Tahlequah Grocery for nostalgia and some extra lunch supplies, and from it scramble down to the beach. In the first ½ mile are Tahlequah Creek, continuous bulkheads, and cozy homes. Views are east to Commencement Bay, downtown Tacoma, pulpmill steam plume, ships, and mountains.

Rounding Point Dalco shifts the mood to wildness, the jungle-drift wall rising a steep 260 feet. Views focus now on the greenery of Point Defiance, the mouth of The Narrows, and the mouth of Gig Harbor. New vistas open north up Colvos Passage, tugs hauling log rafts, fishermen dragging lines. At 1 mile from the point is a wild valley where grow, mysteriously, tall poplars. Step in a bit from the beach and find by the creek a haunted cottage, flowers and beanstalks of a garden gone wild, overgrown by hellberries. A bit farther up the beach is a larger valley where part of a mosquito-fleet dock still stands, old houses line sides of the valley, and one on a bulkhead by the beach bears faded lettering, "Miramar—Board and Room—And Lunches." This is Spring Beach; close your eyes and see the excursion steamer docking, hear the singing around the beachfire.

Revert to the wild mode 1 long mile to a wildland protected by the Seattle-King County Council of Camp Fire Girls. Here is Camp Sealth, a wonderland fondly remembered by generations of girls and more than a few boys; it was in the spring of 1939 that Troop 324 voyaged here on the *Virginia V* to perform, as was the troop's wont, a Good Deed, working on trails. The trail system must be left alone; while walking rapidly by on the beach, admire the nature preserve and the snug buildings tucked in and around the valley.

Keep a sharp eye for functionaries (male) employed by Campfire but unfamiliar with what the organization and the beach are all about. Should you be confronted and given a lecture on Privacy and child-molesting, smile sweetly and offer to buy a box of mints. If they threaten to kick you off the beach, ask for a choice of direction.

"Sealth Point" is rounded to Paradise Cove. Houses start. At ³/₄ mile from the point, 4 miles from Tahlequah, a public street-end at an old boathouse provides a take-out for the loop.

Walk the country road up a forest ravine to the island top, 480 feet. Turn left on 131 Avenue SW a short bit, then right on SW 248 Street, which becomes 123 Avenue as it goes right and becomes curvy on its downhill run to Vashon Island Highway. Cross to a public lane that deadends on Magnolia Beach. This cross-island walk on quiet country roads totals 2 ¹/₄ miles.

Magnolia is a hotbed of Privates who stand 24-hour guard against Public cars. However, a pedestrian who is a guest of a resident—like, say, the Reizenheimers, who just moved in—can readily walk from the deadend.

Watch the tides—ahead lie feeble-wave beaches overhung by alder and maple, cool retreats on hot days, but not so lovable when full of water, requiring a person to swim or fight hillside brush. The first 1 ¹/₂ miles south along Quartermaster Harbor, by Indian Point and Harbor Heights, views to Dockton on Maury Island, are mostly bulkheaded and populated, many boats moored.

In ¹/₂ mile more is "Lunch Spit," a tiny jut of sand enclosing a tiny lagoon. To the south 2 miles can be seen Neill (Kelp) Point, and in all that distance, no sign of man. A second little spit is passed, several inviting ravines. Then houses do indeed exist, up in the trees, no interruption of the mood. (And providing emergency escapes to an overland return if, as happened on the survey, the beach is totally swallowed up.) Piner Point on Maury Island is passed and the water panorama widens, climaxing at Neill Point with a prospect east and north on the Sound to Redondo, Tacoma again, and Rainier. A final 1 mile beside bulkheads and houses leads back to Tahlequah.

Loop trip 11 miles, allow 8 hours
High point 480 feet, elevation gain 480 feet

Maury Island (map—page 120)

Miles of beaches lightly populated or purely wild, a lighthouse built in 1915, some of the most stupendous gravel mines in the western world, and views across ships and barges and sailboats in East Passage to the Whulge Trail from Three Tree Point to the Ruston smelter stack. And Cascades. Public accesses permit beach walks short or long — up to a complete circuit of the island. Leave the car on the mainland and travel by ferry, bus, and foot.

The hike may be started (or ended) at Dockton. In summer 1988 convenient Metro buses leave the Vashon ferry terminal at 6:30 A.M. and 1:00 P.M.; arrive Dockton 7:00 A.M. and 1:26 P.M. The last bus from Dockton to the ferry leaves at 7:13 P.M. Be sure to check a current schedule.

For an alternate start, drive Vashon Island Highway from Vashon Heights or Tahlequah to 1.7 miles south of beautiful downtown Vashon and turn east on SW 204 Street, which in 1 long mile descends to the beach. Turn south on Ellisport-Portage Road 0.7 mile and park anywhere on the wide shoulders near Portage Grocery (1910).

Lighthouse on Robinson Point

Walk the shores of Tramp Harbor, leaving behind the low isthmus that connects Maury to Vashon, looking over boat-busy waters to Issaquah Alps. Though several gulches and benches permit houses near the beach, most of the way a 100-foot wildwood bluff keeps the peace. Stubs of pilings speak of the mosquito fleet. Bulkheaded dwellings of Luana Beach break the greenery for ³/₄ mile, then solitude resumes to the jutting spit and grassy fields of Robinson Point.

Here, 3-¹/₂ miles from Portage, is a scenic climax and satisfying turnaround. The lagoon is filled but not otherwise intruded, the open fields grow wind-waving grass and wildflowers. Water views are unsurpassed. The lighthouse and keeper's house are picturesque; inquire at the office for possible touring of the light station, with a past dating to 1893.

To put in at Robinson Point for hikes south, drive from Portage 0.7 mile to a Y. The right leads in 3 miles to Dockton (King County) Park. Go left on SW 228th (Portage-Robinson Road), descending in 2.5 miles to a T. Go right on Wick Road 0.3 mile to a parking area on top of the hill above the lighthouse. A gated road drops to the keeper's house and the beach.

Rounding the corner, the pilgrim's vistas open southward past Des Moines Marina to Tacoma. Now begins the famous Gravel Coast from which a substantial portion of the mass of Maury has been removed. Two barge-loading docks are active (are they still?), two are in a condition of handsome dilapidation, and others are reduced to piling stubs. The two active (or recently) pits are awesomely vast desolations. Those recently abandoned have grown up in grass and madronas; in early summer, poppies, vetch, yarrow, and ocean spray in orange-blue-white-cream bloom, are winsomely California-pretty. The oldest abandoned pits are so wooded one wouldn't know from a quick look they aren't enigmatic features of a natural landscape.

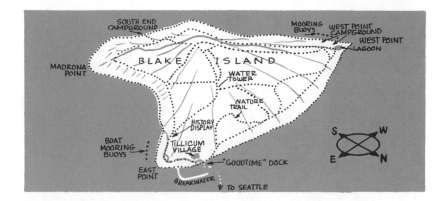

The first half of the 6 miles from Robinson Point to Piner Point is mostly uninhabited, partly due to on-going mining and partly the imposing 300-foot bluff that plunges from the island plateau. The second half alternates between scattered houses and solid homes, notably at Gold Beach, where the removal of the primeval bluff by excavation has created a terrace ideal for subdivision. Piner Point is a wildwood bulge with views across to Dash Point and Commencement Bay, downtown Tacoma and Rainier, and the tallest finger of masonry in the West. A nice spot for lunching and turning around.

If stubbornly intent on doing the total Maury, proceed the 4 miles to Dockton County Park. The bluff drops to naught, a hodgepodge of dwellings rich and poor push close to the water, but the narrow waters of Quartermaster Harbor have charm. Dockton Point is rounded; the protected cove is full of pretty boats and cruddy garbage that impedes feet. The park is a good spot to contemplate the heavy-industrial past. The cove once was the site of a floating drydock employing 400 workers, another 200 at other shipyards; many a vessel of the mosquito fleet was built there.

The older surveyor gazed upon the narrow, tree-obstructed, boot-sucking beach leading past Burton Peninsula to the Inner Harbor and decided he wasn't stubborn enough to stick by the water the last 3 miles back to Portage; the road is by the shore and has nice views. And a bus.

Round trip from Portage to Robinson Point 7 miles, allow 5 hours
Round trip from Robinson Point to Piner Point 12 miles, allow 8 hours
Maury loop trip 16 ½ miles, allow 10 hours

Blake Island (map—page 125)

In the middle of Main Street, ferries rushing this way and that, big ships and little boats and tugs and barges tooling around, jet airplanes booming and propellor jobs clacketing, cities and suburbs humming on every side, are 475 acres of green peace. The beach, and the big-tree forest, are as wild now as when Chief Seattle (reputedly) was born here, and tribes gathered for parties. Bought by William Pitt Trimble in 1904 and kept by him as a summer home until 1929, in 1957 the sanctuary became Blake Island State Marine Park.

For non-boaters, access is by craft of Seattle Harbor Tours serving Tillicum Village, an Indian-longhouse restaurant on 4 ½ leased acres. The *Goodtime* leaves from Pier 56 in Seattle, at the foot of Seneca Street just north of the ferry terminal and just south of Waterfront Park and Seattle Aquarium, attractions suitable for combining with a Blake trip while awaiting the boat. Park in an Alaskan Way lot or on the street, or come by Metro bus. On a vessel reminding of the mosquito fleet, the trip from Blake to Seattle takes 45 minutes, with long views up and down the open Sound, north to

Indian long house at Tillicum Village

Whidbey Island, south to Rainier, then threading through Elliott Bay traffic. The trip to Blake is 60 minutes, including a waterfront tour.

The boat schedule dictates the hike itinerary. To learn the current schedule and make reservations, call Tillicum Village Tours, (206) 329-5700.

The fare (1988) is—without the salmon feast at the longhouse—$12.97 for adults, $5.41 for children; with feast, $29 for adults, varied amounts for children, $26 for seniors.

From May 1 to September 11 (1988) the boats run more and more often as the season advances, mainly to serve feasters. For walkers, throughout this period there is a Sunday boat at 1:30 P.M. and in the middle weeks are 11:30 A.M. boats Saturdays and most or all weekdays. For October 17 to April 30, call the office.

A 2-hour layover suffices to circle the beach and sidetrip in the woods, or to circle the perimeter trail in the woods and sidetrip to the beach. By arriving on a morning boat and leaving on an evening boat, a person can do the whole trail system plus the entire beach, and then lazy around watching the sunset and eating a picnic supper— or buying the salmon dinner served at Tillicum Village, Indian-baked, with dances performed and crafts displayed. Of course, the supreme plan is to combine any trip of one day with any trip of the next, camping at one of the three beachside campgrounds, marveling at the all-around skyglow of the billion-eyed megalopolis. (The east campground, by the dock, is $6 a night. The west and south camps are no-fee.)

At any but high tides the circuit of the longest purely wild beach so near downtown Seattle is the first priority. Walk up the dock toward the longhouse, turn left, and go. (Left is advised in order to do the largely cobble east-southwest beach first, saving the mainly sand north beach for the end.) Village, picnic area, and campground are soon left behind, East Point rounded, and solitude attained—since few of the *Goodtime* crowds venture far from the longhouse. Grand fir, madrona, and maple overhang the beach. Views are to West Seattle and the Fauntleroy-Vashon ferry, Rainier and Issaquah Alps, Space Needle and grain terminal and Magnolia Bluff. At 1 ¼ miles Madrona Point is rounded and the view shifts down Colvos Passage between Vashon and Point Southworth, then across Yukon Harbor to Colby and Colchester. South End Campground, on a spur from the perimeter trail, is passed; the jungled bluff of glacial drift rears up 200 feet from the beach; fleeing herons "gark! gark!" The elevated terrace of a fossil beach begins, and on it is West Point Campground. Then the noble sandspit thrusts out in the waves, driftwood line and dune line enclosing a (usually) dry lagoon. At a scant 2 miles from Madrona Point is the tip of the spit, the climax delight; plan to sit a long while watching Seattle-Bremerton ferries dashing through Rich Passage between Orchard Point and Bainbridge Island. See the Olympics. A final 1 ¼ miles leads back under an alder canopy, in views to the Seattle-Winslow ferry and the metropolis, to the longhouse, completing a 4½-mile loop.

That's the half of it. Now, inland. Logged in the 1850s (except for some wolfish Douglas fir on the south side), the island has regrown a mixed forest that offers every variety of Puget Sound woodland experience—and meetings with some of the island's puny, half-starved 120-odd deer, striving to survive in a habitat that can support only 50 or so. To start the perimeter counterclockwise, walk by the right side of the longhouse to a bridge over a little gulch. To do it clockwise, meander through the campground any old way and near its end turn inland on the old road to the foundations of the Trimble house. A few steps beyond is a Y; left is the island loop trail, right is the cross-island trail. The loop is the basic trail but the cross-island trail offers additional green mystery, as do the nature trail and various lesser paths. Frequent spurs lead to the beach, permitting easy switches from one Blake mode to the other.

Beach loop 4 ½ miles, allow 3 hours
Perimeter trail loop 4 miles, allow 3 hours
High point 200 feet, elevation gain 500 feet
All year (but call (206) 329-5700 for current *Goodtime* schedule)

THE NORTHERN ISLES—
CAMANO, WHIDBEY, FIDALGO

Though a bridge from the mainland long ago de-islanded Camano, the 20-mile length still is ringed by water, 50-odd miles of beach. Despite the Privatizing by generations of summerers and decades of retirees, enough beach people are relaxed enough and enough bluffs rise high enough that excellent wild walking is to be found. To get there, drive I-5 to Exit 212 and follow Highway 532 across the Stillaguamish delta to the bridge over West Pass, whose slim width is all that makes the island so, technically.

In 1985 the U.S. Supreme Court ruled that Long Island, 110 miles long, is not the longest island in the old 48 states because it's a peninsula. One has to wonder why the nine jurists felt compelled to meddle in the business of geographers. One further must ask if Isle Royale loyalists intend to seek *their* justice. In any event, Whidbey Island newly is the longest. How long *is* it? As the crow flies, about 35 miles. As the shoreline curves, 45—or 60—or some other number. The miles of tidelands total (?) 135. Of these, only 30-40 are secure from the discredited but persistent doctrine of "private" beaches, but bluffs leaping steeply to 300 feet and more protect twice that many miles.

The walker who comes for the beaches may be delayed in getting there. A visitor from Puget Sound City is entranced, driving back roads, by the visions of Old America. Farms. Stumpranches. Moss-green barns. Cozy old cottages. "Affordable" housing. The walker is a problem, too frequently dashing back home to pick up the family and move in. Preserving the rural character is a continuing and often desperate battle. The beaches were virtually built out by the end of the 1960s, and in the 1980s the view slopes are filling in fast and suburbanization is advancing through the near-ferry southern part of the island. Still, the only Uglyville is Oak Harbor, symbiont of the jet strip from which Top Guns take off in hydrocarbon explosions to serenade the vicinity—and the wilderness of the Olympics and Cascades—with what a highway billboard calls "The Sound of Freedom." The quality of life on Whidbey varies with the square of the distance from Ault Field.

Another sort of "freedom fighters"—the environmentalists—have had some victories over hammer-and-dash developers. Their greatest triumphs have been in preserving scenic climaxes that are also historic sites. From end to end the island is a history feast. Space here prevents more than a few vignettes, most supplied by Richard K. McDonald, who in December of 1981 sent the older surveyor and a few other friends, as Christmas card, *A Traveler's Guide to Whidbey Island*, 10,000 words of history and geography and comment.

(Speaking of travel, the best approach normally is to drive I-5 to Exit 189, go off west to Mukilteo, ferry to Clinton, and drive the main island road, Highway 525, which becomes Highway 20. On jammed-up summer Sundays the long way around via Deception Pass Bridge may be the shortest way home.)

As for scenery, the southwest is the weather shore, exciting as a voyage around Cape Horn, beneath the magnificent tall bluffs famous as landmarks everywhere from Seattle to the Cascades.

The east side, the lee shore with deeply indented bays, was first to be settled. Beaches are quiet. History is thick in the old towns.

The "West Coast Trail" is something else. A visitor from Puget Sound City feels an exhilarating escape from claustrophobic, mountain-walled confines of the inner Whulge, a wondrous enlargement of the world, in gazing to the water horizon. On a clear day you can see Asia—from whence roar the gales that stir oceanic surfs, sculpt the bonsai forests, wave the grass of the Mendocino-like sea meadows. Despite subdividers braving the winds to trash the flats, the bluffs remain unconquerable and here is the longest stretch of natural beach this side of Olympic National Park. There

Driftwood in Lake Hancock

are other attractions, too: the Olympic rainshadow; Main Street traffic of ships and boats; the Weird Pits of Point Partridge, old-lakebed Ebey's Prairie, spits and baymouth bars and lagoons, mementoes of ancient wars, and—climaxing all—Ebey's Landing National Historic Preserve.

The supreme walk of the island is—the whole thing, of course. In 1962 four teenage boys did the entire shore in a single backpacking go. We would like to hear more about the journey. The report gives the shoreline distance as 201 miles and says the feat was accomplished in five days and nights.

Next, Fidalgo Island. (Marrowstone is a superb Northern Isle but the approach is via the Kitsap Peninsula and thus it is treated in that chapter.) Fidalgo is covered in detail by Marge Mueller's book, *The San Juan Islands, Afoot and Afloat*. The geology tends to make it better for floating than footing. The geology—and the sociology. Anacortes entered the 1970s endowed with thousands of acres of public lands, some given for parks, others disused watersheds. The city had no management plan or policy. As happened everywhere in that decade, motorcycles flowed in to fill the vacuum. Doing a systematic inventory in 1978, the older surveyor fled, spreading the warning cry, "Unclean! Unclean!"

In 1981 a leader arose in the community, mobilized other citizens of like mind, and great things happened. Heart Lake, menaced by a proposed motel, was made a state park. The city adopted the Anacortes Community Forest Land Management Plan for the 2400 acres. The Citizens Advisory Board published the excellent *Trail Guide to Anacortes Community Forest Lands* (ask at your bookstore) for the 18 principal trails, 25-30 miles total. Before he went away, the Leader Who Arose was moving along to promote a Fidalgo Island Trail, to start in the city at the old San Juan Island ferry dock (now used by the Guemes Island ferry) and follow the shore to the new San Juan Island ferry dock; among the features would be the depot of the narrow-gauge Anacortes Railway which commenced in 1887 and the moorage of the sternwheeler, *W.T. Preston*, retired from active service with the U.S. Army in 1981. The way would proceed through Washington Park to the old city watershed at Little Cranberry Lake, to Heart Lake State Park, the old city watershed at Whistle Lake, Mt. Erie, Lakes Erie and Campbell, to a terminus (or connection) in Deception Pass State Park.

When the plan is realized, Anacortes will become a "destination city," hailed by hikers from sea to shining sea. The time of great praising is not yet. Returning for inventory in 1988, the older surveyor rejoiced at the prospect of bringing good news to off-islanders. He broke off the survey prematurely and went away weeping and raging. The trails of the 2400 acres are the same as in 1978, only deeper—deeper trenches, that is, dug by spinning wheels. The city has been badgered and cowed by motorcycles. Every foot of trail in the 2400 acres is open to dirtbikes. The admirable trail guide is too ashamed to say so. The sole mention of trailbikes is to ask the jockeys to "Yield the right of way to horses." Walkers are not given that much.

When Anacortes faces up to off-road machines (perhaps in the return of the Leader Who Arose) the surveyors will take another look. Until then the recommendation for folks who come from as far away as, say, Issaquah, is to drive to the summit of Mt.

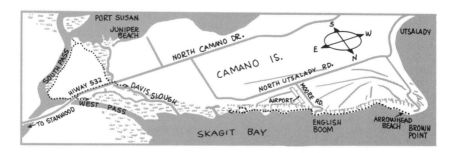

Glacier-scratched rock near top of Sugar Loaf Mountain

Erie for the views (though they are just as good from car-free Sugarloaf) and then, for hiking, go to Washington Park or Deception Pass State Park.

USGS maps: Mukilteo, Maxwelton, Hansville, Freeland, Langley, Juniper Beach, Camano, Coupeville, Port Townsend North, Utsalady, Deception Pass, Anacortes
Walkable all year

CAMANO ISLAND

Though the parts are securely hitched together, "Camano" is a number of quite distinct places—windward and leeward, hip-to-hip houses and lonesome beaches, great walking and poor. As a ground'rule, the farther south, the better.

North End (map—page 130)

Where the Stillaguamish delta wraps around the end of Camano Island are two non-private, okay-anytime shore walks.

Davis Slough

A dike hike along Davis Slough, a small tidal channel connecting Port Susan and Skagit Bay.

Drive about 0.4 mile west on Highway 532 from West Pass Bridge to a parking area on the south, signed "Skagit Habitat Management Area—Davis Slough Access."

Walk the dike path south 1 mile, between salt meadows and slough on the right, farm on the left, birds everywhere. At the waters (or mudflats) of Port Susan the dike turns east, passing a grassy peninsula that leads out through ducks and dunlins to South Pass, one mouth of the Stillaguamish. Look down the west shore of the bay to Barnum Point and the Olympics, down the east shore along the Whulge Trail.

Skagit Bay from English Boom

This is the most interesting part of the loop. However, to complete it, follow South Pass to farmhouses and the split of the river, continue on West Pass to the highway bridge, and walk the shoulder back to the car.

At a low enough tide one can cross under the highway bridge and walk saltgrass meadows 1 mile north to the mouth of West Pass in Skagit Bay. Also, dikes and roads north of the highway, not surveyed, follow Davis Slough toward Skagit Bay.

Loop trip 2 ¹/₂ miles, allow 1 ¹/₂ hours

English Boom

Here's the compulsory north-end trip. Views are breathtaking over Skagit Bay and delta to the mountains. History is thick, and so are the birds.

Drive Highway 532 just beyond Milepost 2 and turn north at the sign, "Utsalady Road-Good Road-Airport." In 2 miles on Utsalady Road, just past the airstrip, turn north on Moore Road 0.6 mile to a large public parking area by the beach. Just before the parking area Eagle Tree Estates are in process (1988) of civilizing the beach, but access has not been blocked, yet.

This is the site of the booming grounds of the English Logging Company, where logs from the Stillaguamish and Skagit were assembled and enclosed by booms in rafts for towing to the mill. That's what the forest of old pilings was for.

The wild shore, secluded by a tanglewood bluff, is open both ways. However, the 1 mile to the west is under the scrutiny of Eagle Tree eyes. If they smile upon the walker, those of Arrowhead Beach on Brown Point will not; the Privates here are hostiles. To the east the delta immediately begins; creek-incised saltgrass meadows were surveyed 1 mile, and perhaps can be walked 1 more to the mouth of West Pass.

Views on a crisp-clear winter day are stunning. The ice mound of Baker and Twin Sisters dominates but also grand are peaks enclosing the Skagit delta—Wickersham-Woolley-Lyman, Chuckanut, Elephant, Devils, Cultus. South are Three Fingers, north are Canadian giants. The centerpiece is the broad expanse of Skagit Bay from

132

Whidbey Island to Ika and Craft Islands, the entire Fir Island segment of the Skagit delta, and the whole Stillaguamish delta.

Round trips 6 miles, allow 4 hours.

Camano Island–East Side (map—page 133)

The lee, Port Susan shore of Camano is infested with houses, only becoming wild near Camano Head. The Conjunction of Four will wreak havoc here; routinely each winter, during the average C/2, the natives call for the aid of the Red Cross and Boy Scouts to help pile up sandbags. Among the hikes that will be opened up after the C/4 is one closed since the previous edition of this book, south from Lona Beach to Barnum Point—a naked bluff at the mouth of Triangle Cove, across whose mouth is a spit solid with homes whose living-room carpets are about three inches above a spring tide.

The surveyor found but a single put-in on the east side of the island where a Public can set foot without being scolded by Privates. At Cavalero Beach County Park you can eat your tuna fish sandwiches and drink your strawberry pop at a veritable Public picnic table.

From the end of Highway 532 go left on East Camano Drive 2.5 miles to a Y. Camano Hill Drive goes right; stay left on East Camano Drive another 2.5 miles and turn east on Cavelero Road 0.5 mile to the park.

Read the peaks from Baker to Cultus to Pilchuck. On glummy winter days a person may be let alone by the houses adjoining the park on both sides and permitted to walk north 1 1/4 miles, and south 1/2 mile, beneath nice wild bluffs.

Round trips 3 1/2 miles, allow 2 hours

Camano Island—West Side: Camano Island State Park (map—page 134)

Though Whidbey Island takes the brunt of the howlers from the ocean, the west side of Camano Island, the weather shore, gets its share of waves, enough to give the pounded look walkers like. Saratoga Passage is busier than Port Susan, fishing boats going to and fro and log rafts south to Everett mills.

Two wild beaches used to offer good lonesome walking. Now there is one. This is not to report anything bad has happened to the beaches of Onamac Point, so praised in the previous edition. To the north of the thrusting spit there still are 1 1/2 miles of bluff-guarded wildness. Erratics are notable. An undisturbed kitchen midden is passed and a forlorn, ruined beach cabin. South from the point the beach and its monster erratics are bluff-safe 1 mile to the old village of Camano; beyond, the 3 miles to Camano Island State Park have only several short stretches of habitation. The problem at Onamac is that the point is Private and so is the road down from West Camano Drive.

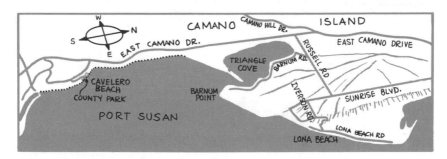

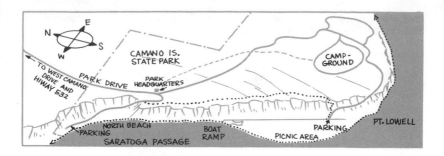

Lone and quiet Publics have been known to park on West Camano Drive, walk down the ³/₄ mile of road (the cavalry patrols are only out in force on Sunday), and hit the beach.

The last remaining sure-fire way to get on the beach is Camano Island State Park, 134 acres of path-interlaced forest and 1 mile of splendid beach rounding Lowell Point.

From the end of Highway 532 take a left, East Camano Drive, 6 miles to a Y, both forks confusingly signed "East Camano Drive." Go right, signed "State Park," 2 miles to an intersection at Elger Bay Grocery. Turn west on West Camano Drive 1.7 miles and turn left on Park Drive. The park is entered and in 1 mile the headquarters passed. Just beyond is a Y, the left leading to parking on the beach at Lowell Point, the right to parking by North Beach. Take your pick.

Near the entrance is the ¹/₂-mile Al Emerson Nature Trail. A 6-mile perimeter trail through the woods is planned. Presently there is a blufftop, wide-view path, the north end at the switchback on the road to North Beach, the south end in a ravine cutting the Lowell Point road at the foot of the bluff.

From North Beach to Lowell Point is 1 long mile of 100-foot cliffs of sand and gravel and varved blue clay, madronas hanging over the brink. Views extend across Saratoga Passage 2 miles to Whidbey Island, the Olympics beyond, far north up the waterway, and south to the island end at Camano Head and beyond to Gedney (Hat) Island.

Keep in mind that on Sundays the walking off the end of public parks irritates residents. Still it must be noted, for lonesome seasons and days, that north of the park the beach is marked only by scattered communities the scant 4 miles to Onamac

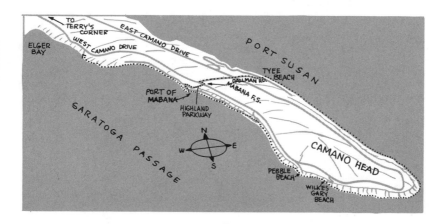

Point, and southward the shore goes 2 miles into and around Elger Bay and another 3 miles to Mabana Shores (see Camano Head).

Round trip (Sundays) 2 miles, allow 1 ½ hours

Camano Head (map—page 134)

Whatever else you do on the island, don't fail to drive to the southern tip, Camano Head. From the airy brink of the 320-foot bluff, look giddily down naked cliffs and sliding tanglewood to the waves, and out over Possession Sound to Hat (Gedney) Island and Port Gardner and Everett's ships and pulpmills, and to Mukilteo's ferry and pastel oil tanks and, on the hill above, enormous buildings of Boeing's Paine Field complex, and to Cascades and Olympics. As of early 1978 this incredible viewpoint was "for sale by owner." Owner! Nobody but the Almighty "owns" such spots. It ought to be dedicated as a temple. At the very least, made a public park. Go see before the access (at the U-bend where West Camano Drive becomes East Camano Drive, a woods road goes to the brink) is closed off; write a letter to Island County or State Parks demanding justice. As of 1988 there was still time.

The beach walk around the base of Camano Head is a classic of the Whulge, 3 miles purely wild beneath that formidable cliff, the rest only spottily inhabited. But the

Camano Head and Gedney (Hat) Island

135

beach is all "private" and the putting-in and taking-out must be done circumspectly; the loop trip suggested is best done by small parties on lonesome weekdays.

Drive to Elger Bay Grocery (see Camano Island State Park) and continue on West Camano Drive a scant 4.5 miles to the Mabana fire station. Turn west 0.2 mile on Highland Parkway. Where it bends right, the second time, take the gravel road switchbacking down to parking space at the Port of Mabana (a relict of steamer days) public boat-launch.

(Note: Not surveyed but mighty attractive is the shore north 4 miles to Elger Bay; a beachwalker down there below the bluff would scarcely see a house the whole way.)

The beach goes south under a bully sand cliff footed by blue clay. Jungle then alternates with bare walls; trails and perilous ladderways, and one aerial tram, come from unseen homes 100 feet up. At 1 ¼ miles a road descends to a dozen homes on a beach-invading fill that must be passed via an inland detour. Then beach solitude resumes to Pebble Beach at 2 ½ miles; the jutting spit encloses a driftwood-filled lagoon; several houses are here. Immediately south is Wilkes Gary Beach, ¾ mile of cottages, and then undiluted wildness.

Across Saratoga Passage are Langley, on Whidbey Island, and Sandy Point and Columbia Beach, the ferry shuttling to Mukilteo. Now, around the bend, appears Hat Island—and Everett. The bluff rears up to its full 320 feet, becomes naked white till and brown sand and blue clay, horridly vertical. At 4 ½ miles from the put-in the shore turns sharply.

What a spot! Camano Head. Sit for lunch. From remote wildness look to the harbor of Everett and buildings downtown. See the ferry and sailboats and mountains.

Now turn north into Port Susan. The bluff is less steep but still an appalling (to property owners) 300 feet high. The view is over to the Whulge Trail and Index, Pilchuck, Three Fingers. On the survey a pair of (nesting?) bald eagles were seen, and herons and ducks and fishing boats. A concrete chunk jutting into the beach suggests an old boat-tie-up for a camp. Loot of recent cedar-mining has been hauled away by a small boat. Nearly rusted-away iron rails in the beach, set in aged concrete, and an odd gully above, suggest a log skidway from the era of World War I. The view opens to the head of the bay, Chuckanut, Baker. At 2 ½ miles from the Head start houses of Tyee Beach. In a scant ½ mile a community boat-launch serves as take-out onto the road, which climbs the bluff ½ mile to East Camano Drive. Cross Dallman Road and in ¾ mile return to the fire station and thence to the Port of Mabana.

Loop trip 9 miles, allow 7 hours.

WHIDBEY ISLAND

The beachwalker can get just about anything he might want at the Whidbey Island restaurant. Short walks on the lee side, where the storms are rarely furious and the history is always thick, and long rambles in horizons that extend to China and the dragons, which in season come raging in from the Ocean Sea to roar at the continent's soft flank and chew at it with big white teeth.

Whidbey Island—South End (map—page 140)

From beaches far south on Puget Sound, from peaks high in the Cascades, the tall, naked bluffs on the south end of Whidbey Island are prominent landmarks. A person canny in the ways of the Whulge admires them from afar and suspects they must be dramatic places to walk. And so they are, so they are. Between broad, shallow, storm-open, useless bays, the jutting bluffs feature solitude, a chaos of erosion, and a big

Bald eagle flying near Maxwelton

parade of Main Street water traffic—tugs towing barges and log rafts, ships going to and from the ocean, fishing boats, pleasure boats, ducks.

Glendale

Though near the ferry landing at Clinton, the smidgeon of a settlement on a slender and short strip of accreted beach retains the feeling of olden times. A building that in 1911 was a ground-floor store, a hotel upstairs, is now a private home. A second old building also has been remodeled. The shore was too exposed for dependable steamer service, but the only railroad ever built on Whidbey extended 4 miles inland.

The history starts in Clinton, established in 1884 as supply point for logging camps. Steamer service from Seattle began in 1907 and lasted into the 1930s. The Mukilteo ferry commenced in 1927. From the town's commercial center just up the bluff from the ferry dock, turn south on Humphrey Road, which runs a scenic route on high and then slants down the slidey bluff. At 2.6 miles from Clinton, immediately on reaching beach level, turn sharp left to a rudimentary boat-launch. However, to avoid inconveniencing the residents, park elsewhere. And never on Sunday. A blustery Tuesday in February is ideal.

Harbor seals in the Whulge

To the north, beyond a few homes, the beach is crazy-wild for 1 mile beneath a superb bluff. In the next mile solitude is intermingled with scattered clusters of population. The final 1 ½ miles to Clinton are solidly housed.

To the south, once past several houses, the way is lonesome for 1 ³/₄ miles under the bluff, with few and minor human intrusions. A final ¼ mile through the village of Possession leads to Possession Park.

Round trip to Clinton 7 miles, allow 4 hours
Round trip to Possession Park 4 miles, allow 3 hours

Possession Park-Possession Point

Sailing past on the day he took possession of New Georgia for his king, Captain Vancouver named the southern tip of the island for the event. Separating Puget Sound from Possession Sound, it is a magic spot to stand with steep bluff at your back and gaze across the broad waters. As of 1988, a brand new park provides good parking and beach access.

Drive Highway 525 north 1.9 miles from the ferry and turn left on Campbell Road. In 1.6 miles turn left on Cultus Bay Road. In 4 more miles, where this turns right, stay straight on Possession Road. In 2 miles more, turn right on Possession Park Road, 8 miles from the ferry. (The Possession Road proceeds 0.2 mile farther to the 12-mailbox hamlet of Possession; no parking.) Possession Park, built by the Port of South Whidbey and turned over to Island County, has picnic tables, boat-launch, bridges over the lagoon between bluff and duneline, and great views, even on Sunday. However, due to habitations on both sides, the off-season and midweek are best for walking.

The beach to Glendale, 4 miles, is very attractive. However, the big show is the other way. For ¼ mile the driftwood is populated. Lonesomeness comes abruptly at a 100-foot wall of vertical till, the edge of wildness. Views north to the Mukilteo ferry, Three Fingers, and Baker yield to views south to the Edmonds-Kingston ferry, Seattle's West Point, and Rainier. The bluff leaps to its towering maximum of 380 feet. Boats cluster, fishing the legendary Possession Hole. Then the shore rounds to views of the Olympics and the 1 mile of wild beach ends at the flats of Cultus (Chinook jargon for "useless") Bay. Until the recent past the walk would have climaxed in a wondrous ½ mile along the spit of Sandy Hook, a superb lagoon on one side, the ¾-mile-wide bay (at low tide, mudflats) on the other. The Skagits had two longhouses here, the better to harvest the clams. Now the lagoon has been dredged to harbor a hundred or two stinkpots. Spit and upland slopes are densely populated.

One speculates that at a very low tide Cultus Bay might be so utterly drained the sand-mud would be walkable across to Scatchet Head.

Round trip to Sandy Hook 2 ½ miles, allow 2 hours

Indian Point-Scatchet Head

Though a bit less high than that of Possession Point, the bluff from Indian Point to Scatchet (a variant of Skagit) Head is longer—more than 2 continuous miles—and more vertical—a steep leap of 300 feet—and more naked. It thus is unmolested by subdividers, the longest stretch of wildness on the island's southwest shore.

Drive Highway 525 from the ferry 3.7 miles and turn south on Maxwelton Road 4.7 miles to Maxwelton. Park at Dave Mackie Memorial (Island County) Park.

Maxwelton dates back to the 1890s as a resort community. A bit later, steamers from Seattle and Everett brought city folk to an amusement park and Chautauqua auditorium. The past remained alive in a venerable general store until its conversion to a home. Happily, in 1989 it was again a store.

To the north, a long mile along the baymouth bar (the former lagoon is pasturized, though not occupied) brings the end of homes. A bluff as high as 200 feet rises, wild and free, 2 long miles to the double spit enclosing Deer Lagoon. The totally Private, built-out spit (Sunlight Beach) once was home for hundreds and hundreds of seals. It will be again after C/4.

The feature journey is the other direction. Walk the beach away from the village-on-the-sandflats in views over Useless Bay to Double Bluff, out to ship traffic of Main Street (here, still Puget Sound), the winking light of Point No Point, Foulweather Bluff and the mouth of Hood Canal, and Olympics from Angeles to Zion to Constance and south. In ¾ mile is Indian Point and its 200-foot cliff, at first tanglewooded, then bare. The precipice steepens, rises to an awesome 260 feet in one lift from the beach, bare drift capped by vertical till. Among clay beds is a layer of leaves, twigs, cedar bark, and fir cones—not years or decades old, but millennia. So steep the bluff becomes, the top a straight-up 300 feet, that chunks constantly fall, slides of huge clay boulders tumble out in the water to be battered by waves.

At 1 ½ miles from Indian Point a nameless point thrusts out, the bluff lays back, and a well-used trail descends from the rim, 340 feet up. Now the view is south up the Sound to Edmonds, the ferry, Appletree Point, West Point. The bluff loses its woods and is again steep and naked to Scatchet Head. A final ½ mile leads to a boulder bulkhead and a subdivision that is not thriving, due to the heavy-heavy-hangs-over-thy-head location of the homesites.

Round trip 5 ½ miles, allow 4 hours

Double Bluff

The sand cliff of Double Bluff is truly a noble eminence, the most prominent naked bluff on the entire Whulge, rising 367 feet from the water in a single leap. A public

WHIDBEY ISLAND

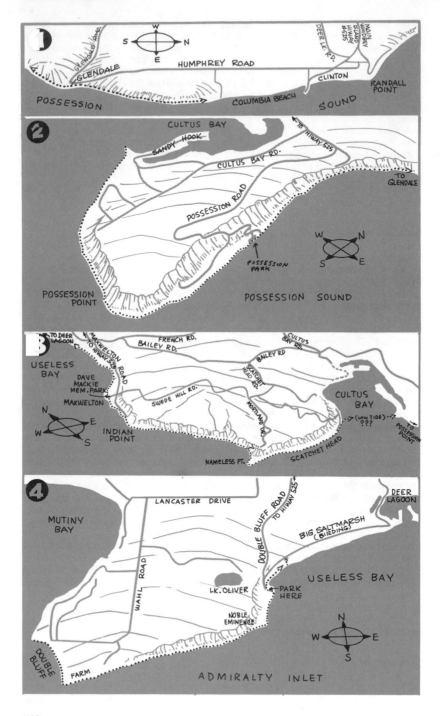

140

Saratoga Passage from Camano Island State Park

access, and protection of an (undeveloped) state park, draw Sunday throngs to the superb wildland beach.

Drive Highway 525 from the ferry 8.3 miles and turn left on Double Bluff Road, which proceeds 1.9 miles to the end on Useless Bay. The unsigned public access has paved parking for some two dozen cars, but no boat-launch, and that's a mercy. (Kayaks don't need a ramp.)

Birders should not ignore the wetlands east of the parking. Though the baymouth bar is built up solid the 1 1/2 miles to the mouth of Deer Lagoon, the saltmarsh behind the bar, a square mile of it, is partly pasture, partly wild grass and reeds and blending of fresh and salt wetness. Abandoned dikes and lines of fence posts testify to a victory of Mother Nature over the Pale Galilean. Approaches from Sunlight Beach and the adjoining upland are guarded by the Privates, though lone Publics are rumored to slip through the defenses to walk the old dikes. Accesses via the baymouth bar and the Double Bluff Road appear feasible.

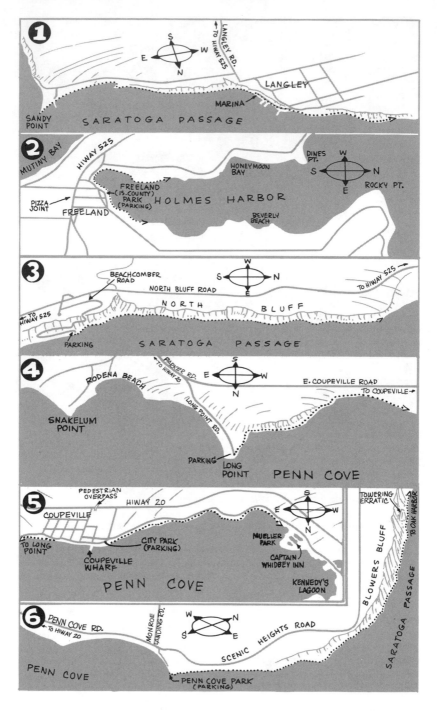

①
S W E N
TO HIWAY 525
LANGLEY RD.
LANGLEY
MARINA
SANDY POINT
SARATOGA PASSAGE

②
MUTINY BAY
HIWAY 525
HONEYMOON BAY
DINES PT.
W N S E
ROCKY PT.
FREELAND (IS. COUNTY) PARK (PARKING)
HOLMES HARBOR
PIZZA JOINT
FREELAND
BEVERLY BEACH

③
BEACHCOMBER ROAD
NORTH BLUFF ROAD
W N S E
TO HIWAY 525
TO HIWAY 525
PARKING
NORTH BLUFF
SARATOGA PASSAGE

④
PARKER RD.
TO HIWAY 20
S E W N
E. COUPEVILLE ROAD
TO COUPEVILLE
RODENA BEACH
LONG POINT RD.
SNAKELUM POINT
PARKING
LONG POINT
PENN COVE

⑤
PEDESTRIAN OVERPASS
HIWAY 20
COUPEVILLE
S E W N
TOWERING ERRATIC
TO OAK HARBOR
TO LONG POINT
CITY PARK (PARKING)
MUELLER PARK
COUPEVILLE WHARF
CAPTAIN WHIDBEY INN
KENNEDY'S LAGOON
PENN COVE
BLOWERS BLUFF
SARATOGA PASSAGE

⑥
PENN COVE RD.
TO HIWAY 20
MONROE LANDING RD.
W N S E
SCENIC HEIGHTS ROAD
PENN COVE
PENN COVE PARK (PARKING)

The other direction is the way to go for beach, bluff and view. The sand beach — slender even at quite high tides — quickly leaves domiciles and bumps against the foot of the noble eminence. A safe path weaves between sand cliffs to the top for a majestic panorama of seas and shores. Hereabouts the name of Main Street changes from Puget Sound to Admirality Inlet; the traffic is the same—heavy. Directly across the street is Foulweather Bluff at the mouth of Hood Canal, south is Edmonds, north is Marrowstone Island. Beyond rise the Olympics, from foothills of Zion and Walker to snowy heights of Townsend and Constance. Himmel.

Jump-slide-erode back down to the beach and proceed by an exceptional variety of glacial drift from two ages, by eagle snags and maybe the eagles, by a Grand-Canyon-like gulch sliced in the sand.

The bluff dwindles and at 2 miles rounds a point, atop whose low bank is a light and spacious green cow pasture, now as for a century. An idyllic scene. Will State Parks find the funds to buy the farm before it is cut up in lots? In $1/2$ mile more is the point named Double Bluff on maps, but that seems a mistake; surely the noble eminence is the nameworthy feature of the vicinity. Anyhow, here starts Mutiny Bay and another mob of houses, so turn back.

Round trip 5 miles, allow 4 hours

Whidbey Island—East Side (map—page 142)

A lee shore, more comfortable for living and thus more heavily settled than the stormy west. Beaches that are generally less dramatic, yet appealing when the weather shore is too thrilling. Views over the water to the Cascades. Much, much history. The entire shore is walkable—or runnable when the militia turns out with flintlocks and mastiffs. However, a number of public put-ins permit sampling the scene on short strolls or long.

Langley (map-page 142)

Settled in 1880 and for some years the major steamer port of the area, Langley now contests with Coupeville for honors as the coziest village on the island. An engaging row of shops—books, candy, ice cream, antiques, collectibles, a theater, "rooms to let"—can combine with beach strolls for a happy day.

Drive Highway 525 north from the ferry dock at Clinton 2.6 miles and turn right on Langley Road 3.5 miles.

A blufftop walkway gives views over Saratoga Passage to Camano Head, Everett, and Cascades. Staircases in the shop blocks descend to the city park-beach promenade.

For beach-walking, park on the blufftop and walk down the entry road, just north of 2nd, to the public marina. Guarded by the 100-foot bluff, it's just you and the wavelets for 1 $1/4$ miles east to the start of the spit of Sandy Point. Except on Sundays, when the Privates have sentries posted, a quiet person might continue unchallenged the $1/4$ mile to the tip of the spit.

The shore bends northwesterly from Langley. The kindly bluff keeps the way mostly lonesome the 4 miles to the first major fortress of the Privates, on the bar of Bells Beach.

Round trip to tip of Sandy Point 3 miles, allow 1 $1/2$ hours

Holmes Harbor (map—page 142)

The deep and broad indent of the bay, 6 miles long and up to 2 miles wide, attracted early mariners. Wilkes named it in 1841, and not many years later the loggers were sawing and the farmers delving. In 1900 a splinter group from the Equality Colony on the Skagit delta moved here as the Free Land Association. By 1904 the splinter splintered apart. As a farming and logging community, Freeland rated a regular mailboat into the 1920s. So, there is history to be soaked up by the sensitives, and that is a main attraction of the beach-walking.

WHIDBEY ISLAND

    Drive Highway 525 to Freeland. At the Gay Nineties (pizza) turn right on Stewart Road to Freeland (Island County) Park.

    West from the park is most of the history—old docks and pilings. Under a bluff up to 100 feet high, the beach east, then north, is wild for 2 miles. The photographer saw two eagles.

Round trip 4 miles, allow 3 hours

North Bluff (map—page 142)

    A splendid stretch of wild shore beneath the 200-foot wildwood of North Bluff, a dominant feature of Saratoga Passage.

    Drive Highway 525 to Greenbank Country Store and turn right on North Bluff Road, passing the largest loganberry farm in the world. In 2.3 miles turn right on Beachcomber Road and switchback 0.4 mile down to the beach. Turn left to the unsigned public parking area.

    The beach extends north under partly naked bluff civilized only by a trail or two, in views to Camano Island, 1 $\frac{1}{2}$ miles before an encampment of Privates blocks the way. Hikers who visit in the wake of the C/4 will proceed north on nearly 2 miles of public tidelands to which the boat-lacking public presently has only sneaky access.

Round trip 3 or 7 miles, allow 1 $\frac{1}{2}$ or 5 hours

Holmes Harbor

Coupeville

Long Point (map—page 142)

In a region where spits are man's favorite squats, how did this beauty (the tip of it, anyhow) escape? Amazing. With no private eyes staring darts, even on Sunday the Publics can stand amid the waves and winds and gulls at the mouth of Penn Cove.

Drive Highway 20 north from Greenbank to Smith Prairie, where the Navy has a simulated carrier deck the Top Guns use to practice simulated takeoffs and landings, giving folks on the highway simulated hysterics. At the second of two right-angle turns to the left, go straight ahead north on Parker Road, passing the State Game Farm. In 3.2 miles go right on the road signed "Long Point." This immediately Ts at Marine Drive. Turn left 0.4 mile to the road-end on Long Point.

Sit on a log and gaze across Penn Cove to Blowers Bluff and beyond to Oak Harbor, west up Penn Cove to Coupeville, and east to the Cascades. Homes occupy most of the spit leaving only the point open. In toleration time a person quickly can skip west past homes and enjoy the privacy beneath a 200-foot bluff extending most of the 1 1/4 miles to Lovejoy Point. Another scant 1/2 mile around the corner leads to the heart of Coupeville.

To the east it's 1 1/4 miles to Snakelum Point, named by Wilkes for a Skagit chief. In 1841 Wilkes saw several fortified Skagit villages in the vicinity. The Skagits had enemies, including the Klallams from the Olympic Peninsula, not to mention the dreaded Raiders from the north. Other enemies, including the smallpox and measles germs, ended those hostilities. The walking to Snakelum Point is too privatized to be recommended.

Round trip to Coupeville 3 ½ miles, allow 2 hours

Coupeville (map—page 142)
Coupeville is the island's hotbed of history (see Ebey's Landing National Historical Reserve). The blockhouse, the museum, the old houses, the preserved wharf, combined with the fun shops—good things to eat, interesting things to look at or even buy—can make a very nice day indeed. But there is beach, too.

Drive Highway 20 to Ebey's Prairie and just east of the pedestrian overpass turn north through town to the waterfront. Turn left, past the wharf, to parking; there is more just beyond, in the city park.

A 50-foot bluff secludes the walking for 1 mile of securely Public tidelands. These (but not the bluff) continue 2 more miles, to the head of Penn Cove, to lagoons and peninsula of Mueller (private) Park, location of the old (1907) log restaurant, Captain Whidbey's Inn, and the wildlife delights of Kennedy's Lagoon. Then, back to Coupeville for an ice cream cone.

Round trip 6 miles, allow 4 hours.

Blowers Bluff (map—page 142)
California-like golden fields slope gently down to the hamlet of San de Fuca on the north shore of Penn Cove. At the turn of the shore into Saratoga Passage is Blowers Bluff, the tallest and steepest piece of geography in these parts.

Drive Highway 20 north from Coupeville, then east along the shore of Penn Cove. At San de Fuca Store go off right on Penn Cove Road. In 2 miles, where Monroe Landing Road goes left, turn right to Penn Cove Park, unsigned, undeveloped.

Coupeville wharf

From a wide sandspit-lagoon the beach is close under the road ½ mile. Then the bluff leaps up and enwildens the way. The view back to the head of Penn Cove includes Coupeville and the Olympics. As the shore bends, the view is over Saratoga Passage to Pilchuck and Three Fingers, Cultus and Higgins, Baker and Shuksan. Rounding more, the view is into Oak Harbor and the Naval Air Station and out to Strawberry Point.

Meanwhile the bluff has grown to 150 feet, including a stretch of vertical till. At 2 ½ miles is the chief spectacularity, a monster erratic of quartz-veined gray metamorphic rock, 20 feet high, topped by till and grass. Beyond the Towering Erratic the bluff leaps to 200 feet, steep and naked. In ¾ more mile bluff and wildness drop off to the mouth of Oak Harbor.

Round trip 6 miles, allow 4 hours

Oak Harbor (map—page 148)

The EA-6B Prowlers and A-6 Intruders come in low, touching down on the runway, then whining and howling up to the sky, circling and slanting in again. From 1980 to 1985, the annual total of takeoffs-landings was about 10,000; in 1987, it was 30,000, or 2500 a month, 80 a day, an average of one every 15 minutes. The highway billboard says, "Please pardon our noise. It is a sound of freedom." In 1942, the population of Oak Harbor was 375. In 1987 it was 7000, mainly purveyors of fast food to a transient population of 21,000 military personnel and dependents. Few pedestrians seeking a quiet day are likely to visit the area on purpose. However, there is no way to avoid the presence of Oak Harbor, no matter where a person goes. On an ocean beach a walker may be stunned by a jet screaming 50 feet above his head, thousands of clams squirting in unison. A climber in the Cascades or Olympics may awake from unconsciousness and in the distance see the speeding dot that knocked him out. Oak Harbor is the headquarters of the Top Guns, the dirtbikers of the sky.

Drive Highway 20 to Oak Harbor. Side streets lead off to the water. At the west edge of downtown is City Beach Trailer Camp. Farther along east is a park with beach access, picnic tables, Dutch windmill, and sewage plant. At the east edge of downtown is Flintstone Park, named in honor of Fred Flintstone and Barney Rubble.

The visitor unavoidably detained in Oak Harbor might park at the City Beach Trailer Camp and walk the 2 ½ miles, mostly wild, to Towering Erratic (see Blowers Bluff).

From Flintstone Park a shore walkway parallels East Pioneer Way a scant ½ mile to a Y at Whidbey Branch Skagit Valley College. The sidewalk goes right on Catalina Drive a long ¼ mile into Oak Harbor Marina, for close examination of the Money of Freedom. The view ahead is tantalizing—the picturesque peninsula tipped by Maylor and Forbes Points. Why the Navy needs the peninsula is not clear. Originally it was a seaplane base, but there aren't any of those anymore. At low tide, says the eye, the feet could find a way off the marina onto the beach, and 2 mainly wild miles to Maylor Point, and perhaps another mile or so around Forbes Point.

Round trip to Towering Erratic 5 miles, allow 4 hours
Round trip to marina 1 ½ miles, allow 1 hour

Crescent Harbor (map—page 148)

The 5 miles of beach from the Maylor-Forbes peninsula to the tip of Polnell Point are purely Navy, yet not necessarily off-limits.

Drive from downtown Oak Harbor (Flintstone Park) east on East Pioneer to a block short of Skagit Valley College. Turn north on 70th, not signed at this point, then right on Crescent Harbor Road. A short way beyond the crossing of Taylor Road, spot on the right a sign, "Oak Harbor Game Management Area—public hunting." Park here, elevation 200 feet.

An opening permits the public feet through the Navy fence into a huge empty field sloping to the shore. It may be that another fence bars access to the beach; the Top

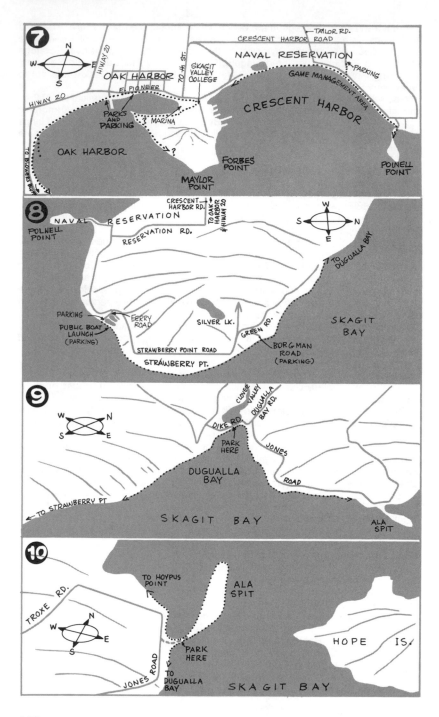

Guns made the surveyor too nervous to linger. A ½-mile descent of the field would lead to the water. The tempting target then would be Polnell Point, a tombolo tenuously attached to Whidbey at the east end of Crescent Harbor. The beach distance would be 2 ½ miles. If intercepted, reach for the sky and sing "Yankee Doodle."

Round trip 6 miles, allow 4 hours plus federal prison

Strawberry Point (map-page 148)

Now, this is more like. The longest recommendable walk on Whidbey's east side only quits when feet and tide dictate; actually it goes on and on to Deception Pass. Saratoga Passage now ends and the views are over Skagit Bay past the tip of Camano Island to the awesome width and flatness of the Stillaguamish-Skagit deltas, the Cascades jutting abruptly up beyond. As the miles wear on, there come into view the funny little islet-peaks of the southernmost San Juans, in the head of Skagit Bay.

At the south edge of Oak Harbor, where Highway 20 turns left, go straight through town onto E Pioneer Way. A block short of Skagit Valley College, turn left on (unsigned) 70th, then right on Crescent Harbor Road, which becomes Reservation Road. At about 9 miles from downtown Oak Harbor, turn right on Ferry Road (remembering the ferry to Camano island), to Mariners Cove, as the realtor's sign calls it. In several hundred feet is a T. Drive right 0.4 mile to the road-end, where an opening in the wall of houses has no signs, and thus must be a public access. This is the put-in for the short walk southwest. For the put-in for the long walk north, back at the T drive left 0.5 mile to an opening between houses which is an unsigned public boat-launch; spot it by a means of a public facility—a bench; confirm it by the concrete ramp.

The short walk, surveyed only by the eyeball, quickly scoots under the shelter of an up-leaping bluff and remains lonesome-wild 2 miles to the sand neck of Polnell Point. A Navy road can be seen going the ½ mile out to the tip for unknown reasons.

The long walk begins with a quick pace past the picture windows on the baymouth bar whose lagoon has been dredged for yacht basins. The bluff of glacial drift rises up, and except for brief breaks remains at a height of 50 to 150 feet to Dugualla Bay, permitting only small and scattered structures on or near the lonesome beach.

In 1 mile from the boat-launch is Strawberry Point, bringing in sight the long, low horizon of the Skagit delta dikes. An ancient boathouse of big timbers bears the faded advertisement, "Apples for Sale 50¢ Sack."

At 2 wild miles from the point are a wide valley, several houses, and a public beach access at the deadend of Borgman Road. (Drive past Mariners Cove on Strawberry Point Road, as Reservation Road becomes, 2.2 miles; where it turns left, go right on Green Road, then right on Borgman Road—unsigned, just past "Davis Landing Mt. Baker Circle Private"—to the beach.)

Wildness resumes. Nice creeks are crossed. Alders lean a hundred feet over the beach. Enormous erratics are passed, one as big as a house, a forest of ferns atop. Each bulge in the shore yields new views north—to "Fish Town Island," Ika and Bald and Craft and Goat Islands, Quarry Mountain, the mouth of Swinomish Channel, Hope and Deception Islands.

How far to go? There's nothing stopping feet or dulling interest in the 5 miles to the next put-in, take-out on Dugualla Bay.

Short round trip 5 miles, allow 3 hours
Long round trip up to 10 miles, allow up to 7 hours

Dugualla Bay (map—page 148)

The bay mudflats, covered with log rafts and assorted trash, do not invite boots, but the bay itself is interesting and the dike leads to fine beaches south and north.

WHIDBEY ISLAND

Drive Highway 20 north from the Oak Harbor stoplight 6 miles and turn east on Dugualla Bay Road. In a scant 1 mile turn right on Dugualla Dike Road 0.2 mile to a diketop parking turnout.

The bay is the east end of the swale, Clover Valley, across Whidbey island; when sea level was 35 feet higher it split off Whidbey's north tip in a separate island. Now the vale contains a large lake, formerly a tidal lagoon, a great flat farm, and jet airfield that harasses the countryside for hundreds of miles around.

The easy access dike leads to wild beach 5 miles south to Strawberry Point (which see) and 3 miles north to Ala Spit (which see).

Round trip to Ala Spit 6 miles, allow 4 hours

Ala Spit (map—page 148)

Magicland! Particularly appealing for a short, slow, amusing walk among the birds and toy islands, the spit also is a put-in for long walks to Dugualla Bay and north the scant 2 miles, wild all the way, to Hoypus Point in Deception Pass State Park (which see).

At the Y where Dugualla Dike Road goes right (see above), go left on Jones Road 3 miles. Upon descending to the shore, take the unsigned dirt road right, down to public parking on Ala Spit.

Ah! On one side of the 1/2-mile-long driftwood-heaped spit is the bird-busy lagoon. On the other, across the narrow channel, are grass-tawny rock buttresses of Hope Island. South in the bay are Deadman Islands, Seal Rocks, Goat and Ika Islands, the opening to Swinomish Channel. North are Skagit and Kiket Islands—and Fidalgo. Here the glacier-drift islands end, the rock-hearted San Juans begin.

Round trip 1-4 miles, allow 1-3 hours

Abandoned barge visible at low tide on Ala Spit. Mt. Erie beyond

Beach trail at South Whidbey State Park

Whidbey Island—West Coast Trail

A decade or so ago a proposal was put forth by the International Boundary Commission to establish an international park to knit together Canadian and American shores from Vancouver Island to Whidbey Island. It was like sticking a firebrand in a bee tree. Speculators and developers of two nations came out a-buzzing and a-stinging. That was that. And will be until a Conjunction of Four. Or perhaps a C/5 (for this, throw in an 8.2 earthquake).

The significance of the Whidbey west coast already has merited a federal presence. Deception Pass State Park was shaped in the 1930s by CCC crews working under National Park Service direction. The Park Service is again on the island, supervising creation of Ebey's Landing National Historic Reserve. However, we are not here suggesting a new park, merely noting that the area by no means would be out of place in the national park system.

There is the history, to an unusual extent preserved from the ravages of developers, and re-developers. There are the plant and animal communities of sea and land, abiding side by side in a state of relatively undisturbed nature. And there is the beach.

Why is this the most-famed, most-acclaimed beach of the Whulge? Because of the vigorous weather and surf of the weather shore, where storms blow freely in from the ocean. Because of the wilderness that prevails due to the discouragement of dense habitation by the weather plus the sea cliffs. Because of the storm-tortured forests, so much like those of the ocean coast, and the tawny sea meadows, so much like those of green-and-gold California. Because of the busy Main Street waterway, always something going this way or that, somewhere, and views from Baker to the San Juans

151

WHIDBEY ISLAND

to the Olympics to Rainier. Because of eagles and old forts. That's some of it. And unlike the wilderness ocean of Olympic National Park, it's all close enough to Puget Sound City for easy day hikes.

We here describe the beaches of the west coast as a "trail" because one leads inevitably to another and a hiker cannot but wish to connect them with his feet. When word gets around the trip is likely to become as de rigueur as backpacks along the Olympic Park beaches.

South Whidbey State Park (map—page 153)

Walk on the beach, walk in the forest of old-growth Douglas firs and companion cedars and hemlocks, an island of antiquity amid second-growth. Sky-open waters and green-twilight woods combine for an experience greater than the sum of the parts.

Drive Highway 525 north from Freeland and turn off west on Bush Point Road, which becomes Smugglers Cove Road and in 6 miles from the highway reaches South Whidbey State Park. Park at the entry lot, especially if the park gate is closed, or at the main lot a short way north, or in the campground, farther north. Elevation, 200 feet.

Several routes savor the 87 acres of park on the west side of the highway; these were acquired from the University of Washington in the 1960s. From the parking lot-picnic area at the entry, the Loop Trail goes ¹/₂ mile south on the bluff rim and returns inland for a 1-mile total. On a quiet winter day, the entry gate closed to vehicles, the campground loop roads provide a fine forest "trail," some 1 mile total. The Beach Trail and the Hobbit Trail take off from the network of paths in the vicinity of the main parking lot and campground and switchback down ¹/₂ mile in a mix of big old conifers and the younger deciduous trees typical of a bluff that in the geological sense is always on the move; put the trails together with the beach between their outlets for a loop of 1 mile.

On the inland side of Smugglers Cove Road are the 250 acres of the "Classic U" tract added to the park in 1985. The tract was part of the University of Washington trust lands, managed by the state Department of Natural Resources to produce income for the University trust. When the DNR announced an impending timber sale in 1977, giving it the identification tag of "Classic U," local folks rose in rage to protest the clearcutting of what they had thought either was part of the existing park, or was planned to be, or should be. Environmentalists throughout the region joined the battle, one of their tactics being to file the Plaintiff Trees lawsuit, claiming for the trees legal standing in court. In 1980 the longtime (very) incumbent head of the DNR was defeated for reelection. The new head negotiated a settlement of the suit and then the sale of lands to State Parks.

The result is the preservation of a forest which is partly second-growth getting on to be a century old and partly true old-growth, Douglas firs and western red cedars more that 250 years of age. Called "the true gem of South Whidbey," directly across the road from the park entry is the Wilbert Trail, dedicated in 1982, named for the island resident who led the fight to save the trees. The 1 ¹/₂-mile path winds about to take in the choice groves, including a really big tree, and exits on Smugglers Cove Road at 0.3 mile from the park entry.

Total trips 5 miles, allow 5 hours

On the Trail—Mile 0–12: South Whidbey State Park-Lagoon Point-Lake Hancock-Crockett Lake-Keystone Harbor

Let it be noted that after the C/4 the Trail may very appropriately be extended south 2 miles under a green riot of bluff to the village on Bush Point and beyond (after ³/₄ mile of houses which will then have been removed) another 2 more wild miles to Mutiny Bay, which after Nature's cleanup job will be excellent walking to Double Bluff.

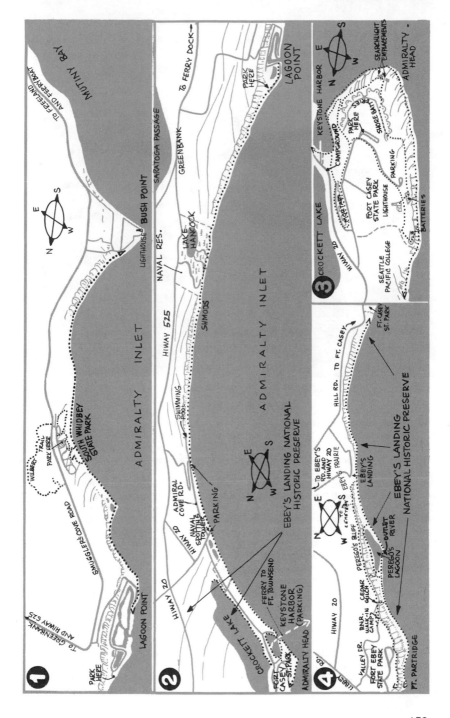

Old Gun mounts at Fort Casey

However, the subject here and now is the way north.

The 1 mile of beach in the state park presently is the first mile of the Trail. The next 1 ½ miles to Lagoon Point, and the 1 ¼ miles around the point, will not be worth a visit until cleansed. Primevally, the lagoon was among the finest on the island. However, the developer not only has put picture windows elbow to elbow along the duneline and the bluff foot but has dredged two stinkpot harbors and used the spoils to build a peninsula between them and cover that up with houses as well. Finally, though a county park is reputed to exist on the point, residents have seen to it that no development has been done that would encourage visitors. The park, wherever it may be, isn't even signed. There is a public beach access at the very north end of the spit, accessible from Smugglers Cove Road, and the Privates might not be too hostile to a visiting Public on winter weekdays.

The 1 ¾ miles north from Lagoon Point are splendid, the exceptionally steep bluff too formidable to let Privatizers near the water. When the cliff lowers to naught, a baymouth bar ¾ mile long has completely cut off an ancient bay, producing a half mile-square lagoon, mostly tidal marshes, partly Lake Hancock. The Navy has the lake and lagoon in its clutch. On the survey for the previous edition, a faded sign warned "Danger. Absolutely No Trespassing. Bomb and Rocket Target Area." However, the gate on the access road was in ruins and locals obviously drove ¾ mile past the marsh to a gate picnicking-and etc. area at the beach. As of 1988 the Navy has repaired the gate to keep out vehicles and resorted to a new threat: "Warning. Keep out. Helicopter Practice Landing Area." The path around the gate testifies that the locals now walk the 3/4 mile to the etc. at the beach. A person driving Highway 525 cannot help but note Lake Hancock, close by the highway a scant 1 mile north of Smugglers Cove Road. Just north of the lake will be seen the access road; there is no parking on it or very near. Undoubtedly, once the Navy gives up the property, it will go directly into a State Wildlife Department game sanctuary. For the present, most birders will approach via the beach, south or north.

The 3 miles from the baymouth bar of Lake Hancock to the baymouth bar of Crockett lake (the latter bar called Keystone Spit) have only one flaw—poor access. From the south there are Lagoon Point and Lake Hancock. From the north there is Admirals Cove subdivision, squatting on the beach, the picture windows extending to the south end of the bar, bounded by a community swimming pool. Don't start there. Instead, turn east from Highway 20 where it hits the shore, park, and hit the beach.

The 3 miles are totally lonesome except for a handful of houses on a slump terrace at the halfway point. The bluff rises as high as 150 feet, in places vertical and stark naked. Particularly striking is a section of till just north of Lake Hancock where erosion has carved a badlands of cleavers and chimneys and pillars. The beach pebbles are outstanding, with many agates. The most fun are the hard concretions formed in clay strata and now strewn about. The traditional name is "mud babies," but fans of Li'l Abner see his friends, the Shmoos.

The aforementioned 1 mile from the swimming pool along the bar to Highway 20 is all public tidelands, and that's good, and all glass eyes staring at the walker, and that's bad. The final 1 ³/₄ miles along Keystone Spit to Keystone Harbor are also on the bar, but thanks to environmental heroes of the 1960s-70s, almost entirely houseless; here is the longest beach walk on the island that (1) is essentially natural and (2) has no bluff; one is reminded of Dungeness Spit.

However, many a hiker will leave the beach, cross Highway 20, and walk beside 600-acre Crockett Lake, feeding and resting ground for hundreds of waterfowl at a time, plus herons and their sort; one winter the older surveyor, driving by, exclaimed at the disgraceful roadside litter of white plastic bags, until he noted that some of them were snowy owls down from the Arctic. Developers once proposed to do the Lagoon Point job here, on a vastly larger scale, but were prevented by massed outrage and a phalanx of attorneys. Crockett Lake is not yet finally secure. Neither is the empty stretch of Keystone Spit. As of 1988 State Parks is trying to buy it. Money is the problem. The lack of it.

Lake, spit (bar), and beach end at Keystone Harbor, where Fort Casey Picnic Area is located on an enormous fill. The former site of the Keystone Ferry was so exposed the Army Engineers dredged the harbor for a new landing, as well as a stinkpot shelter. The longshore currents that built the bar continue to dump loads, requiring the Army to return every half-dozen years to dredge.

One wonders that the ferry was so important to the nation. Still, the voyage makes a dandy sidetrip, for a passenger (no car) across Admiralty Inlet to Port Townsend and back again. Because the ferry must thread through ship traffic, barge traffic, and tug-and-log-raft traffic—all of which have the right-of-way—the crossing sometimes takes an hour. In a storm the experience is thrilling, though to date no vessel has gone down.

Fort Casey State Park (map—page 153)

The history and the views are sufficient to keep a hiker happy even when tides are too high to permit doing the beach.

For the complete tour, drive Highway 20 to Keystone Harbor and park at the Fort Casey Picnic Area. (Other parking areas are across the harbor, at the entry to the campground, and at several spots in the park, on heights of Admirals Head.)

At the turn of the century, when the United States were conquering the Sandwich Islands, bullying rickety old Spain, and annexing the Caribbean and Pacific, it behooved the military to expect such truculence to make somebody angry. To guard Puget Sound from naval assault by any possible (or impossible) foe, Admiralty Inlet was fortified with the "Triangle of Fire," or "Death Triangle," or "Devil's Triangle,"

155

composed of Fort Casey, Fort Flagler and Fort Worden. The guns of Fort Casey were mounted in 1900, test-fired in 1901, and melted down after 1922. In World War II the fort was reactivated as a training center, but in 1950 no further military use could be devised; in 1956 State Parks acquired 137 acres.

The recommended complete tour ascends a path from the campground entrance to the site of the mortar batteries hidden behind the hill from enemy ships at sea; proceeds along the park-entry road to the shore batteries, the concrete-and-steel emplacements so preserved and safeguarded that warlike little children can easily spend an afternoon playing games; and examines the spotting bunkers and searchlight emplacements. The walk culminates in the domain of Peace, the lighthouse. The original house, built in 1860, was torn down to make way for the shore batteries. The successor, erected in 1902, was retired in the 1920s and now serves as the park museum and interpretive center. So neat and tidy is the structure, metalwork painted black, walls white, and roof red, it's a pity the light is no longer there, keeping company with those still winking through the night from the other old forts of the Triangle.

Admiralty Head is the climactic viewpoint of the "West Coast Trail." North are San Juan Islands, farther around Vancouver Island, and then, out the water horizon, China. There are Olympics from Angeles and Blyn Hill and Big Skidder Hill to Zion and Walker and Constance. In the distance is the plume of the mill at Port Angeles, and directly across the waters is the pulpmill plume of Port Townsend; the lighthouse winking at the tip of Point Wilson marks Fort Worden State Park. Farther south is the third member of the Triangle, Fort Flagler State Park. And here is the most exciting Main Street marine-traffic view in the region—merchant ships and fishing boats and tugs and barges and pleasure craft and Navy vessels and, dodging through it all, the Keystone-Townsend ferry.

Round trip 2 miles, allow 3 hours

On the Trail—Mile 12–16: Keystone Harbor-Admiralty Head-Ebey's Landing
At Fort Casey State Park begins the longest stretch of undeveloped beach on the island, only minor intrusions north 9 1/2 miles to Hastie Lake Road, and the most of it in government hands. The rounding of Keystone Harbor and the jut of Admiralty Head covers 1 1/2 miles of ferry landing, campground, and the beach below the guns. A portion of the old fort, some 87 acres, was acquired by Seattle Pacific University, which sporadically behaves like a Private, not having heard about *Caminiti v. Boyle*.

The distinctive "Ebey-type" sand bluff (largely loess blown here by dry glacial winds) rises up, lowering on the north to Ebey's Landing. These 2 1/2 miles are exceeded in beauty and popularity only by the beach and bluff north from the landing.

Ebey's Landing National Historic Reserve (map—page 153, 161)

Many millennia ago the ancestors of the Salish arrived here, even before the saltwater flowed in to form the Whulge. First hunters, then fishers, always gatherers, they became farmers, annually burning the forests and undergrowth to provide more growing room for the camas, the blue-flowering plant whose bulb made so tasty a change from a heavily protein diet, and the bracken fern, whose root was ground into flour. In the early 1830s the Skagits, the island people, obtained potatoes from the Hudson's Bay Company; the tuber from the mountains of South America, via Europe, rewarded cultivation much more richly than native plants. So envious were neighbors across the water, the Klallams, that the Skagits looked to the fortification of their villages on Penn Cove.

European germs, and then European settlers, brought a new era. In 1850 Isaac N. Ebey filed his claim on lands from which the Skagits had ejected Thomas Glasgow two years earlier. By the next spring Samuel B. Crockett had filed on Crockett Lake. The Alexanders and the Hills soon arrived. Also in the 1850s came sea captains, first to trade, particularly for the oak that made stout hulls and the Douglas fir that made tall masts, and then to settle down as businessmen. Thomas Coupe gave his name to what became the dominant town.

On January 22, 1855, Governor Isaac Stevens swindled the Indians with the Treaty of Point Elliott. This and other thefts brought on the Indian Wars (White Wars). Many leaders of the Whidbey community of Europeans served in the Territorial Volunteers, an armed force whose savagery frequently appalled the U.S. Army. Though the local Skagits didn't take up arms, the European squirearchy wasn't sure of their mood and built eight blockhouses. It wasn't a bad idea. The Northern Raiders took advantage of the disquiet to intensify their regular raids. In the fall of 1856 a party got away with the Nisqually homesteaders' potato crop. A U.S. Navy ship caught up with them and on October 20 fought the famous Battle of Port Gamble, killing and wounding half of the hundred-man force, capturing the survivors and dumping them at Victoria. Having lost a principal chief, reconnaissance parties of Northerners returned in January of 1857 to seek a suitably eminent enemy to provide them "a head for a head." Ironically, they

Perego's Lagoon and Strait of Juan de Fuca from bluff north of Ebey's Landing

Old fort in Ebey's Landing National Historic Reserve

decided on Dr. John Coe Kellogg, the medicine man, but after waiting three days for him to return from a trip to Olympia, they went for their second choice. The night of August 11 they removed Colonel Ebey's head and carried it away up north. In 1859 a diplomatic mission by the Hudson's Bay Company recovered the head for burial with the rest of the colonel.

The prairies entered into a shifting, tortuous, often hardscrabble, but continuous farming history—wheat, oats, potatoes, onions, other garden truck, sheep, milk cows, whatever the market would accept. The farming continues to this day, the longest continuously farmed land in the state, the Europeans starting in the 1850s, the Skagits 20 years earlier with potatoes—and many centuries earlier with camas.

In the 1960s the farming, as inevitably as the Indians the Europeans, met its natural enemy—the subdivider. Keystone Spit and Crockett Lake were fated to become picture window-stinkpot communities. Ebey's Prairie was to be cut up in city-sized lots and covered with houses and carports and scrappy little lawns. It was a consummation not to be endured by the Friends of Ebey. Their efforts culminated in November of 1978 with establishment by Congress of Ebey's Landing National Historic Reserve—the first such in the nation.

The reserve—created to commemorate the exploration of the Whulge by Vancouver in 1792, the settlement by Ebey and friends, the Donation Land Law of 1850-55, and the growth since 1883 of the town of Coupeville—also must necessarily remember the Skagits. Their disease-decimated and demoralized remnant was deported in the 1850s, perhaps 13,000 years after their ancestors arrived. The boundaries of the Reserve encompass Fort Casey State Park, Crockett Lake and Keystone Spit, part of Smith Prairie, Coupeville and the entire shore of Penn Cove, Fort Ebey State Park, and the shore of the adjoining Whulge. The National Park Service has purchased some lands where subdivision threatened and, elsewhere, development rights and scenic easements. Ultimately, when the Reserve has achieved its aims, management will be turned over to a non-federal agency.

As of 1988, the Park Service lacks funds to supply interpretive materials and maintain a local staff. The best introduction to the Reserve is the kiosk by the entry to the Coupeville Wharf (1900), where maps and text tell the history in some detail and point the way to the historic structures and sites. In Coupeville itself is a bit of the cross the Skagits made for Father Blanchett when he came in 1840 to instruct them; the 1853 house of Thomas Coupe; the Methodist church of 1853; the Alexander Blockhouse moved here from its original site; and the museum of the Island County Historical Association. But that's only Coupeville.

On the Trail—Mile 16–18 ¹/₂: Ebey's Landing-Perego's Lagoon (Lake)

Some walkers like to start the Ebey Loop on the beach, saving the China View for the climax. Some start on the bluff, to have less distance to carry the stones and driftwood they loot from the beach. The most sophisticated start from the cemetery, to fully marry prairie and sea. However they do it, the sum of the somes is everybody who knows as much as a thing or two about walking the Whulge. If not the best of the shore tours, as many would insist, there's surely none better.

Sunnyside Cemetery is the choice beginning. Drive Highway 20 north 1 mile from the Coupeville pedestrian overpass and turn left on Sherman Road, then right on Cemetery Road, and 0.3 mile from the highway enter the cemetery and park, elevation 200 feet.

Tour the headstones, marking graves dating back to 1861. Find memorials to Ebey, Crockett, Alexander, and others of the pioneer community. George W. Samuel H. Perego was a latecomer, taking up a claim on a bluff he felt the Army would want. He was almost right, but chose the wrong spot for gunnery purposes and anyway he died in 1897, just as the Death Triangle was being built. Until then he lived as a hermit, up on the bluff with three dogs, watching for a hostile navy. Also at the cemetery is the Davis Blockhouse, one of the eight of 1855; it was a mercy for the settlers that they never had to stand a siege here.

A trail runs 1 mile from the cemetery to Perego's Bluff, and this is the quintessential experience of Ebey's Prairie, described in the Park Service brochure: "The square mile of primitive prairie that was Isaac Neff Ebey's by right of entry . . . without question the prize acres of the whole of Whidbey Island, if not the whole of Washington Territory. No matter how you come upon it, you know when you are there. . . . The special ambience it radiates reaches to the visual horizons, and beyond, on all sides. It is not that this area has not changed; it is that the landscape has absorbed the impact of 13,000 years of human habitation and changed so little—and so gracefully." Contouring through cultivated fields on the slope, a hundred feet above the table-flat (old lakebed? old bay floor?) prairie, the dark soil exposed where newly plowed, the green carpet lush where crops are growing, the walker's eye mingles the land with the water; in early April the eye may spot blue flowers around the unplowed edge of the prairie—the camas—and gaze into that past where the entire prairie bloomed blue.

The more usual approach is to drive Highway 20 to a short bit north of the Coupeville pedestrian overpass, turn west on Terry Road, and when this bends left continue straight on Ebey Road, which in 2 miles from the highway dives off the brink of the table to Ebey's Landing. (Just before the brink, look south to the Ferry house, built in 1860. Ebey's home was a few yards south.)

A ten-car parking lot at the beach is supplemented by a long, wide shoulder on the road south to Fort Casey State Park (an alternative approach.) A few steps north of the parking lot is Landing Gully, via which wagons trenched through the 60-foot bank to the prairie. Passengers and mail from the metropolis of Port Townsend destined for Coupeville ascended the gully. In boomer days a canal was projected over the prairie to Penn Cove. A city was laid out at the west end of the canal and named "Chicago." But its three-storey hotel collapsed and by the end of 1891 the bubble had burst altogether.

From the gully a staircase climbs the bank to a brink trail at the edge of the cultivated fields; this is the way to Perego's Bluff. If the beach beginning is chosen, 1 3/4 miles of sublime shore leads to the north end of spit-enclosed Perego's Lagoon (Lake). (Note: Some years storms rip a hole in the spit and the usually brackish lagoon becomes subject to the tides. The outlet is then a wide and perhaps a roaring river—in and out. In such case it may be necessary to detour on a path along the lagoon at the bluff foot.)

From the north end of the driftwood-filled lagoon a steep path climbs the tawny sand and green grass and (in season) brilliant flowers to the lip of Perego's Bluff, as high as 240 feet above the brown-white driftwood line, the gray beach, the white breakers, and the gray-green sea. Views are glorious over Main Street traffic on Whulge to three mountain ranges—Vancouver Island, Olympics, Cascades. And way out there is the water horizon, the edge of the world, source of the winds that so buffet the Douglas fir and Sitka spruce they have the appearance of being tortured for centuries by a Japanese bonsai artist. The path passes the Cemetery Trail, a mandatory sidetrip 1 mile to the headstones, and descends to the Prairie and the Landing.

On the Trail—Mile 18 1/2–22 1/2: Perego's Lagoon-Point Partridge-Libbey Beach County Park

Nobody lives on the beach. Nobody lives atop the 200-foot bluff, largely composed of the distinctive "Ebey sand," blown by winds from glacial outwash plains. The 3 1/4 wild miles on the shore of the vasty Whulge can be walked from either end or two places in-between: Fort Ebey State Park and the DNR Point Partridge Beach Area (for driving instructions, see below).

At 3/4 mile from the north end of Perego's Lagoon the bluff is deeply notched by Cedar Gulch, which occasions a stimulating exercise in geomorphological theorizing. A DNR staircase-trail ascends the north side of the gulch to the walk-in camps and picnic tables of the DNR recreation site. (As of 1988 a slippage of the bluff has taken out a section of the trail, which is signed "DANGER. STAY OFF." The access road is gated shut as well. But repairs may be made any year.) Inland, this section of Whidbey Island is notable for the Weird Pits, the holes up to 100 feet or more deep which pock the ground east to Penn Cove, separated by ridges just as mysterious. The older surveyor, noticing them from the highway, supposed they were old gravel mines. In time he began to wonder who on earth (or in outer space?) ever had such an insatiable appetite for gravel. It was on the bluff at Point Partridge the revelation came: this is hill-and-kettle topography. The glacier from Canada, in retreating, left behind chunks of ice buried in moraine; eventually melting, these produced the deep holes—the kettles.

From Cedar Gulch the way lies beneath the blufftop Fort Ebey State Park and Point Partridge Lighthouse 1 1/2 miles to a little driftwood-filled lagoon the sharp eye recognizes as a kettle broken into by the waves. Here a major access trail comes down the slope from a parking area in the state park near Lake Pondilla.

A final mile leads to Libbey Beach County Park. (To get there by car, turn west from Highway 20 on Libbey Road to its end at the water, 1.3 miles.) Non-walkers come here to stand atop the beach meadows and gaze over the Whulge to the broad gap between America and Canada, to the Oceane Sea.

Fort Ebey State Park (map—page 153, 161)

Authorities differ on the antiquity of this fort. One faction says the fort was first built before World War I to cover a blind spot not directly in line with the guns of the Death Triangle; never mind, they say, the "1942" set in the concrete of the ammunition lockers. The other faction says the fort dates from World War II, by which time the guns were long gone from the Triangle forts. The Army emplaced guns at several spots on the entry from the Pacific Ocean, including two six-inchers at Fort Ebey.

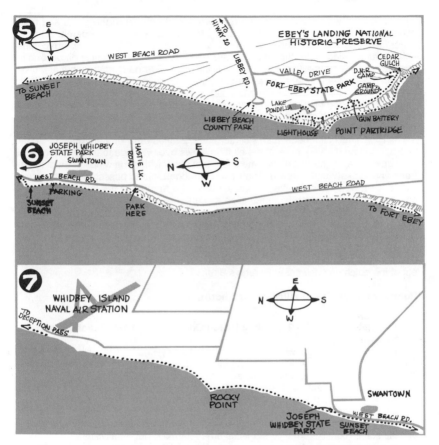

Evidently, a major Japanese task force was not expected; it would, however, have been embarrassing for a suicide squadron of destroyers to land a force of Imperial Marines on Whidbey and capture Coupeville.

From Highway 20 go off west on Libbey Road 1 mile and turn left on Valley Drive 0.6 mile to the entrance to Fort Ebey State Park. (As of 1988, Valley Drive is gated just beyond the entry, temporarily blocking car access to the DNR Point Partridge campground and beach trail.)

The park was established on 227 acres donated to the state by the Army in 1968 and developed and opened to the public in 1981. In 1985 a 350-acre parcel of DNR land was transferred to the park. Most of the land is hill-and-kettle, second-growth Douglas fir, and thickets of salal and rhododendron, broken by old "prairies" cleared by the military. The walking interest is close to the shore, on the beach and atop the bluff.

For the north section of the park, turn right at the T just inside the entry gate. In 0.3 mile is a parking lot for the Bluff Trail and just beyond, parking for the Lake Pondilla Trail, which drops a short bit to the bilious green water beloved of ducks and binoculars; it is, of course, a kettle, the best of the bunch.

Behind and above the restrooms at the Pondilla trailhead, a path leads to the north end of the Bluff Trail, described below. Another breaks through the fringe of wind-deviled trees to the sea meadow above Broken Kettle Lagoon and descends to the

WHIDBEY ISLAND

beach. But the walker should not hurry down. He should sit in the grass and train glasses on the enormous kelp bed, watching for diners, winged or flippered.

For the south section of the park, turn left at the entry T. In 0.3 mile a sideroad goes right to the parking lot for the gun batteries—and the Bluff Trail. A little bit beyond is the entry to the campground; this is not a proper day-hiker parking area, but at the far end, on the seaward side, are walk-in camps extending out to the brink of the bluff, other entries to the Bluff Trail. On one visit the older surveyor encountered winds so strong on the open bluff he could scarcely stand—and a dozen yards inland, behind the screen of wolf trees and head-high salal, the air in the camps was virtually still— beneath a mighty river roaring in the treetops.

The Bluff Trail is the pedestrian's centerpiece, 2 miles from Broken Kettle to Cedar Gulch, often on the very brink of the bluff, in views over Whulge to the Olympics and Vancouver Island, the rest of the time a few feet away within the windscreen of tough trees and thickety undergrowth. The Point Partridge Light is passed; it's not a great old house-tower, merely a little automated box. The mounts of the 6-inch guns have some interest. The concrete ammunition lockers are open to the public and can be explored by flashlight. A broad terrace below the guns was bulldozed to permit the guns to bear straight down on the Imperial Marines as they waded ashore. Barb-wire barricades were supplemented by plantings of gorse, which blooms a pretty yellow the year round and viciously stabs anyone coming in touch. The trail continues south past the campground 1/2 mile to Cedar Gulch. Plans are to extend it down into and up out of the gulch and onward to Perego's Bluff.

Round trip Bluff Trail 4 miles, allow 3 hours

On the Trail—Mile 22 1/2–25: Libbey Beach County Park-West Beach-Hastie Lake Road

For every dozen hikers who head south from Libbey Beach, only one heads north. The better for the solitude. Though rather different, the beach north is equally fine and, in its own specialties, more spectacular.

Public tidelands extend 6 miles north, eliminating any concern about Private harassment. The bluff rises to over 200 feet, stunningly precipitous much of the way. keeping houses from the beach the entire distance. Unlike the "Ebey-type" sand bluff south of Point Partridge, here the mix is a more standard clay and sand and gravel and till, some rock-like, from older glacial times, forming noble tall cliffs.

The view rounds to northward vistas into Rosario Straight, past the lighthouse on Smith Island and supertankers carrying oil to the refineries, to the San Juan Islands, to the heights of Erie and Constitution.

Then the bluff drops to houses and Hastie Lake Road.

On the Trail—Mile 25–28 3/4: Hastie Lake Road-Sunset Beach-Joseph Whidbey State Park

From Libbey Beach the West Beach Road runs along the top of the bluff, which falls to nothing at Hastie Lake Road, access to the public tidelands south and north.

Northward, beyond a short row of houses, the bluff leaps up once more. In 1 mile the beach rounds 100-foot-high "Vertical Till Point" and enters a shallow cove. Now the clay-sand precipice rises steadily higher, finally to 250 feet—as exciting as anything south of Point Partridge. In a most impressive "Grand Canyon" stretch the alternating strata of sand and clay form steps.

Then the bluff drops to nothing and man snuggles up to the water. A public parking area and beach here are reached by driving West Beach Road north 2 1/2 miles from Hastie Lake Road.

The former bay, now great, wide Swantown Valley, presents 1 mile of Sunset Beach houses, not appealing. However, at the north end of the baymouth bar and row of houses there is good news again.

162

Great blue heron fishing along the shore

On the Trail: Mile 28 ³/₄–31 ³/₄: Joseph Whidbey State Park-Clover Valley

Where the homes of Sunset Beach end, an undeveloped parking lot and public beach access mark the unsigned boundary of Joseph Whidbey State Park, 112 acres leased from the Navy. A few yards east on the road to Highway 20 is the official park entry, "undeveloped and held for the future."

The park ends in a long ¹/₂ mile but the local folk obviously walk on, enjoying a 3-mile stretch of beach lonesome-wild except for Navy-only recreation sites. A drastic change takes place in the shore from Swantown Valley to the north tip of the island. The bluff lowers, recedes inland, and virtually vanishes, replaced by a series of cutoff bays where the winds blow free, blowing up sand dunes, or trying—the Navy flattens them out.

At 1 ³/₄ miles the drift bluff briefly rears up. Here, at Rocky Point, is Whidbey's southernmost west-side exposure of non-glacial bedrock, picturesquely eroded by the waves. In another 1 ¹/₄ miles of solitude a little bluff rises to a Navy park. Beyond its bulge are Clover Valley and Ault Field. It is technically conceivable for a walker to scamper across the 1 mile of jet strip to resume the walking of West Beach, as described under Deception Pass State Park. However, given the average of one takeoff-landing every 15 minutes the day around, the year around, the odds are in favor of having the brains scrambled by a Top Gun.

DECEPTION PASS STATE PARK

If a person were compelled to select a single spot for all wanderings of saltwater shores and forests, there could be no better choice than Deception Pass State Park. One would think Mother Nature felt cramped for space in Creation, forced to stuff such richness of goodies in such small room: virgin forests of Douglas fir up to 9 feet in diameter; other forests of grand fir, Sitka spruce, shore pine, juniper, and madrona contorted and sculpted by storm winds blowing from the Pacific Ocean with nought in the way to blunt their fury; grassy sea meadows, flower-bright in season, and rock gardens of moss and lichen on headlands looking out to the San Juan Islands; myriad surprising little coves and secluded pocket beaches, and islands and off-shore rocks, and former islands (tombolos) connected to the mainland by sand necks; kelp beds and rafts of waterfowl, seals cavorting, eagles nesting and hawks soaring, and mobs of herons flying to and from a rookery; pretty-pebble beaches, tidal marshes, and a sand-floored, tea-water, sea-level lake, enclosed by a baymouth bar topped by the best sand dunes on the Whulge; buttresses of heavily metamorphosed volcanic rock polished and rounded and scratched by the glacier. To this man adds small boats (and sometimes, amazingly, log rafts pulled and pushed by tugs) navigating cliff-walled Deception Pass, where at turns of the tide the water runs river-swift and turbulent; and history of Indians, explorers, and the CCC—and a penal colony. All in the rainshadow of the Olympics, where mossy citizens of Puget Sound City flock in winter for a chance to see the sun.

The bulk of the modern park was preserved in virginity (or near such) as a military reservation until turned over to the state in 1925. In 1933 the Civilian Conservation Corps, supervised by the National Park Service, began developing roads and trails and building shelters, the craftsmanship in stone and timber contributing a rustic charm. The 3500-acre park hosts some 1,800,000 people a year for camping (254 sites), swimming, boating — and hiking the dozens of miles of trails and beach.

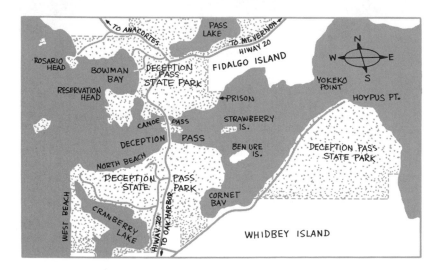

Canoe Pass and Deception Pass bridge

So many are the delightful nooks, so intricately interwoven the paths, and so many the convenient parking areas, a pedestrian can assemble the ingredients into a virtually infinite number of superb recipes. Short walks can be taken, a mile or less, fun enough to keep a child—or adult—entertained all day. Or these can be linked in longer rambles. Described here, to stimulate the imagination, are combinations that among them pretty well sample the park.

(Note: the park is notable for cliffs from which the rangers annually rescue scores of bold idiots trapped by their bravery. Please stay on safe paths and beaches.)

From I-5 drive Highway 20 onto Fidalgo Island and take the south arm, signed "Deception Pass." The park is entered at Pass Lake and lies on both sides of the highway and both sides of Deception Pass.

Pass Lake, Deception Pass State Park

Rosario Head-Bowman Bay-Lighthouse Point-Canoe Pass (map—page 164, 169)

Quintessential, that's what it is—most of the raptures promised by the introduction are delivered here. Three short strolls can be taken separately or combined.

From Highway 20 at the south end of Pass Lake, turn right, signed "Rosario." Pass the sideroad down to Bowman Bay (an alternative parking and starting point), continue 1 mile, and turn left down to the Rosario Beach parking and picnic area.

Stroll #1, a ½–1 mile loop. Walk out the grassy neck of the picnic area and up the forest-and-meadow heights of Rosario Head, with broad views over Rosario Strait to Lopez Island, little lighthouse-blinking Smith Island, and the water horizon of Whulge and the Strait of Juan de Fuca. Look across the Northwest Pass to Lighthouse Point, next on the agenda.

Stroll #2, 1 mile to junction, then a 1-mile loop. Returned to the picnic area, take the "Canoe Pass, Lighthouse point, Bowman Bay" trail by the restrooms, into woods, along cliffs, ½ mile to Bowman (Reservation) Bay and the picnic area. On trail or beach proceed ¹/₂ mile more, by a boat-launch and one-time fish-rearing ponds and old dock, along a marsh, to a wooded sidehill above the low neck connecting to Lighthouse Tombolo. Here is a Y; take the right, down onto the neck. On the far end the trail goes left around a corner and starts up the hill; spot a less-good path taking off from it straight up the hill—this is the return loop.

Actually, the best plan is to return the way you came, on good trail. But by picking rude paths carefully to avoid peril, one can finish the loop in order to experience all variations on the view.

Stroll #3, a 1-mile loop. Returned to the Y, go left, round forest slopes, pass a sidetrail left (the loop return), switchback up a peaklet, and contour. Then take a sidetrail down to overviews of Canoe Pass, Deception Pass, Canoe (Pass) Island, the bridge, and boats; another path drops to the beach at the west entrance of Canoe Pass. Complete the loop back through a saddle and return as you came to Rosario Beach.

Three-stroll round trip 4 ¹/₂ miles, allow 3 hours
High point 150 feet, elevation gain 500 feet

Pass Lake-Lake Campbell (map—page 164, 169)

Around and north of Pass Lake is an undeveloped area which in its wildness memorializes the Heilmans, who tended and loved this land so long and fended off taxmen and developers to preserve it for the people. Eventually a trail system through the forest, selectively logged before World War II but very lovely, will connect duckpond-quiet Pass Lake and Lake Campbell at the foot of Mt. Erie.

Adventurous walkers can sample the area on a fire-protection trail and the rude fishermen's Pass Lake Perimeter Trail. If the trees aren't huge the woods are really wild; on a survey in a winter twilight were heard alarming crashings in the brush, one merely a deer but the other suspected of being a chimera or basilisk.

Loop trip 3 miles, allow 2 hours
High point 500 feet, elevation gain 400 feet

Bowman Hill-Canoe Pass-Prison Camp (map—page 164, 169)

The Bowman Hill segment never was developed by the CCC, the only travel routes being long-overgrown military patrol roads and brushed-out powerline service roads, along which walkers have beaten out a rude trail system. The rangers would just as soon not have too many folks getting lost here and falling off the cliffs, so the area is suggested only for the experienced hiker. The accompanying sketch map indicates the general route, starting from the turnout just north of the bridge.

The scenery is more of the same (terrific), though with a different perspective. The history is novel: From 1909 until 1923, an average population of 25 prisoners lived on a bench by the shore and worked the quarry in the north wall of Canoe Pass. Concrete footings and a large concrete cistern are about all the traces of the colony to be seen; the quarry is best viewed from Canoe Island.

Round trip to prison camp 2 miles, allow 2 hours
High point 450 feet, elevation gain 800 feet

Canoe (Pass) Island (map—page 164, 169)

No short walk in the park is more scenic, more popular, and more dangerous. So take it easy. But by all means take it.

From the trail on Hoypus Point

Drive the highway over the bridge to the island-top parking area and go. Descend the alpine-meadow-like rock-garden path, strawberry-blossom-bright in spring, and with grass widows and mahonia blooming as early as February, to the east tip of the island and look east to Strawberry Island and Hoypus Point and Yokeko Point. Stroll close by frightening eddies and whirlpools of loud waters, under the bridge, to the west tip and look west to Deception Island.

You're really in the middle of things here, in the waterway called "Boca de Flon" by a Spaniard in 1791 and given the modern name next year by Vancouver, who'd been deceived into thinking he'd found a peninsula until his man Whidbey explored the passage.

Round trip ³/₄ mile, allow 1 hour
High point 175 feet, elevation gain 250 feet

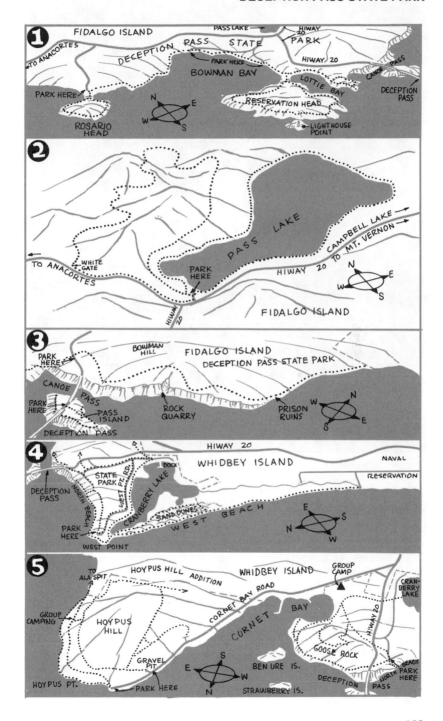

Calypso (lady slipper)—a flower only rarely found outside old, virgin forest

West Beach-Sand Dunes-North Beach-Cranberry Lake (map—page 164, 169)

Here's another melange of three strolls, partly quintessential but also with two unique features—unique not only in the park but the entire Whulge. Though each stroll can be a delicious afternoon by itself, the combination is suggested because the contrasting flavors enhance each other.

The combination can be done from several parking areas. For one (no better than the others) drive the highway south of the bridge to the park headquarters entry. Following West Beach signs, drive to the large parking area at West Beach.

Stroll #1, a partly looping round trip of 4 ½ miles. Head south on West Beach, walkable at all tides, in views to San Juans and Olympics and the water horizon of Whulge and the Strait of Juan de Fuca. At ¾ mile is the park boundary, beyond which houses have invaded the dunes, but set back far enough not to disturb enjoyment of waves and waterfowl, and the parade of ships south to Puget Sound, and the Taiwan merchant marine carrying billions of quarts of oil to the refineries. At 1 ⅓ miles from

170

the park the walk must halt, blocked at the outlet creek of Cranberry Lake by the U.S. Naval Reservation and Ault Field; the danger in going on is not so much in being captured as a suspected spy but in being on the beach when a Top Gun passes inches overhead, the noise of his sky motorcycle turning you into a vegetable.

The beach is great. An inland-looping return, however, leads to The Unique. Here where the rainshadow sun shines and the wild west winds blow there were, until the recent past, miles of sand dunes, far and away the grandest such display on the Whulge. The 1/2 mile preserved by the park from Navy and developers still is the grandest such display on the Whulge. In order to help the preservation, please view the dunes, and the sprawling mass of spruce, hemlock, and fir, from the blacktop paths; indiscriminate walking erodes. See the innermost and highest duneline, standing above the marsh-lake lagoon area, representing a drier climate of the past and now mostly anchored by forest. See the outermost dunes, lightly vegetated, moderately active. From the dunes walk by Cranberry Lake, admiring the unusual sand beach in water of "ocean tea."

Stroll #2, a round trip of 2 miles. Returned to the parking area, walk north to the jutting rocks of West Point and take the trail along North Beach, in views over boiling waters of Deception Pass to Fidalgo Island. North Beach consists of four gravel arcs separated by rock points; at moderate tides the route can combine beach and trees, at high it can stay on the forest trail. In 1 long mile North Beach is terminated by up-leaping cliffs.

Stroll #3, 2 miles one way. To complete the melange, from the picnic area short of the cliffs walk the trail in big trees up to the North Beach parking lot (alternative start) and proceed up its access road through an "Avenue of the Giants," huge Douglas firs and Sitka spruces and western hemlocks and western red cedars, and also-huge sword fern, to the park headquarters (alternative start).

Here is a 1/4-mile nature trail interpreting the plant community. After walking that, descend by road or trail to the Cranberry Lake picnic area (alternative start), 1 mile from North Beach. Walk out on the dock to survey the lake, in mood and vegetation reminding of Ozette Lake in Olympic National Park. Follow the shore path, tunneling through 8-foot-high salal, to the West Point Road. Soon leave it for trail again and walk by contorted shore pines out on a plank bridge to an islet with a rock point, giving the sensation of being on an alpine lake at 10,000 feet in the High Sierra.

Three-stroll round trip 7-1/2 miles, allow 5 hours
High point 175 feet, elevation gain 250 feet

Cornet Bay-Goose Rock (map—page 169)

More waterscapes and forestscapes and cliffscapes. But also a miniature mountain, 475 feet high, giving broad views to far horizons. Goose Rock can be conquered from any number of starting points and by several routes. The surveyors' choice is a loop starting from the North Beach parking lot (closed in winter—park then at park headquarters).

Where one big wide trail drops from the road to the beach, find another boulevard contouring east into big firs, then climbing a rock-garden wall to cross under the bridge. The trail goes through woods, gradually dropping near the water, madronas leaning over the beach. Strawberry Island (park) is passed, and then Ben Ure Island (private), as the shore rounds into Cornet Bay, with marina and houses. At a Y of two good-looking forks, take the right uphill (the left deadends on cliffs) to a glorious moss-garden grass-meadow bald high above the boat-dotted bay. The trail then switchbacks down through walls covered with saxifrages and succulents to the beach and a junction 1 1/4 miles from North Beach.

The path straight ahead leads in 1/4 mile to the mudflat head of Cornet Bay and the park's Group Camp, site of one of the CCC work camps (others were at Bowman Bay and park headquarters). Two trails lead from the camp back over the highway, for variants on the suggested loop.

However, from the junction reverse-turn right, uphill, on the Goose Rock trail and switchback ³/₄ mile through rhododendrons and big, fire-blackened firs to mossy balds and onto the broad peak. Proceed over the ice-rounded rock domes to the west peak and the best views.

Zounds. See far down Camano and Whidbey Islands and Skagit Bay and Rosario Strait, out to Olympics and Vancouver Island and Lopez and a mess of other San Juans. Especially interesting is the perspective on Cornet Bay, Cranberry Lake, and the dunes. And, on the Whulge, ships and boats, always something going somewhere.

For the looping descent, at the summit note another big obvious trail dropping into the woods. Descend it ¹/₂ mile to intersect the North Beach Discovery Trail (starting at the Group Camp). Following a former county road, the trail goes through stunningly huge fire-blackened firs, crosses under the highway, and in ¹/₂ mile from Goose Rock trail hits the North Beach road at ¹/₄ mile uphill from the end at the picnic area.

Loop trip 3 ¹/₂ miles, allow 3 hours
High point 475 feet, elevation gain 900 feet

Hoypus Hill-Similk Bay (map—page 169)

Here is the forest primeval, the park's purest wilderness, most jaw-dropping trees. More sheltered from ocean blasts, the trees grow notably tall and straight—it was here the CCC cut the timbers for park structures. The trails largely overgrown, here too is adventure, and solitude. (For a truly mystic experience, walk these woods on a foggy morning.) And aside from all that, beachwalking. And entirely different views. Plus, probably, eagles.

Drive south past the park headquarters and turn east on Cornet Bay Road. Pass the Group Camp, private land with a marina, and reenter park. Pass the boat-launch parking area and in 0.2 mile note a gated woods road climbing the hill to the right—this is the return of the Hoypus Hill loop. Drive on a scant 0.5 mile more to a gravel pit and park.

This is not a view walk, it's a tree walk through the Hoypus Point Natural Forest Area. Climb the woods road past the white gate. Soon the eyes bug, the Douglas firs are so incredibly big and tall. In a long ¹/₄ mile a sideroad goes right; this is an alternative return of the loop (see below). The fire-road trail tops out and contours, passing trails down left to group pack-in camps (used by reservation) served by a hand-pumped well. At 1 mile from the start the trail hits private property, steeply climbs the hill, and sets out on a compass course due east on the park's south boundary. To the left is the Hoypus Hill Addition, obtained from the state Department of Natural Resources, containing groves comparable to those in the Natural Forest Area, and wetlands as well. Though not surveyed for this guide, it has trails beloved by the local folks who fought the good fight to save it from logging. There is so little old-growth left in the state—and especially so little at sea level—every tree is precious.

At 1 mile from where private property was hit is a junction. The fire trail goes straight; instead, take the road-trail right. Pass two sideroads right which are alternative, shorter returns (see above). Switchback down to the shore road, reached at the white gate in 1 mile of walking from the park south boundary. Walk the paved road—or the beach—to the gravel pit to complete the loop.

Loop trip 3 ¹/₂ miles, allow 3 hours
High point 350 feet, elevation gain 350 feet

A second Hoypus Hill hike combines monster trees with Similk Bay beach and views, plus a spice of history.

Drive past the gravel pit 0.3 mile to the road-end at Hoypus Point. What's this concrete bulkhead for? The ferry. What ferry? The one that until the bridge was built in 1935 crossed to Dewey Beach on Fidalgo Island.

At low tide the beach can be walked 2 miles south to Ala Spit (which see). Over the waters are Kiket and Skagit Islands in Similk Bay. South are Goat and Ika Islands. Trees lean over the beach, including a grand fir that is horizontal 70 feet, its limbs rising straight up as a row of little trees. Look out for seals. (Or was that an otter swimming in the winter twilight?)

At any time the forest can be enjoyed. From the road-end scramble up the bank to what was in CCC days a big wide path but now, maintained only by thrusting bodies, is a slow go. But worth it for the gulper firs. In 1 mile are the pack-in campsites and then private property.

At the right tide the correct route is forest one way, beach the other.

Forest round trip 2 miles, allow 1-¹/₂ hours

FIDALGO ISLAND

Not loose sands and gravels and clays but hard rock is the essence of Fidalgo. The rock-hound and the rock-climber are thereby delighted. The walker, too, finds pleasure not common farther south. Yet if he is a native of that glacier-drifted south, he perceives he is in a very different sort of land—and sea.

Sugarloaf (map—page 175)

As discussed earlier, the Anacortes Community Forest Lands presently are not worthy of attention by a hiker traveling from, say, the Issaquah Alps, where similar large tracts of public land have been rid of trailbikes. However, a companion summit of Mt. Erie has the views of that peak without the intrusion of a road. In spring, on the rocky balds, the flowers bloom tra la, not crushed to death under the weight of beer cans and broken glass. The outlander come on a tour of inspection surely will drive to the top of Erie, because it is there. He should then walk the short path to Sugarloaf.

From I-5 drive Highway 20 toward Anacortes. Where 20 splits, take the south fork, signed "Deception Pass." In a scant 2 miles, where 20 turns left along Lake Campbell, go right on the unsigned (?) road. Drive past Lake Campbell 1.5 miles to a Y at Lake Erie. Go right a scant 1.5 miles. Watch for a prominent sideroad right, diverging from the highway and shortly rejoining it. Turn in on this road—narrow, winding, paved Ray Auld Drive—and climb 0.6 steep mile to the saddle between Mt. Erie and Sugarloaf. Park here, elevation 750 feet.

The trailhead is signed "Anacortes Community Forest Lands—Sugarloaf Trail." Marked by "15" signs, the path ascends through such scrub growth as can eke out existence in the thin soil or from cracks in the rock (a very ancient, hard metamorphic),

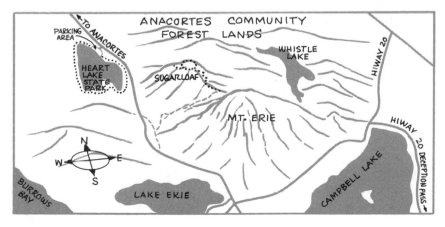

From Sugarloaf Mountain

and in the winds from the ocean. The madrona and lodgepole pine and Douglas fir are so scattered, gnarled, and charred they never have so much as registered in a logger's eye. In ⅓ mile the way emerges on the mossy balds that ring the grove of tough trees huddled for mutual protection on the summit, 1055 feet.

The moss alone is worth the walk. In early spring, before the sunball dessicates the heights, flowers dot the rocks. A network of sidetrails goes out on the west side of the peaklet to views from cliff brinks. Look out to the San Juan island-mountains, blue seas of the Whulge and green seas of the Skagit delta, to Cascades and Olympics and British Columbia Coast Range and Vancouver Island Mountains.

Round trip with sidetrips 1 mile, allow 1 hour
High point 1055 feet, elevation gain 300 feet

Washington Park (map—page 176)

Better not schedule anything else the day you come to 220-acre Washington Park. Don't be deceived by the shortness of the walk, which any hotfoot could crank out in an hour. The long halts for views over waterways to islands near and far, to examine juniper and madrona groves and granite boulders dropped by the glacier which also polished and scratched the buttresses, and sidetrips on sea-meadow bluffs and down balds to rocks jutting in the waves—well, better bring lunch, because you could be all day at it.

From I-5 drive Highway 20 into Anacortes, turn left, following signs to "Victoria Ferry," and when the highway turns downhill right, to the ferry dock, continue straight on Sunset to the park entrance. At a Y the right fork, signed "Beach Area," drops to Sunset Beach; go left, signed "Camp Area, Loop Road, Boat Launch." At the next Y go right, toward the boat-launch, and park, elevation 25 feet.

The park has innumerable trail signs pointing to Fidalgo Head Loop, Sunset Beach, Green Point, Rosario Strait, Juniper Point, Burrow Bay, Havekost Monument; the walker will want to take in all these spots. Mileages on the signs are given to the second decimal—".01, .24, 1.06" etc.; the walker needn't burden his brain with the numbers. The basic walk is a big and simple loop around Fidalgo Head on Loop Road, single-lane, blacktop, speed bumps to enforce slow, quiet driving. Frequent sidepaths lure to wonders. Connector paths link many of these, eliminating returns to Loop Drive. And so the whole day just melts away.

Find the Loop Road above the boat-launch. Walk a roadside path in views over Rosario Strait to Cypress, Orcas, Blakely, Decatur, and Lopez Islands. See the ferry from Anacortes to Vancouver Island. In ½ mile round Green Point and from the green

Burrows Pass from Washington Park

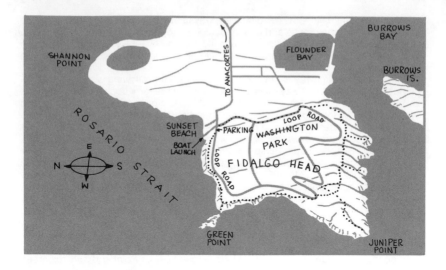

lawns look south to the Olympics. On or beside the road (at low tide, after a sidetrip down to West Beach), climb grassy opens.

After the road switchbacks left into forest, spot a good trail switchbacking right. Follow it away from the road and to the top of Juniper Point, 1 mile from the start. Now sidepaths proliferate, slowing progress, as do carpets of moss and grass and flowers, old, gnarled, wind-sculpted junipers reminding of the Sierra, views across the water to Burrows Island, Mt. Erie, fishing boats.

Following this path or that, likely the Loop Road will be touched here and there. And likely as not more trails will beguile, down ravines to secluded coves, out on high meadows. Chances are that after walking about 2 miles, exclusive of sidetrips, one will hit the Loop Road at a view over the Flounder Bay Marina to Erie. If so, the Havekost Monument, commemorating the pioneer of 1871 who gave Anacortes this park, will be passed, as well as concrete footings of the reservoir that served the lumber mill at Flounder Bay until demolished in 1961 (all except the planing mill, now a boat shed). A final scant 1 mile on the Loop Road, through fine cool woods, returns to the parking area.

As of 1990, Burrows Island has a spacious state park. Splendid walking — if you can paddle or swim to the trailheads.

Loop trip 3 miles, allow 2 hours
High point 250 feet, elevation gain 400 feet

NORTH KITSAP AND
OLYMPIC PENINSULAS

Whan that Aprille with his shoures soote
The droghte of March hath perced to the roote. . .
Thanne longen folk to go on ferry rides. . . .

Granted, the ferrying from Seattle or Edmonds cannot be done in less than an hour, what with the loading-unloading and waiting in line; this, with the driving, compoundly fractures the Two Hour Rule. But the water road is nothing like the concrete road. Ferries aren't part of the agony, the disease—they're part of the fun, the cure. Even on a pell-mell-paced jumbo a person can hotfoot around the decks 1 mile or more during a crossing, soaking up scenery and drinking in salt air like wine.

Two walks on the Kitsap Peninsula can be done by parking the car in Kingston and paying only foot-passenger fare (cheap). Even when the car must be ferried (expensively), the Kitsap beaches are so different from those facing across Puget Sound they're worth it. Wilderness! On Main Street! Also, history back to the earliest days of mowing down old-growth forests to load on square-rigged ships, of the U.S. Navy firing cannons at the Haidas. And history forward to Bangor Doomsday.

The next step, by bridge (sometimes) over Hood Canal, entails a moderately to very long day, though a very comfortable overnighter. The Olympic Peninsula (to which a bridge has attached Marrowstone Island) is worth a long day or two. When a walker yearns for a change from the intimate beauties of Home Whulge, yet hasn't the two-three days required by the Dragon Whulge, there is the Middle Whulge, the beaches long and wild and lonesome, the surf often ocean-crashing, seascapes and mountainscapes enormous, Main Street traffic busy. Here, too, is where mossy citizens of Puget Sound go on pilgrimage to the rainshadow of the Olympics, the Great Blue Hole in the semi-eternal grays.

Also on the Olympic Peninsula are mountains. In the season when a person wants that ferry ride but the High Olympics welcome only snowshoers, or when the rhododendrons are blooming, the mountain front may well be judged worth breaking the Two-Hour Rule and the budget for the flower show and for fresh perspectives on Whulge and the Cascades.

USGS maps: Duwamish Head, Bremerton East, Shilshole Bay, Suquamish, Poulsbo, Edmonds West, Brinnon, Port Gamble, Lofall, Quilcene, Mt. Walker, Tyler Peak, Hansville, Port Ludlow, Center, Uncas, Nordland, Port Townsend South, Port Townsend North, Gardiner, Sequim, Carlsborg, Dungeness

Indianola To Kingston (map—page 178)

A mere 5 miles across the waters is the throbbing (and roaring, banging, rumbling, generally racketing) heart of Puget Sound City, and along Main Street the traffic hurries between points on the Whulge and the Seven Seas. But here one walks in wildness for miles, just waves and gulls for company.

Drive to Indianola. From Winslow ferry the route is via Highway 305 to Agate Pass, then north on Suquamish Highway to the head of Miller Bay, then south on Indianola Road. From Kingston ferry the route is south around Appletree Cove on Indianola Road. Parking space is scanty in the old old summer-cottage settlement. Some room is available by the post office and delightful Indianola Country Store. But don't come on summer Sundays to complicate a quiet community that has zero provision for public entertainment. Lonesome winter is the season—there then is also easy toleration of the put-in, the only part of the route that poses the slightest problem.

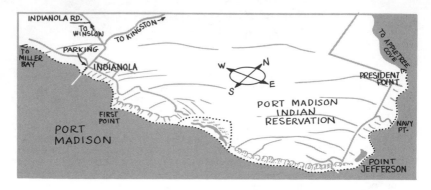

Walk down to the dock (the Port of Indianola, from mosquito-fleet days) and take the stairs to the beach.

(Note: In toleration season the beach is inviting the 1 mile to the base of the spit reaching nearly across the mouth of Miller Bay. The spit was wanted as a public park but a developer snuck in, providing joy to a dozen families, denying thousands of families a picnic visit. Rectification can come after C/4.)

The wild walk is east along Port Madison. A couple houses-on-bulkheads are passed and then man retreats to his proper place atop the bank. In a long ½ mile "First Point" is rounded and the bluff rears up a steep, partly naked 200 feet of till and sand and clay. The view back down Port Madison to Agate Pass is lost, that of Bainbridge Island continues, and across Main Street is Seattle.

At ½ mile from First Point is the most unusual feature of the trip. The bluff swings far inland around an ancient bay, long since closed off by a baymouth bar, within which is a lagoon-mudflat, a mass of bleached driftwood, and a broad marsh and great swampy forest. Birds! What a crowd! What secrets lurk here in the heart of the Port Madison Indian Reservation? Marred by a single structure only, the entirety of closed-off bay and surrounding forest hills appears wild. At medium-to-high tides the lagoon-mouth channel must be waded to the knees or detoured around on the driftwood; at low tides the channel can be hippety-hopped over, the baymouth bar walked, ½ mile to a resumption of bluff.

After ¾ mile more of bluff wildness, a dock and road intrude. In ¼ mile more is Point Jefferson, with duneline, lagoon, and a half-dozen modest cottages. Now the view opens north past Carkeek Park to Richmond Beach, oil tanks of Point Wells and Edwards Point, and Edmonds. This may be far enough for many walkers, 3 miles from Indianola.

But onward ½ wild mile is "Navy Point"; atop the bluff is some aged war-like structure, below it another lagoon. And in ¾ bluff-wild (though the blufftop is inhabited) mile more, complicated by a beach-invading stretch of riprap requiring scrambling at medium tides, are the wide flat and lagoon of President Point, sparsely dotted with houses. Now the view is north to Whidbey Island and Mukilteo. Here, 4-¼ miles from Indianola, is a good turnaround—though in only 1-¼ more (civilized, now) miles, past a beached hulk, is the point at the mouth of Appletree Cove, with close views of the Edmonds ferry arriving at and departing from Kingston.

Round trip to President Point 8-½ miles, allow 6 hours

Kingston To Eglon Beach (map—page 180)

A terrific beach, right on Main Street yet wild much of the way beneath a formidable guardian bluff. What's really sensational about the trip is you don't need to ferry your wheels over the waters, just your boots and attached body.

Drive (or Metro bus) to Edmonds and park in the Port of Edmonds lot by the ferry dock. Walk to the second (foot-passenger) ticket booth. Voyage carfree and liberated over the waves to Kingston. Walk up from the dock, take the first road right, and from it find the broad trail dropping to the beach. And away you go.

The 1 ½ miles to Appletree Point are beneath a two-step bluff 60-100 feet high, keeping houses distant from the beach except at the halfway mark, where a boulder bulkhead briefly invades, requiring a short wade at medium tides. The couple dozen modest cottages on the Point are readily passed, no scowls usually, but at the north end is a wicked 100-foot bulkhead that is non-detourable via bluff, non-clamberable due to a house, and at middle tides and above requires a knee-deep to nose-deep wade. Face it—to do the whole trip to Eglon you're going to have to get feet and knees wet here, going or coming. The beach then widens. North of the point begins an amusing ½ mile, a half-dozen quirky little cottages-castles, trail-access only, scattered along a slump terrace.

Now, 2 ½ miles from the ferry, begin 2 ½ utterly wild miles, the bluff a steep 300 feet. Chunks of bluff slide onto and across the beach. Gullies slice the clay. Waterfalls

Appletree Cove and Kingston ferry

cascade out of greenery. Jungle ensures solitude. It's as wild a beach as is to be found anywhere on the Whulge.

Trails and staircases foreshadow the start of civilization, on the flat of a coastal bulge at the mouth of a creek. Oddly, the only development is a couple small farms, several beach houses, and several bleached ruins. Very nice. Wildness resumes, though of a lower order, the bluff a mere 60 feet, the final ³/₄ mile to Eglon Beach Park.

Sit for lunch. Enjoy views of Main Street traffic, Whidbey Island's imposing bluffs, the Edmonds ferry dock whence you came, Pilchuck, Glacier Peak, Rainier. Far across the waters, hear the rumble of trains on the Whulge Trail.

Round trip 12 miles, allow 8 hours

Point No Point to Eglon Beach (map—page 180)

A big-view, lighthouse-tipped point jutting through the rabble of gulls and crows and ducks and fishing boats toward the passing parade of ships on Main Street. And a long, bluff-wild beach intruded by civilization only briefly at the middle.

Drive to Hansville. From Winslow ferry the route is Highway 305 to just west of Agate Pass, then north on Suquamish Highway to the Hansville Road. From Kingston ferry the route is west 2.5 miles to the Hansville Road. Upon descending to the shore plain, turn right on Point No Point Road 0.7 mile to the resort entrance. Park on a road shoulder back toward Hansville.

Walk through the resort to the beach, thence to the point; or, where the resort road turns left, walk the road straight ahead to the lighthouse, where very limited parking is available during visiting hours (Wednesday-Sunday, 8 A.M. to 4 P.M.). Dating from 1879, the light is worth a tour.

The view west is past Hansville over Skunk Bay to Foulweather Bluff, and north is across Puget Sound to the gray-white cliffs of Double Bluff and Indian Point and Scatchet Head on Whidbey Island.

South from the spit, jungled cliffs of glacial drift enwilden the beach. Bald eagles may be seen; a pair or two perhaps nest here. The view now is past Possession Point to densely inhabited slopes of Edmonds, oil tanks of Edwards Point and Point Wells, Richmond Beach, and towers of downtown Seattle. Beyond are Cascades from Rainier to Glacier to Baker. And always ships passing, birds flying and swimming.

Paths indicate unseen residences above. Then, at Pilot Point, 2¹/₂ miles from Point No Point, a half-dozen cabins occupy a beach-side flat. Wildness resumes the final

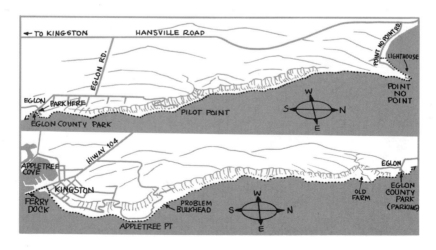

Point No Point Lighthouse

1 ¼ miles to Eglon Beach Park. To do the walk starting here, from Hansville Road take Eglon Road.

Round trip 8 miles, allow 5 hours

Foulweather Bluff (map—page 183)

Talk about weather shores! Foulweather Bluff juts out where Hood Canal, Admiralty Inlet, and Puget Sound meet, and the weather comes at it every which way. The skinny beach at the base of the vertical jungle is a terrific viewpoint, resounding finale to a walk by two great spits and a marvelous nature sanctuary.

Drive to Hansville (see Point No Point) and keep going. Upon reaching the beach, Hansville Road turns west as Twin Spits Road. At 2.8 miles from the bend watch for a wide marsh to the left; summer vegetation can make it hard to see. A bit beyond, spot an obvious path into the woods, signed only by demure "Nature Conservancy" tags and a little plaque identifying this as a Nature Sanctuary. If you come to Skunk Bay Road, you've gone 800 feet too far. Alternatively, drive on 0.7 mile to the road-end and a public beach access beside Twin Spits Resort.

However, the Sanctuary is the special treat. Walk the footpath through the woods past the marsh, then the broad lagoon, ⅓ mile to the beach. To appreciate how glorious a spot this is, and how fortunate we are that the Conservancy saved it, walk 1 ¼ miles southeast, first along the baymouth bar that encloses lagoon and marsh, then under an 80-foot-high naked bluff, to the monster development on the spits of Coon Bay.

But the main show (other than the Sanctuary, which a birdwatcher just may not want to leave) is the other way, on what was, when sea level was 20 feet higher, Foulweather Island. Houses are safely atop the 60-foot till wall the 1 wild mile to the

Madrona trees near Foulweather Bluff

southern of the Twin Spits, where are located Last Resort, Twin Spits Resort, and the public beach access. Proceed by several beach-near houses ¼ mile to the northern spit and a resumption of wildness. At low tide walk across the lagoon outlet onto the spit and stick with the beach; otherwise follow the foot of the bluff until saltgrass and driftwood can be walked around the lagoon to the beach. Views are superb south along Hood Canal to Hood Head, the floating bridge, Port Gamble, the mouth of Port Ludlow directly across the Canal, and Zion, Townsend, Walker, and Constance.

The spit beach is ¾ mile long, a lonesome splendor of grass-anchored sand dunes, driftwood, and waves on the Canal side and birds on the lagoon side. Two modest summer cottages at the spit base only briefly break the solitude, which resumes under the bluff leaping to 100 feet, then 220 feet, and too steep and clay-slidey to permit trails from the top. The shore rounds from northerly to east, the view extending to Marrowstone Island and Fort Flagler State Park, to the distant San Juans. Directly across Main Street is Double Bluff, between Mutiny Bay and Useless Bay on Whidbey Island. Ocean freighters race by, making wonderful crashing waves, ocean-size, to delight the beachwalker. Fishing boats work and sailboats play. Ah, but what's missing from the scene? The Edmonds-Ludlow ferry, scuttled soon after War II.

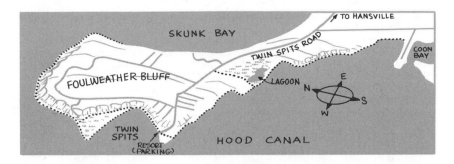

Foulweather Bluff was a famous landmark, in those distant days, to voyagers en route to the high Olympics, Trapper Nelsons lashed to fenders of the Model A.

At 1 mile from the northern Twin Spit the bluff shore turns sharp south into Skunk Bay. About 1/2 wild mile more and the bluff dwindles to naught and houses begin.

Round trip to end of bluff 7 miles, allow 5 hours

Port Gamble (map—page 183)

No museum specimen under glass is this, no artist colony or row of shoppes, but a lived-in, working mill town, with the oldest operating sawmill in North America. The place seems too old for this raw young corner of the country, looks like it belongs in New England. Indeed, when A.J. Pope, Captain William Talbot, and Cyrus Walker founded the town in 1853, they built it to resemble their native East Machias, Maine. Take away the cars and TV antennae, fill the bay with square-rigged ships, and the scene would be straight out of the 19th century.

Parking areas in town permit walking tours from a number of starts. A nice way to grasp the geographical setting is to approach via beach from Salsbury Point County Park. Drive Highway 104 from Kingston, or, from Winslow, Highways 305, 3, and 104, to 0.5 mile east of Hood Canal Floating Bridge, and turn off on Wheeler Street to the beach.

The little park is hedged by homes but in toleration season one can walk the beach to the shelter of Teekalet Bluff, in views south on Hood Canal to the Olympics, north to Port Ludlow and Foulweather Bluff. In 1 mile is the millyard, from which a road-path climbs to the town and the parking area across from the post office (Land Office) and the Port Gamble General Store (1853). Here too is the Pope and Talbot Office; the company restored and maintains the town and runs the mill on timber from lands it has been logging all this while, in some cases now milling a third crop as the fourth grows.

In the basement of the General Store is the Historical Museum, the basic introduction when open and providing a walking-tour pamphlet-guide. But there's plenty of history out in the open. Stroll the sidewalks along tree-shaded streets, by workers' by-no-means-humble homes and capitalists' mansions, in views down to the

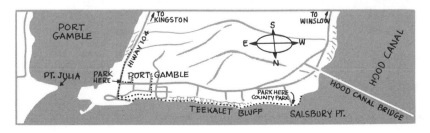

mill, rafted logs, and over Port Gamble to where the Indians lived, watching all this with mixed emotions.

Ascend the bluff-rim lawn westward to the hilltop cemetery, where headstones bear such legends as "died at Teekalet W. T. 1860." Note the memorial to "Gustav Englebrecht—Germany—Cox US Navy—Indian War—November 21, 1856." When the Haida attack came, the millworkers called for help from the *Massachusetts*. During the desultory skirmish known to history as the Battle of Port Gamble, the coxswain poked his head over a bulwark for a better view of the action and became the first U.S. Navy man to be killed in a Pacific Ocean war.

Salsbury Point County Park, the floating bridge that for a time failed to do so, and Olympic Mountains

Pope & Talbot mill at Port Gamble

Admire the view to Hood Canal Floating (?) Bridge, Olympics, Marrowstone Island, the plume of the pulpmill at Port Townsend, Foulweather Bluff. In mind's eye see the tall ships spreading sail to carry Washington lumber the world around.

Round trip 3 miles, allow 3 hours

Hood Head State Park (map—page 186)

Stroll shores of a secluded little bay, poke around amid ducks and herons thronging a lagoon half-ringed by saltmarsh and forest, explore spits, venture out on a former island, now a tombolo, and from its tip look up and down Hood Canal. All this on assuredly public beaches of an undeveloped state park.

Drive to the west end of the Hood Canal Floating Bridge and turn right on Paradise Bay Road, signed "Port Ludlow." Immediately turn right again on Termination Point Road, steeply down to the beach. Drive past the Puget Power transformer to a sign, "Shine Tidelands. Limited Public Facilities. Held for Future Development. Camping Permitted." Park here.

The state park is said to have 131 acres, including a forest of sizable firs and cedars crisscrossed with paths. However, the bulk of that forest seems to be private—or why would houses be springing up like so many toadstools? Never mind. The nearly 4 miles of public tidelands offer exercises short and long. Termination Point provides a guaranteed access.

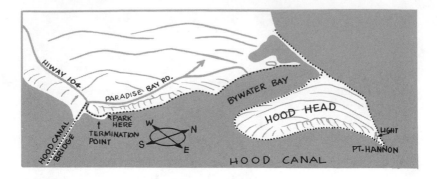

Begin by walking 1 mile on the shore of Bywater Bay to a former beach access now fenced and signed "Private." Continue north ½ mile, by a log-filled lagoon, on South Spit, to its tip. The spit thrusts out so far it nearly cuts off the head of the bay, forming a large inner bay-lagoon, a mudflat at low tide, a duck pond at high.

Round trip to tip of South Spit 3 miles, allow 2 hours

As of 1988 there appears to be no public access from the mainland onto the base of North Spit; the spit itself, however, connecting mainland to the island-now-tombolo of Hood Head, is public. What a person must do is study the tide charts and time the visit for quite low water—and prepare to accept with equanimity a wetting of the feet and ankles, perhaps the knees. Don't try in rough weather—storm surfs sweep entirely over the North Spit, and perhaps the South Spit as well.

From the tip of South Spit it's no more than a child's pebble-toss to North Spit east of the midpoint of its ½-mile length. Walk the spit from end to end. Then go off the east end onto Hood Head. Walk the north shore beneath a high bluff of tree-tangled glacial drift the 1 mile to Point Hannon, a superlative viewpoint thrust out in Hood Canal. Look north to the entrance portals, Tala Point and Foulweather Bluff, and beyond to Marrowstone Island. Look across to the mill and town of Port Gamble, Rainier rising above.

The first edition of this book, delivered to the stores in February of 1979, said "Look south to the bridge floating in the Canal (floating, that is, until the next approximately twice-in-a-century event, the last coming in the 1930s, a northerly gale on a bull tide, a combination for which the bridge was not engineered, and thus the fittingness of the location near Port Gamble)." On February 13, 1979, the bridge sank. A new one was built. One must ask, how will it handle the C/4?

Though the uplands of Hood Head, rising to a near-mountainous 220 feet, were not surveyed, they are an intriguing wildwood, 1 mile long and averaging ½ mile wide. The shore, too, is perfectly wild except for the dozen-odd cottages on the west side. Though this stretch depends on toleration, the logical completion of the trip is to round the island, in a scant 2 miles from Point Hannon returning to North Spit.

Complete round trip from Termination Point 7-½ miles, allow 5 hours

Marrowstone Island–Fort Flagler State Park (map—page 189)

An embarrassment of riches! Miles and miles of grand beaches with views of Main Street traffic and of mountains from Olympics to Baker to Glacier Peak to Rainier. And absolutely the bulliest of the three forts of the Death (or Devil's) Triangle that once protected cities of Puget Sound from naval bombardment. A pity the Spanish battle fleet never attempted to force a passage through Admiralty Inlet. See the ships of the gallant, foolish hidalgos, staggering and burning, riddled with shells! Absolutely a bully show!

Yet the old fort is a fraction of the treasures. Though the island is not very distant in hours from Seattle, it's very far away in the past. The same water shortage (the sky is the only supply) that restrains development on Vashon Island has, in combination with the commuting distance, held Marrowstone, 6 miles north-south and up to 1 mile east-west, to a population of 500. "Pleasure driving" is still a reality. And—oh—the pleasure walking. A day trip from Puget Sound City can be olden-day relaxed. A better plan is to camp a night or two or several and be for that long an islander.

Drive Highway 104 west 5 miles from Hood Canal Bridge and turn north at the sign, "Fort Flagler State Park, Port Townsend." In 1.6 miles turn right on Oak Bay Road, signed "Port Ludlow." In 9.8 miles more turn right on Flagler Road. (This junction can be reached in the same driving distance, the scenery different but just as good, via Chimacum and Hadlock, as the highway map reveals.)

But first. Back up from the junction 0.5 mile and turn onto the road signed "Oak Bay Park." Descend to the beach and drive out on the spit to the road-end, 0.4 mile from the highway. Park. Walk. To the spit tip, then along Portage Canal, which splits off Indian Island. From the canal shore be surprised to see Port Townsend, pulpmill

Rain at Fort Flagler State Park

Lighthouse at Fort Flagler State Park

plume and all. Binoculars at the ready, return along the ¹/₂-mile length of the excellent lagoon. The campground at this Jefferson County park is stark, the way RVs like it. A single picnic table comforts the tenters who appreciate that amenity.

Now, back to Flagler Road. Drive from the Y 0.9 mile across the bridge onto Indian Island and, immediately, to Hadlock Lions Public Park, picnicking and looking and access to the Indian Island beach, 2 miles with nary a house, the highway out of mind atop a short but sufficient bluff.

Next, proceed on the main road 0.8 mile from the bridge and turn right on an unsigned gravel road which drops to the beach and turns to follow the shore to the road-end and two picnic tables, 0.2 mile from the highway. Though no signs say so, this is another segment of Oak Bay (County) Park—which indeed takes in most of the Indian Island shore. Let us say this about that: the shore is a saltwater museum, most of the length oozy-rich saltgrass on the bluff side of a system of bars, clean gravel on the wave side. A lagoon ¹/₃ mile long empties into the bay (or in flood, sucks in the bay) exactly at the picnic tables.

All this and not yet on Marrowstone! At 1.7 miles from the Portage Canal bridge begins the causeway-isthmus which artificially-naturally separates-connects Oak Bay from Scow Bay and Indian Island from Marrowstone Island. Park here, too. Walk the beach 1 mile to the south tip of Marrowstone, Kinney Point. The state DNR has 80 acres here, ultimately to be a park—developed only to an extent compatible with preserving the wildlife habitat, which includes eagle nests, one said by the State Wildlife Department to be the most productive in the Northwest. Local folks see eagles every day of the year.

Drive on north. Nordland is your next stop. To buy an ice cream bar at the Nordland Store, mail a postcard at the Nordland post office. No tourist boutiques here. This is the authentic 1930s. Pause for a look-in at Mystery Bay (State Park) Recreation Area, where the recreation is driving water-razzers up and down Kilisut Harbor. The historical eye looks across to Indian Island, which is targeted for atomic obliteration on Doomsday because it is the storage site for U.S. Navy atomic obliterators, and reflects that there are still living on Marrowstone folks who remember when the U.S. Army was waiting for the Spanish Navy.

North of the Nordland Store 0.4 mile, turn right at the sign "East Beach Park" and drive 0.3 mile to the driftwood, a picnic shelter, inviting beach (at low tide, broad sand) north and south, and to views: Rainier, the shore of Whidbey Island, Baker and Shuksan, Main Street traffic up and down Admiralty Inlet.

At last, Fort Gate, and at 3 miles from Nordland, the main intersection of Fort Flagler State Park. Each of three roads puts the feet on the beach.

The road right leads in 0.4 mile, passing a gun battery with two 3-inch guns, to Fort Flagler Fishing Pier, a long reach of planks out into views. A beach access is the start for a ¾-mile walk to Marrowstone Point or some 7 miles to Kinney Point.

The road straight ahead from the main intersection passes through the main campus (handsome old officers' homes, utilitarian enlisted men's barracks—and now, park headquarters, interpretive center, hostel, etc.) and in 0.7 mile ends at

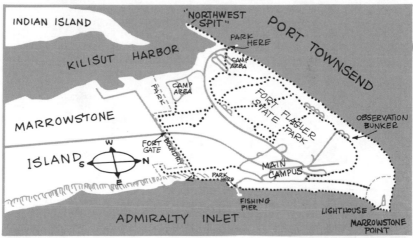

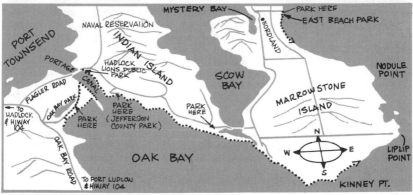

Tern

Marrowstone Point Lighthouse. Look across to the loess bluffs of Ebey's Landing and the green plain of Ebey's Prairie. Look south between Foulweather Bluff and Double Bluff to Puget Sound; the mainland shore is a distant blue silhouette, seemingly at the foot of Mt. Rainier.

For the suggested introductory walk, drive left from the main intersection 1.4 miles to the road-end at Northwest Spit. (On the way are a mortar battery, trails, and two campgrounds, up on the bluff and down on the filled lagoon. Here is the sublime base for a Marrowstone vacation.)

First off, walk west 1/3 mile to the tip of the spit pushing across the mouth of Kilisut Harbor. Look over Port Townsend bay to the pulpmill and town and Fort Worden, to Olympics from Constance to Zion to Blue to Angeles.

Returned from this sidetrip, head east, leaving the spit flat for the base of the 120-foot vertical bluffs Vancouver called "marrow stone"—what we call glacial drift, here represented by concrete-like till and some of the finest sand cliffs around. Ships, tugs and barges, sailboats, waves, birds, the Keystone-Townsend ferry. Across Admiralty Inlet, the Ebey's Landing section of Whidbey Island, Baker, Shuksan, Wickersham-Woolley-Lyman, Cultus, Chuckanut, San Juans. In a scant 2 miles are the flats of Marrowstone Point, the lighthouse on the tip, and views south to Whitehorse, Glacier, Rainier, and Foulweather Bluff at the mouth of Hood Canal.

Leave the beach (4 miles with never a Privatizer to be seen) and follow the road up the hill to the main campus and its well-kept 1900-era frame buildings. Keep right on an old, barricaded road-become-trail. The route from here the 2 miles back to the campground is partly on this or that old road, partly on trails; the rule is, stick with the easy going as near the bluff edge as feasible and safe. The way is in forest and sky-open, wide-horizon sea meadow, passing (explore with care!) concrete emplacements of the 10- and 12-inch disappearing guns and 12-inch mortars, and underground fire-control posts. Set aside as a military reservation in 1866, the fort was developed from 1897-1900 and declared surplus in 1954. Three wars in the memories here. Stand in the wind on the brink of the meadow-top precipice and look over the waters to the other forts of the Death Triangle and visualize the climax, here, of a fourth war that never was; only in phantom history books is there, to rank with Trafalgar and Midway, a Battle of Admiralty Inlet.

Fort Flagler State Park is an enormous 783 acres, mostly a forest getting on to be a century old. The miles of woodland paths were not surveyed for this guide because a person wouldn't drive from Puget Sound City for their sake. Come for a stay of several days, though, a walker surely will want to intermingle the big sky of the sea with sorties into the little green rooms of the trees.

Introductory Flagler beach loop 6 miles, allow 4 hours

Quimper Peninsula-Fort Worden State Park (map—page 192)

How impoverished our park systems would be without wars—and foolish fears of implausible wars. Forest wildlands are preserved, and miles of lonesome beaches, all wonderfully haunted. Even if a person lacks a taste for ancient bloodshed the Quimper Peninsula has plenty to enchant—history that is not military, ocean-like beaches, and unsurpassed water-and-mountain views.

Drive a scant 4 miles west from Hood Canal Bridge and turn north on the highway signed "Port Townsend." At all junctions pursue this destination.

But first, turn in to clearly signed Old Fort Townsend State Park. Unlike neighbors, this was an Indian War fort, established in 1856, abandoned in 1895, the 377 acres deeded to the state in 1953. The beach is a dandy, extending north under guardian bluffs 1 mile to Glen Cove, nearly to the steam-spewing pulpmill, and south 1 ³/₄ miles to Kuhn Spit and Kala Point, all in broad views. The park is almost entirely a lonesome woodland full of paths; a loop trail of some 3 miles can be readily figured out and is especially attractive in May when the rhododendrons are in bloom.

Now, onward. Enter Port Townsend on Highway 20 and before downtown turn left at the sign, "Fort Worden State Park," and turn right and left and right and left (always signed) and voila, the park entrance. The car can be parked and the walk begun at any number of places. Three sample tours are suggested.

History Tour (War) (map—page 192)

Had the enemy (who was that?) tried to storm on through from the ocean into Puget Sound, the batteries of this corner of the DeathTriangle would've fired the first shells, perhaps leaving Flagler and Casey little to do but finish off cripples. Work on gun emplacements began in 1897 and in 1904 Worden became headquarters of the Harbor Defense of Puget Sound. In 1911 the 12-inchers of Battery Kinzie were in place. In 1920 aerial warfare arrived with the construction of balloon hangars. On December 8, 1941, the fort briefly revived. In 1953 it was closed, to become a 339-acre park.

To absorb all this, first drive around the parade ground to the flagpole and park office to obtain a copy of the park map and chronology. A methodical way to do the history is with a periphery tour. From the chapel at the entrance walk by the guardhouse, turn left to the balloon hangar and cemetery, turn right up the boundary

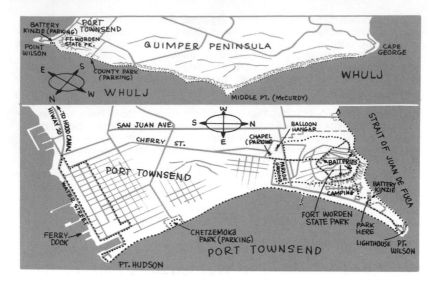

to bluff-edge views over the Whulge, turn right and prowl gun batteries, return right to the neatly white buildings of the old barracks, now the Conference Center, and stroll the parade ground to the mansions of Officer's Row, now leased as vacation homes.

Loop trip 2 1/2 miles, allow 2 hours.

On the Beach From Lighthouse to Old City (Map—192)

Drive by the parade ground, down the beach, and north to the parking area at Battery Kinzie, just short of the Point Wilson Lighthouse.

First, of course, tour the lighthouse (visiting hours, weekdays 1-3, weekends 1-4) on the tip of the superb spit poking into Main Street, the Strait of Juan de Fuca on one side, Admirality Inlet on the other, great ships often passing close to make the turn, sloshing great waves on the beach. Views are overwhelming across to Victoria on Vancouver Island, the full east-west width of the San Juans, the high sand bluffs of Whidbey Island, the shuttling Keystone-Townsend ferry, Cascades from Baker to Shuksan to Glacier to Whitehorse and Three Fingers.

Walk south along the spit beach (wide, sandy, all-tides-walkable) by the driftwood line, the grass-grown dunes, the (filled) lagoon. South 3/4 mile from Point Wilson is the pier, providing out-in-the-water perspectives. Leave the spit for the foot of a wild bluff, pass under Chetzemoka Park (alternative in-town start), and at 2 1/4 miles from Point Wilson come to the end of beach, start of port facilities, at Point Hudson (parking, alternative start).

Port Townsend is a town worth walking. Turn onto Water Street, main drag of the lower, below-bluff city, visit the ferry dock, and tour the scene. A thriving seaport when Seattle was a real-estate speculation, Port Townsend lost the race to hugeness. That's our good luck, because the long languishing in limbo preserved much of the 19th-century would-be metropolis. The 1891 City Hall at Water and Madison houses an historical museum; the basement, when a jail, offered hospitality to Jack London. The Bartlett Building, when a tavern, specialized in shanghaiing seamen. The 1874 Leader Building is claimed to be the oldest remaining all-stone structure in the state. The upper town has many well-kept Victorian homes.

Beach round trip 4 1/2 miles, city tour 2 miles, for both allow 4 hours

Point Wilson Lighthouse

Cape George

Long Wild Beach (map—page 192)

If it's a good leg-stretching you seek, a good lung-filling with salt winds, a good eye-filling with ocean-like marine vistas, the north shore of Quimper Peninsula is for you. What do you want? A few-minutes' stroll? Or a long day's journey into night?

Park at Battery Kinzie and hit the north beach, walkable at all but the highest tides. Views are east by the Point Wilson Lighthouse to Whidbey Island bluffs and the white tower of Baker, north by ships to Vancouver Island. When a tall freighter rushes past, the surf turns ocean-size, sort of scary there under the tall bluff of old glacial drift, hard and steep. Cormorants perch atop erratics. Grebes dive, oystercatchers squeal, gulls soar, crows caw, plovers scurry, peep run over the sands. After 1 mile of splendid isolation is the park boundary and a dropping-away of the bluff to a flat. Here are fields and homes and North Beach (Jefferson) County Park, an alternative start (from Fort Worden entrance drive west, then north).

After 1/2 mile the bluff rises, with homes atop. But at 2 3/4 miles from Point Wilson the houses end, the bluff rears up to a frightful precipice, sand strata topped by vertical till, the brink 280 feet from the water, the tallest naked vertical wall encountered in *Footsore* surveys. A long 1 mile Champion Cliff continues, then diminishes somewhat to McCurdy (Middle) Point, 4 miles from Point Wilson and a logical turnaround.

But the wildness, the splendid isolation continue under a more-than-ordinarily-vertical bluff rising to as much as a daunting 200 feet of clays and gravel and tills. Watch those tides, folks! Escape routes are few and cruel and mostly dangerous, not a single deep-slicing ravine to breach the wall. Spice is added by the fact that at high tides there is no beach much of the way, just clay walls battered by breakers and

194

clawed by fingernails. Yes, a wilderness to sing in, and no fear that any developer will invade the combat zone where waves buffet the clay cliffs, great chunks of which slide down to counterattack.

At 3 ¼ miles from McCurdy Point (atop which is an abandoned military reservation) is Cape George at the mouth of Port Discovery, views to Olympic foothills, Miller Peninsula, and Protection Island. Time to turn around, because soon start houses of Cape George Colony, and after all these wild miles who needs that?

Round trip (Point Wilson to Cape George) 14 ½ miles, allow 9 hours

Miller Peninsula: Diamond Point to Rocky Point to Travis Spit (map—page 195)

Views across the great embayment to Canada and the northern mountains. Ships of many nations passing to and from Vancouver and Seattle. Waves of those ships washing up to the foot of the bluff, reinforcing the surf the next thing to oceanic. Seals poking heads out of the water to watch the seal-watchers on the beach. Bald eagles circling above, guarding their nest. Peregrine falcons, too. It is good, very very good. But the best, perhaps, is that in 5-odd miles of Miller Peninsula shore there is (1988) no intrusion by human machines or homes. Not very much by humans. The powerful longshore currents slim the beach so drastically that quite a low tide is required to do any walking. Few ravines breach the 200-foot bluff; the trail described here is just about the only practical way to the beach on public lands. The DNR parcel contains 1444 acres, more than 3 miles of tidelands. A major park can be expected here in years ahead — but *please*, no fancy-dancy resort. Keep it wild!

Drive US 101 west from Gardiner about 1.5 miles and turn north on Diamond Point Road. In 2.2 miles the road curves left to an obscure sign, "Northwest Technical Industries." A dirt road goes off left a short way to a locked gate. To the right of this road and gate is a muddy, potholed lane, possibly drivable, but why fight it? Park on the wide shoulder, elevation 360 feet.

Walk, passing a sign, "DNR Research Plots," a scant 1 ½ miles through forest of cedar and hemlock, and huge cedar stumps notched for springboards, reminding of the old forest. Where the road curves and goes up a bit, spot an old road-now-path on the right. This is the route to the beach, down the ravine of what would be the

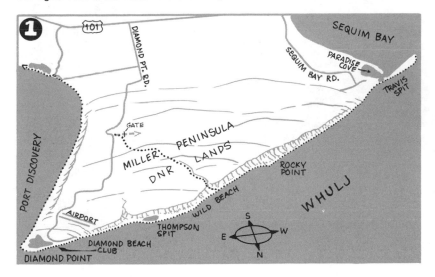

Driftwood on Dungeness Spit

peninsula's largest creek were it not a dry gulch. At 2 miles is the beach—and a striking view out to Protection Island.

Walk east 2 miles to Diamond Point. Well, maybe not the whole way; the magnificent spit has been littered with cabins and trailers set up in a row for the C/4 to bash to splinters and deposit in the lagoon. (Many lots remain unsold as of 1988, permitting Public feet to slip through the Privates onto the beach, temporarily providing an alternative start for the walk.) The best of the trip comes in ·/2 mile, Thompson Spit—actually almost a baymouth bar. Behind the driftwood line the duneline is greenly grassed. At the tip of the spit is a lone shore pine, tortured by storms to a stunted bonsai. Back of the murky orange-brown lagoon is an old hovel. The map shows a cross here and says "Grave." The surveyor saw six seals and four bald eagles.

Walk west ³/4 mile to Rocky Point, distinguished by two enormous glacial erratics. The point cannot be rounded except at a low tide. Not surveyed for this guide were the 2 ¹/4 miles onward to the base of Travis Spit (on the way the bluff dwindles to naught) nor the ³/4 mile of that spit, which very nearly closes off Sequim Bay and makes it a lagoon.

Note: Early in 1989 a plan surfaced to develop the Miller Peninsula into a $100 million resort area, largely on DNR property. The future lies ahead.

Total round trip (Road-Diamond Point-Rocky Point) 9 ¹/2 miles, allow 5 hours
High point 360 feet, elevation gain 360 feet
All Year

Dungeness Spit (map—page 198)

The longest natural sandspit in the United States thrusts 5 miles out from Olympic Peninsula bluffs into the Strait of Juan de Fuca, so far that on a stormy day a walker feels wave-tossed and seasick, and on a foggy day wonders if he's passed over to another and totally watery planet. Birds run the sands and swim the waters and fly the air. Seals pop heads out of breakers to marvel what you're at.

Drive US 101 west from Sequim's town-center stoplight 4.5 miles and turn north on Kitchen Road, signed "Dungeness Recreation Area." In 3.2 miles the road makes a right-angle turn east and just beyond is the entrance road to the recreation area, a 240-acre Clallam County park. Drive 1 long mile, passing the head of the horse trail, going by the picnic area and through the campground, to the road-end parking area and restrooms and trailhead, elevation 120 feet.

As a prefatory note, there's more great walking here than just the spit. Southwest are at least 4 miles of open-to-boots big-surf beach, totally wild below naked, vertical, 100-foot bluffs of glacial drift. In the same direction, an unsurveyed distance, runs a blufftop path through grass and wind-tortured scrub trees and broad views.

However, the spit calls. The trail ("no camping, no fires, dogs on leash, no guns, no wheels") enters forest, then emerges to a viewpoint of spit and Whulge, joins the horse trail coming from the right, and drops to the mouth of a nice little creek valley, in a scant ·/2 mile reaching the beach and the base of the spit.

So, there you are. Go. Via the outside route or the inside, separated by the driftwood jumble along the spit spine. The outside is the surf side, with views to tankersful of oil, one in every so many of which spills, to Vancouver Island, San Juan Islands, Whidbey Island, and Baker-dominated Cascades. The inside is the bay side, the first half a lagoon, often glassy calm and often floating thousands of waterfowl come to enjoy amenities of Dungeness National Wildlife Refuge; the view is to mainland bluffs, delta of the Dungeness River, and the Olympics. The best plan is to alternate routes.

Both end in the standard pretty government-issue lighthouse, the foghorn, and the tip of the spit ¹/3 mile beyond. A light has been on this site since 1857, earliest in the state. Note that the precise name is New Dungeness Lighthouse; when Captain Vancouver gave the name in 1792 he was observing the resemblance to Dungeness

Kelp on Dungeness Spit

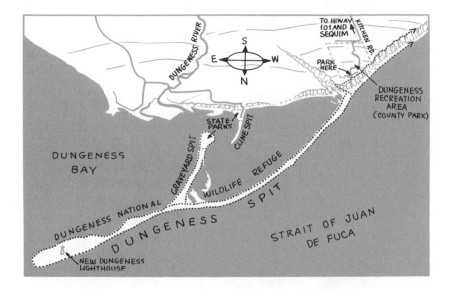

"in the British channel" of Olde England. Note, too, that the beach is wheel-traveled; when the Coast Guard had the lighthouse keeper maintain contact with shore by boat, we were denied the pleasure of the company of his jeep.

There's a sidetrip. Graveyard Spit, commemorating the day in 1868 when 17 Tsimshians were massacred by the Klallams, branches off, extending 1 ½ miles south, nearly touching Cline Spit reaching from the mainland, the two enclosing the inner lagoon.

Round trip 11 miles, allow 8 hours

Mount Zion (map—page 200)

From a fragrant garden of rhododendron blossoms on a bald-rock knob, see mountains on Vancouver Island, waterways of the Whulge far south on Puget Sound and north to the Strait of Georgia, islands and towns and cities of the plain, and Cascades from Rainier to Baker, and—but why go on? Especially since all the older surveyor saw on a first assault was the white insides of a cloud enwrapping a snow-white ridge. Returning next day he found the cloud broken a bit, revealing to the west, over the valleys of Gold Creek and the Dungeness River, snowy peaks of Graywolf Ridge, and, over Bon Jon Pass and the head of the Little Quilcene River, the white barrens of Mt. Townsend. But in the other direction the cloud remained, thinning just enough to reveal Port Discovery close enough below to see the fish jumping. Nevertheless, usually reliable sources declare Zion verily is the promised land for fans of the big picture.

From US 101 at 2 miles north of Quilcene, take the paved Lords Lake Loop Road. In 3.4 miles, just below the (Port Townsend) reservoir dam, go left on a gravel road signed "Mt. Zion Trail 7, Little Quilcene Trail 9." In 4.2 more miles is a triple fork; keep right, signed "Mt. Zion Trail 3," in views down the Little Quilcene valley to the end of Quilcene Bay. In 1.2 miles, at Bon Jon Pass, 2900 feet, take a right, contouring the northeast side of Gold Creek valley. At 2 miles from the pass, 11.2 miles from US 101, is the trailhead, elevation 2900 feet.

In a corner of the Olympics with roads for fun-loving squirrelers everywhere, why the Forest Service should permit wheels on this last surviving scrap of trail is a

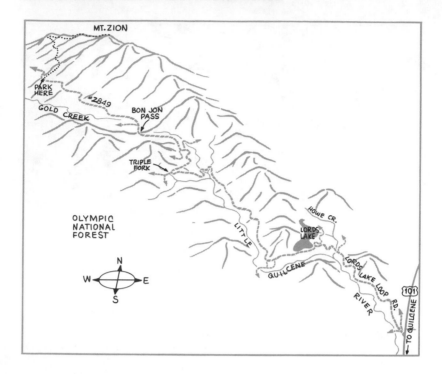

mystery. Why these scant 2 miles cannot be reserved for feet is a question every hiker should ask the ranger.

The summit ridge of Zion seems secure from logging; regrowth since the 1916 forest fire is so scrawny that not for generations will a log-exporter salivate here. The trail quickly switchbacks to the first windows out on Gold Creek valley and its clearcuts. Cliffs of rubbly basalt, then conglomerate, provide scenic rest-stop perches.

The summit is pleasantly open, all trees diminutive, if only a few are alpine-seeming, and in early summer the flower show brilliantly culminates in the rhododendrons. Sit on the site of the long-gone lookout cabin and enjoy the views. An "island mountain" cut off from the main range by deep valleys, Zion is a very high peak to be so far out. There's absolutely nothing to block the view from Seattle to Bellingham to Vancouver to Victoria. Unless, maybe, a cloud.

Round trip 4 miles, allow 3 hours
High point 4273 feet, elevation gain 1400 feet
May-November

Big Quilcene Lookout (map—page 202)

Mt. Constance is so close you can see the mountain goats begging cookies from the mountain climbers, and Quilcene pastures are just a long moo below, and if a Navy torpedo ever went astray on the Dabob Bay practice range you'd have to dodge splinters of the fishing boats. All this and more from a scalped summit at the edge of the Olympics.

Drive US 101 southerly 1 mile from the Quilcene Ranger Station. Just past Milepost 296, where the highway curves left, go straight ahead right on an unsigned (probably) road pointed at a small quarry. Stay on this road, eventually revealed to be road No. 2812, through a batch of junctions, to wit: At 1.2 miles from the highway, go left, signed "Big Quilcene Trail 14." At 3.2 miles, go straight. At 4.2 miles go right, "Big Quilcene Trail 11." At 4.6 miles, pass a sideroad left, signed "Lower Big Quilcene Trail ½." And so forth. Climbing steadily, the way bends around the end of the Quilcene Range ridge, following the valley of the Quilcene River far below. At a creek crossing 7 miles from the highway, 2812 continues up the valley and road No. 2752, the summit route, switchbacks right. Park here, elevation 2200 feet.

Yes, but 2752 all too often is readily drivable. The ascent must be finished afoot because the views are perilously attractive. But because of sporting wheels the walk is recommended as a snowline-prober in winter.

Road No. 2752 passes a deadend spur left and rounds the south end of the ridge, curving north through a saddle to the east side of the ridge. Clearcuts of the 1950s-70s open wide windows on the view, alternating with virgin forest of hemlocks and cedars hung with yellow-green lichen. All the way are rhododendron—an argument for walking the road in early summer to sniff the blossoms. In 2 miles, at 2900 feet, is a Y, 2752 going straight; switchback right on 2752B the final long ½ mile to the summit, 3450 feet.

Mt. Constance from Big Quilcene Lookout site

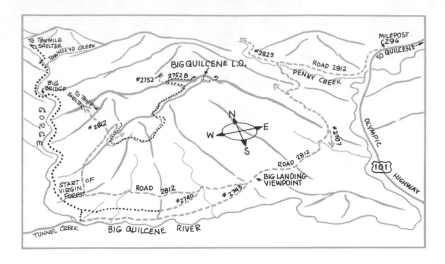

All the horizons have been seen on the ascent; now they all are seen at once. (But from no lookout tower—that's gone.) The ridge juts into the Big U Turn of the Quilcene River. East across its gorge is Mt. Walker, blocking much of the world in that direction, but big windows open southeast through Walker Pass and northeast down the Quil valley to Hood Canal and its arms, notably Quilcene Bay and Dabob Bay, the village of Quilcene, cows and boats, and cars on the highway. If Walker gives the broader view east, this summit is much more intimately involved with snowfields and crags of Constance, and Warrior, Buckhorn, Townsend, plus looks straight down to the Quilcene River, Townsend Creek, Tunnel Creek.

Round trip 5 miles, allow 4 hours
High point 3450 feet, elevation gain 1300 feet
February-December

Lower Big Quilcene River Trail (map—page 202)

Why was a road built up the Big Quilcene River in the early-middle 1930s? For some years the only perceivable excuse was to save Scouts 10 miles of walking from Camp Parsons, on the shore of Hood Canal, to Bark Shanty Shelter. But that was no good reason. Scouts liked to walk. Probably the road simply was Olympic National Forest's notion of Progress. Loggers came to the valley in the 1950s. But they never used the upper portion of the road. The river runs there in a gorge with walls so steep that even as the Forest Service was rushing to shear the entirety of an area that ought to have been put in Olympic National Park, it could figure no way to do a clearcut. And so it happened that the 1930s road, dwindled to trail width, became what it had been in the 1920s—a trail. A trail through the same forest as that of the 1920s. The 1820s. The 1620s. And the elevation is low enough that when the Buckhorn Wilderness is plugged up with snow, the virgin forest is open to feet.

From US 101 drive 4.6 miles on road No. 2812 (see Big Quilcene Lookout) and turn left on road No. 2740, signed "Lower Big Quilcene Trail ½." Descend to a nice two-party campsite and the trailhead, elevation 1400 feet.

The one complaint hikers can make is that the Forest Service allows motorcycles.

At a junction and pretty waterfall in ½ mile an old road-path drops to a parallel lower road, No. 2743, and Tunnel Creek. At ¾ mile is a sign, "Entering Watershed of City of Port Townsend." In a short bit more the Quilcene Trail turns sharply north, away from roads, into virgin forest of the wild gorge. Now everything is as it was, before. The huge cedars and hemlocks have somehow anchored themselves to the green precipice. In snowmelt time the hiker looks up through them, watching for loosened rocks to come hurtling and bounding down. The river is a constant roar close below. Two tributaries add their splash, waterfalling in chasms. When snow covers the trail it can be seen to be a coyote freeway.

At 2 1/4 miles Big Bridge spans the river, an opportunity to be mesmerized, looking down. A step farther is the confluence with Townsend Creek and at 2.4 miles (says the sign at the trailhead) is the site of Bark Shanty Shelter, where the Big Red Truck from Camp Parsons used to unload Scouts to begin the Three Rivers Hike. The shelter is long gone but the camp is lovely as ever—the river loud, the trees big, the forest floor a green carpet of moss. Elevation, 1500 feet.

The trail crosses the river on a motorcycle bridge and continues 3 1/2 miles, partly through clearcuts, partly through superb old forest, to Ten Mile Shelter, 2500 feet. There it intersects the modern logging road. But there, also, it enters Buckhorn Wilderness and proceeds onward and upward to Marmot Pass.

Round trip to Bark Shanty 4 3/4 miles, allow 3 hours
High point 1500 feet, elevation gain 100 feet
All year

Round trip to Tenmile Shelter 12 miles, allow 8 hours
High point 2500 feet, elevation gain 1300 feet
March-November

Mount Walker (map—page 204)

The absolute easternmost summit of the Olympics, zapping straight up from Hood Canal, sitting out by its lonesome cut off from neighbors by a deep glacier trough, Walker is, apart from skyline peaks, the most prominent point in the range as seen from Seattle. It follows that from Walker one can readily see Seattle. And so one can. And all the other neighborhoods of Puget Sound City and everything in between. The only thing wrong is a road to the top. On second consideration, that's not so wrong. In winter (October through April) the road is gated at the highway and thus is a trail. In other seasons there is the other and veritable trail.

Drive US 101 to the Mt. Walker Viewpoint road, No. 2730, at Walker Pass, 5 miles south of Quilcene. Elevation, 727 feet.

The Road

The 1978 survey was in utter solitude on a crisp February Wednesday in four inches of overnight snow, plenty for animal tracks and pretty tree decorations but not enough to hinder feet. Plan your trip to be so lucky. The narrow, steep road ascends virgin forest, passing basalt walls and windows opening to views this way and that. In 1 1/2 miles, at 1300 feet, are a half-bridge across a cliff and the first exclamation-point view, east over the Big U Turn Gorge of the Big Quilcene River to Constance. The way circles the peak, passing small windows north; at 4 miles, 2300 feet, is Wow Window, east over Hood Canal to Seattle. In a scant 1 mile more the road tops the forested summit ridge at 2760 feet and divides.

Left a scant 1/4 mile, at 2804 feet, is North Point Lookout, the tower gone but the basalt garden of rhododendrons and other shrubs intact and the views enormous over Walker Pass, up the Big Quilcene valley to Constance, Warrior, Buckhorn, Townsend, and their supporting cast of green ridges. Closer are clearcuts of Turner, Buck, and Crag. The Quilcene Range, Big Quilcene Lookout at the tip of the ridge, runs north toward Zion and Big Skidder Hill, and San Juan Islands and Canada.

Right a scant 1/2 mile, at 2750 feet, is South Point Observation, another garden and panorama. The foreground is saltwater at the foot of the mountain—Quilcene Bay off

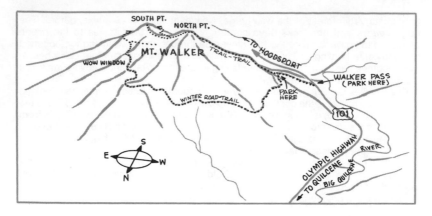

Dabob Bay off Hood Canal. The middleground is the Kitsap Peninsula. The background: Cascades from Baker to Glacier to Rainier to St. Helens; cities and towns from Everett to Seattle to Bremerton to Tacoma. Look at a map of Whulge country— whatever is on the map you probably can see from Walker. (Alternatively, as on the day of the survey, the east may be a shining cloudsea from horizon to horizon, only volcanoes poking above. But that's not bad either, on a winter day when the Olympics are carved from white ice and the forests are sugar candy.)

Round trip 11 miles, allow 8 hours
High point 2804 feet, elevation gain 2600 feet
February-December

The Trail
The trail was there before the road but for some years was lost in the brush before volunteers came a-whacking, after which, in 1988, came the surveyor. Views are less plentiful than on the road-trail. But the distance is less, by half. Wheels are banned. In June you may go blind from the color show.

Drive a scant 0.2 mile up from the highway to the clearly marked trailhead, elevation 775 feet.

The path ascends steeply, unpleasantly so under a boot-depth of snow, and is so slippery when wet that many hikers then prefer to ascend the trail and descend the road. But in rhododendron time! As the feet move slowly up the trail, the nose is thrusting through masses of blossoms.

At 1 1/2 miles, 2450 feet, is the only view comparable to those from the road. The trail switchbacks over a large rock outcrop. Off the trail, at the outcrop top, is a vista of Buck, Turner, Crag, Constance, Warrior, Buckhorn, and Townsend. At the summit, of course, are the road views. The trail comes out at North Point, just west of where the lookout used to be.

Round trip 5 miles, allow 4 hours
High point 2804 feet, elevation gain 2000 feet
February-December

INDEX

INDEX